RELIGIOUS TROJAN HORSE

Brannon Howse

Worldview Weekend Publishing
Collierville, TN

RELIGIOUS
TROJAN HORSE
Published by Worldview Weekend Publishing
a division of Worldview Weekend

© 2012 by Brannon Howse
All rights reserved.
International Standard Book Number:
0–9785014–9–7

Cover Design by Joe Potter

Unless noted otherwise, Scripture quotations are from
The Holy Bible, New King James Version (NKJV)
© 1994 by Thomas Nelson, Inc.

For Information:
www.worldviewweekend.com

Printed in the United States of America

Here Is What Christian Leaders Are Saying about

Religious Trojan Horse

As I read Brannon's new book, *Religious Trojan Horse,* I noticed the extensive research that had gone into the writing of this major work on some of the most pressing issues of our day. The footnoting in this great project will assure every reader that this is not just one man's opinion but a compilation of materials gathered from many researchers.

Since I started "partnering in ministry" with Brannon and began listening to his dynamic presentations I have been impressed with his quick mind, ability to communicate, and the clarity with which he communicates a message needed in the days we are living, days very close to the return of Jesus Christ.

That same method of public presentation has been put in this published work and will be available for the next generation to read and digest for the purpose of decision making as they will live in times far worse than ours, should the Lord tarry in His call for us to join Him in the heavens at the Rapture.

Thank you, Brannon, for working so hard to present this vital information for me as well as for the countless brothers and sisters in Christ to read at such a time as this.

Dr. Jimmy DeYoung
www.prophecytoday.com

Religious Trojan Horse is a valuable and much-needed resource for the Church. Brannon Howse not only reveals how secular subversives are destroying Christianity in our culture, but also how some leaders in the conservative community are using the Church for their own ambitions and political schemes. While crying out for the preservation of "liberty" in America, they seem to have forgotten that our only true freedom comes by faith in our Lord Jesus Christ. These men often redefine Christianity and deny the true Gospel, so as to join themselves to apostates and unbelievers in the pursuit of power. Brannon's testimony is especially imperative, because he was once part of the movement he now confronts with biblical truth. His new book shows how the faith that was once delivered to the saints is being betrayed on behalf of a Dominionist agenda, and it sets forth a powerful warning to sincere Christians against becoming entangled in a man-centered concept of religion.

Christian J. Pinto
www.noiseofthunder.com

Christianity is under attack. Formidable forces are actively working to undermine what remains of the biblical worldview once prevalent in the United States and to distort the Gospel around the globe. These forces are powerful, well connected, well funded. They dominate key christian media outlets and constitute the single greatest threat to the Church today. What is most frightening, however, is that they profess to be and are widely believed to be Christian.

Brannon Howse, in his book *Religious Trojan Horse*, courageously exposes these false teachers peddling false doctrine. Ironically, many false teachers now embraced by today's evangelical and pro-family leaders not so many years ago were widely recognized as heretical—and even banished by some denominations. That what was once recognized as heresy is now being endorsed as Christian is indicative of the stunning biblical illiteracy and lack of discernment among most professing believers.

As someone who has studied these movements in depth, written my Master's thesis on them, and currently teaches seminars on them both domestically and abroad, I can attest to the thoroughness, soundness, and contextual integrity of Brannon's research.

In a day and age in which most people desire to have their ears tickled (2 Timothy 4:3), Brannon, at considerable cost to himself and his family, has chosen the noble and biblical duty of being a Berean (Acts 17:11) and earnestly contending for the faith (Jude 3). *Religious Trojan Horse* is a must-read for the discerning believer who cares about the doctrinal purity and authoritative supremacy of the Gospel. I enthusiastically and without reservation recommend it.

Justin Peters
Justin Peters Ministries
www.justinpeters.org

Religious Trojan Horse is a must-read for all discerning followers of Christ. Spiritual confusion is running rampant in our world today, and unfortunately, as Brannon reveals, much of it is within the Church!

Jason Carlson
President, Christian Ministries
International
www.jude3.com

If you're a Pastor, read this book! You will find areas in which you've been blinded and deceived by a religious system that has drifted so far from orthodoxy that normal is our enemy. This book will wake the frog in the kettle. If your church doesn't agree with the teaching in this book, get a new church!

Dr. Randy White
Randy White Ministries
www.randywhiteministries.org

As the church is tossed here and there by waves of deception and carried about by every wind of doctrine, it needs faithful preachers of God's Word to take a stand and contend for the Gospel. With a passion for the truth, Brannon Howse does this and more in *Religious Trojan Horse*. Seeking the approval of God over man, he exposes the evil deeds of darkness by naming those who are diverting people away from the purity of their devotion to Christ.

Error has always been more popular than truth, but those who expose the fatal errors of Satan with the light of God's truth are not always popular in the Church. With very few men warning of the growing apostasy which is leading many into a counterfeit Christianity, Brannon's book *Religious Trojan Horse* is vitally important. I urge Christians everywhere to examine the fruit of Brannon's tireless research and experience in exposing the ecumenical movement. This book will help us prepare for the spiritual battles which lie ahead.

Mike Gendron
www.pro-gospel.org

Finally, someone who has the courage to expose what is taking place inside and outside the Church that was remarkably predicted 2,000 years ago. Think I'm kidding? Then read *Religious Trojan Horse*.

Pastor Steve Holley
Pastor of Ministries
Immanuel Bible Church, Springfield, VA

DEDICATION

Ron Carlson: June 6, 1950 – June 16, 2011

When I was in seventh grade, Dr. Ron Carlson was a guest speaker at my church. I remember standing near him in the church foyer listening to him talk to a few adults. Little did I know that evening that many years later, I would establish the Worldview Weekend conferences and that Ron Carlson would not only become one of our regular speakers, but he would become one of my closest friends and advisors. Ron and his wife, Marge, traveled with Melissa and me to more than 35 cities in 24 months just before his unexpected passing.

Ron was the kind of godly example described in Titus 1 and 2 that the older men of the church are to be to the young men.

Titus 2:1–2:
But as for you, speak the things which are proper for sound doctrine: that the older men be sober, reverent, temperate, sound in faith, in love, in patience;

Titus 2:6–8:
Likewise, exhort the young men to be sober-minded, in all things showing yourself to be a pattern of good works; in doctrine showing integrity, reverence, incorruptibility, sound speech that cannot be condemned, that one who is an opponent may be ashamed, having nothing evil to say of you.

Ron was committed to sound, biblical doctrine and to the instruction of others in accord.

Since Ron's passing, I have truly missed his godly counsel as well as his constant encouragement and affirmation of the work to which the Lord has called me. Ron not only had the gift of teaching but also of encouragement. Ron and I spent countless hours together over the years, and I can truly say that Ron was a consistent, godly example.

I thank God for allowing Ron Carlson to be my friend and mentor, and I look forward to the day we are once again together and discussing the things of the Lord. However, the next time we have such fellowship it will be in the very presence of our Lord and Savior Jesus Christ.

ACKNOWLEDGMENTS

I would like to thank my editor, Greg Webster of The Gregory Group, for his excellent editing and work on this book. This is the seventh book Greg has edited for me. Greg is a true talent, and I am very fortunate to have him as a part of my team.

I would also like to thank Bob Heyer for his excellent work in laying out the pages of this book. This is the seventh book Bob has worked on with me, and I appreciate his late hours of work and gracious spirit when making the last-minute changes.

TABLE OF CONTENTS

The Bible Predicted the Religious Trojan Horse, and We Are Called to Expose It

The great burden of my heart is to use the projects of Worldview Weekend and Worldview Weekend Foundation to encourage and equip true believers to understand our great need to proclaim the Gospel and to suffer, defend, and rejoice as we do. I am encouraged in this by Acts 20:28–31, which declares:

> Therefore take heed to yourselves and to all the flock, among which the Holy Spirit has made you overseers, to shepherd the church of God which He purchased with His own blood. For I know this, that after my departure savage wolves will come in among you, not sparing the flock. Also from among yourselves men will rise up, speaking perverse things, to draw away the disciples after themselves. Therefore watch, and remember that for three years I did not cease to warn everyone night and day with tears.

The great need of the hour is for you and me to warn the Church about false teachers that have come in among the Church through what I call a "religious Trojan horse". These false teachers speak perverse things (the word *perverse* actually means "to speak distorted or twisted things"). Today, false teachers promote a form of godliness but deny the power of the Gospel spoken of in 2 Timothy 3:5 ("having a form of godliness but denying its power. And from such people turn away!").

Jude 3 also warns of the religious Trojan horse when we read:

> ...for certain men have crept in unnoticed, who long ago were marked out for this condemnation, ungodly men, who turn the grace of our God into lewdness and deny the only Lord God and our Lord Jesus Christ.

Second Peter 2:1–2 further reveals the need for us to guard ourselves and the flock from the deception of the religious Trojan horse:

> But there were also false prophets among the people, even as there will be false teachers among you, who will secretly bring in destructive heresies, even denying the Lord who bought them, and bring on themselves swift destruction. And many will follow their destructive ways, because of whom the way of truth will be blasphemed.

It is from this growing false church that I believe Christians are going to receive a great deal of persecution. For this reason, we must equip and train the Church to understand that persecution is to be expected for the true believer who contends for the Gospel. Paul, in 2 Timothy 3:12, tells us to expect this: "Yes, and all who desire to live godly in Christ Jesus will suffer persecution."

This threat is why Worldview Weekend and Worldview Weekend Foundation work to equip and encourage the Church to proclaim the Gospel and endure persecutions. Here are some verses I pray will encourage you as they have me:

- Defend the Gospel—1 Timothy 6:20, 2 Timothy 1:13, 2:25
- Proclaim the Gospel—1 Corinthians 15:3–4, 2 Timothy 1:8, 2:15, 4:2
- Suffer for the Gospel—2 Timothy 1:8, 2:3, 2:8–9, 3:12, 4:2
- Rejoice in the Gospel—Romans 8:18, 2 Timothy 4:7–8

Romans 8:18 is particularly encouraging: "For I consider that the sufferings of this present time are not worthy *to be compared* with the glory which shall be revealed in us" (emphasis mine). And 2 Timothy 4:7–8 is what I pray will be true of both you and me:

> I have fought the good fight, I have finished the race, I have kept the faith. Finally, there is laid up for

me the crown of righteousness, which the Lord, the righteous Judge, will give to me on that Day, and not to me only but also to all who have loved His appearing.

Is It Negative and Unbiblical to Name False Teachers?

After a Worldview Weekend Rally in Rockford, Illinois, on Sunday night, November 21, 2010, I was informed that the church we had been renting for the previous several years did not want us to return. What makes this especially sad is that this is the church in which my wife grew up, and it has raised five generations of her family, dating back to the great grandparents on both sides. One set of great grandparents, in fact, were two of the original 13 founders of the church. The reason given for rejecting us is that our 2009 rally was thought by some of the church staff to be too negative. They thought it inappropriate to publicly call false teachers by name. I asked what their senior pastor thought about that evening's Worldview Weekend Rally but was informed that the senior pastor had chosen not to attend the conference at all.

I am not going to name the church because the people who attended the conference and live in the area know which church I'm talking about. I am not telling you about this incident because of any personal offense but to highlight how biblical truth has become an offense to some of America's churches.

Many churches claim to love truth, but what people really love is a man-centered Christianity that helps them obtain success in their marriages, finances, and family lives, as well as a positive attitude that produces health and success without the pain of dying to self, picking up the cross of Christ, and being persecuted for proclaiming truth. Second Timothy 4:3 warns that eventually many Christians will only want to hear what makes them feel good and appeals to their flesh: "For the time will come when they will not endure sound doctrine; but after their own lusts shall they heap to themselves teachers, having itching ears."

That weekend I spoke on the topic of my book *Grave Influence*, and I did name such Emergent Church false teachers as Brian McLaren, who has said the cross and hell are false advertising for God. I named Bill Hybels, who signed the Yale document stating that Muslims and Christians worship the same God. Hybels has also hosted McLaren at his church. And I mentioned Rick Warren, who sits on the advisory board of the Tony Blair Faith Foundation, which seeks to bring the religions of the world together. I named Rob Bell, who has proclaimed an abundance of heresy and who has also spoken at Bill Hybels's church.

I spoke on why the number of adherents to pagan spirituality is doubling in America every eighteen months and explained that many New Age practices—such as "Christian" yoga and contemplative prayer—have come into the churches of America. I told how Christians could proclaim the Gospel to a postmodern culture that has become more interested in spirituality than theology. I also warned that many churches are being compromised from within by church staff who do not adhere to the biblical mandates and purposes of a New Testament church. Many are an inch deep and a mile wide in their doctrinal and theological understanding and commitment. I warned that the remnant should understand that our greatest opposition will not come from the government but from those who have the title "reverend" or "pastor."

I and the other two speakers who joined me at the conference used many scriptures to equip those in attendance to understand the times and know how God would have them to respond.

Worldview Weekend is thankful for the churches that still allow us to rent their buildings, but we are being forced to rent more and more hotel ballrooms because so few churches have leaders, staff, and pastors with clear discernment, courage under fire, and an unwavering commitment to biblical truth in our age of nonjudgmentalism, tolerance, and Christian happy talk.

No one ever said being a watchman on the wall and warning of impending danger would be a popular job, but if popularity is what we seek, then we are not seeking to be faithful to the One we serve. Thus, we will have failed in our calling.

Warning the Church of emerging dangerous, unbiblical trends as well as false teachers, a false gospel, and unbiblical theology and doctrine has now become negative in the eyes of many of today's hirelings. In John 10:11–13, Jesus says we will encounter some who claim to be shepherds or pastors but really have little concern for the sheep:

> I am the good shepherd: the good shepherd giveth
> his life for the sheep. But he that is an hireling, and not
> the shepherd, whose own the sheep are not, seeth the

wolf coming, and leaveth the sheep, and fleeth: and the wolf catcheth them, and scattereth the sheep. The hireling fleeth, because he is an hireling, and careth not for the sheep. (KJV)

Worldview Weekend will not be deterred in speaking truth, no matter how unpopular it becomes with individuals or members of a church staff.

Needless to say, I was concerned about how my wife would respond to the Rockford criticism, since she was raised in that particular church, but her response revealed to me (again!) how blessed I am that God gave Melissa to me as a helpmate. She said, "Why are you surprised? You knew this church was becoming increasingly liberal over the past few years. I was shocked they let Worldview Weekend return for the 2010 rally."

Melissa encouraged me to shake the dust from my shoes and go out and find a hotel ballroom. She also encouraged me to continue taking Worldview Weekend to Rockford because of the people—including her lifelong friends—who come up to her each year at the resource table to express their gratitude that Worldview Weekend returns to Rockford, Illinois.

In fact, on our last night there, a physician who is a member of that church handed my wife a letter he had written to his children after the previous year's Worldview Weekend. He wrote:

> ...I attended a Worldview Weekend Rally at [name of church removed] on Sunday evening, November 22nd, and found it to be very helpful, informative, stimulating and timely.

This father went on to recommend that his children read some of the books written by the speakers:

> At this point in time, all three books impress me as being coherent, credible, plausible, relevant, responsible, strategic and timely. I believe that they qualify as priority reading for serious Christian believers and church leaders who need and want to be alert to the crucial times in which we and our families are living.

The doctor's letter reveals a common response and a common problem I've seen all across America: lay leaders are often more biblically grounded, discerning, and committed to truth than some of their own church staff.

So, is it negative and unbiblical to name false teachers? Negative? Are you kidding? I think it is very positive. And unbiblical? Not at all. The Bible is filled with examples of Jesus and others calling false teachers by name. In 2 Timothy, for example, the apostle Paul names numerous people:

- 1:15—Phygellus and Hermogenes
- 2:17—Hymenaeus and Philetus
- 3:8—Jannes and Jambres
- 4:10—Demas
- 4:14—Alexander the coppersmith.

In 3 John 9, John names Diotrephes. Jesus rebuked false teachers in Matthew 23 and Luke 11.

I believe God allows false teachers in order to test whether or not the Church will be faithful in its biblical mandate to expose false teachers and protect the sheep from spiritual poison and wolves in sheep's clothing. Ephesians 5:11 makes it clear we are to expose false teachers: "And have no fellowship with the unfruitful works of darkness, but rather expose them."

If a pastor will not point out the wolves among the sheep, then this should be a clear warning to the flock that the shepherd does not have its best interest in mind. Such a hireling is not called of God but is simply involved in an occupation for personal gain as revealed in 1 Timothy 6:5 ("...who have been robbed of the truth and who think that godliness is a means to financial gain"). Such nonshepherds show that they are more interested in their reputations and in being seen by the larger, unsaved community as tolerant and nonjudgmental.

False teachers give sheep the opportunity to test the commitment of their shepherds/pastors. If the pastors on your church staff fail this biblical test, then it is time for the church to replace its hirelings with real shepherds. If your church will not do this, then it is time for you to find a new flock.

Show me a shepherd who will not name false teachers, and I will show you a false teacher. Pastor Jim Bublitz offers further insight into the positive results of identifying false teachers by name:

> From those words it is clear that God allows teachers of error for the same reason as He does persecutors of His people: to test their love, to try their fidelity, to show that their loyalty to Him is such that they will not give ear unto His enemies. Error has always been more popular than the Truth, for it lets down the bars and fosters fleshly indulgence, but for that very reason it is obnoxious to the godly.
>
> The one who by grace can say "I have chosen the way of Truth" will be able to add "I have stuck unto Thy testimonies" (Psalm 119:30, 31 KJV), none being able to move him therefrom.
>
> "For there must be factions among you in order that those who are genuine among you may be recognized" (1 Corinthians 11:19).[1]

Committed Christians must publicly name false teachers because it is impossible to privately correct public false teaching.

While writing this book, I received an email from a junior in high school near Atlanta, Georgia. This young lady explained that because she had attended two Worldview Weekend rallies in Atlanta and heard me expose the false teaching of Emergent pastor Rob Bell, she was equipped to reject his false teaching when a Bible study group at her Christian school decided to read one of his books. She had the courage and conviction to politely hand the book back to the group leaders and warn them of Bell's false teaching.

This student's testimony has come to mind many times and has deeply encouraged me to continue speaking truth no matter how negative or offensive it may be to the nondiscerning. If I had not named Rob Bell, how would this student have known to reject his book and false doctrine? If I had not named Rob Bell, would she now be spiritually deceived? If I had not named Bell, would this young woman have been able to warn her peers about Bell's spiritual poison?

The late Vance Havner wrote, "We live what we believe; the rest is religious talk." Living what we believe includes our willingness to name false teachers and to endure the criticism and persecution that will surely follow. To do any less is treason to our calling, to our mandate, to our Lord and Savior Jesus Christ.

When we expose false teaching and false teachers, we proclaim and defend the authority, accuracy, and application of God's Word—the very thing false teachers seek to undermine. Living what we believe requires speaking biblical truth and warnings no matter how offensive it may be to the spiritually immature, the nondiscerning, or the wolves that creep in among the sheep.

Jude 3–4 commands *all believers* to contend for the faith that is under attack from false teachers:

> Beloved, when I gave all diligence to write unto you of the common salvation, it was needful for me to write unto you, and exhort you that ye should earnestly contend for the faith which was once delivered unto the saints. For there are certain men crept in unawares, who were before of old ordained to this condemnation, ungodly men, turning the grace of our God into lasciviousness, and denying the only Lord God, and our Lord Jesus Christ. (KJV)

Truth is never negative to those who seek to serve the truth.

False Arrest—Confronting the Politically Correct Matthew 18 Police

If you've read some of my articles, you know I point out the intolerance of people who scream about how important it is to be tolerant. Ironically, many who advocate not judging others are the most judgmental of opinions with which they disagree. Now I've found a new set of hypocrites who try to bully us into doing as they say but not as they do, and I've christened them the Politically Correct Matthew 18 Police (PCM18). Usually I go after liberals, but some of the PCM18s are misinformed and naïve, yet genuinely well-meaning, Christians. They're also dead wrong.

What exactly do PCM18s have to do with Matthew 18:15–17? They twist truth to fit their convenience and use it against people like *me* who blow the whistle on bizarre or heretical claims made in the name of Christ.

Recently, several members of the PCM18s (they're stationed all over the country) confronted me about several articles. I had produced a three-part series on the false teachings of Christian happy-talk superstar Joel Osteen. And exposing him, by the way, was incredibly easy. All I did was quote from Osteen's interview on *Larry King Live* and from his book, *Your Best Life Now*. His statements obviously contradict the Word of God.

I also released an article on 85 "evangelical" leaders who had signed a left-wing global warming initiative funded by radical, anti-Christian foundations. A few in this group held press conferences and interviews and even launched a series of national television commercials and radio spots to ballyhoo their "insights." Then I did what may have been the most unpardonable, un-PC act of all: I wrote an extensive article on the dangerous and unbiblical beliefs of the Emerging Church and some of its leaders.

Citations from the PCM18s rolled in like a tsunami. But did they email privately to chastise me for my "unbiblical" conduct of writing and speaking out against false teachings? No, of course not, even though that is exactly what they were writing to tell me *I* should have done. (You'll notice, if you haven't already, that the hallmark of any "tolerance officer" is that they want you to do what they would never do themselves.)

The PCM18s ignored my private email address—which is clearly posted on our website—and posted their virulent objections in the feedback section. I had to laugh. Without first coming to me in private as the scripture they quoted says to do, they publicly blasted me for not first going in private to those about whom I had written. Hmm. Can you say, "Disconnect"?

Now don't get me wrong. I think Matthew 18 is a great chapter of the Bible and one that should be followed (of course!). However, the PCM18s strip Matthew 18:15–17 from its context in order to force their politically correct, "nonjudgmental" tolerance agenda on Christians who challenge unbiblical beliefs, doctrine, or worldviews. In context, it is clear the verses address how to handle a private issue or a personal offense. They detail the steps to take for church discipline of an individual who has sinned. If the offending person does not repent when you confront him or her privately, then you are to take one or two people with you. If the individual still will not repent, take the issue before the church. If even that doesn't work, the person is to be removed from fellowship until he or she does admit to the sin and repents.

PCM18s would have you believe Matthew 18 means you should never write or speak publicly to oppose one of their gurus unless you first speak to that person privately. This is just an absurd manipulation of Scripture. In reality, the PC police seek to intimidate and manipulate by guilt those with whom they disagree. Apparently, such childish techniques are the best they can muster when backed into the proverbial corner by solid biblical facts. With finger wagging and heaping helpings of self-righteous indignation, they offer verbal or email lashings about how you are sinning and should repent and cease at once from speaking out against false teachers and their accompanying doctrines. PCM18s drone on about how you are not loving or are creating disunity among Christians and how this is such a bad witness to unbelievers.

A bad witness? It would be a better witness to allow false teaching and a false gospel to go uncorrected and unchallenged? What the police don't want you to know is that throughout the New Testament the great apostle Paul himself publicly denounced false teachers by name *without* first going to them in private. After all, how can one *privately* correct *public* false teaching? It can't be done, and that's exactly why we are to publicly point out erroneous teaching once it has been promoted in books, television, radio, websites, and other public forums.

So now you're ready. If you should ever happen to get "pulled over" by the Politically Correct Matthew 18 Police for boldly refuting someone's public false teaching, take the law into your own hands and make a Christian citizen's arrest by pointing out their illegal handling of the Scriptures.

Churches and Christian Media Censor the Truth

Much of what I share in this book I would never be allowed to present in most "evangelical" churches or on "Christian" radio or television stations. Most are either hostile to biblical truth or are afraid of the public-relations fallout from the truth we speak at Worldview Weekend conferences.

In 1983, Walter Martin spoke at the ordination service for my friend and mentor, Ron Carlson. I have played Dr. Martin's sermon on my radio program because it is still so timely. He told those assembled in the California church that they needed to understand that people who speak biblical truth are not censored primarily by the secular media but by the Church and "Christian" media:

> You see, the attitude of the Christian media is don't rock the boat, and the Christian Church is suffering from that disease today by its Latin name, non rock-a-boat-us. Whatever you do, non rock-a-boat-us ecclesiastic-us. Don't shake, rattle and roll the boat of the Church. Leave us alone....
>
> They're always screaming about secular humanism censoring the Christian Church, but they're the ones that are censoring the Christian Church. They don't want to get on television and on radio and tell it like it is. You know why? Because then they won't get any checks from people out there whose feelings they hurt.
>
> So, they are not governed by the Holy Spirit. They are not governed by the authority of the Scriptures, which commands them to tell the truth. They are governed by the almighty checkbook of the people that are listening.

The "soft" persecution and censorship now taking place in America is coming largely from self-professing Christians. I have a file of emails from "Christian" leaders who, through the years, have criticized me for speaking about false teachers. Some of these are highly visible authors or Christian radio and television hosts. Many have the public reputation of being bold and committed to truth, but in reality they are very shrewd about the issues they will address. If an issue will impact the bottom line or upset their "good old boy club," the truth becomes a casualty. I have personally witnessed many of evangelicalism's well-known personalities clam up when a biblical stand might negatively impact their book and DVD sales, speaking invitations, attendance of their conferences, donors to their organization, or how many stations carry their radio programs.

Is it any wonder that a religious Trojan horse has slipped into the camp of evangelicalism when so many "perceived" watchmen or watchwomen will only warn the Church when it does not impact their bottom line, personal well-being, or reputation? May neither you nor I allow the love of money to cause us to stray from proclaiming the truth as 1 Timothy 6:10 warns: "For the love of money is a root of all kinds of evil, for which some have strayed from the faith in their greediness, and pierced themselves through with many sorrows."

Speaking of God

As you will see, I aim many of my criticisms at people who claim revelation or direction from God in a manner not consistent with Scripture. Let me assure you up front, however, that I do believe God is active through His Holy Spirit in leading those called by His name. But some ways of "hearing from God" are scriptural, and some are not. God does not speak to people today in an audible voice, for instance, and He never reveals new doctrine. So how does He "speak" to us?

The Holy Spirit convicts people of sin and works in our lives in powerful ways. A true Christian who is walking in the light of God's Word and studying the Scriptures can have a prompting of the Holy Spirit—not an audible voice, but a prompting to pray for someone or to call another person on the phone or to visit someone in order to minister to him or her. The Holy Spirit can direct a Christian to share the Gospel with a stranger—someone who, you might find out later, had been longing to talk with a believer about Christ.

Affirming such leadings and promptings is entirely scriptural. Nothing in the Bible discourages a believer from accepting this as appropriate. My dispute in the following pages is only with those who teach or demonstrate by their actions that they are open to "extra-biblical" or new doctrinal revelations. May God bless your own understanding of His work in your life as you read.

A Note to My Critics

I recognize there will likely be much criticism of what I've written in this book. While I am willing to accept such criticism, I ask one favor of my critics: please document any errors you find and allow me to correct them in the second edition with apologies to anyone I have misread or misunderstood. Please understand that all my opinions and commentary are not directed toward anyone personally. My intent is not to focus on personal issues but on theological issues. My intent is to examine the doctrinal and theological fruit of those discussed and the biblical ramifications produced from their philosophies, values, ideas, and actions. I pray that this book is received in the spirit in which it was written.

CHAPTER 1

The Grave Influence
of the Religious Trojan Horse

So how did I come to write *Religious Trojan Horse*? While researching and writing my last book, *Grave Influence: 21 Radicals and Their Worldviews that Rule America from the Grave*, I noticed that the influence and philosophies of most, if not all, of these 21 radicals had found their way into the Church. (You can purchase *Grave Influence* as a hardcover book or e-book at the WorldviewWeekend.com bookstore.)

And these ideas have not just infiltrated the mainline, liberal denominations but also many denominations often referred to as "evangelical." Let me give you a quick overview of just a few of the 21 radicals I expose in *Grave Influence* and how their worldviews influence evangelicalism and aid in building the religious Trojan horse.

Alice Bailey (1880–1949)

Alice Bailey wrote 24 books totaling thousands of pages, books she claimed to have written under the direction of a spirit guide called Djwhal Klul or the Tibetan. But to be clear: I believe Bailey was communicating with a demon, a practice strictly forbidden in the Bible. As we will examine in detail later, many churches today practice contemplative prayer (Christian code word for transcendental meditation) in hopes of hearing from God. There are many reasons I believe they are hearing from the demonic spirit world. For starters, God speaks to us today through His Word. He does not use occult practices to communicate with His people.

The Tibetan made a number of provocative claims about the future:

> This coming age will be as predominantly the age
> of group interplay, group idealism and group con-

sciousness. ...for the will of the individual will voluntarily be blended into group will.[2]

The future, in other words, will be about socialism—collectivism
or group-thinking—not individualism or dissent. Group-think, collectivism, and group consensus is now deliberately used in many mainline and "evangelical" churches to emotionally manipulate church
members to conform to the desired goals and philosophies of church
leaders. This process is also used by neo-evangelicals and the New Religious Right (NRR) to silence those who do not agree with their brand
of "Christian" activism and compromise of biblical truth.

Bailey and her demon predicted that the future and new order will
be about pluralism (the belief that all religions are equal) and universalism (the belief that all roads lead to God):

> I refer to that period which will surely come in
> which an Enlightened People will rule; these people
> will not tolerate authoritarianism in any church....they
> will not accept or permit the rule of any body of men
> who undertake to tell them what they must believe in
> order to be saved...[3]

Most people know pluralism is promoted by the religious left, but
few realize that, whether knowingly or unknowingly, many within evangelicalism and the New Religious Right promote pluralism through
political and spiritual ecumenical initiatives. Numerous members of
the New Religious Right refuse to publicly refute the false Jesus and
false gospel of Mormonism and the Catholic Church because to do so
would cost them financial contributions and destroy their political coalitions. Some neo-evangelical and NRR leaders openly proclaim that
those who follow the Jesus of Mormonism or the Jesus of the Church
of Rome are following the same Jesus of the Bible. I will explain later
why this is not only false but how the Bible warns Christians not to
follow another Jesus or to accept another gospel.

To clarify my "religious right" terminology: the original Religious
Right developed in the mid-1970s during the administration of
President Jimmy Carter. Some of its founders included the late Pastor
Adrian Rogers of Bellevue Baptist Church in Memphis, Tennessee;
former president of the Southern Baptist Convention, the late Dr. D.

James Kennedy of Coral Ridge Presbyterian Church in Ft. Lauderdale, Florida; and the late Dr. Jerry Falwell of Thomas Road Baptist Church and Liberty University in Lynchburg, Virginia.

The next generation of Religious Right leaders, unlike the previous generation, has largely abandoned the early leaders' commitment to biblical theology and doctrine and unite openly with false teachers when it furthers their political and cultural goals. For this reason, I refer to the Religious Right as the New Religious Right.

I will say, however, that the more I research the founding of the 1970s Religious Right, the more I see how some (but not all) of its founding members sowed seeds guaranteeing the failure of the Religious Right and set a poor example for today's leaders. For example, Jerry Falwell's son, Jerry Falwell Jr., revealed on Glenn Beck's radio program in 2010 the concept to which his father had introduced him:

> If we don't hang together we'll hang separately. I mean, that's what my father believed when he formed Moral Majority, an organization of Mormons, Catholics, Protestants, Jews, people of no faith. And there are bigger issues now. We can argue about theology later after we save the country.[4]

"We can argue about theology later after we save the country." I believe this statement reveals a great deal about the theology of Jerry Falwell Jr. Not only will God not bless such compromise, but it will invite His judgment.

Alice Bailey did not hide the fact that her worldview was founded in occultism, and she predicted that future churches—even those that once rejected her worldview—would eagerly accept it in order to attract the masses. Within a generation, countless American churches have wandered from defending a biblical worldview to teaching that the Word of God is subjective, that all roads lead to God, and that mysticism and pagan spirituality should be embraced to further one's religious experiences. If that sounds "seeker sensitive," it is. It's all part of the quest for a spiritual salve to dull the ache in the human soul. Bailey saw it coming (perhaps because her demonic guides had it planned all along?):

> It can be expected that the orthodox Christian will at first reject the theories about the Christ which

occultism presents; at the same time, this same orthodox Christian will find it increasingly difficult to induce the intelligent masses of people to accept the impossible Deity and the feeble Christ which historical Christianity has endorsed.[5]

The occult and mysticism have gone mainstream within evangelicalism thanks to the teachings of people like Joel Osteen, John Hagee, Kenneth Copeland, Rick Warren, and Robert Schuller. The occult has also infiltrated evangelicalism as neo-evangelicals and leaders of the New Religious Right have publicly entered into spiritual enterprises with some of the pastors I have just mentioned as well as members of the New Apostolic Reformation (NAR). The NAR is nothing less than occultism wrapped in Christian language. A false dominant church is being built through a religious Trojan horse, and some of its designers have been influenced directly or indirectly by Alice Bailey.

Julius Wellhausen (1844–1918)

In 1878, a German theology professor and author of numerous books "discovered" that the Bible is a book of stories but not the divinely inspired Word of God. He proclaimed his new truth to countless Germans and taught that the Bible could not be trusted, but human reason could. Known as Higher Criticism or German rationalization, this was the contribution Julius Wellhausen offered to Germany's cultural demise.

European Christianity was compromised and changed into a false religion from within as Higher Criticism led people into an essentially humanistic religion. Germany was Hitler's for the taking because absolute truth and the Gospel of Jesus Christ had long since been betrayed. Thus the German people came to believe that "the end justifies the means." In return for regaining national pride and financial abundance, the people would grant Hitler his dream of hope and change.

History screams that ideas have consequences, that worldview matters. Most Germans—including German Christians—willingly traveled the road to Hitler's hell, largely because they had lost the courage of their convictions. They had sold out to paganism, pragmatism, and a new gospel that promised everything while requiring nothing. Does this not sound like churches, seminaries, Christian colleges, and some of the best-selling Christian authors in America today?

Wellhausen's liberal philosophy eventually jumped the ocean, became popular on the East Coast, and has spread throughout the United States. Many American Christians are all too willing to go down a path that will surely lead to the destruction of our once great nation. Incredibly, many self-professing Christians are not just following but are leading the way over the cliff. A domineering false church is rising, largely due to pansies in the pulpit. False teachers have turned the grace of God into lewdness, and they deny the only Lord God and our Lord Jesus Christ (Jude 3–4).

Søren Kierkegaard (1813–1855)

Although many Christians don't know the name Søren Kierkegaard, they know well his essential philosophy of life. In the mid-1800s Kierkegaard, who claimed to be a Christian, denied any consistent morality. Known as existentialism, his ideas gained steam in America a hundred years after his death. The central tenet of existentialism is that there is no absolute truth. "Christians" practicing existentialism introduced what is called neo-orthodoxy. The American version of this movement grew popular in the 1960s and virtually took over in the '70s and '80s.

David Breese explains how it happened:

> A careful neglect of Calvary, the blood of Christ, divine forgiveness, original sin, and other great Christian themes. Salvation becomes experience-oriented, theology becomes contextual, and ultimate truth becomes contradictory. They announce that Jesus Christ came into the world to bring economic liberation to the oppressed masses of the earth.[6]

Kierkegaard's existentialism proclaimed that "truth is subjective," a worldview very much alive today. "Existentialism is a philosophical movement that became associated with the philosophy of Jean-Paul Sartre (who rejected the name as too confining) and whose roots extend to the works of Søren Kierkegaard and Martin Heidegger."[7]

Martin Heidegger's existentialism and that of Kierkegaard differed in some ways—as did the existentialism of Kierkegaard and Nietzsche—but there is room for both on the highway of postmodern thinking. "Kierkegaard and Nietzsche differed radically, most famously in their approach to religion (Christianity in particular). Kierkegaard was devout, while Nietzsche was a blasphemous atheist. But so, too, twentieth-century existentialism would include both religious and atheistic philosophers."[8] In other words, Nietzsche applied the idea of subjective truth to the natural world as an atheist while Kierkegaard applied subjective truth to his brand of spirituality and called himself a Christian.

The wide way of existentialism is described by Walter Kaufmann in his book *Existentialism: From Dostoevsky to Sartre*:

> Existentialism is foreshadowed most notably by nineteenth-century philosophers Søren Kierkegaard and Friedrich Nietzsche, though it had forerunners in earlier centuries....Although there are some common tendencies amongst "existentialist" thinkers, there are major differences and disagreements among them (most notably the divide between atheistic existentialists like Sartre and theistic existentialists like Tillich); not all of them accept the validity of the term as applied to their own work.[9]

There is really nothing new under the sun, and I contend that this neo-orthodoxy laid the foundation for what we now call the Emergent Church (EC). Some Christian authors and pastors have claimed that the Emergent Church is a fad, but that is like saying Gnosticism is a fad even though Gnosticism is as popular today as it was in Paul's day. Paul warns of Gnosticism in Colossians 2:8–23; 1 Timothy 1:4; and 2 Timothy 2:16–19.

Gnosticism includes the worship of angels; the belief that salvation is not gained exclusively through the death, burial, and resurrection of Jesus Christ; and that truth can be obtained through mystical experience and practices. As we will discover later in this chapter, Gnosticism also elevated women to a role of savior of mankind, and it helps explain why the worship of Mary is so prevalent in the Gnosticism of the Catholic Church. Gnosticism and feminism are inextricably linked.

John MacArthur describes Gnosticism this way:

> Gnosticism took Greek rationalism, that is the musings and the mind of man, and Eastern mysticism, those intuitive esoteric fanciful imaginary experiences that mystics supposedly have, and wed them together and said this is the higher knowledge, this is the lofty knowledge, this is a superior knowledge. The Bible is mundane, earthy, common and wrong.[10]

Gnosticism is very much alive today in many forms, especially in the Emergent Church. While the term "Emergent Church" may no longer be in vogue, its philosophies will become some of the foundational beliefs of the one-world religion, described as Revelation 17's woman who rides the beast.

Nietzsche and Kierkegaard believed a person could not know truth, that we should embrace the mysticism of the world and reject absolutes. We can see this influence of Kierkegaard and Nietzsche on both the American culture and many of America's churches, seminaries, and Christian colleges.

Postmodernism, which is closely tied to existentialism, was introduced through the English departments of many American colleges and universities. The study of literature offered a convenient vehicle to teach the idea that one can never know what an author means to convey. Interpretation is subject to each individual reader.

Western society is denying absolute truth even in the disciplines of reading and writing. Postmodernists within the Church deconstruct Christianity—as did Kierkegaard—by proclaiming that the Bible is not the absolute, inerrant, divinely inspired Word of God.

The Emergent Church is gaining ground in spreading this false message. In rejecting traditional morality and values, existentialists uphold what they call an ethic of authenticity. You will also hear this phrase from the Emergent Church as it rejects traditional, orthodox Christianity for an "authentic" Christianity.

The Emergent Church, like many liberal, mainstream churches, has rejected the idea of the return of Jesus Christ and His judgment of the world. Instead, they see it as their responsibility to build God's kingdom through utopian ideals of the redistribution of wealth, the social gospel, disarmament, and a world community committed to social justice and pluralism. This commitment to dominionism, or building God's kingdom on earth now, is not only embraced by the Emergent

Church but also by the Church Growth movement, New Apostolic Reformation movement, Word of Faith movement, and many within the New Religious Right. All four of these can be traced back to a few seminal leaders.

Friedrich Nietzsche (1844–1900)

"Postmodernism" is a term so widely known these days that you might think it is simply a word arbitrarily attached to a vast but vague set of contemporary ideas. Yet its origin is very traceable. Friedrich Nietzsche, along with Michael Foucault, founded postmodern thought.

Postmodernism holds that truth and reality are created by man and not by God, that something is true "if it works for you." They believe that truth is neither absolute nor binding over the entire globe, but merely situational and subjective. Postmodernism is a dominant worldview in America today, largely because Friedrich Nietzsche is one of the most widely read authors on college campuses.

The Emergent Church has picked up on Nietzsche's thinking and has incorporated it into its attitude toward Scripture. EC leaders such as Rob Bell have declared that the Bible is not absolute truth. *Christianity Today,* in November 2004, reported that: "The Bells started questioning their assumptions about the Bible itself—'discovering the Bible as a human product,' as Rob puts it, rather than the product of divine fiat."[11]

How ironic that a church movement would be built on the worldview of a man best known for declaring "God is dead." Nietzsche said not only that God is dead but that "we have killed him." Nietzsche hated Christians. "Christianity has been the most calamitous kind of arrogance yet," he wrote. "I call Christianity the one great curse, the one enormous and innermost perversion, the one moral blemish of mankind....I regard Christianity as the most seductive lie that has yet existed."[12] Nietzsche believed Christianity made his fellow Germans weak, so he described himself as "The Anti-Christian Friedrich Nietzsche" or sometimes as just "The Antichrist" (also the title of one of his books—*Antichrist*).

It does not take a rocket scientist to realize that Nietzsche's war on Christianity and Nietzsche's acceptance within a false dominant church portends the increase in "soft" persecution of Christians in the West. This may well lead to the kind of persecution of the true Church that is common in nations like China and Cuba.

One sure way to lay the foundation for persecution is to dull man's God-given, internal mechanism for determining what is right or wrong, just or unjust. Nietzsche championed the eradication of guilt from the human conscience and elevated Darwin's survival of the fittest to the next level. He proclaimed, "Life simply is will to power." Whatever it takes, one should purpose to be a ruler, a master over the less desirable. Promoting his master-and-slave morality, Nietzsche, in his book *Beyond Good and Evil*, proclaimed the need to look past Christian definitions of good and evil to whatever it takes to gain power, part of which means endorsing cruelty when necessary to accomplish the goal. Nietzsche explained:

> We should reconsider cruelty and open our eyes....
> Almost everything we call "higher culture" is based on
> the spiritualization of cruelty, on its becoming more
> profound: this is my proposition.[13]

"Master morality" means the strong rule over the weak. Nietzsche includes Christians among the weak because of their compassion for the sick, aged, and vulnerable. Anyone who holds to a fixed morality, he maintained, would become slaves—and deservedly so. Nietzsche thoroughly rejected the Christian worldview, its absolute truth, standards of justice and injustice, righteousness and unrighteousness. For Nietzsche, the only standard that matters is what puts and keeps someone in power. He believed "...that the demand of one morality for all is detrimental for the higher men...."[14] Notice that this is why today's cultural elite have set one standard for the masses and a completely different one for themselves.

In contrast to Nietzsche, why do Christians have such a strong commitment to the life of the unborn, the sick, the disabled, and the elderly? Because we understand that man is created in the image of God, and therefore every person has a right to life, liberty, and property. With the loss of the Christian worldview and the ever-increasing acceptance of Nietzsche's postmodernism, Bible-believing Christians in America risk being portrayed as the enemies of the State—intolerant, out of touch, bigoted, extremist, or even domestic terrorists—all because their worldview conflicts with that of "the higher man," the cultural elite, or the master morality.

America's sick, handicapped, and elderly will also be at risk as man's intrinsic, God-given worth is replaced by a value measured only according to what a person can do for the State. Once national healthcare is a reality and the majority of Americans come to see it as a right, only the threat of its removal will be needed to convince younger, postmodern generations that the lifeboat is too full, and it is time to toss the weak overboard.

Nietzsche promoted the concept of a "Superman" race, which Hitler also embraced after studying Nietzsche. Today, the Superman concept is welcomed through "spiritual evolution," which declares that man is evolving to new levels in the spiritual realm as more and more individuals discover their "god consciousness."

In Germany, a false church not only assisted Adolf Hitler in coming to power but also in maintaining power. Many German "Christians" had accepted the worldviews of Nietzsche and Wellhausen. These same two radicals and their worldviews are now accepted within many churches and denominations throughout the world. This fast-rising, global false church will give credibility to internationally recognized political and spiritual leaders who will in turn give their power and authority to a one-world leader. After appearing to be a man of peace and justice, this one-world leader will reveal his true intentions and will rival Hitler's brutality in immeasurable ways. Like Hitler, he will have largely achieved his position through the help of a global false church that embraced the postmodernism of Friedrich Nietzsche.

The Frankfurt School

In 1923, a group of German intellectuals started what has become known as the Frankfurt School. William Lind explains that the name originally planned for the institute had to be abandoned in order to conceal from the public its true agenda:

> The intended name for the Frankfurt School was the Institute for Marxism. The Institute's father and funder, Felix Weil, wrote in 1971 that he "wanted the Institute to become known, and perhaps famous, due to its contributions to Marxism as a scientific discipline...." Beginning a tradition Political Correctness still carries on, Weil and others decided that they

24

could operate more effectively if they concealed their Marxism; hence, on reflection, they chose the neutral-sounding name, the Institute for Social Research (Insitut für Sozialforschung).[15]

The Frankfurt School was directly connected to Karl Marx, Sigmund Freud, George Hegel, and Friedrich Nietzsche. Dr. Lind writes:

> The Frankfurt School blended Marx with Freud, and later influences (some Fascist as well as Marxist) added linguistics to create "Critical Theory" and "deconstruction." These in turn greatly influenced education theory, and through institutions of higher education gave birth to what we now call "Political Correctness." The lineage is clear, and it is traceable right back to Karl Marx.[16]

In 1933, when the Nazis came to power in Germany, many members of the Frankfurt School found refuge in America at the invitation of John Dewey (one of the radicals to whom I devote an entire chapter in *Grave Influence*). Dewey was on staff at Columbia University in New York and saw the opportunity to place these Marxists at leading colleges and universities around the country. He and his cohorts specifically targeted education and media as the means by which to inculcate their worldview into American culture. As Chuck Morse points out:

> The original strategy to destroy America, employed by the Frankfurt School, came from Italian Communist Antonio Gramsci, who realized that in order to achieve a Socialist victory, cultural institutions would have to be infiltrated and subverted. Gramsci realized that America, steeped in traditions of freedom and liberty, would never succumb to a frontal assault.[17]

Gramsci seems to have obtained his ideas from the Catholic Jesuits. Catholic author George Marlin writes:

> Gramsci advised Marxists to achieve power by democratic means and then to use it to destroy

Christian hegemony. "Gramsci's principle," French journalist Jean-François Revel pointed out, "was that [Marxists] must begin by influencing the culture, winning the intellectuals, the teachers, implanting itself in the press, the media, the publishing houses." Somewhat surprisingly, Gramsci pointed to the Jesuits' response to the Reformation as a model: Marxists had to create a cultura capillare ("capillary culture") that would infuse itself into every nook and cranny of the body politic.[18]

The phrase "make love, not war" shouted during the counter-culture revolution of the 1960s was coined by Frankfurt School faculty member Herbert Marcuse. The 1960s student rebels implemented strategies laid out by Marcuse in writings influenced largely by Gramsci. American campus radicals were inspired by Marcuse's cultural revolution proclamations such as:

> One can rightfully speak of a cultural revolution, since the protest is directed toward the whole cultural establishment; including the morality of existing society...there is one thing we can say with complete assurance. The traditional idea of revolution and the traditional strategy of revolution has ended. These ideas are old-fashioned...what we must undertake is a type of diffuse and dispersed disintegration of the system.[19]

An all-powerful and intrusive government that robs you of freedoms is the ultimate goal of what you may know only as political correctness. It is, in general, a masking term for cultural Marxism.

Although people regularly laugh about political correctness, losing our freedom of religion, freedom of speech, property rights, and parental authority is no laughing matter. Thought control is not funny, and many Christians already have been prosecuted under hate-crime laws for sharing the Gospel and for publicly speaking out against homosexuality.

Cultural Marxism intends to destroy Christianity in all areas of American life. The elimination of the Christian worldview will create the chaos necessary for Marxism to have its day. Once chaos has reached a fevered pitch, the public will cry out for government to solve the problem, and people will welcome socialism. I believe our new financial system will be a mixture of socialism and capitalism called communitarianism.

Another of the goals of Frankfurt School faculty was the promotion of feminism, which is closely tied to Marxism and Gnosticism. Dr. Gerald L. Atkinson, CDR, USN (Ret.), describes the attack on the American male through the propaganda of the Frankfurt School:

> The Frankfurt school studied the "authoritarian personality" which became synonymous with the male, the patriarchal head of the American family. A modern utopia would be constructed by these idealistic intellectuals by "turning Western civilization" upside down. This utopia would be a product of their imagination, a product not susceptible to criticism on the basis of the examination of evidence. This "revolution" would be accomplished by fomenting a very quiet, subtle and slowly spreading "cultural Marxism" which would apply to culture the principles of Karl Marx bolstered by the modern psychological tools of Sigmund Freud. Thus, "cultural Marxism" became a marriage of Marx and Freud aimed at producing a "quiet" revolution in the United States of America. This "quiet" revolution has occurred in America over the past 30 years. While America slept! "The Authoritarian personality," studied by the Frankfurt School in the 1940s and 1950s in America, prepared the way for the subsequent warfare against the masculine gender promoted by Herbert Marcuse and his band of social revolutionaries under the guise of "women's liberation" and the New Left movement in the 1960s. The evidence that psychological techniques for changing personality is intended to mean emasculation of the American male is provided by Abraham Maslow, founder of Third Force Humanist Psychology and a promoter of the psychotherapeutic classroom, who wrote that "...the next step in personal evolution is a transcendence of both masculinity and femininity to general humanness." The Marxist revolutionaries knew exactly what they wanted to do

and how to do it. They have succeeded in accomplishing much of their agenda.[20]

Betty Friedan (1921–2006)

If "tolerance" is the core value of political correctness, feminism is its most cherished cause, and the implications of our cultural devotion to feminism are monstrous. Feminism is not about equal rights for women but about the feminization of the American male. The feminist ideology is antifamily and antifather—and virtually guaranteed to bring about the wholesale destruction of the family.

Among the champions of feminism have been Gloria Steinem, Elizabeth Cady Stanton, and most prominently, Betty Friedan. Friedan was also cofounder of the National Organization of Women (NOW), one of America's most radical feminist organizations.

Friedan's book *The Feminine Mystique* could be described as the Feminist Manifesto. Released in 1963, it was a major force behind the 1970s explosion of the radical feminist agenda. Like many of the "Grave Influencers" I've discussed, Friedan was an atheist who embraced Marxism. As Benjamin Wicker points out:

> Before she published *The Feminine Mystique*, Friedan had spent years in Marxist-inspired agitation on behalf of mistreated lower-class workers—and the abstractness of her analysis is fundamentally Marxist. She had been a Marxist since her college days at Smith in the late 1930s and early 1940s. In the years after, she belonged to, worked for, or wrote positively about a string of leftist organizations and publications—like the Popular Front, the Federated Press, UE News, Congress of American Women, Jewish Life—that had significant Communist membership or Soviet sympathies. Knowing that the call to revolution in *The Feminine Mystique* would be damaged if it was associated with the call to revolution in the *Communist Manifesto*, she hid her radical past.[21]

The bottom line is that feminism has been a tool of humanists to destroy the family. Leading humanist Paul Kurtz said, "Humanism and feminism are inextricably interwoven."[22] Humanists and communists have sought the destruction of the American family because they know that the family has been the instrument for passing on Christian values and a biblical worldview—the source and foundation of our freedoms and constitutional republic.

With the help of the feminist movement in the late 1960s, divorce laws were liberalized. The resulting drastic increase in divorce began to break down the strength, respect, and permanency of the marriage covenant in the civil arena. No-fault divorce made separation fast and allowed couples to split up without admitting fault or accepting responsibility.

In the 1972 Stanley v. Illinois case, the U.S. Supreme Court ruled that custody laws distinguishing between married and unmarried fathers was "constitutionally repugnant." Fathers would be given the same rights and face no consequences for fathering a child outside of marriage. Thus, one of the main reasons for entering into the religious and civil covenant and contract of marriage was removed. Those who were married and those who were not married were given the same respect and legal standing.

Divorce and illegitimacy have undercut the institution of the family. The incubator for nurturing offspring who would safeguard the republic and, for Christians, discipling children in biblical truth is now relatively in shambles.

Friedan and the cultural Marxists have used civil law, courts, and the media to destroy the family and fathers and to make possible the rise of the welfare nanny state. The break-up of the family has been the leading cause of generational poverty and the permanent underclass. And the chaos is having its intended effect: the American people increasingly call for government to solve the problem by greater intervention into family life.

Feminism has some natural appeal. One consequence of the fall of man in the Garden of Eden is that women will challenge men for leadership (Genesis 3:16). But this does not mean women really want it—even if they think they do. If a woman takes the leadership position, she ultimately doesn't find it satisfying and usually ends up discontent with her man. What women really want in a marriage is the protection, provision, and servant leadership of a loving husband. Whether people admit it or not, it is evident there are God-ordained roles for men and for women—each complementing the other. This is what makes a great marriage great—the different and sometimes opposite but complementary gifts, abilities, insight, and interests of each spouse.

Many people in the Church now embrace feminism, and as a result, the biblical roles of men and women are not taught in most churches. While once only mainline liberal churches permitted women to teach men in the church, today many "evangelical" churches encourage women to teach men. In a sermon series on the biblical role of women, John MacArthur accurately describes the impact feminism has had on the Church:

> One of the most devastating and debilitating and destructive movements in our day is the Feminist Movement. It is changing not only the world but sadly it is changing the church. And as a result, the Word of God is being dishonored, opponents are having plenty bad to say about us, and God, our Savior, is being dishonored and shamed. Radical feminism has brainwashed our culture. It has brainwashed our culture to the degree that even the church has fallen victim to this. Church leaders, theologians, professors of theology who are supposed to be profound in the Scripture, as well as lay people in the church have bought the feminist lies. There is even an organization in America called "CBE" having to do with Christians for equality. And this is an evangelical group advocating a feminist agenda....
>
> The real feminist agenda is frightening. The real feminist agenda is satanic....Feminism with all of its assorted features and its unique companionship with homosexuality is an old, old heresy that is meant to destroy God's design. It really started in the Garden when Eve, the original feminist, stepped out from under Adam's authority and thought she would act independently and led the whole race into sin, and thus the first act in Satan's feminist agenda was successful....
>
> What you see today in the feminist agenda is a repackaging, a reincarnation of ancient Gnosticism. In fact, the parallels are very striking....Ancient Gnosticism focused on women. This is what it said, for ex-

ample, "Eve was a spirit-endowed woman who saved Adam...." They said, "Final salvation for the whole world from the imprisonment of matter will come through female power." And the key is, "Female self-actualization, self-realization, self-knowledge in which a woman becomes so fully in tune with herself and so well knows herself and actualizes and realizes and fulfills herself that she becomes fully divine, and as she becomes divine she will rescue the rest of these lame men just like Eve fully divine rescued poor Adam...."

By the way, if you look at Hinduism you see where some of this stuff comes from because the Savior in Hinduism is a goddess. Radical feminism today is being moved along by the idea that women must be liberated, and they can redeem humanity, they can save humanity.[23]

How many pastors today do you hear talk from Scripture about feminism? Some pastors, like John MacArthur, understand the prevailing antibiblical philosophies of the day and warn their flocks by not only explaining these philosophies but also by destroying them through faithfully teaching God's Word. However, many "evangelical" pastors are among the most uneducated men I know when it comes to understanding the times, the worldviews, and the philosophies ruling our day and how to biblically destroy arguments raised up against the principles of the Lord as we are called to do in 2 Corinthians 10:5. As a result, much of the flock unknowingly eats the poison served up by false teachers and the culture.

William James (1842–1910)

William James is known for many things, including his lectures entitled *Pragmatism: A New Name for Some Old Ways of Thinking*. But concerning pragmatism, Dr. John MacArthur warns:

> Pragmatism is the notion that meaning or worth is determined by practical consequences....Pragmatism has roots in Darwinism and secular humanism. It is inherently relativistic, rejecting the notion of absolute right and wrong, good and evil, truth and error. Pragmatism

ultimately defines truth as that which is useful, meaningful, helpful. Ideas that don't seem workable or relevant are rejected as false....But when pragmatism is used to make judgments about right and wrong, or when it becomes a guiding philosophy of life and ministry, it inevitably clashes with Scripture.[24]

MacArthur is right to be concerned. Pragmatism has influential advocates within the Church. For instance, the Rev. Jim Garlow, pastor of an evangelical church, was a guest on a talk show in January 2012, one day before the Iowa caucuses. In this interview Garlow explained why he believes Christians should vote for Newt Gingrich. His choice of candidates is not the critical issue here. The problem is the reasoning he brought to defend his recommendation. He called for Christians to practice "biblically founded pragmatism":

> ...we do not as Christians assess the problem quickly enough with a healthy, biblical, biblically founded pragmatism. For example, I see people hyper-spiritualizing this election. They say, "Well, God parted the Red Sea." Well, he did it once! But he told Noah to build a boat. In other words, get in there and float on this thing. So we're being out-fought, unfortunately, because we hyper-spiritualize way too much.[25]

Ironically this is coming from a man who worked with "prophet" Lou Engle of the New Apostolic Reformation (NAR) in prayer and fasting events in California. The NAR and Word of Faith (WOF) members are well known for their "hyper-spiritualizing" and spiritual allegorizing. *Charisma Magazine* reported on this prayer rally sponsored by NAR and WOF:

> Organized by California pastor Jim Garlow and Prison Fellowship founder Chuck Colson, Pray & Act has gained support from a cross-section of Christians, including Bible teacher Kenneth Copeland, former Arkansas Gov. Mike Huckabee, Generals International co-founder Cindy Jacobs, Southern Baptist Convention leader Richard Land, Atlanta pastor Creflo Dollar, and Campus Crusade for Christ co-founder Vonette

Bright....The Pray & Act kickoff, to be broadcast on
the American Family Association (AFA) website Sunday at 8 p.m. Eastern, will feature leaders attending
the AFA's Values Voters summit this weekend. The
speakers—ranging from conservative politicians to
pastors—will be interviewed by Garlow and will join
him in calling Christians to 40 days of prayer and fasting. A final simulcast will be held on Oct. 30 from the
Lincoln Memorial.[26]

It is pragmatism at work when self-described evangelicals unite
with false teachers in prayer, fasting, and other spiritual enterprises in
hopes of winning the culture war, passing legislation, or winning elections. For several years, I have warned against the New Religious Right
and today's neo-evangelicals' practice of pragmatism.

Jim Garlow (who has also appeared on the television program of
New Age Mormon Glenn Beck and who participated in Beck's Restoring Honor rally in August 2010) shows his pragmatic approach to
spirituality:

Glenn Beck is being used by God—mightily....
Based on all I know about him, I am proud to stand
with him at the Restoring Honor Rally this weekend.
Glenn does not see that this is about him, because it is
not. It is about Restoring Honor. That is the issue. It is
much bigger than Glenn Beck, and he knows it. And
God knows, we need it.[27]

To the contrary, I believe Glenn Beck has been used by Satan—
mightily—and that he is a victim of Satan's strategy to leverage President Obama for satanic purposes. The president scared self-professing
Christians right into the waiting arms of Glenn Beck, his ecumenical
friends, and the Church of Rome. The strategy has been successful so
far in getting evangelicals to embrace false teachers, their false Jesus,
and the accompanying false gospel. The process will culminate in the
building of the harlot church described in Revelation 17.

Glenn Beck is a Catholic-turned-Mormon who bragged that when
he was at the Vatican, he was shocked to discover that they knew who
he was. His comments were recorded:

We are entering a, we are entering a dark, dark period of man. I was, I was in the Vatican, and I was surprised that the individual I was speaking to knew who I was. And they said: "Of course we know who you are. What you're doing is wildly important. We're entering a period of great darkness, and if good people don't stand up, we could enter a period unlike we have seen in a very long time." It was odd to stand in the Vatican and hear those words. Of all places that would understand the Dark Ages. We are dealing with people who want to deconstruct the world. They say they are for progress, but their progress is to deconstruct. Their progress is to go backwards. Instead of inventing our way out of something. Instead of heralding achievement and merit, they destroy it. Instead of respecting life, we devalue it.[28]

In February 2012, Beck's website proclaimed that Beck had once again traveled to the Vatican, and this time it was for very high-level meetings to discuss a global spiritual plan "to build bridges between various faith traditions so that the collective can have a stronger voice in fending off secular attacks."[29]

His website also reported that "In addition to the support Beck offered to the church, he also announced the 'We Are All Catholics Now' movement…"[30] which further plays into the ecuemencial agenda of the Church of Rome.

The Hegelian Dialetic process is not only a favorite tool of Satan but also of the Church of Rome and its Jesuit Order, which was founded in 1540. It is interesting how political and religious opposites are pitted against each other with the end result being a political and religious campaign that declares "we are all Catholic now." Former Jesuit Malachi Martin wrote in his 1987 *New York Times* bestseller *The Jesuits* that Francis Carney, a prominent Jesuit of the 1970s, argued that "dialectical conflict" should be "treasured as the key to the future of Catholicism."[31]

Former Catholic Glenn Beck, the Vatican, and the "we are all Catholics now" agenda lie at one end of the spiritual and political spectrum. At the other end is President Obama, who was helped into office largely by a Jesuit priest. While researching the Jesuit Order for the next book in this series (*Harlot Church*), I discovered this remarkable revelation in a Chicago magazine:

> It has now been more than four years since Barack Obama threw an arm around Gregory Galluzzo in Iowa and confided that whenever anybody asked how his presidential campaign had so quickly assembled its grass-roots operation, he would credit Galluzzo's mentorship. A former Jesuit priest who'd been drawn to Chicago by the work of Saul Alinsky, the father of community organizing, Galluzzo had good reason to feel proud: He was indirectly responsible for bringing young Barack Obama to Chicago to be an organizer. Obama's subsequent election was "like a son winning an office," says Galluzzo.[32]

Obama's campaign "quickly assembled its grass-roots operation" through the efforts and mentoring of a Jesuit. If this begins to help you understand how the game is being played, you are one of the fortunate few who do. Because so many do not, some of the biggest evangelical leaders in America and around the world have been "useful idiots" of the Church of Rome. Many of today's evangelical leaders, knowingly or unknowingly, have assisted in building the Harlot Church, the one-world religious system described in Revelation 17 as "the woman that rides the beast." (I'll explain in *Harlot Church* how the Church of Rome takes both sides of every major issue because of its "dialectical conflict" strategy.)

As I will examine in more detail in a later chapter, there are many problems with Glenn Beck's theology and doctrine, and I *do not* believe God is using Glenn Beck to restore righteousness in America. Nevertheless, a Christian broadcaster emailed me in August 2010 to say he was aware of my criticism of the Restoring Honor Rally and of the evangelicals who were publicly standing with Glenn Beck in his "spiritual" events. The man asked me if I didn't think it would be just like God to use a former alcoholic and his messed up Mormon theology to ignite revival in the American Church. I told him that God's Word specifically forbids Christians from uniting in spiritual enterprises with nonbelievers (see 2 Corinthians 6:14; 2 John 9–11; Romans

16:17–18), and thus God would not contradict His Word and bless that which He forbids.

In Summer 2011, pragmatism led this same broadcaster to promote The Response prayer rally in Houston, Texas, which included a circus of false teachers from the Word of Faith movement and the New Apostolic Reformation. Listed and pictured on The Response website as "endorsers" were individuals including Jim Garlow, David Barton, Cindy Jacobs, Che Ahn, Mike Bickle, John Hagee, Catholic priest Bob Hogan, and C. Peter Wagner, just to name a few. The honorary co-chairs listed and pictured on the website included James and Shirley Dobson, Tony Evans, Tony Perkins, and others. I believe many evangelicals and members of the New Religious Right, whether knowingly or unknowingly, have embraced pragmatism in order to "reclaim the country."

In the January 2012 interview I mentioned earlier, Garlow also emphasized his call for biblically founded pragmatism in a wide range of political involvement:

> Let me make it real, ground-tested and practical, and this will probably disturb some people. Michele Bachmann is wonderful, but she has no cash and no traction. Rick Perry is wonderful; I think he's absolutely fabulous; I hope he has strong influence in the nation in the future, along with Michele Bachmann. He has lots of cash, but his articulation skills have harmed him seriously, and he cannot overcome them, not now. Rick Santorum is wonderful, but he has no cash and no machinery. If he wins Iowa, he needs to be spending $3 million a week minimum to carry him through to try to keep up with the Romney machine, so Romney's best interest is to land Rick Santorum right up there at the top. People are not thinking through a strategy, and by lack of a biblically founded pragmatism that the Holy Spirit can show us, the lack of a strategy, we are being defeated and frankly humiliated, and our biblical rights are being robbed from us.[33]

I believe calling for "biblically founded pragmatism" is like calling for "biblically founded moral relativism" or "biblically founded situational ethics." Pragmatism, moral relativism, and situational ethics are fundamentally at odds with Christianity. Christians are not to practice them but are to make decisions based solely on the absolute truth of God's Word. John MacArthur agrees:

> What is pragmatism? Basically it is a philosophy that says that results determine meaning, truth, and value—what will work becomes a more important question than what is true. As Christians, we are called to trust what the Lord says, preach that message to others, and leave the results to Him. But many have set that aside. Seeking relevancy and success, they have welcomed the pragmatic approach and have received the proverbial Trojan horse.[34]

William James would likely be pleased that his term "pragmatism" is being used affirmatively by evangelical leaders and even more pleased that it is being tied to the Bible. Why? When pragmatism is tied to the Bible in a positive manner, it undermines the authority of God's Word. What more could an enemy of the cross and radical like William James ask for?

Saul Alinsky (1909–1972)

Antonio Gramsci advised World War II dictator Benito Mussolini that violence was not the way to bring about a lasting revolution people would embrace and maintain. Gramsci wrote eloquently of a "quiet" revolution—one that would transform a culture from within by changing the basic worldview of each and every institution in society. He also cautioned that this revolution would be "a long march through the institutions," not a blitzkrieg of change. So clear was his strategic thinking that Gramsci targeted Christianity specifically as the greatest philosophical adversary along the way.

Later in the twentieth century, Gramsci's vision captivated another rising neo-Marxist who codified the Gramsci dream in a 1971 book, *Rules for Radicals: A Pragmatic Primer for Realistic Radicals*. In it, Saul Alinsky detailed the need to penetrate the middle class and re-organize from within. Alinksy articulated tactics for infiltrating every conceivable social institution, including churches.

Alinsky had no compunction about speaking "against the Most High" because his allegiance lay elsewhere. The depth of Alinsky's evil intent is clear from the dedication page of his book:

> Lest we forget at least an over-the-shoulder acknowledgement to the very first radical; from all our legends, mythology, and history...the first radical known to man who rebelled against the establishment and did it so effectively that he at least won his own kingdom—Lucifer.[35]

Here you see a rare, forthright declaration of the basic force behind all the *Grave Influence* thinkers. Alinsky betrays the secret that the globalist vision is threaded through a diverse assembly of influencers thanks to a strategy created by the devil himself. It explains their hatred of Christians and the biblical worldview. It also reaffirms the point that we are in a spiritual battle, and the prize is hearts and minds. Here are a few eye-opening excerpts from *Rules for Radicals*:

> A Marxist begins with his prime truth that all evils are caused by the exploitation of the proletariat by the capitalists. From this he logically proceeds to the revolution to end capitalism, then into the third stage of reorganization into a new social order of the dictatorship of the proletariat, and finally the last stage...the political paradise of communism. (p. 10)

> An organizer working in and for an open society is in an ideological dilemma to begin with, he does not have a fixed truth...truth to him is relative and changing; everything to him is relative and changing....To the extent that he is free from the shackles of dogma, he can respond to the realities of the widely different situations.... (pp. 10–11)

> The first step in community organization is community disorganization. The disruption of the present organization is the first step toward community orga-

nization. Present arrangements must be disorganized if they are to be displaced by new patterns.... All change means disorganization of the old and organization of the new. (p. 116)

An organizer must stir up dissatisfaction and discontent.... He must create a mechanism that can drain off the underlying guilt for having accepted the previous situation for so long a time. Out of this mechanism, a new community organization arises.... The job then is getting the people to move, to act, to participate; in short, to develop and harness the necessary power to effectively conflict with the prevailing patterns and change them. When those prominent in the status quo turn and label you an "agitator" they are completely correct, for that is, in one word, your function—to agitate to the point of conflict. (p. 117)

It is important to understand the tactics of Saul Alinsky because his ideas are being used to transform churches from within and turn their members into community organizers:

From the moment the organizer enters a community he lives, dreams... only one thing and that is to build the mass power base of what he calls the army. Until he has developed that mass power base, he confronts no major issues.... Until he has those means and power instruments, his "tactics" are very different from power tactics. Therefore, every move revolves around one central point: how many recruits will this bring into the organization, whether by means of local organizations, churches, service groups, labor Unions, corner gangs, or as individuals.... Change comes from power, and power comes from organization. (p. 113)

In one respect, I must tip my hat to Saul Alinsky. He knew what he believed, why he believed it, and he made disciples. As Alinsky demonstrates, the radical, godless left is often more committed to making disciples than are Christians. And regrettably, his disciples have ended up in some very, very high places—like the White House. President Obama studied Alinsky and community-organized many of his ideas into practice. Hillary Clinton's senior honors thesis at Wellesley College was on Alinsky. Yet we're told that 28 percent of evangelicals voted for Obama or Clinton. And this in spite of the fact that the Harvard/San Francisco wing of the Democratic Party is the most pro-abortion, pro-homosexual and pro-socialist party in the history of the United States.

Sigmund Freud (1856–1939)

"To demolish religion with psychoanalytic weapons," Freud biographer Peter Gay reported, "had been on Freud's agenda for many years."[36]

Sigmund Freud, like Friedrich Nietzsche who strongly influenced him, hated God and Christianity. In his book *The Future of an Illusion*, Freud describes his "absolutely negative attitude toward religion, in every form and dilution."[37]

Benjamin Wiker, in *Ten Books that Screwed Up the World*, explains the roots of Freud's attitude:

> We cannot forget Nietzsche's assumption that religion was an entirely human creation. Since Freud read Nietzsche, this may have done as much as anything to help form his presentation of religion in *The Future of an Illusion*.[38]

With that concept at the core of Freud's thinking, Wiker goes on to describe the psychoanalyst's resultant, perverted worldview:

> His rebellion took the form of baptizing as natural the most hideously unnatural sins, sins condemned by every society as the most unholy and unthinkable.... Freud damned as unnatural the Christian-based morality of Western society.[39]

Freud himself points out several of these "unholy and unthinkable" inclinations: "Among these instinctual wishes are those of incest, cannibalism, and lust for killing."[40]

Freud believed that it is the people who reject a biblical worldview and follow their "natural" desires that are truly sane. As Dr. Wicker explains:

> He [Freud] claimed that psychological disorders were the result of the unnatural repression of our naturally unholy and anti-social desires, and that some people just couldn't handle the repression....Therefore, neurotics are the only sane people because they react to unnatural frustration by training to reclaim their original, natural, asocial and amoral state. The result: the anti-social psychopath who kills without conscience is the most natural of all. The interesting effect of Freud's proclamation that evil is natural was the seemingly unintended consequence of making psychopathic insanity natural.[41]

The Bible declares that all have sinned and fallen short of the glory of God. It also holds that the world will become increasingly wicked. People will do whatever seems right in their own eyes and will call evil good and good evil. Indeed Freud, Maslow, Fromm, and others in their line of psychologists prove that this has come true. Calling "evil good and good evil," they declare Christians insane and those who act out compulsions such as child molestation and murder sane.

The Soul of a Soulless Discipline

The word *psychology* derives from the Greek word "psyche," the study of the soul—which, ironically, should be impossible for secular humanistic psychologists who deny the spiritual world and the soul. Author Alan Bloom notes that for secular humanists "the self is the modern substitute for the soul." And when humanists refer to the mind, they really mean the brain.

Contrast the significance the Christian worldview places on this realm that Freud insists doesn't even exist. The biblical worldview, of course, acknowledges both the spiritual and natural worlds. The brain is part of the natural world, but the mind and heart, as described in the Bible, are connected to the soul—the spiritual side of man.

Scripture mentions the heart 826 times, where "heart" refers to the core of a person's being. Proverbs 4:23 says the heart is "the source of life." From the heart proceeds our good and bad thoughts, emotions, and behavior. The Bible admonishes us to love the Lord our God with all our heart, soul, strength, and mind.

In Scripture, the words "heart" and "mind" are often interchangeable, and other times, they complement one another. Jeremiah 17:9, for instance, describes the heart as "more deceitful than anything else and desperately sick," so the mind must moderate the heart. The Bible also describes the nature of those who ignore God as it tells us how to practice godliness:

- Psalm 14:1—"The fool has said in his heart, 'There is no God.'"
- Proverbs 23:19—"Hear, my son, and be wise; And guide your heart in the way."
- Proverbs 23:7—"For as he thinks in his heart, so he is."

Your heart and mind are part of your soul, the core of your being that will still exist after you die. Souls will live forever and be judged by God (Romans 2:5; Revelation 2:23). The person who repents of sin and surrenders his or her will to the Lordship of Jesus Christ is the person who has received mercy and grace. That person has been saved by God on the basis of Christ's complete payment for sin at Calvary.

According to Romans, the moral law is written on the heart and mind of every person—thus the conscience. "Con" means with and "science" means knowledge. So every time people sin or rebel against God, *they know it is wrong.*

We don't murder fellow human beings because murder goes against the character of God. We are not to lie, steal, or break any of the other Ten Commandments because doing so would go against Who God is. Romans 1:21 reminds us, "although they knew God, they did not glorify Him as God, nor were thankful, but became futile in their thoughts, and their foolish hearts were darkened." And Romans 2:15 points out that people "show the work of the law written in their hearts, their conscience also bearing witness, and between themselves their thoughts accusing or else excusing them."

Did you catch that? Romans 2:15 tells us that the conscience is one way in which man can know he has violated the character and nature of God. The conscience is part of the soul, and yet psychology denies the conscience by denying the soul. John MacArthur explains that killing the conscience is one of the objectives of psychology:

> The goal of modern psychology is to train people to ignore their conscience. Your conscience is making you feel guilty? That's wrong. You're not a bad person, you're...what?...you're good, you lack self-esteem. In fact, you're so much better than you think you are that it's really troublesome and most of your problems are because you don't know how good you really are. So when conscience says you're guilty, you're guilty, this is wrong, this is wrong, this is wrong, you silence that conscience.[41]

People can either accept the guilty feeling of the law upon their conscience that accuses them of transgression when they sin or they can excuse the guilty feeling and learn to ignore it. If they ignore the guilt long enough or often enough, they will become people "speaking lies in hypocrisy, having their own conscience seared with a hot iron" (1 Timothy 4:2).

You can see, then, that people who listen to Freud and his devotees—believing that sinful thoughts and impulses are natural instead of understanding that guilt is a sign they have violated the character and nature of God—are headed in a seriously wrong direction. The end result can be true insanity if their rebellion against God goes too far. This is the effect of having a "seared" conscience, yet no one will have an excuse at Judgment for rejecting God. Romans 3:19–20 warns:

> Now we know that whatever the law says, it says to those who are under the law, that every mouth may be stopped, and all the world may become guilty before God. Therefore by the deeds of the law no flesh will be justified in His sight, for by the law is the knowledge of sin.

Everyone has broken the law. No one can justify his or her entry into heaven by claiming to have "lived a good-enough life." God's standard is to keep the complete moral law, and no one has done that, except Jesus.

To further underscore the reality that committing sin is breaking the moral law, 1 John 3:4 says, "Everyone who commits sin also breaks the law; sin is the breaking of law." And Romans 3:10 explains, "There is none righteous, no, not one." Finally, Romans 3:23 concludes: "... all have sinned and fall short of the glory of God."

Humanist, psychologist, and member of the Frankfurt School, Erich Fromm greatly respected Freud. And while disagreeing in some areas, Fromm and Freud were united in their attack on Christianity. Fromm declared, "[M]an challenges the supreme power of God, and he is able to challenge it because he is potentially God."[43]

In a similar vein, psychologist Abraham Maslow developed the idea of self-actualization—which means a person's innate goodness has evolved. David Noebel describes self-actualization this way:

> Abraham Maslow refers to those in touch with their inherent goodness as self-actualized. He categorizes this drive to get in touch with our inherent goodness as a need that can be attended to only after we have satisfied our lower needs—namely, physiological, safety, social, and ego needs. We must satisfy these needs as well as our need for self-actualization before we can truly be declared mentally healthy.[44]

Humanistic psychologists deny our sinful nature that results from the original sin of Adam and Eve. Instead, they believe man is simply a product of his environment. When they apply Darwinian evolution to their worldview, they contend that society is evolving along with nature and that things will get better and better as we become more enlightened—or, as Maslow claimed, self-actualized. In truth, the twentieth century was the bloodiest of all centuries. In other words, things are *not* getting better.

As part of the denial of original sin and man's depravity, psychology elevates man and claims that our problems do not stem from a sinful nature but from a lack of self-esteem. John MacArthur explains the result of this way of thinking:

Humanistic psychology has had a devastating effect on Christians and on Christian theology for a number of reasons. But one of these reasons is built into the very basic humanistic philosophy that man exists for his own satisfaction. It is the very bottom line in humanism that man to be happy must have all of his perceived needs and desires met. And so humanism says that the goal of life is to have all of my wants fulfilled, all of my desires accomplished, all of my needs met. Man will be happy, say the psychologists, man will be content, man will be satisfied when his desires are met, when his longings are met, when his needs are met, when he is fulfilled. Contemporary presentations of the gospel have sucked up this humanistic psychology and philosophy unwittingly. And you have the good news of self-worth, the good news of the value of you as a person, the good news of security, the good news of significance, the good news of prosperity, of health, wealth and happiness, the psychological gospel, the prosperity gospel.[45]

Karl Marx (1818–1883)

As a young man, Karl Marx was dismissed from several universities for his radical, revolutionary views. An atheist and a Secular Humanist, he wrote the *Communist Manifesto* with his friend Friedrich Engels. Marx did not believe in the spiritual world or life after death, only in the natural, material world, and he valued people only for what they could do for the State. Is it any wonder, then, that the worldview of Marx—Communism—has been responsible for the murder of as many as 500 million people?

Marx hated the free market and capitalism—and their roots in the Protestant Reformation—perhaps because he was a lazy slob who wanted other people to take care of him. He lived largely off of his friend Engels, who drew an income from the family business. How perversely ironic that Marx spread his hatred of capitalism while drawing his livelihood from the fruits of capitalism! Isn't that always the mode of operation for those who follow the economic philosophy of Communism, the most virulent form of socialism?

Marx was such a reprobate that out of his six children, three died of starvation while still infants, two others committed suicide, and only one lived to become an adult. The Marx family was often hounded by creditors. Yet, when Marx received a gift of 160 pounds (about $500), he neglected to pay his bills, his rent, or to buy food for his starving family. Rather, he went on a two-month drinking binge with his intellectual buddies while his wife and infant children were evicted from their apartment. Marx, the parasite, also spent his wife's inheritances from her mother and uncle, causing his family to live on the edge of financial ruin for years.

Among the many infectious ideas Marx promoted was his hatred for the traditional family. Instead, he favored "a system of wives in common." Needless to say, Marx did not have a great marriage, and when his wife died, Marx didn't even attend her funeral. Not only was he a negligent husband and father, Marx was such an uncaring, arrogant bully that he had few friends. Even those who agreed with his teachings did not like him as a person. As a result, when he died, less than a dozen people attended his funeral.

The basis of Marxism is atheism. As Marx said, "Religion is the sigh of the oppressed creature, the sentiment of a heartless world, as it is the spirit of spiritless conditions. It is the opium of the people."[46]

This obsession to obliterate Christianity manifests itself in many ways. Richard Wurmbrand was imprisoned for 14 years in Romania for preaching the Gospel. He also railed against Communism. After his freedom was purchased, he found his way to America.

A month after arriving in 1966, Wurmbrand testified before the United States Senate, and for the next three years, his testimony was the most-sold government document. The testimony is available online (http://members.cox.net/wurmbrand/communist.html), and if you read it, you'll understand why it is so popular. It warns that Communism cannot tolerate Christianity, and the Communist strategy in America is to infiltrate religious institutions and use them to further the Communist cause. Wurmbrand pleaded with Americans to oppose Communism in any form:

> The church can never have a peaceful coexistence with atheism. Everybody would laugh if I would say that health can peacefully exist with the microbe of

tuberculosis, that the FBI can coexist peacefully with gangsters, that the church can peacefully exist with drunkenness, but communism and atheism is much worse than drug addiction and drunkenness. You drink a little wine and the next day it passes, but communism poisons youth and our children since 50 years. How can there be peaceful existence with this on the side of churchmen and the church leadership I cannot understand.[47]

Pastor Wurmbrand explained that Communists do not really care whether or not people become Communists per se but only that they do not oppose Communism. Pointing out the unbiblical ideas and values of Communism leads to cruel and murderous actions against dissenters. In outlining the Communist approach, Wurmbrand explained that churches do not need to teach Communism, just a liberal Christianity that allows for the acceptance of what Communists want to accomplish:

> Romanian Communists are very interested in the fact that you have here in the States, something like 300,000 [liberal clergy] on their side. They can't very well win them for Communism, but they can win them for a leftwing Christianity which supports Communism.[48]

In addition to his congressional testimony, Wurmbrand wrote several books cautioning against Communism. Unfortunately, Wurmbrand's warnings have largely gone unheeded, and we are now suffering the consequences. Numerous churches throughout America and the world promote the Communism of Marx under the umbrella of social justice, but Christians should pursue biblical justice, not social justice. Social justice is a masking term for the economic philosophies of Communism and socialism.

Social justice promotes the redistribution of income in the name of "the common good." Among world influencers, it is important to note that "common good" is used by the Vatican and the pope over and over. That should not come as a surprise when we realize the term "social justice" was coined by a Catholic Jesuit.[49] Luigi Taparelli

D'Azeglio, who lived from 1793 to 1862, was an Italian Catholic scholar of the Society of Jesus who coined the term "social justice."[50]

My friend and frequent Worldview Weekend radio guest Carl Teichrib explains that many denominations now actively promote "social justice":

> In today's Christian world—and Western culture in general—there's a myriad of changes taking place, and with it comes new language. "Social Justice" is certainly in the spotlight. Jim Wallis of Sojourners uses this term repeatedly. Brain McLaren's book *Everything Must Change* seeks to reframe Christianity in a social justice context. The Christian Reformed Church has a social justice office, as does the Salvation Army; and the Mennonite Church USA, the United Methodist Church, the United Church of Canada, and an endless list of other denominations and church bodies speak of "social justice."[51]

FBI founder and director J. Edgar Hoover, in his 1958 book *Masters of Deceit,* explains why Communists insert their people as the heads of churches and other such organizations to promote Communism in the guise of social justice:

> To make a known Party member president of a front would immediately label it as "communist." But if a sympathizer can be installed, especially a man of prominence, such as an educator, minister, or scientist, the group can operate as an "independent" organization.[52]

Marx was educated at a secularized Jesuit high school,[53] and interestingly enough, he and Jesuit Taparelli were contemporaries:

> Marx and Engels fleshed out their "science of socialism" during the same time frame as Luigi Taparelli D'Azeglio's "social justice." And *The Communist Manifesto* was published the same year that the Society of Fraternal Democrats called for social justice. Under Communism, wealth redistribution was to be used for social

ends. In this structure, private property for personal gain was viewed as the cornerstone of the class system and was seen as the cause of social injustices and strife. Wealth redistribution, therefore, was aimed at producing a society where all people were economically equal. Hence, the abolition of bourgeois property (that of the capitalist class) was the key to Communism.[54]

The Church of Rome via its Maryknoll and Jesuit orders has promoted, aided, and propped up Communism when it served its interests. The pope's 2012 visit to Communist Cuba more than proves the point. Roman Catholic Humberto Fontova wrote an article entitled "Pope Blesses Castroism."[55] Read the article and weep for those suffering under Castro's police state. And yes, the pope had time for the Castro brothers but no time for those languishing under them. In fact, the day after the pope left the island, Castro's thugs arrested "at least 43 Cuban dissidents."[56]

This sort of thing is not brand new. In 2009, the Vatican, through a Jesuit newspaper, praised Karl Marx. Richard Owen of *The Times Online* reports:

> *L'Osservatore Romano*, the Vatican newspaper, said yesterday that Marx's early critiques of capitalism had highlighted the "social alienation" felt by the "large part of humanity" that remained excluded, even now, from economic and political decision-making.

> Georg Sans, a German-born professor of the history of contemporary philosophy at the pontifical Gregorian University, wrote in an article that Marx's work remained especially relevant today as mankind was seeking "a new harmony" between its needs and the natural environment. He also said that Marx's theories may help to explain the enduring issue of income inequality within capitalist societies.

> "We have to ask ourselves, with Marx, whether the forms of alienation of which he spoke have their origin in the capitalist system," Professor Sans wrote. "If

money as such does not multiply on its own, how are we to explain the accumulation of wealth in the hands of the few?"

Professor Sans's article was first published in *La Civiltà Cattolica*, a Jesuit paper, which is vetted in advance by the Vatican Secretariat of State. The decision to republish it in the Vatican newspaper gives it added papal endorsement.[57]

As we will see in chapter 5, Communism also hides within a mixture of socialism and capitalism known as communitarianism or "Communism lite" and is being aggressively promoted by the Church of Rome and prominent neo-evangelicals.

Today's young people get a heavy dose of social justice curriculum written by individuals such Bill Ayers. As a result, many people tell me they are pleased that their church or denomination is involved in social justice. But Carl Teichrib explains why social justice is completely unbiblical:

"My church has a social justice mandate…. This is something I support."

Sounds nice, but can you tell me what you mean? The usual response I get, thankfully, centers on feeding the poor, helping at a homeless shelter or safe house, assisting the elderly, working with troubled teens, or supporting an orphanage.

Sorry, that's not social justice. The dominant social justice concept for the past 150 years has been centered on the sliding slope of Papal-advocated wealth redistribution, and a Marxist version of Collectivism. Feeding the poor and assisting the helpless, from a Christian perspective, isn't social justice—its biblical compassion, a generous act of love. Such acts of compassion engage individual lives, and are based on the Christian call of loving others more than self. This is the heart of compassion: An individual sees a need, and operating out of love, reaches to meet that need.

Churches too are to function in a similar manner. A need is evident, and moved by compassion, the congregation works to solve the dilemma. Coercion never enters the picture, nor does a political agenda emerge, nor is a call for economic equality heard.

The biblical parable of the Good Samaritan demonstrates true compassion (Luke 10). A Jewish man has been beaten, robbed, and left to die on the road. Various people pass him by, including the religiously pious. However, a Samaritan traveler sees the individual, and although the Samaritan is culturally alienated from the beaten man, he recognizes the desperation and individually takes action—dressing his wounds and providing a place of rest and refuge. And the Samaritan pays for it himself without demanding remuneration or compensation, either from the victim, his family or community, or from the government or ruling class.

However, if the Samaritan were a supporter of the dominant theme in social justice, he would have acted with a different motive for different ends. The Samaritan would have used the occasion to lobby for social transformation.

1. The robbers were really victims of an unjust economic system, and had acted in response to the oppression of the ruling class.
2. In order to bring justice to this oppressed class, and to steer them back to a caring community, equitable wealth redistribution should take place. The rich must be taxed to fund necessary social programs. A more equitable society is needed.
3. Who will pay the victim's medical bills? The community or the rich.
4. This tragic event, the Samaritan would tell us, is a graphic reminder of the class struggle. We are all victims of an unjust economic order. Therefore, we must be the "voice of the voiceless" and advocate for radical social change.

In the social justice framework there is another agenda that lurks behind the tragic: A political/economic cause is piggybacked and leveraged—the cause of economic equality through wealth redistribution. This isn't about truly helping the victim; it's about using the victim.

Biblical justice, on the other hand, never seeks to dismantle class structures. Evil actions are condemned, but this isn't specific to a particular social strata. Consider the words of Leviticus 19:15: "You shall do no injustice in judgment. You shall not be partial to the poor, nor honor the person of the mighty. But in righteousness you shall judge your neighbor."[58]

Mark W. Hendrickson complements the commentary of Mr. Teichrib when he writes:

[Biblical] Justice not only means that nobody is to be picked on because he is poor or favored because he is rich, but that (contrary to the doctrine of "social justice") nobody is to be picked on because he is rich or favored because he is poor.

The fundamental error of today's "social justice" practitioners is their hostility to economic inequality, per se. Social justice theory fails to distinguish between economic disparities that result from unjust deeds and those that are part of the natural order of things. All Christians oppose unjust deeds... [but] it isn't necessarily unjust for some people to be richer than others.

God made us different from each other. We are unequal in aptitude, talent, skill, work ethic, priorities, etc. Inevitably, these differences result in some individuals producing and earning far more wealth than others. To the extent that those in the "social justice" crowd obsess about eliminating economic inequality, they are at war with the nature of the Creator's creation.

The Bible doesn't condemn economic inequality. You can't read Proverbs without seeing that some people are poor due to their own vices. There is nothing unjust about people reaping what they sow, whether wealth or poverty.

Jesus himself didn't condemn economic inequality. Yes, he repeatedly warned about the snares of material wealth; he exploded the comfortable conventionality of the Pharisaical tendency to regard prosperity as a badge of honor and superiority; he commanded compassion toward the poor and suffering. But he also told his disciples, "you have the poor always with you" (Matthew 26:11), and in the parable of the talents (Matthew 25:24–30) he condemned the failure to productively use one's God-given talents—whether many or few, exceptional or ordinary—by having a lord take money from the one who had the least and give it to him who had the most, thereby increasing economic inequality.

The Lord's mission was to redeem us from sin, not to redistribute our property or impose an economic equality on us. In fact, Jesus explicitly declined to undermine property rights or preach economic equality when he told the man who wanted Jesus to tell his brother to share an inheritance with him, "Man, who made me a judge or divider over you" (Luke 12:14).[59]

Many within the apostate church, civil government, the educational establishment, national and international corporations, charities, foundations, and nongovernment organizations (NGOs) have bought into what is called the sustainable development version of communitarianism. Henry Lamb explains this danger:

From the highest rafters of academia comes another enemy of freedom: Communitarianism. This is a belief system that opposes both authoritarianism and individualism, and promotes instead a social organization that is governed by policies designed by civil society to limit individual freedom as required for the benefit of the community. Dr. Amitai Etzioni is credited with founding this communitarian movement.

For more than 200 years, all these questions were addressed by elected representatives of the community. Individual members of the community have always been free to propose projects to meet unmet community needs. Elected officials who failed to respond to the wishes of the community could always be replaced at the next election.

In the 1980s and 1990s, the environmental movement, joined by "social justice" advocates, grew impatient with the rate of change under this traditional policymaking procedure. That's why the President's Council on Sustainable Development declared, "We need a new decision process...." This new decision process is constructed on a communitarian philosophy and employs the consensus process.

Typically, these councils have been initiated and funded by special interest groups or by the federal government—not by the local community. These councils inevitably create a plan that incorporates the recommendations set forth in Agenda 21, the U.N.'s bible on sustainable development. These plans limit individual freedom and impose individual responsibilities in order to create a community that the vision council has determined to be in the best interest of the whole.[60]

Satan has used socialism, Communism, and Marxism to build his "new order"—his own kingdom. He seeks to destroy Christianity, free nations, national sovereignty, and laws based on the character and nature of God. The devil has used dictators committed to Marxist/Leninist philosophies to kill countless Christians. Why? Only committed Christians build God's Kingdom in the spiritual realm by preaching the Gospel, making them one of Satan's greatest obstacles.

In every way possible, Satan encourages people to violate the Ten Commandments. The doing away with private property (stealing), for instance, forces service to the State alone in order to survive. This fulfills the enemy's plan that people ultimately are not really serving the State but the one who stands behind the authoritarian State—Satan himself. In John 10:10, Jesus points out that "the thief does not come except to steal, and to kill, and to destroy." Satan—and his tool, the Communist State—is a thief. He loves Communism, socialism, and Marxism because any version of such a government does, indeed, steal, kill, and destroy.

Later in John 10:10, Jesus offers the good news: He came so we would have eternal life. This is a precious promise for the untold numbers of Christians who have refused to worship at the altar of Satan (serving the State) and who have been imprisoned or murdered as a result.

Christians can take hope that God's Kingdom will come and crush Satan's dominion, as foretold in the book of Daniel. Until that day, believers must realize that failure to oppose socialism, Communism, and Marxism is to agree with a satanic plan that fuels injustice, cruelty, antifamily values, and anti-Christian worldviews.

One final quote captures the essence of what Marx believed and what he thought should be done: "The idea of God is the keynote of a perverted civilization. It must be destroyed."[61] He was dead wrong, but that doesn't change the reality that the worldview of Marx is alive and well in America and around the world.[62] The influence of Marx's ideas is overwhelming, and his vile legacy continues despite the indisputable failure of his atheistic, Communistic worldview wherever it has been tried.

Charles Darwin (1809–1882)

The spectacular scope and intensity of Darwinism's influence on virtually every arena of thought is breathtaking. In a sense, Darwin "started it all." His books *The Origin of Species by Means of Natural Selection or The Preservation of Favored Races in the Struggle for Life* and *The Descent of Man* crystallized the worldview he would come to stand for.

The Descent of Man is essentially a call to embrace eugenics, which Darwin euphemistically called "survival of the fittest." Although Darwin initially described a farm animal breeding program, he eventually made it clear he was talking about human "evolution" as well. The legacy of this one idea has led to the deaths of millions. Here's how Darwin put it:

> With savages, the weak in body or mind are soon eliminated; and those that survive exhibit a vigorous state of health....We civilized men, on the other hand, do our utmost to check the process of elimination; we build asylums for the imbecile, the maimed, and the sick; we institute poor-laws; and our medical men exert their utmost skill to save the life of every one to the last moment. There is reason to believe that vaccination has preserved thousands, who from a weak constitution would formerly have succumbed to smallpox. Thus the weak members of civilized societies propagate their kind. One who has attended to the breeding of domestic animals will not doubt that this must be highly injurious to the race of man. It is surprising how soon a want of care, or care wrongly directed, leads to the degeneration of a domestic race; but excepting in the case of man himself; hardly anyone is so ignorant as to allow his worst animals to breed.[63]

Darwin spins this into his prescription for how to assure the continuing upward progress of mankind:

> If...various checks...do not prevent the reckless, the vicious and otherwise inferior members of society from increasing at a quicker rate than the better class of man, the nation will retrograde, as has occurred too often in the history of the world. We must remember that progress is no invariable rule.[64]

While Darwin's theory of evolution has been readily accepted by all mainstream liberal churches (those belonging to the National and World Council of Churches), it also has made great inroads into evangelical churches and colleges. This issue alone could comprise a book, but the one major surprise is certainly the Nazarene denomination and its pro-evolution colleges.

Nazarene churches for the most part were at one time fundamental, evangelical, evangelistic, and orthodox. Yet, many of their colleges (Point Loma Nazarene University, Eastern Nazarene College, etc.) reek with Darwinism. Their college bookstores promote Darrel R. Falk's *Coming to Peace with Science: Bridging the World Between Faith and Biology* (InterVarsity Press, 2004), but you will not find any anti-Darwin works so students can get both sides of the issue. Why not allow students to at least read Stephen C. Meyer's article in the August 4, 2004, *Proceedings of the Biological Society of Washington,* which challenges the theory of Darwinian evolution? It probably won't hurt the students, but it might hurt their evolutionary professors' claims to fairness and scholoarship.

Point Loma's biology professor, Darrel R. Falk, is also the head of BioLogos, a theistic evolution organization which brings its evolution message to hundreds of evangelical churches. It is a scandal in the making. I bet you will not find any information or even a word of warning from this organization on Darwin's relationship to Adolph Hitler and his Nazism or Joseph Stalin and his Communism. Darwinian evolution was the biological basis of both of those death-dealing political movements. BioLogos is also weak on Adam and Eve. Most theistic evolutionists deny our first parents, and most theistic evolutionsists avoid like the plague any discussion relating to the Cambrian period's trilobite fossils (there was no duobite or monobite) and the coelacanth fish!

Pastor Tim Keller, as we shall examine in a later chapter, embraces social justice, but he also supports BioLogos. *Christianity Today* reported on March 30, 2012, that "evangelical evolutionists meet in New York." The article explains:

> Attending were such luminaries as N. T. Wright, Alister McGrath, John Ortberg, Tim Keller, Scot McKnight, Os Guinness, Joel Hunter, and Andy Crouch.... This year's program centered on concerns for the church—especially for young people who feel torn between science and the Bible.[65]

(Please take note of the name Joel Hunter, as he is a neo-evangelical whose beliefs we will examine later.) Tim Keller is quoted in the article as saying, "To develop a BioLogos narrative is the job of pastors."[66] Really? So the job of pastors is to undermine the authority of Scripture and dilute the purpose and need of the death, burial, and resurrection of Jesus Christ due to original sin? This is what BioLogos is doing when they deny the biblical and historical persons of Adam and Eve and the original sin that entered into the world through the Fall.

Dr. Albert Mohler, president of Southern Baptist Theological Seminary, addresses the distorted theology and worldview of Biologos:

> Writers for BioLogos have repeatedly made the case that we must relinquish the inerrancy of the Bible and accept that the biblical writers worked from a defective understanding of the world and its origins. They have asserted, for example, that the Apostle Paul was simply wrong in assuming that Adam was an historical person from whom all humans are descended. They have been bold and honest in rejecting the biblical account of the Fall as historical. They have warned that an affirmation of biblical inerrancy has led evangelicalism into an "intellectual cul-de-sac."[67]

Mohler continues:

> They are embarrassed by the fact that a majority of evangelicals reject evolution, and they honestly believe that some people will not come to know Christ because they are so offended by our unwillingness to accept evolution. They have repeatedly asserted that the credibility and integrity of our Christian witness is at stake.
>
> The writers for BioLogos have been unsparing in their criticism of evangelicals who believe in the inerrancy of the Bible or are proponents of either Intelligent Design or creationism.[68]

John Upchurch with Answers in Genesis wrote an article in 2011 entitled "The Danger of BioLogos" in which he makes the case that BioLogos attacks the Gospel:

In their effort to reconcile evolution with the Bible, proponents of theistic evolution also wipe away the cosmic impact of the Curse and of Christ's full redemptive work. Romans 8:22 makes it clear that the whole creation groans as a result of Adam's sin. Acts 3:21 and Colossians 1:15–20 teach that when Christ, the Creator of all things, comes again He will restore all things. At that time, the Curse of Genesis 3 will be removed, and a glorious new heavens and earth will exist (Revelation 22:3).

The denial of a "first couple" similarly attacks the gospel. "Jesus and the apostle Paul clearly consider Adam and Eve to be historical," explains theologian Cal Beisner. "Paul makes our whole understanding of the relationship between the redeemed and Christ contingent on Adam's being a historical individual just as Christ is (Romans 5:12–19; 1 Corinthians 15:22, 15:46–49). Take away Adam as a historical person, and the whole understanding of the federal (covenantal) relationship between Christ and believers collapses—and with it the gospel of justification by grace alone through faith alone in Christ alone because of the federal (covenantal) imputation of His righteousness to believers."[69]

Then there is the disturbing fact that the John Templeton Foundation provided funds to launch BioLogos. The website for the foundation explains its purpose:

These grants support the launch of the BioLogos Foundation with the creation of a website and a series of workshops on the compatibility of theism and evolutionary science. The website will serve as a forum for Francis Collins and other expert consultants to address common questions about the relationship between faith and science. The invitation-only workshops will bring scientists and evangelical leaders together to seek a theology more accepting of science, specifically evolutionary biology.[70]

John Templeton was a promoter of pagan spirituality who wanted to establish a world religion "about God that doesn't rely on ancient revelations or scripture."[71] If a man is known by the company he keeps, this tells us a lot about the discernment of N. T. Wright, Alister McGrath, John Ortberg, Tim Keller, Scot McKnight, Os Guinness, Joel Hunter, and Andy Crouch, does it not?

Darwin and Spiritual Evolution

Darwin helped lay the foundation for natural evolution that has now produced a belief in spiritual evolution. One of the leading proponents of spiritual evolution is Michael Dowd. According to his website, Reverend Dowd is a graduate of the Assemblies of God school, Evangel University. (While this school does not embrace Dowd's worldview, I mention this only to reveal that many of today's leaders of the New Spirituality are not coming just out of far left, mainline denominations but from what have historically been evangelical denominations, colleges, and universities.)

Dowd describes himself as an "evolutionary evangelist" and is the author of *Thank God for Evolution*. On September 24, 2011, *The Ventura County Star* ran an article on Dowd that, not surprisingly, reveals what appears to be his hostility to the authority of the Word of God. Quoting Dowd:

> I hope to help attendees celebrate facts as God's native tongue and to truly get that scientific, historic, and cross-cultural evidence to reveal God's word for today far more accurately than the Bible could ever hope to.[72]

Dowd makes it clear that he does not believe in the authority of Scripture or that God's Word has been delivered once and for all to the saints as declared in Jude 3. Dowd believes that "God's word for today" is revealed through science and other extrabiblical methods. He also seems to believe that Christians such as I (and I pray you as well), who believe that the Word of God equips us for every good work (2 Timothy 3: 16–17), are involved in "idolatry of the written word." Evidently, biblical Christianity has become out of date because as nature, individuals, and society have evolved, the Word of God has remained static:

He believes his upcoming talk is important "because idolatry of the written word has rendered the church deaf, dumb, and blind to what God's been faithfully revealing through evidence the past 200 years," Dowd said. "Consequently billions of human beings not only don't appreciate the evolutionary significance of religion and religious differences, their inner GPS is so wildly out of date that it's no wonder they suffer and struggle needlessly. Their views of history, death, and human nature are not aligned with reality."[73]

The article continues:

"On behalf of the United Church of Christ in Simi Valley I was eager to invite Michael because he is a critical voice in the evolution versus creationism/intelligent design conversation," said June Goudey, a United Church of Christ minister. "That conversation has to do with the compatibility of science and religion, which many conservative people of faith discount."

Dowd's teachings "support the insights researchers have made into the importance of human consciousness in the evolving universe," Goudey said. "By understanding that human beings are the universe becoming conscious of itself, he offers a powerfully transcendent and liberating view of human nature without undermining the role of divine presence and purpose."[74]

Did you have to read that last paragraph twice to make sure Dowd is saying what it sounds like he's saying? Dowd believes "human beings are the universe." This is pantheism and panenthiesm.

You will not be shocked that Dowd's speaking schedule for 2011 and 2012 included a majority of Unitarian and Universalist churches. (Unitarians are really Cosmic Humanists or New Agers.) Dowd's website also reveals that he spoke on January 21, 2012, to "Jesuit Alumni in Arizona." This is especially interesting because one of the fathers of the New Age Movement was a Catholic Jesuit by the name of Teilhard de Chardin.

In *Grave Influence*, I explain more about the significance of de Chardin's thought. I devote a chapter to the worldview of Marilyn Ferguson and her book *The Aquarian Conspiracy*. In her book, Ferguson reveals that she surveyed New Agers and asked them who had influenced them the most. The two names that topped the list were Carl Jung and Teilhard de Chardin.[75]

As I studied Dowd, I could hear the influence of de Chardin, who wrote:

> Without the process of biological evolution, which produced the human brain, there would be no sanctified souls; and similarly, without the evolution of collective thought, through which alone the plentitude of human consciousness can be attained on earth, how can there be a consummated Christ?[76]

Former U.S. vice president Al Gore wrote in his book, *Earth in the Balance*, that de Chardin believed "the fate of mankind, as well as of religion, depends upon the emergence of a new faith in the future."[77] Such a faith is certainly growing in popularity, but it is not new. The lies of Satan from Genesis 3 have simply been repackaged.

On the Internet, I found a video of Michael Dowd preaching at "Renaissance Unity in Detroit, Michigan, one of America's largest progressive churches." Dowd proclaims that he believes God did not create everything at one time but that everything evolved and that the energy or creativity that assisted in the evolutionary process is God. Michael Dowd proclaimed that we are part of that process, and thus we are also God:

> So we see this at all nested levels: creativity exists and what we now know, and I say know rather than believe, is that ultimate creativity—God, the Goddess, whatever your name for ultimate creativity—didn't really make everything at the beginning of time like a potter makes a pot or a carpenter makes a table. The divine creativity, God's creativity, exists throughout the entire universe in a nested sense, and from this vantage point, God is not a supreme landlord residing off

the planet and outside the universe—no, a supreme engineer who, you know, who made this clockwork universe. God is nothing less than a sacred proper name for that ultimate creative reality, the largest creative reality that includes it all yet transcends it all.[78]

Dowd goes on to explain that his worldview lines up with what the Greek Stoics believed. But remember: Paul on Mars Hill preached to a group of people that included Stoics, the New Agers of their day. Dowd is openly admitting that he agrees with the Stoics' description of God:

> This is God beyond belief or disbelief; this is a God that is undeniably real in every drop of experience. You may or may not choose to call ultimate reality God, but that reality is itself undeniable. In fact, the Stoic Greeks, you know what the Stoic Greeks called ultimacy...or largest nesting reality? Cosmos. A proper name. An "I, thou" relationship. Cosmos. Not the cosmos, little "c" like, you know, the pulpit. No, then it would be an object. No, Cosmos, a living being they were a part of. See, we are a subset of the whole. We can't get outside the whole to examine it. So I have to use some analogies and metaphors to describe the nature of ultimacy. What this means, of course, is there's no one right way to talk about ultimate reality. Which I realize is probably preaching to the choir here, but this may be news to many of your neighbors.[79]

There is no single, ultimate reality? It is standard New Age spirituality to declare that God is a force or energy field you can use to your advantage through the power of your mind. New Age doctrine declares there is no such thing as absolute truth—which in itself is a truth claim they *absolutely* believe in. New Age doctrine declares that we are all part of God, and therefore divine, co-creatures with God, but we were not created by the God of the Bible. And the process has been in the works a long time:

> Probably the most important thing I am going to say this morning: human beings are literally the uni-

verse after some 14 billion years of unbroken evolution now becoming conscious of itself. We are literally creation becoming aware of itself. We are the universe becoming conscious of itself. We didn't come into the world. We grew out of it in the same way that apples come out of an apple tree. We are organically related to the whole.[80]

I have warned my radio audience numerous times that just because someone says he believes in Jesus does not mean it is the Jesus of the Bible. Just because someone says she believes the gospel does not mean she believes in the biblical Gospel proclaimed by the Jesus of the Bible. The apostle Paul warns us of men like Reverend Dowd in 2 Corinthians 11:3–4:

> But I fear, lest somehow, as the serpent deceived Eve by his craftiness, so your minds may be corrupted from the simplicity that is in Christ. For if he who comes preaches another Jesus whom we have not preached, or if you receive a different spirit which you have not received, or a different gospel which you have not accepted—you may well put up with it!

Dowd is clearly preaching another Jesus and another gospel when he declares:

> As this knowledge is integrated into our religious traditions, which over the course of the next several decades it will be, each religion will see that its own core insights, its own core doctrines, are larger, more meaningful, and have more this-world-reality than ever before. This is part of the gospel, the good news of evolution. It helps us know:
>
> A) We are not separate from the divine. B) The divine is up to something, and we co-create with the divine when we work for justice, for peace, for sustainability, when we, when we work, when we just listen to someone, we are the divine; we are God in that process doing

God's work in this world. And part of the good news is that the sacred understanding of evolution, which is not the same thing as a meaningless understanding of evolution. I don't fault people who reject evolution. In fact, it's not a surprise, because for most of us the only version of evolution that we have ever been exposed to is a chance, meaningless, purposeless, cruel, godless, directionless process. So if that's what you think of as evolution, please continue to reject it. The evolution that I am talking about is nothing like that at all. It's a sacred, meaningful process that values religion and helps us to live lives of greater integrity, great love, greater compassion, greater generosity, and where we see the science and religion war end.[81]

Notice Dowd claims to reject the "chance, meaningless, purposeless, cruel, godless, directionless" evolution promoted by Charles Darwin. But Dowd has simply taken Darwin's secular naturalism and given it a spiritual source and context. Dowd echoes the "14 billion years of unbroken evolution."

What Dowd and his fellow spiritual-evolution proponents believe is that everything is biologically and spiritually spiraling up to a place of perfection that will allow man to usher in a New Age—a new world order, God's kingdom on earth:

> How did life create greater complexity, interdependence, and cooperation at larger and wider scale? When we learn that and align our laws, our medicine, our politics, our economics, our education with the way life works, with the way God works, we can move into a healthy future. We can co-create thy kingdom come, thy will be done on earth as it is in heaven.[82]

Dowd tells his audience that spiritual evolution restores the hope that mankind can save itself as man learns and embraces his own divine nature and the common ground found in all world religions. He says that in the end it will not be the Jesus of the Bible Who saves mankind and the earth; it will be mankind as we embrace spiritual evolution which:

...restores realistic hope. Not other-worldly hope. Not Jesus; the Cosmic janitor is going to come and clean up the mess we've made. But real hope, real believable, spiritual, practical, material hope. So that we can work together across our differences. One of the things I love about the diversity here is that we have virtually every kind of worldview represented and yet we can stand shoulder to shoulder and co-create a just, healthy, sustainably life-giving future. And that, for me, is the richest aspect is that we have realistic hope. A sacred understanding of evolution builds bridges, provides guidance, and gives us realistic hope so we can wake up each morning and not just grow spiritually, as important as that is, or grow personally. But in our growing personally, in our growing spiritually, in our growing in integrity as individuals and couples and families and so on, we also become a blessing to our neighborhood, to our community, to our city, to our country, to our world. And as we grow together in integrity, we truly participate in what God has been doing for billions of years and that, that is holy work.[83]

What Dowd is preaching would please Alice Bailey and her demon very much. Bailey declared that biblical Christianity must be destroyed in understanding that "all is one":

World unity will be a fact when the children of the world are taught that religious differences are largely a matter of birth....He will learn that religious differences are largely the result of manmade quarrels over human interpretations of truth. Thus gradually, our quarrels and differences will be offset and the idea of One Humanity will take their place.[84]

Compare this teaching of Bailey's with what I've shown from Dowd:

There is, as you well know, no angry God, no hell, and no vicarious atonement... and the only hell is the earth itself, where we learn to work out our own salvation....This teaching about hell is a remainder of the sadistic turn which was given to the thinking of the Christian Church in the Middle Ages and to the erroneous teaching to be found in the Old Testament agent Jehovah, the tribal God of the Jews. Jehovah is not God....As these erroneous ideas die out, the concept of hell will fade from man's recollection and its place will be taken by an understanding of the law which makes each man work out his own salvation... which leads him to right the wrongs which he may have perpetrated in his lives on Earth, and which enable him eventually to "clean his own slate."[85]

Alice Bailey had a huge influence on the United Nations through such people as Robert Mueller, who served for many years as assistant secretary general of the United Nations. Not surprisingly, Michael Dowd, according to various news reports, has spoken to audiences at the UN.

What makes this so important is that New Age spirituality or spiritual evolution will be one of the worldviews that unites all religions. Dowd's website reveals that the spiritual evolution he teaches is embraced by many religions—which is no surprise, since the coming one-world religion is going to be based on Satan's old and tired lie that man is God and man can save himself. And by the way, endorsers noted on Dowd's website reflect this wide-ranging inclusivity: Roman Catholics, mainline Protestants, Mennonites and Quakers, Evangelical/Emergent, Unity/New Thought, Unitarian Universalists, Jewish, Buddhists, Hindus, Evolutionary Enlightenment, Spiritual Dynamics, and Religious Naturalists.

It makes sense that Dowd would be approved by the Emergent Church, since the EC leans heavily on the teachings of German theologian Jurgen Moltmann, whose philosophy was based largely on spiritual evolution. In the 1960s, Moltmann created what he called "a theology of hope," following the philosophy of Friedrich Hegel. What makes this so critical is that Hegel had a major influence on the German people in a way that helped lay the foundation for Adolf Hitler. Yet, how many Bible-believing Christians are aware that Hegel's philosophies, as promoted by Moltmann, are now being promoted by some of America's most well-known "Christian" authors, pastors, and conference speakers? Bob DeWaay reveals that the heretical teachings of the Emergent Church find their source in Moltmann:

> The Hegelian synthesis denies absolutes, such as absolute truth or knowledge, and instead claims that everything evolves as incompatible ideas merge into something new and better. Two incompatible opposites, such as good and evil, combine and evolve into an improved third option that surpasses both. Moltmann applied Hegel's synthesis to theology and eschatology, deciding that because incompatibilities were evolving into new and better things, God could not possibly allow the world to end in judgment. Instead of judgment, Moltmann set aside scripture to declare that the entire world and all of creation was heading toward paradise and progressively leaving evil behind.[86]

Danielle Shroyer, author of *The Boundary-Breaking God* and pastor (yes, female pastor) of Journey Church in Dallas, Texas, provides an excellent example of Moltmann's thinking put into practice. Bob De-Waay explains what she teaches at her church:

> [S]he was the one who was teaching people what the basics of Moltmann's theology is all about. She is a disciple of Moltmann...on the cover is an endorsement of her book by Jurgen Moltmann. Now, what did she call Jurgen Moltmann's theology? Neo-Hegelian, panentheistic, universalism; that is what they call themselves.[87]

The Emergent Church, like many liberal, mainstream churches, rejects belief in the return of Jesus Christ and His judgment of the world. Instead, they see it as their responsibility to build God's kingdom through utopian ideals like the redistribution of wealth, the social gospel, disarmament, and a world community committed to social justice and pluralism:

> As we shall see with the Emergent Church's theology, which is derived from Moltmann and others, a serious problem exists. The problem is that this hope

is based on the idea that history is not headed toward cataclysmic judgment in which those who do not believe the Christian gospel are judged and lost for eternity but is headed toward the kingdom of God on earth with universal participation.[88]

The Trojan Horse Moves In

In his introduction to *The Crucified God*, Moltmann writes:

> ...I now turn to the questions of "negative dialectic" and the "critical theory" of T. A. Adorno and M. Horkheimer, together with the experiences and insights of early dialectical theology and existentialist philosophies.[89]

Note that Adorno and Horkheimer were on faculty in the Frankfurt School. While many Christians are aware of Charles Darwin and his belief in naturalistic evolution, few are aware of how his worldview laid the foundation in the minds of many to accept spiritual evolution, but he is behind much of this thinking.

Now that you have an understanding of the grave influence of the religious Trojan horse, let's look at the philosophies, worldviews, individuals, and groups that are aiding in building and establishing the religious Trojan horse. In the process, I'll also show how you can keep your family, friends, and, most importantly, the Gospel and the Church from riding along.

CHAPTER 2

Religion, the Foundation for the New World Order

Click on your favorite TV news channel or surf to the online news site of your choice, and the headlines that greet you will likely blare something about the economy, the latest natural disaster, or a speech by the president, but probably not much about religion. Sure, there's a religion section buried in the website somewhere and an occasional report on the subject, but unless a clergy sex scandal or televangelist financial corruption story has just surfaced, or someone is bold enough to mention Islam in a report about the latest terrorist attack, you won't find it on the home page. Religion is second-class news.

Strange. The most influential force in creating a new world order and transforming life on earth for the majority of its people stays off the radar screen. It's almost as if there's a conspiracy to keep it out of view. And there's a good reason for that: religion will be the foundation for the new world order, and those perpetrating that are not interested in publicity. The Bible is clear, though, that a one-world religion will be established—and it's not a good thing. Second Thessalonians 2:3–4 makes it very clear:

> Let no one deceive you by any means; for *that Day*
> *will not come* unless the falling away comes first, and
> the man of sin is revealed, the son of perdition, who
> opposes and exalts himself above all that is called
> God or that is worshiped, so that he sits as God in
> the temple of God, showing himself that he is God.
> (Emphasis mine.)

So, there's going to be an apostasy, a falling away from traditionally held biblical truths, and then a one-world religion will be established: "All who dwell on the earth will worship him, whose names have not been written in the Book of Life of the Lamb slain from the foundation of the world" (Revelation 13:8).

Another part of the plan is to establish a one-world economy. The Bible again is ahead of the game in recognizing that this will happen. Revelation 13:16–17 prophesies: "He causes all, both small and great, rich and poor, free and slave, to receive a mark on their right hand or on their foreheads, and that no one may buy or sell except one beast, or the number of his name."

We also see in the Scriptures there will be a one-world government, as noted in Revelation:

- 13:2–4—The dragon gave him his power, his throne, and great authority. And *I saw* one of his heads as if it had been mortally wounded, and his deadly wound was healed. (Emphasis mine.)

- 13:7—It was granted to him to make war with the saints and to overcome them. And authority was given him over every tribe, tongue, and nation.

- 17:12–13—The ten horns which you saw are ten kings who have received no kingdom as yet, but they receive authority for one hour as kings with the beast.

The one-world religion will be the vehicle that brings about the one-world economy and one-world government. My goal in this chapter is to explain exactly how religion will be the vehicle that brings about the one-world economy, one-world government, and eventually a one-world leader.

Fiscal Currents

At the core of economic functioning lies the currency of each nation, yet there has been much discussion and promotion in recent years of consolidating national monetary systems. The prime example, of course, is the creation of the euro. What is generally lacking from secular, left-leaning analyses of the situation is that a nation's sovereignty depends on the country having its own healthy currency. When a sovereign currency is dissolved into a "group currency," national sovereignty is seriously undermined.

The transition to a one-world economy begins with a change in currency. As countries switch to a different currency, sovereignty goes away. If the American dollar ceases to exist (and I believe it will by design) and America agrees to a regional (i.e., North American) currency, or a global currency, America thus surrenders its national sovereignty. This holds true for any other nations that give up their national currency and transition into a regional or global currency.

For many years there has been the discussion of regional currency modeled after the euro of the European Union. However, it is possible that a global financial crisis could become so severe that regional currencies are bypassed and the world transitions directly to a global currency. A one-world economy naturally lays the foundation for a one-world government through a common currency.

But the picture grows in intrigue. Once the one-world religious system has been turned to the advantage of the antichrist and his ten assistants as described in Revelation 17, the antichrist and his minions will turn and devour the woman riding the beast and will eat of her flesh. I believe the beast the woman is riding is a symbol of the one-world system. The Bible tells us that at some point, the antichrist and his ten assistants will turn against this one-world religious system and destroy it—eat its flesh—and then the antichrist will set himself up to be worshiped.

Creeping, Creepy Socialists

One of the greatest forces behind a one-world religious system may at first seem surprising. I believe Fabian socialism or communitarianism will be at the heart of the new way of things. If it seems odd that a secular worldview would embrace religion, simply consider that the evolutionary doctrines of infiltrating cultures to make them socialist is based on an ideology that will use any and all means available to secure their ends. The Fabians know that cloaking their actions in religiosity will accelerate the acceptance of their ends among many people.

Communitarianism and Fabian socialism are twin sisters, but we generally do not call communitarians by the label of Fabian socialist because most have never belonged to the Fabian Socialist Society. But make no mistake, communitarians and Fabian socialists are united in the common goal of merging capitalism with socialism, promoting social justice, and establishing a new world order. Later, we will look at such popular communitarians as Peter Drucker and Rick Warren (yes, *the* Rick Warren!).

Fabian socialism started in London in 1883. Fabians pursue socialism by evolution, not revolution (as compared to communists who advocate revolution). One Fabian socialist who has greatly damaged America is John Maynard Keynes, from whom we get Keynesian economics. (For a more in-depth look at John Maynard Keynes, read *Grave Influence*.)

Keynes is likely the world's best-known economist. Yet, the values represented by Keynesian economics are contrary to much of what makes for healthy financial living for individuals or nations: love of debt and hatred of savings. The wholesale implementation of his ideas caused the Great Depression to be much deeper and last much longer than was necessary. He believed that during an economic downturn or recession, government should borrow or inflate the currency and dump large amounts of cash into the economy by being the primary source of spending and employment. The end results are inflation, the devaluation of currency, and debt.

Many members of America's two dominant political parties are committed to socialistic Keynesian economics, and many are likewise Fabians or communitarians. The true goal of Fabian socialism is not merely national socialism but globalism. Fabianism dovetails well with corporate fascism, the merging of big government and big business. In my second book, published in 1995, I predicted that America would jump on a fast track toward corporate fascism. As is now obvious, that has happened, and the pace is increasing.

John Strachey, a long-time communist and author of the pro-Marxist/Leninist *The Theory and Practice of Socialism*, entered the British Fabian Society in 1943 and became war minister in the Labor Government of Great Britain in 1950. He explains Keynesian economics this way:

> The positive part of Keynes' work was a demand that capitalism should now be regulated and controlled by a central authority....The principal instruments of its policy should be variations in the rate of interest, budgetary deficits and surpluses, public works and a redistribution of personal incomes in equalitarian direction. This positive side of Keynes' work requires an

authority to do the regulating, and that authority can be, in contemporary conditions, nothing else but the government of a nation state.[90]

Keynes himself admitted that by

...a continuous process of inflation, governments can confiscate, secretly and unobserved, an important part of the wealth of their citizens. By this method, they not only confiscate, but confiscate arbitrarily: and while the process impoverishes many, it actually enriches some. The process engages all of the hidden forces of economic law on the side of destruction, and does it in a manner that not one man in a million can diagnose.[91]

Keynesian economics is tied directly to Fabian socialism and communitarianism. Keynes's observation that "not one man in a million can diagnose" what they are doing fits perfectly with the social evolution tactics of the Fabians. As the controllers inflate currency and steal money from the people, they cease to be capitalists.

In America, the Federal Reserve has been the institution used to inflate our currency. While it has achieved that unspoken goal, the Federal Reserve has failed to accomplish what it was supposedly created to do. According to economics writer Walter Williams:

The justification for the Federal Reserve Act of 1913 was to prevent bank failure and maintain price stability. Simple before and after analysis demonstrates that the Federal Reserve Bank has been a failure.

In the century before the Federal Reserve Act, wholesale prices fell by 6 percent; in the century after they rose by 1,300 percent. Maximum bank failures in one year before 1913 were 496 and afterward, 4,400. During the 1930s, inept money supply management by the Federal Reserve Bank was partially responsible for both the depth and duration of the Great Depression.[92]

America's Early Warning

Americans cannot say they were never cautioned about the dangers of a central bank. As long ago as 1832, President Andrew Jackson worked to abolish the Bank of the United States, which at the time operated much like today's Federal Reserve. During his tenure, Jackson vetoed a bill that would have rechartered the bank, and in his farewell address President Jackson cautioned Americans never again to allow the creation of a central bank. But less than a century later, we ignored his warning and created the Federal Reserve System. In the portion of Jackson's speech noted below, see if you recognize the degree to which we are suffering the consequences he outlined and that resulted when our elected officials created the Federal Reserve and eventually ceased to back our currency by gold or silver:

> In reviewing the conflicts which have taken place between different interests in the United States and the policy pursued since the adoption of our present form of Government, we find nothing that has produced such deep-seated evil as the course of legislation in relation to the currency. The Constitution of the United States unquestionably intended to secure to the people a circulating medium of gold and silver. But the establishment of a national bank by Congress, with the privilege of issuing paper money receivable in the payment of the public dues, and the unfortunate course of legislation in the several States upon the same subject, drove from general circulation the constitutional currency and substituted one of paper in its place.

> It was not easy for men engaged in the ordinary pursuits of business, whose attention had not been particularly drawn to the subject, to foresee all the consequences of a currency exclusively of paper, and we ought not on that account to be surprised at the facility with which laws were obtained to carry into effect the paper system. Honest and even enlightened men are sometimes misled by the specious and plausible statements of the designing. But experience has now

proved the mischiefs and dangers of a paper currency, and it rests with you to determine whether the proper remedy shall be applied.

The paper system being founded on public confidence and having of itself no intrinsic value, it is liable to great and sudden fluctuations, thereby rendering property insecure and the wages of labor unsteady and uncertain.

The corporations which create the paper money cannot be relied upon to keep the circulating medium uniform in amount. In times of prosperity, when confidence is high, they are tempted by the prospect of gain or by the influence of those who hope to profit by it to extend their issues of paper beyond the bounds of discretion and the reasonable demands of business; and when these issues have been pushed on from day to day, until public confidence is at length shaken, then a reaction takes place, and they immediately withdraw the credits they have given, suddenly curtail their issues, and produce an unexpected and ruinous contraction of the circulating medium, which is felt by the whole community. The banks by this means save themselves, and the mischievous consequences of their imprudence or cupidity are visited upon the public. Nor does the evil stop here. These ebbs and flows in the currency and these indiscreet extensions of credit naturally engender a spirit of speculation injurious to the habits and character of the people.

My humble efforts have not been spared during my administration of the Government to restore the constitutional currency of gold and silver, and something, I trust, has been done toward the accomplishment of this most desirable object; but enough yet remains to require all your energy and perseverance. The power, however, is in your hands, and the remedy must and will be applied if you determine upon it.

Our growth has been rapid beyond all former example in numbers, in wealth, in knowledge, and all
the useful arts which contribute to the comforts and
convenience of man, and from the earliest ages of history to the present day there never have been thirteen
millions of people associated in one political body who
enjoyed so much freedom and happiness as the people
of these United States. You have no longer any cause
to fear danger from abroad; your strength and power
are well known throughout the civilized world, as well
as the high and gallant bearing of your sons. It is from
within, among yourselves—from cupidity, from corruption, from disappointed ambition and inordinate
thirst for power—that factions will be formed and liberty endangered. It is against such designs, whatever
disguise the actors may assume, that you have especially to guard yourselves. You have the highest of human trusts committed to your care.

In March 2009, David Noebel, on my national radio program, described Keynesian economics to my radio audience. Notice how much
his warning sounds like that of President Jackson:

Keynesianism or interventionism or socialism is
contrary to nearly every aspect of the Christian worldview in economics. Today, Keynesianism is called interventionism. Interventionism is where the government itself gets involved in the economic sphere and
passes laws that destroy what we would call sound,
basic economics. And what we had with Fannie Mae
and Freddie Mac and the whole deal of going now
into debt by trillions is nothing more or nothing less
than Fabian, Keynesian economic philosophy. So this
is what every Christian needs to get a handle on, ...
or we are finished as a nation. Austrian economics
was just basically classical economics....For 6,000
years, the economics of the world was basically money, sound money. You've got to have something that
you can judge by, and even though over the history of

the world for the last 6,000 years we've tried various things, they always ended up with gold and silver as being the standard of money. And you could judge it. The dollar itself comes from the word *thaler*, which was a measurement of what an ounce of silver would entail, or a percentage of a gold piece would entail.... in fact, the U.S. Constitution identifies money as gold and silver.

Keynesian economics is unbiblical for many reasons, but even a quick reading of the Ten Commandments reveals two. The commandments against coveting and stealing are broken when the government covets what you own and seeks to steal it from you through inflation. Further, in Deuteronomy 25:13–16, God declares His hatred of unjust weights and scales used to cheat people. Our government and the Federal Reserve use the "unjust weights and scales" of monetization (printing money) of our national debt to steal from Americans for the government's self-serving financial gain and harvesting of power.

Note, too, that according to the Bible, mere "consumer confidence" is not considered adequate backing for a currency. Haggai 2:8 proclaims, "'The silver is mine, and the gold is mine,' saith the Lord of hosts." Real wealth is not stored or found in paper but in gold and silver.

Keynes was also a blatant pervert. Zygmund Dobbs, who conducted research for the book *Keynes at Harvard,* describes Keynes and his socialist buddies this way:

> Singing the Red Flag, the highborn sons of the British upper-class lay on the carpeted floor spinning out socialist schemes in homosexual intermissions....The attitude in such gatherings was anti-establishmentarian. To them the older generation was horribly out of date, even superfluous. The capitalist system was declared obsolete and revolution was proclaimed as the only solution. Christianity was pronounced an enemy force, and the worst sort of depravities were eulogized as "that love which passes all Christian understanding." Chief of this ring of homosexual revolutionaries was John Maynard Keynes....Keynes was characterized

by his male sweetheart, Lytton Strachey, as "a liberal and a sodomite, an atheist and a statistician." His particular depravity was the sexual abuse of little boys.[93]

Notice that Christianity was pronounced an "enemy force." Fabian socialists hate Christianity. But that does not mean they will not call themselves Christians or be friendly to Christians as they build the religious Trojan horse.

Joan Robinson, a Marxist economist who worked with Keynes, declared that "the differences between Marx and Keynes are only verbal." I contend that many elected officials at the state and federal level are Fabian socialists committed to a social revolution in America by deliberately creating an environment in which chaos and crisis can flourish for the purpose of bigger government—and moving us toward globalism. The end game for a Fabian socialist is global governance. So, whether you call it Fabian socialism or communitarianism; whether you call it internationalism or statism—whatever you want to call it—they're all working together. The worldviews vary, but all are headed toward the same goal of global governance, a one-world economic system, and a one-world government.

George Bernard Shaw was a famous Fabian. In a letter to Henry James on January 17, 1909 he observed:

> I as a socialist have had to preach as much as anyone the enormous power of the environment. We can change it. We must change it. There's absolutely no other sense in life than the task of changing it. What is the use of writing plays? What is the use of writing anything if there's not a will which finally molds chaos itself into a race of gods.

That sounds a lot like Genesis 3:1–5, when Satan appears to Adam and Eve in the form of a serpent and says, "You will be like gods." Shaw is preaching that Fabian socialism will help change man into "a race of gods."

But where does religion fit in the Fabian scheme? In his book *The Open Conspiracy: Blueprints for a World Revolution*, H. G. Wells, another Fabian, declares:

> This is my religion, the way of salvation, the political work of the Open Conspiracy must weaken, efface, incorporate and supersede existing governments. The character of the Open Conspiracy will now be plainly displayed. It will be a world religion.

What an amazing confession of the Fabians' ultimate goal: a world religion just as the Bible predicted thousands of years ago. How exciting it is that we are watching this biblical prophecy being fulfilled even in our lifetimes. Predictive prophecy reveals the supernatural nature of God's Word, and so much of what is happening in the world today is daily confirmation of the Bible's trustworthiness. Fabian socialism dovetails with the progression to the one-world government foretold in God's Word.

Economics, London-style

In 1895, Fabian Society members Sidney Webb, Beatrice Webb, and George Bernard Shaw founded the London School of Economics. The school taught Fabian socialism and Keynesian economics and is still at it today. The school currently "has around 8,700 full-time students and 1,300 academic staff."[94] The *Sunday Times* profile on the London School of Economics for the 2008 *Sunday Times University Guide* stated:

> There are many who have achieved in the world of politics, business or academia who can trace their success to the years they spent at LSE. Inspired by tuition from academics who are often familiar faces, if not household names, LSE students take their first steps to greatness in the debating chambers, cafes, bars—and even occasionally in their seminar groups—during three or four years of studying.[95]

During the Egypt crisis in the winter of 2011, Fox News interviewed a man who, at the end of the interview, was revealed to be a guest commentator from the London School of Economics. Most Americans have no idea what the LSE is or its significance. They don't know that it teaches Fabian socialism, and even if they did, they likely wouldn't know what that is and how Fabianism, Keynesian economics, and communitarianism are destroying America, along with many other nations.

The Fabian Window

Regardless of what anyone claims, every person has a religion. A religion is simply a system, set, or collection of beliefs, and everybody has that whether they articulate it or not. Even the U.S. Supreme Court, in a footnote to a key decision in 1961, ruled that Secular Humanism is a religion. And many religions use stained glass windows to communicate their beliefs—including the Fabians.

The Fabian stained glass window was created and designed by George Bernard Shaw in 1910. The playwright designed and commissioned the window to exemplify Fabian beliefs. For many years, the window was not publicly displayed. It was stolen in 1978, and then in 2005 it reappeared at an auction of Sotheby's. The next year, the Fabian window was unveiled in a ceremony at the London School of Economics. And who was there to deliver the keynote address for the unveiling? The Fabian socialist, former prime minister of Great Britain, Tony Blair.

If you look up the Fabian window on the Internet, you will see that it features the earth or globe sitting on a red-hot anvil. A man in a green outfit is grabbing the world with tongs because it is too hot to touch. Why? This symbolizes the world coming out of some kind of crisis. Behind the man is the fire. The Fabians have just pulled the earth out of a fire, and they're hammering the world on an anvil with two hammers. Across the top of the window is a phrase that enlightens the intent of the image: "Remold it near to the heart's desire." What are we to remold? Fabians intend to remold the world.

The window is predictive of what I think is likely to come upon us. At some point (likely sooner rather than later), a crisis will heat the world to the boiling point. It will be a crisis manufactured by globalist world leaders who will take advantage of the crisis to remold the world nearer to their hearts' desire.

Crisis Manufacturing

Pulitzer Prize-winning author James MacGregor Burns promotes globalism, and in his 1984 book *The Power to Lead,* he reveals that a crisis will cause the American people to reject our founding documents, give up our sovereignty, and embrace globalism. The globalists/socialists are intentionally creating just such a crisis:

> Let us face reality. The framers [of the Constitution] have simply been too shrewd for us. They have outwitted us. They designed separated institutions that cannot be unified by mechanical linkages, frail bridges, tinkering. If we are to "turn the founders upside down," we must directly confront the constitutional structure they erected.
>
> Others might press for major constitutional restructuring, but I doubt that Americans under normal conditions could agree on the package of radical and "alien" constitutional changes that would be required. They would do so, I think, only during and following a stupendous national crisis and political failure.[96]

Days before Barack Obama was sworn into office as president of the United States, Nobel Peace Prize winner and former secretary of state Henry Kissinger gave an interview on CNBC at the New York Stock Exchange. Speaking of President-elect Obama, Kissinger said, "His task will be to develop an overall strategy for America in this period when, really, a new world order can be created. It's a great opportunity, it isn't just a crisis."[97]

The crisis is a great opportunity? Barack Obama's White House chief of staff, Rahm Emanuel, told business leaders in a November 2008 meeting that the financial crisis presents "an opportunity to do things you could not do before." Emanuel has also said, "You never want a serious crisis to go to waste."

It sounds as if Kissinger, Obama, and Emanuel are singing from the same songsheet, but there's another voice in the chorus Americans should find alarming. Mikhail Gorbachev, the last leader of the Soviet Union, is president of the International Foundation for Socio-Economic and Political Studies in Moscow and has been pushing one-world religion and one-world government ideas for years. Remarkably, Gorbachev has conducted much of his work right here in America, from an office in San Francisco.

On January 1, 2009, Gorbachev wrote a column in the *International Herald Tribune* in which he seemed gleeful over the financial crisis and the "opportunity" it provides for furthering the globalist agenda:

The G-20 summit meeting in Washington foreshadowed a new format of global leadership, bringing together the countries responsible for the future of the world economy. And more than just the economy is at stake. ...The economic and political balance in the world has changed. It is now a given that a world with a single power center, in any shape or guise, is no longer possible. The global challenge of a financial and economic tsunami can only be met by working together.[98]

Working together for what purpose? Gorbachev reveals:

> A new concept is emerging for addressing the crisis at the national and international levels. If current ideas for reforming the world's financial and economic institutions are consistently implemented, that would suggest we are finally beginning to understand the importance of global governance.[99]

On the heels of Gorbachev's New Year's comments, a January 8, 2009, Associated Press article by Emma Vandore reported on a two-day meeting hosted by French president Nicolas Sarkozy. The event roster included former British prime minister Tony Blair, who has been calling for a one-world interfaith dialog for years and who used the platform to promote a new financial order based on "values other than the maximum short-term profits." Sarkozy argued that:

> In the 21st century, there is no longer a single nation who can say what we should do or what we should think.... We cannot accept the status quo.... In the capitalism of the 21st century, there is room for the state.[100]

When the State moves in, capitalism ceases to be capitalism, and that is exactly the goal. The demise of capitalism brings the fulfillment of the humanist and socialist dream: global government.

On January 12, 2009, Henry Kissinger published an article in the *International Herald Tribune* entitled "A Chance for New World Order" in which he declared:

> As the new U.S. administration prepares to take office amid grave financial and international crises, it may seem counterintuitive to argue that the very unsettled

nature of the international system generates a unique opportunity for creative diplomacy.... An international order can be permanent only if its participants have a share not only in building but also in securing it. In this manner, America and its potential partners have a unique opportunity to transform a moment of crisis into a vision of hope.[101]

In a twist of irony—or perhaps in a plan well laid and patiently implemented since 1883—the British Fabian socialists are going to dominate America's financial system. Dick Morris's April 7, 2009, article, "European Socialism to Run Our Financial System," explains:

On April 2, 2009, the work of July 4, 1776, was nullified at the meeting of the G-20 in London.

The joint communiqué essentially announces a global economic union with uniform regulations and bylaws for all nations, including the United States. Henceforth, our SEC, Commodity Futures Trading Commission, Federal Reserve Board and other regulators will have to march to the beat of drums pounded by the Financial Stability Board (FSB), a body of central bankers from each of the G-20 states and the European Union.

The mandate conferred on the FSB is remarkable for its scope and open-endedness. It is to set a "framework of internationally agreed high standards that a global financial system requires."

Now we may no longer look to presidential appointees, confirmed by the Senate, to make policy for our economy. These decisions will be made internationally.

And Europe will dominate them. The FSF [Financial Stability Forum and precursor to the FSB] and, presumably, the FSB is now composed of the central bankers of Australia, Canada, France, Germany, Hong Kong, Italy, Japan, Netherlands, Singapore, Switzerland, the United Kingdom, and the United States plus representatives of the World Bank, the European Union, the IMF, and the Organization for Economic Co-operation and Development (OECD).

The Europeans have been trying to get their hands on our financial system for decades. It is essential to them that they rein in American free enterprise so that their socialist heaven will not be polluted by vices such as the profit motive.[102]

The developments in Europe represent what I believe is the revived Roman Empire predicted in Daniel 2:41–43. This sort of prophecy reveals the remarkable supernatural nature of God's Word. Scripture repeatedly predicts, years in advance, what inevitably comes to pass. We are now watching the fulfillment of Scripture as Europe increases and America decreases.

Secular journalists who once laughed at the idea of a world government are now writing on the issue themselves. In the December 9, 2008, *Financial Times*, Gideon Rachman shared his concern in "And Now for World Government":

I have never believed that there is a secret United Nations plot to take over the US. I have never seen black helicopters hovering in the sky above Montana. But, for the first time in my life, I think the formation of some sort of world government is plausible.

A "world government" would involve much more than co-operation between nations. It would be an entity with state-like characteristics, backed by a body of laws. The European Union has already set up a continental government for 27 countries, which could be a model. The EU has a supreme court, a currency, thousands of pages of law, a large civil service and the ability to deploy military force.

So could the European model go global?[103]

Rachman then lays out three reasons why he thinks it is plausible, and one of them is our global financial crisis.

Rachman's worries are well founded. On July 10, 2009, Bloomberg announced in "Medvedev Shows Off Sample Coin of New 'World Currency' at G-8":

> Russian President Dmitry Medvedev illustrated his call for a supranational currency to replace the dollar by pulling from his pocket a sample coin of a "united future world currency."
>
> "Here it is," Medvedev told reporters today in L'Aquila, Italy, after a summit of the Group of Eight nations. "You can see it and touch it."
>
> The coin, which bears the words "unity in diversity," was minted in Belgium and presented to the heads of G-8 delegations, Medvedev said.
>
> The question of a supranational currency "concerns everyone now, even the mints," Medvedev said. The test coin "means they're getting ready. I think it's a good sign that we understand how interdependent we are."[104]

Along with a few other observers, I've predicted for years that a global crisis would be used to implement the freedom-robbing tyranny of global governance, and now here we are.

Socialism, Cloward-Piven Style

Even before Glenn Beck, Rush Limbaugh, and scores of others in the media, I was talking about and revealing the Cloward-Piven Strategy on my national radio program and on our website, www.worldviewtimes.com. One of our columnists, James Simpson, wrote an article on the Cloward-Piven Strategy that we carried on our website. I also interviewed James on my national radio program, and much of the material presented in this book, on my radio and TV programs and on our website will continue to be months and even years ahead of most of the secular talk-show hosts. That's because many of them do not have spiritual eyes and biblical discernment that God, by His grace, gives to Christians who are blessed to study the Scriptures while asking for wisdom, knowledge, and understanding.

After studying the Marxist Saul Alinsky (read *Grave Influence* for an entire chapter on Alinksy), Professor Richard Andrew Cloward and Frances Fox Piven wrote an article in the May 2, 1966, far-left magazine *The Nation*. This husband-and-wife pair of radical socialists from Columbia University developed the Cloward-Piven Strategy, which advocates implementing socialism by swamping the welfare system of states as well as the federal government with new recipients.

Cloward and Piven also called for a protest movement, marches, and rallies to put extreme pressure on politicians to create new benefits. This strategy is also used to stop the elimination of government benefits as we saw in Madison, Wisconsin, in February 2011. If you remember, thousands of union thugs protested as newly elected Governor Scott Walker sought to cut a small portion of the government benefits received by Wisconsin teachers so he could reduce the size of government and the crippling tax burden on Wisconsin families and business.

Cloward and Piven's strategy was to create a financial crisis, to bankrupt city and state governments—and eventually the federal government—through an ever-expanding welfare state. Once the financial crisis blooms, the collapse of state and federal budgets would spawn a socialist state and the nationalizing of failed financial institutions such as mortgage lenders.

Among their many accomplishments, Cloward and Piven inspired an activist named George Wiley to found a liberal organization that set in motion a startling chain reaction. Wiley's work influenced Wade Rathke who, along with Bill Ayers, was a member of the radical Students for a Democratic Society (SDS). The SDS organization was the student offshoot of John Dewey's League for Industrial Democracy. Rathke started Arkansas Community Organizations for Reform Now to employ the Cloward-Piven strategy. He was so successful in Arkansas that the organization expanded and changed the "A" in its name from "Arkansas" to "Association," and it became known as the Association of Community Organizers for Reform— the now infamous ACORN.

James Simpson, writing for worldviewtimes.com, notes:

> As a young attorney in the 1990s, Barack Obama represented ACORN in Washington in their success-

ful efforts to expand Community Reinvestment Act authority. In addition to making it easier for ACORN groups to force banks into making risky loans, this also paved the way for banks like Superior to package mortgages as investments, and for the government sponsored enterprise Fannie Mae and Freddie Mac to underwrite them.[105]

The financial housing crisis that made headlines in 2007 was brought on through Saul Alinksy's ideas, via the Cloward-Piven Strategy of implementing socialism through big-government destruction of contract law and free-market principles. This "economic sabotage" was originally attempted in New York City, and by 1975, the Big Apple was on the verge of financial meltdown. In 1960, New York had a manageable 150,000 welfare cases, but a decade later, the number had soared past the 1.5 million mark.

Barack Obama was a community organizer with Project Vote, an affiliate of ACORN, before he entered public service, and his "organizing" was built on the model of Saul Alinsky.[106] Obama's activities come right from the Alinsky playbook. In *Rules for Radicals*, Alinsky describes his purpose:

> In this book we are concerned with how to create mass organizations to seize power and give it to the people; to realize the democratic dream of equality, justice, peace.... "Better to die on your feet than to live on your knees." This means revolution.[107]

An obvious plug for socialism, Alinksy says radicals "hope for a future...where the means of production will be owned by all of the people instead of just a comparative handful."[108] In *Rules for Radicals*, Alinksy admits that his goal is to "present an arrangement of certain facts and general concepts of change, a step toward a science of revolution."[109] He also reflects on the book *The Prince,* which he says "was written by Machiavelli for the Haves on how to hold onto power. *Rules for Radicals* is written for the Have-Nots on how to take it away."[110] According to Alinsky, an organizer "is in a true sense reaching for the highest level for which man can reach—to create, to be a 'great creator,' to play God."[111] Alinsky notes that out of the chaos, the politician/community organizer can "play God."

Much of the unrest and chaos around the globe is related to central banks and globalists manipulating their nation's money systems and deliberately creating inflation. Inflation means higher fuel costs, higher costs in fertilizer, higher costs in planting and harvesting a crop, and higher costs in driving that crop to market. Runaway inflation offers the real possibility of spawning more and more social unrest. And I believe this is all part of the ultimate plan. A crisis is needed to remold the world closer to the heart's desire of the globalists.

So, as the Fabian window shows, the globe is on fire. There's a crisis or chaos taking place, and the Fabians are banging on the world with these hammers, remolding it on an anvil.

Wolves in Sheep's Clothing

A small sign to the bottom left of the Fabian window offers yet another important insight into Fabian intentions. It says, "Pray devoutly, hammer stoutly." At the bottom of the window, nine people, looking very religious, kneel and pray toward a stack of books or essays. A tenth person is standing and waving his arms. Many believe this man represents George Bernard Shaw himself. Some say he's mocking the nine that are kneeling and praying, because he believes their plans should be out in the open, for everybody to know about. Shaw himself was quite frank about his plans—"I am a communist. I'm just not a member of the Communist Party."[112]

Perhaps the most shocking and revealing aspect of the Fabian window is the image that stands above the globe. A wolf in sheep's clothing clearly represents the Fabians' deceptive intent. Globalists are intently building a religious Trojan horse by which to co-opt the Church. Jesus addressed this issue in Matthew 7:15–16: "Beware of false prophets, who come to you in sheep's clothing, but inwardly they are ravenous wolves. You will know them by their fruits."

What fruits? Jesus is speaking of their doctrinal fruits. Do they teach the exclusivity of Jesus Christ, salvation through Christ alone? Do they teach about the death, burial, and resurrection of Christ? The inerrancy of Scripture? Do they bring to you the doctrines of Christ, as we see in 2 John 9–11? If they do not, then we are not to enter into spiritual enterprises with them:

> Whoever transgresses and does not abide in the
> doctrine of Christ does not have God. He who abides
> in the doctrine of Christ has both the Father and the
> Son. If anyone comes to you and does not bring this
> doctrine, do not receive him into your house nor greet
> him; for he who greets him shares in his evil deeds.

If you want to know who is a false teacher or a wolf in sheep's clothing, then judge by the doctrinal fruits. Many Fabian socialists have been involved in religion as false teachers and wolves in sheep's clothing, just as their logo reveals was planned as far back as 1910 and earlier.

Tony Blair is an excellent example of a Fabian socialist wolf in sheep's clothing. In addition to presenting an address at the unveiling of the Fabian window, today he leads the Tony Blair Faith Foundation, the stated goal of which is to bring the religions of the world together. In Blair's window speech, he declared:

> Despite all the very obvious differences in policy
> and attitude and positioning, a lot of the values that
> the Fabians and George Bernard Shaw stood for would
> be very recognizable, at least I hope they would, in
> today's Labour Party.

The Labour Party in Great Britain, for which Tony Blair was the prime minister, grew out of the Fabian socialist party. And so Blair acknowledges that he wants to see the Fabian socialist ideas coming from the Labour Party.

The November 26, 2010, London newspaper *The Telegraph* offers further evidence of Blair's campaign to use religion to bring about global governance:

> Mr. Blair, who converted to Roman Catholicism af-
> ter he stepped down as Prime Minister in 2007, was
> to address the question, "Is religion a force for good or
> ill?"...[In an] interview with Toronto's *Globe and Mail*
> newspaper, Mr. Blair said, "I think the place of faith in
> the era of globalization is the single biggest issue of the
> 21st century. In terms of how people live together, how

we minimize the prospects of conflict and maximize the prospects of peace, the place of religion in our society is essential....I think religion could be, in an era of globalization, a civilizing force."

Through the Tony Blair Faith Foundation, he promotes the notion that an amalgamated world religion will be "a civilizing force." (Note, too, that Blair is a disciple of the Church of Rome. I will talk more about the significance of this in a later chapter.)

As I will show in more detail in another chapter, Christian colleges in America are embracing Tony Blair despite his worldview. One such example would be Wheaton College. A press release by the Tony Blair Faith Foundation about its newfound relationship with Wheaton announced:

> The Tony Blair Faith Foundation has announced that Wheaton College, Illinois, USA, has become the first American Associate University of the Tony Blair Faith Foundation's Faith and Globalization Initiative (FGI). [113]

Purpose-Driven Socialism

As unpopular as it may be for me to say so, Pastor Rick Warren, author of the best-selling book *The Purpose Driven Life*, is another false teacher garbed in sheep's clothing—and an extremely influential one at that. His website claims he has 500,000 churches plugged into what he's doing. His books have sold millions of copies. He appears regularly on national television and travels the globe holding and speaking at various conferences. Warren is one of the great change agents of our day. But the change is not necessarily for the better.

As of this writing, Warren sits on the advisory board of the Tony Blair Faith Foundation. That raises the legitimate question: Why would any solid evangelical, Bible-teaching pastor sit on the advisory board of a foundation that seeks to bring the religions of the world together? This is a clear violation of 2 John 9–11 (which we have already discussed) and 2 Corinthians 6:14:

> Do not be unequally yoked together with unbeliev-
> ers. For what fellowship has righteousness with law-

lessness? And what communion has light with darkness?

From those two verses alone—and I could cite many more—Rick Warren should not be on Blair's advisory board.

An article in the February 14, 2011, *Christian Post*, "Rick Warren to Interview Tony Blair at Saddleback Church," announced:

> Mega-church pastor Rick Warren will speak to former British Prime Minister Tony Blair on Egypt and peace and a globalized economy next month at Saddleback Church. Warren is expected to award Blair with the Annual International Medal of Peace. The award is given to individuals who exemplify outstanding contributions toward alleviating the five global giants.

Author Roger Oakland and two members of his ministry attended the event at Warren's church and offered the following report on his website:

> At the forum, both Warren and Blair stated that the only way a global peace could happen on planet earth in the future would be for all faiths to work together and do good together. The audience at the forum appeared to be mesmerized and awe-struck as they were wooed with discussion on faith, good works, democracy, and coming together. Beneath the vernacular, however, was another story. During the time that Roger Oakland and his co-researchers were at the Blair/Warren forum at Saddleback this past week, the team only heard one Bible verse mentioned. It was quoted so quickly it was hard to recognize if it was a verse or a paraphrase of a biblical verse. Clearly the Word of God was not included as a crucial element in this inter-faith plan to save the world.[114]

Rick Warren's endorsement of the Tony Blair Faith Foundation appears on Blair's website:

I honestly don't know of anyone better suited for this challenge. It's why I agreed to serve on the advisory board. The Tony Blair Faith Foundation's potential for doing good is staggering.

It is also an interesting side note that in *The Purpose Driven Life,* Warren makes positive references to three Fabian socialists. He quotes George Bernard Shaw on page 33, Aldous Huxley on page 248, and Bertrand Russell on page 17. While Warren acknowledges that Russell was an atheist, he quotes him as saying, "Unless you assume a God, the question of life's purpose is meaningless." Warren quotes Huxley as saying, "Experience is not what happens to you. It is what you do with what happens to you." And he quotes George Bernard Shaw as writing, "This is the true joy of life: the being used up for a purpose recognized by yourself as a mighty one; being a force of nature instead of a feverish, selfish little clot of ailments and grievances, complaining that the world will not devote itself to making you happy."

"Recognized by yourself as a mighty one"? The Bible says that in our weakness the Lord is strong. In 2 Corinthians 12:9–12 we read:

> And He said to me, "My grace is sufficient for you, for My strength is made perfect in weakness." Therefore most gladly I will rather boast in my infirmities, that the power of Christ may rest upon me. Therefore I take pleasure in infirmities, in reproaches, in needs, in persecutions, in distresses, for Christ's sake. For when I am weak, then I am strong.

The warning signs have been around for a long time that Rick Warren is someone that the Church should not be following. He is also a member of the one-world-oriented Council on Foreign Relations.[115]

The (Fabian) Council on Foreign Relations

In 1921, a group of Fabians started the Council on Foreign Relations (CFR).[116] It included a mix of globalists, internationalists, and statists—not all Fabians but all Fabian-friendly. This same group helped give us the United Nations in 1945.

Volumes of books have been written on the unbiblical and anti-Christ objectives of the Council on Foreign Relations, and there is, quite simply, no reason I can see for a Christian to serve on the Council's board. Yet, sadly, Richard Land of the Southern Baptist Convention is also a member. He's spoken extensively about it on the radio and has noted that he was invited to join—which is not unusual. That's the kind of club it is. Land claims to have joined so he can be salt and light, but Christians are never called to compromise biblical principles in order to be salt and light.

While I believe Rick Warren is complicit in his participation with the CFR, I believe Richard Land is simply ignorant about the council. I doubt he's ever read Carroll Quigley's *Tragedy and Hope: A History of the World in Our Time*. The CFR is eager to co-opt religious leaders so the organization will not be viewed as a threat to Christians. This is how they will infiltrate the Church. As my friend Dennis Cuddy has revealed:

> Members of the Round Table Groups, along with members of the Fabian (Socialist) Society, as well as "the inquiry," formed the Royal Institute of International Affairs in Great Britain, and its American branch, the Council on Foreign Relations.[117]

Many of our elected officials in Washington look to the Council on Foreign Relations to set policy agendas. On July 15, 2009, United States secretary of state Hillary Clinton gave a speech to the Council on Foreign Relations and was introduced by the organization's president, Richard N. Haas. In her opening statement, Clinton remarked:

> Thank you very much, Richard, and I am delighted to be here in these new headquarters. I have been often to, I guess, the mother ship in New York City, but it's good to have an outpost of the Council right here down the street from the State Department. We get a lot of advice from the Council, so this will mean I won't have as far to go to be told what we should be doing and how we should think about the future.[118]

In addition, the president of the European Central Bank came to America and gave a speech at the Council on Foreign Relations on

April 26, 2010, in which he used the phrase "global governance" over and over. Similarly, Richard Haas has declared:

> The near monopoly of power once enjoyed by sovereign entities is being eroded ... states must be prepared to cede some sovereignty to world bodies.... Globalization thus implies that sovereignty is not only becoming weaker in reality, but that it needs to become weaker.... The goal should be to redefine sovereignty for the era of globalization, to find a balance between a world of fully sovereign states and an international system of either world government or anarchy.[119]

One of America's most influential families, the Rockefellers, was heavily involved in founding the Council on Foreign Relations. John Ensor Harr and Peter J. Johnson document in their book on the Rockefellers that John D. Rockefeller Jr. was

> [a] committed internationalist, he financially supported programs of the League of Nations and crucially funded the formation and ongoing expenses of the Council on Foreign Relations and its initial headquarters building, in New York, in 1921.[120]

The United Nations was birthed out of the Council on Foreign Relations on October 24, 1945, and the Rockefellers donated the land in New York City on which the United Nations headquarters was built. John D. Rockefeller was also a strong promoter and supporter of ecumenicalism. He once declared:

> Would that I had the power to bring to your minds the vision as it unfolds before me! I see all denominational emphasis set aside....I see the church molding the thought of the world as it has never done before, leading in all great movements as it should. I see it literally establishing the Kingdom of God on earth.[121]

In his memoirs, David Rockefeller admitted to the goals of his family, which many have been alleging for years:

> Some even believe we [the Rockefellers] are part of a secret cabal working against the best interests of the United States, characterizing my family and me as "internationalists" and of conspiring with others around the world to build a more integrated global political and economic structure—one world, if you will. If that's the charge, I stand guilty, and I am proud of it.[122]

Tony Blair's work would make the Rockefellers proud as he set aside "all denominational emphasis" through his foundation.

In 1959, the Rockefeller Brothers Fund report entitled "The Mid-Century Challenge to U.S. Foreign Policy" outlined "the task of helping shape a new world order in all its dimensions—spiritual, economic, political, social." Notice that the first dimension they look to influence for a "new world order" (their words, not mine) is "spiritual."

The globalists are fighting to set up their own "kingdom of God" on earth. And they're getting help from many inside the Church besides just the high-profile folks like Rick Warren. Many who call themselves Christians are part of Dominion Theology or the New Apostolic Reformation. But Jesus made it clear in John 18:36 that dominion theology is not biblical when He declared:

> Jesus answered, "My kingdom is not of this world. If My kingdom were of this world, My servants would fight, so that I should not be delivered to the Jews; but now My kingdom is not from here."

Our call is not to physically build God's kingdom here on earth now. We are to be involved in building His kingdom in the spiritual realm as we preach the Gospel, which brings people to salvation through Jesus Christ alone.

"Sustainable Development" and the United Nations

This "kingdom building" comes at us on many fronts, and environmentalism is a favorite. Mikhail Gorbachev and Maurice Strong were all involved in the United Nations' Earth Summit in Rio de Janeiro in 1992, where they unveiled *Agenda 21*, a nearly 400–page document on how to use "sustainable development" as the framework for global governance. Sustainable development is a code term for restraining developed countries through multinational power. (To get a more complete understanding of sustainable development, please read *Grave Influence*.) Agenda 21 is the global plan for how to implement a one-world economy, a one-world government, a one-world religious system, and radical environmentalism.

Sustainable development promotes abortion on demand, population control, socialized medicine, social justice, welfare programs, public housing, and elimination of national sovereignty, parental authority, and religious liberty. One of its tenets is the criminalization of Christianity. A variety of UN-aligned organizations uses sustainable development as the framework for bringing about global governance.

The approach is now being implemented in more than 2,000 communities in America without any government mandate. The perpetrators are getting federal money for it, but there's no federal mandate to do it. This is all part of a spooky confluence of belief systems. In 1990, Steven Rockefeller co-authored *Spirit and Nature: Visions of Interdependence*, which encourages people to discover "the face of the sacred in rocks, trees, animals... and the Earth as a whole."[123] In his article "The Rockefeller Plan," author Dennis Cuddy reveals that "he [Steven Rockefeller] started writing the Earth Charter for Maurice Strong and Mikhail Gorbachev, both of whom said the charter would be like a new Ten Commandments."[124]

After the Rio Earth Summit, Rockefeller, Strong, and Gorbachev unveiled the Earth Charter, which calls for the equitable distribution of wealth within nations and among nations, social justice, communitarianism or Fabian socialism, depending on what you prefer to call it. It has been housed in the Ark of Hope, an "ark" intended to resemble the Ark of the Covenant that held the Ten Commandments. According to the arkofhope.org website:

> Recognizing that the United Nations is central to global efforts to solve problems which challenge humanity, the Ark of Hope carrying the Earth Charter and the Temenos Books was exhibited at the United Nations during the World Summit Prep Com II in January–February 2002.

The Ark of Hope was also placed on display at the 2002 World Summit on Sustainable Development in Johannesburg, South Africa.

Socialism by Another Name

The "social justice" called for by the Earth Charter is merely socialism or redistribution of wealth. The term has been used by Communists for years, and now it is being used by religious leaders. When social justice comes into the Church, it is called the social gospel, but make no mistake, the social gospel is nothing more than socialism wrapped in religious terminology and unbiblical theology.

Dr. Walter Rauschenbusch is called the father of the social gospel. A member of the Fabian Socialist Society, Rauschenbusch taught at Rochester Theological Seminary. His goal was to indoctrinate seminary students in socialism, global governance, the social gospel, and Fabian socialism and then send them into the churches. Rauschenbusch declared: "The only power that can make socialism succeed, if it is established, is religion. It cannot work in an irreligious country."[125] Rauschenbusch spoke of Jesus "not as one who would come to save sinners from their sins but as one who had a 'social passion' for society."[126]

With the financial support of the Rockefellers, Rauschenbusch and his Fabian colleague Rev. Harry F. Ward (also known as the "Red Dean" for his Communist beliefs) started the Federal Council of Churches, which later became the National Council of Churches. According to a publication of the Federal Council of Churches, Ward sought to produce "a changed attitude on the part of many church members concerning the purpose and function both of the Church and Christianity."[127]

But why would they want to change the purpose of the Church? They wanted to move it away from preaching the Gospel to using it as a vehicle for bringing about global governance, social justice, and the ideas that we see communitarian Rick Warren and other social justice/social gospel proponents promoting. Author Edgar Bundy explains in *Collectivism in the Churches* that

> ...we have seen how Dr. Walter Rauschenbusch... and the leaders of the social-action movements in the churches decided to do away with Christian individualism and turn to outright collectivism, using the church as their instrument.... Religion was only a means toward achieving socialism. And, like all other false prophets who have infiltrated religion through the centuries, [Rauschenbusch] used a "front" or disguise.

This disguise, as we have seen, was "The Kingdom of God." The Kingdom was not pictured as a spiritual society into which men and women had to be born as individuals through a personal relationship with Jesus Christ as Savior, but as a collectivist society which would be brought about by... eradication of poverty, redistribution of wealth... and "economic justice."[128]

Take note of this incredible testimony before the Committee on Un-American Activities of the U.S. House of Representatives in July, 1953. Robert Kunzig, chief counsel for the committee, asked Manning Johnson, a former top member of the Communist Party, a series of questions:

> KUNZIG: ...the name Harry Ward has appeared in so many of these various organizations and groups. It seems as if there is almost an interlacing tie-up... through various sects and denominations. Have you any comment to make on this situation?

> JOHNSON: Yes, I have. Dr. Harry F. Ward, for many years, has been the chief architect for Communist infiltration and subversion in the religious field.

> KUNZIG: ...could you give us a summary of the overall manner in which the Communists have attempted to infiltrate and poison the religious organizations of America wherever possible?

> JOHNSON: Once the tactic of infiltrating religious organizations was set by the Kremlin, the actual mechanics of implementing the "new line" was a question of following the... church movement in Russia, where the Communists discovered that the destruction of religion could proceed much faster through infiltration of the church by Communist agents operating within the church itself. ...the infiltration tactic in this country would have to adapt itself to American conditions.... In the earliest stages it was determined that with only small forces available it would be necessary to concentrate Communist agents in the seminaries and divinity schools.

The practical conclusion drawn by the Red leaders was that these institutions would make it possible for a small Communist minority to influence the ideology of future clergymen.... The idea was to divert the emphasis of clerical thinking from the spiritual to the material.... Instead of emphasis towards the spiritual and matters of the soul, the new and heavy emphasis was to deal with those matters which, in the main, led toward the Communist program of "immediate demands."

Manning explained that religion was the cover for an overall Communist operation:

The plan was to make the seminaries the neck of a funnel through which thousands of potential clergymen would issue forth, carrying with them, in varying degrees, an ideology and slant which would aid in neutralizing the anti-Communist character of the church and also to use the clergy to spearhead important Communist projects....

This policy was successful beyond even Communist expectations. The combination of Communist clergymen, clergymen with a pro-Communist ideology, plus thousands of clergymen who were sold the principle of considering Communist causes as progressive... furnished the Soviet apparatus with a machine which was used as a religious cover for the overall Communist operation.[129]

Benjamin Gitlow, a Communist Party USA founder who turned against Communism, wrote and spoke against Communism until his death in 1965. He, too, testified before the committee:

KUNZIG: What kind of an organization was the Methodist Federation for Social Action, and how did it differ from a Communist-front organization?

GITLOW: The Methodist Federation for Social Action, originally called the Methodist Federation for Social Service, was first organized by a group of Socialist, Marxist clergymen of the Methodist church headed by Dr. Harry F. Ward. Dr. Ward was the organizer, for almost a lifetime its secretary and actual leader. He at all times set its ideological and political pattern. Its objective was to transform the Methodist Church and Christianity into an instrument for the achievement of socialism. It was established in 1907, 12 years before the organization of the Communist Party in the United States in 1919.[130]

As we conclude this chapter, it is crucial to understand that the Scriptures have warned us there would be people just like we've examined. Committed Christians must warn the Church of the wolves in sheep's clothing, just as the Fabian socialists' window depicted. Jude 3–4 warns:

> I found it necessary to write to you, exhorting you to contend earnestly for the faith, which was once for all delivered to the saints, for certain men have crept in unnoticed, who long ago were marked out for this condemnation, ungodly men who turned the grace of our God into lewdness and deny the only Lord God and our Lord, Jesus Christ.

Notice the Word of God warns us to be aware that certain men have crept in "unnoticed." This is why we must be watchmen on the wall. Christ died for the Church, and we should be willing to defend the Church from these ungodly men.

Second Peter 2:1–2 similarly cautions that "there will be false teachers among you, who will secretly bring in destructive heresies, even denying the Lord who bought them, and bring on themselves swift destruction. And many will follow their destructive ways."

When we call out false teachers, the wolves in sheep's clothing, when we call out these men who have crept in unnoticed, who have brought in secret, destructive heresies and doctrines, we will be accused of intolerance, of being divisive, creating factions. Many people have told me, "Howse, you're divisive." And my response is, "I hope so."

I want to be as wise as a serpent and as gentle as a dove, but I hope what I'm saying and writing is divisive because the Word of God is a double-edged sword, dividing between truth and untruth. If we speak biblical truth, it will be divisive to those who contradict the Word of God. True Christians are called to distinguish between what is right and wrong, between truth and untruth. That which is consistent with the Word of God and God's character and nature is truth, and that which deviates is not truth. We dare not fear being divisive if we hope to win the battle against the one-world Trojan horse.

U.S. Senator Barry Goldwater ran for president in 1964, and you may remember that during his campaign, Ronald Reagan cut his political teeth, giving speeches for Goldwater. Much later, in 1979, Goldwater wrote the book *With No Apologies* in which he discussed globalists and the Trilateral Commission. Goldwater explained that the Trilateral Commission (and globalists) "represents a skillful, coordinated effort to seize control and consolidate the four centers of power—political, monetary, intellectual, and ecclesiastical."[131]

Goldwater had the foresight to warn the Church that globalists were working to co-opt the Church with a religious Trojan horse. We should do no less.

First Corinthians 11:18–19 explains that divisions over truth are actually necessary:

> For first of all, when you come together as a church,
> I hear that there are divisions among you, and in part
> I believe it. For there must also be factions among
> you, that those who are approved may be recognized
> among you.

There must be factions. Otherwise, how are you going to know who is being faithful to the Word of God? There is a religious Trojan horse inside the camp of Christianity. The question is: Will you embrace the religious Trojan horse, or will you expose it in order to keep people from being taken spiritual prisoners of war?

CHAPTER 3

Dangers of the New Apostolic Reformation and Dominion Theology

"Dominion theology" may not be a household term for everyone, but for its adherents, few ideas matter more—and that's the problem.

Dominion theology is the belief that God gave Adam and Eve a sort of legal authority over the whole earth. The idea derives from Genesis 1:26 and 28, which reads:

> Then God said, "Let Us make man in Our image, according to Our likeness; let them have dominion over the fish of the sea, over the birds of the air, and over the cattle, over all the earth and over every creeping thing that creeps on the earth."...Then God blessed them, and God said to them, "Be fruitful and multiply; fill the earth and subdue it; have dominion over the fish of the sea, over the birds of the air, and over every living thing that moves on the earth."

Those committed to dominion theology use these two verses as the foundation and justification for their concept. As Don Koenig points out, however, the dominion interpretation wrongly assumes a legal authority instead of the actual intent that we are to be *stewards* of the world:

> All we really see in this passage is God giving Adam administrative rule over the animals and plants on the earth that God created. Any transfer of legal authority is not implied. The word dominion in this passage is "radah," which literally means to "tread down" or

"master." To say that this passage gave Adam legal authority over the whole earth contradicts passages in the Bible that paint a clear picture that God created man to be the steward of God's earth. Scripture does not in any way imply that there was some legal transfer of authority or ownership of the earth from God to man. In the garden, man reported to God and limits were set.[132]

Legal authority implies that God has delegated His authority to man, while stewardship suggests that God is still the Master and Owner of the world of which we have been made the managers, a significant distinction. Al Dager, in *Vengeance Is Ours: The Church in Dominion*, outlines the three beliefs that characterize this approach:

Dominion theology is predicated upon three basic beliefs: 1) Satan usurped man's dominion over the earth through the temptation of Adam and Eve; 2) The Church is God's instrument to take dominion back from Satan; 3) Jesus cannot or will not return until the Church has taken dominion by gaining control of the earth's governmental and social institutions.[133]

One of the fastest-growing movements and key promoters of dominion theology operating inside evangelicalism is the New Apostolic Reformation, also called the NAR. While not everyone who believes in dominion theology agrees with the NAR movement (some would even say that many teachings of the NAR are heretical), many who believe in dominion theology gladly partner with NAR in order to accomplish political and culture-war objectives.

I have explained in great detail to some pro-family leaders the goals of dominion theology and the NAR. Even though these leaders acknowledge that they do not believe in dominion theology or in the heretical teachings of the NAR, they still work with NAR to accomplish mutually held culture-war objectives. Let me explain why that is a problem.

The New Apostolic Reformation is an outgrowth of the Latter Rain Movement, the Word of Faith movement that includes the prosperity gospel (also known as "Name It and Claim It"). The full name of the Latter Rain Movement—the New Order of the Latter Rain— is important to note because the movement is fast becoming mainstream and accepted by many within evangelicalism and pro-family circles of the New Religious Right. The *New Order* of the Latter Rain is helping build the "new order" or "new world order" of the antichrist.

When the antichrist shows up on the world scene, the followers of the New Apostolic Reformation, Word of Faith, New Agers, Mormons, Hindus, and Buddhists will have been well prepared to embrace his message of pagan spirituality and ecumenicalism which will be backed by signs and wonders, as described in 2 Thessalonians 2:9–11:

> The coming of the lawless one is according to the working of Satan, with all power, signs, and lying wonders, and with all unrighteous deception among those who perish, because they did not receive the love of the truth, that they might be saved. And for this reason God will send them strong delusion, that they should believe the lie.

The Church has been warned about this. In 1949, for example, the General Council of the Assemblies of God USA issued the following declaration when it kicked the Latter Rain Movement out of its denomination:

> RESOLVED, That we disapprove of those extreme teachings and practices which, being unfounded Scripturally, serve only to break fellowship of like precious faith and tend to confusion and division among the members of the Body of Christ, and be it hereby known that this 23rd General Council disapproves of the so-called, "New Order of the Latter Rain," to wit:
> 1. The overemphasis relative to imparting, identifying, bestowing or confirming gifts by the laying on of hands and prophecy.
> 2. The erroneous teaching that the church is built upon the foundation of present day apostles and prophets.
> 3. The extreme teaching as advocated by the "new order" regarding the confession of sin to man and deliverance as practiced, which claims prerogatives to human agency which belong only to Christ.

4. The erroneous teaching concerning the imparta-
tion of the gift of languages as special equipment for missionary service.

5. The extreme and unscriptural practice imparting
or imposing personal leading by the means of utterance.

6. Such other wrestings and distortions of Scripture,
interpretations which are in opposition to teachings and
practices generally accepted among us.[134]

Today, offspring of the Latter Rain Movement, the New Apostolic
Reformation (NAR), has become mainstream within many church
denominations and is eagerly embraced even by nonpentecostal or
noncharismatic "Christians" and leaders of the New Religious Right.

Some modern-day forerunners of the NAR are televangelists Pat
Robertson and Oral Roberts. In its current manifestation, the New
Apostolic Reformation pursues the goals I outline below. (As you read
what I have to say about the NAR, please do not confuse the New
Apostolic Reformation with Reconstructionists who also embrace dominion theology. Many Reconstructionists would join me in objecting
to the heretical theology of the New Apostolic Reformation.)

**(1) The New Apostolic Reformation believes the primary pur-
pose of the Church is to take back dominion of the earth from
Satan and to build and establish a physical Kingdom of God on
earth.**

In the last chapter, I quoted David Rockefeller Jr., but it bears re-
peating in the context of this discussion of NAR. Rockefeller said:

> Would that I had the power to bring to your minds
> the vision as it unfolds before me! I see all denomina-
> tional emphasis set aside….I see the church molding
> the thought of the world as it has never done before,
> leading in all great movements as it should. I see it
> literally establishing the Kingdom of God on earth.[135]

The dominion theology crowd, the New Apostolic Reformation,
and the globalists all want to create God's Kingdom on earth. For a
globalist like the late David Rockefeller, that really means the establishment of a New World Order based on communitarianism. This, how-

ever, has not stopped the globalists and NAR crowd from using each other for their own objectives.

Adherents to dominion theology and the New Apostolic Reformation believe they must establish the Kingdom of God on earth before Christ can return. This is completely unbiblical thinking, as Jesus Himself declares in John 18:36:

> Jesus answered, "My kingdom is not of this world. If My kingdom were of this world, My servants would fight, so that I should not be delivered to the Jews; but now My kingdom is not from here."

Only by giving the Gospel message to the lost are Christians used by God to build His Kingdom on earth. The Bible does not instruct Christians to build a physical kingdom here on earth. Building a physical kingdom has more in common with globalism than it does with biblical Christianity.

The false church referred to in Revelation 17 as "the woman that rides the beast" will work with globalists toward their common goal of building a kingdom on earth, and any Christians that speak against social justice, social gospel, dominion theology, new world order, and global governance will be declared the enemy.

C. Peter Wagner, who originally came to prominence for his studies of church growth, is one of the leaders and founders of the New Apostolic Reformation. Wagner's influence in developing the NAR is even documented by National Public Radio: "The international 'apostolic and prophetic' movement has been dubbed by its leading American architect, C. Peter Wagner, as the New Apostolic Reformation (NAR)."[136] While not all of today's "prophets" and "apostles" are part of Wagner's NAR, they often embrace many of the same heretical beliefs.

In a letter posted online in May 2007, Wagner declared:

> Our theological bedrock is what has been known as Dominion Theology. This means that our divine mandate is to do whatever is necessary, by the power of the Holy Spirit, to retake the dominion of God's creation which Adam forfeited to Satan in the Garden of Eden.[137]

Reports from the Arise Prophetic Conference in October 2004 indicate Wagner declared there that the Church needs to form a government in order to overthrow the government of Satan:

> See, the problem is, that Satan has had too much of his way in our society because he has a government! And the only way to overthrow a government is with a government. It won't happen otherwise. So therefore the government of the church has to get into place in the extended church just like we do have it very well in place; we haven't reached our goal yet, but it's very well established in the nuclear church.... These apostles in the workplace are the ones that are going to come into the picture and with them we'll be opening these gates; without them we can have all the prayer meetings we want, all the marches for Jesus we want, all the prayer walking we want, the gates aren't going to be opened. Because it takes a government to overthrow a government. Gate number one, letter A, the gate of social transformation, the gate of social transformation.... This gate will be opened when we understand about the church in the workplace, that the church has a government, that it takes a government to overthrow a government, and when we understand this, if we renew our minds, if we embrace this paradigm shift, if we see, if we hear what the spirit is saying to the churches, if we recognize ministry in the extended church and government in the extended church, the revival we've been praying for is just around the corner. We will see it.... And now I pray for every individual here, before you, who is in the workplace, who tomorrow and in the days to come will be going out to their ministries in the workplace, and I impart to them an anointing, I impart to them an anointing for not seeing a job, but seeing a ministry in the workplace. And I impart an anointing to them and to this whole community to recognize and raise up apostles who will set the

church in the workplace in order so that our cities, our communities, our states, and our nations will be transformed for Your glory, in Jesus' name.[138]

In order to take dominion back from Satan, the NAR and Word of Faith teach that Satan must be bound. Thus, the NAR and Word of Faith run around the globe holding prayer and fasting services in their attempts to bind Satan and take dominion neighborhood by neighborhood, town by town, city by city, state by state, and nation by nation.

In an interview with National Public Radio, Wagner explained the strategy of spiritual mapping and binding of demons:

> When you talk about demons over cities, we're talking about what—sometimes what we refer to as territorial spirits, and they're more high-ranking spirits in the hierarchy of darkness, and they're more powerful and they require different approaches, and it's not as easy as commanding them to leave in the name of Jesus. So sometimes there has to be repentance, sometimes there has to be—there has been bloodshed in that city that needs to be repented of, there has been idolatry in the city that has ruined the land. There's been immorality that needs to be repented of, and there are several social things that people really need to acknowledge that they're bad and repent of them and ask forgiveness.... There are certain individuals in our whole movement that have special gifts for doing that, and they're helping lead the way in weakening the power of the spirits. We don't believe we can kill demons, and sometimes we don't believe we can completely get 'em out, get 'em away from a city, but we can reduce their power. We can bind them, and then we can move strongly with the kingdom of God into the city.[139]

To justify this "binding of Satan," NAR and Word of Faith teachers often use Matthew 16:19 and 18:18. However, they use them out of context to support their teaching that Jesus' words instruct people to "bind Satan." Matthew 16:18 reads: "And I also say to you that you are

Peter, and on this rock I will build My church, and the gates of Hades shall not prevail against it." And Matthew 18:19: "Again I say to you that if two of you agree on earth concerning anything that they ask, it will be done for them by My Father in heaven."

Matthew 18:19 and 16:18 have nothing to do with binding Satan but, rather, are talking about church discipline. The verses teach that if church leadership declares someone is bound by sin and their declaration is in accord with what the Bible describes as sin, then heaven agrees with that assessment. If the individual who is bound in sin repents as described in the Word of God, then heaven agrees with that as well. These verses describe how church leaders can determine if someone is forgiven and has repented of a sinful practice or lifestyle or if he or she is still in sin.

The NAR and Word of Faith also use Luke 11:21–22 and Matthew 12:28–29 out of context to justify their binding of Satan. Again, the NAR and Word of Faith are demonic religious systems built on Satan's number one scheme, which is to distort the Word of God. So, we should not be surprised that NAR and Word of Faith leaders are constantly twisting scripture by taking it out of context and even teaching that verses say things they do not say. The verses I have cited are a clear example of twisting scripture. First, it is important to understand that in both Matthew and Luke, Jesus is the One casting out demons. The NAR and Word of Faith teachers are notorious for believing they can do whatever Jesus or the Apostles and prophets did while here on earth—which is a lie and, ultimately, blasphemy to claim to be able to do the work of God incarnate.

Luke 11:21–22 reads:

> When a strong man, fully armed, guards his own palace, his goods are in peace. But when a stronger than he comes upon him and overcomes him, he takes from him all his armor in which he trusted, and divides his spoils.

And Matthew 12:28–29 says:

> But if I cast out demons by the Spirit of God, surely the kingdom of God has come upon you. Or how can one enter a strong man's house and plunder his

goods, unless he first binds the strong man? And then he will plunder his house.

In context, these verses describe Satan as the strong man and Jesus Christ as the stronger man. Jesus defeated—or bound—Satan through His death, burial, and resurrection. Colossians 2:13–15 speaks of this:

> And you, being dead in your trespasses and the uncircumcision of your flesh, He has made alive together with Him, having forgiven you all trespasses, having wiped out the handwriting of requirements that was against us, which was contrary to us. And He has taken it out of the way, having nailed it to the cross. Having disarmed principalities and powers, He made a public spectacle of them, triumphing over them in it.

Hebrews 2:14–15 speaks of the victory that is ours through Jesus Christ Who freed us from the bondage of sin and death and defeated Satan:

> Inasmuch then as the children have partaken of flesh and blood, He Himself likewise shared in the same, that through death He might destroy him who had the power of death, that is, the devil, and release those who through fear of death were all their lifetime subject to bondage.

In Jude 9 we read where Michael the archangel did not attempt to "bind" Satan nor engage him in an argument:

> Yet Michael the archangel, in contending with the devil, when he disputed about the body of Moses, dared not bring against him a reviling accusation, but said, "The Lord rebuke you!"

Satan is on a leash held by God Himself. Our rightful response to Satan is found in James 4:7–8:

> Therefore submit to God. Resist the devil and he will flee from you. Draw near to God and He will draw

near to you. Cleanse your hands, you sinners; and purify your hearts, you double-minded.

A better translation of "submit to God" is to be "lined up under"
His authority. God is our defender and protector when we follow His
will and His authority. A better translation of "resist" is to "take your
stand." Notice, however, that we only take our stand after we line up
under God. Once we have lined up, living in obedience to God and
His Word, then we can take our stand knowing that greater is He that
is in me than he that is in the world.

To "draw near to God" is to take seriously our relationship with
Him through prayer and the study of His Word. It is through God's
Word that we conform our lives to His will and deepen our relation-
ships with Him as we submit every area of our lives to His Lordship.
There is protection from Satan when we are under God's authority and
living in His will.

Notice that 2 Peter 2:9–12 tells us false teachers who rail against
demons are foolishly doing what even the angels, who are more powerful than demons, will not do:

> [T]hen the Lord knows how to deliver the godly
> out of temptations and to reserve the unjust under
> punishment for the day of judgment, and especially
> those who walk according to the flesh in the lust of
> uncleanness and despise authority. They are presump-
> tuous, self-willed. They are not afraid to speak evil of
> dignitaries, whereas angels, who are greater in power
> and might, do not bring a reviling accusation against
> them before the Lord.

The lesson to be learned here is that the NAR, Word of Faith, and
other purveyors of false teaching are highly skilled at taking Scripture
out of context to build their demonic, self-serving, humanistic worldview. Truthful teachers know that we must always study the Scriptures
in context and use the Word of God as our chief weapon to destroy
arguments raised up against the principles of the Lord (2 Corinthians
10:4–5).

Sadly, even the National Day of Prayer organization, led by Shirley
Dobson since 1991, seems to have been influenced by Word of Faith

and NAR teachings. The National Day of Prayer website, under the heading "Why pray?" notes:

> Warfare: (Psalm 149:6–9). This is prayer directed against the powers of darkness. Our praises to God are also a weapon directed against the powers of darkness (demons, fallen angels who are at work in the affairs of the world and the church). We pronounce against them the written judgment by reading the Scriptures of judgment against them (Psalm 149:9), *we command them to be bound or to leave their positions of influence or authority in the name of Jesus.* (Matthew 16:19; Mark 16:17). (Emphasis mine.)

Notice Matthew 16:19 is the often-misused Scripture given for NAR and Word of Faith teachers' unbiblical activity of railing against demons. The verse is about church discipline and has nothing to do with Satan or demons. Mark 16:17 refers to casting out demons and, when considered in context, is clearly written about the apostolic community. Casting out demons is not a gift or power given to Christians in all ages. A common mistake made by the undiscerning, those who are not skilled in the Word, is to believe that the gifts of the early Church expressed in the book of Acts apply to all believers today.

The "Why Pray?" section of the National Day of Prayer website also says:

> We need to pray because it is necessary for men to invite God to act in salvation. God gave the earth to Adam and his descendants. We must invite God to work here. If no one invites God to work here, Satan (the god of this world through man's universal rebellion—2 Corinthians 4:4) will dominate the affairs of men and eventually the judgment of God will come. By inviting God often and specifically, multitudes can be saved that would otherwise be lost.[140]

This is 100 percent false! Nowhere in the Word of God do we read that "it is necessary for men to invite God to act in salvation" in order to save people. Neither do we see that salvation has anything to do with man beating back Satan's dominion.

This unbiblical teaching by the National Day of Prayer (NDP) organization should not come as a surprise if you notice that the website lists among its board of reference Paul Crouch of the heretical Trinity Broadcasting Network. WallBuilders' David Barton is also listed on the website as a member of the board of reference. Barton, when he was a guest on the television program of false teacher Kenneth Copeland, declared that sometimes our prayers can be delayed from reaching heaven for 21 days. Citing Daniel as his justification for his thesis, Barton declares:

> And I can tell this in the U.S. Capitol. When I walk from the House side to the Senate side, I cross the middle line of the Capitol; I can feel a different principality because they have jurisdictions over different things. And there are principalities that sit over different government entities that cause them to think really goofy and you can't get prayers through, they get delayed twenty-one days because the principalities are up there fighting in the Heavenlies.

> Because we're not fighting flesh and blood. And if you don't understand this is a spiritual battle, and if you don't understand there are really big principalities and powers sitting over places of power, whether it be banking, or education. There's principalities that sit over schools to keep those kids from getting knowledge, there's principalities that sit over financial institutions. They sit over households. That's why you have principalities in powers, that gradation, you have the corporals, and you have the sergeants, and you have the lieutenants, the captains and the generals, and the generals have a bigger principality and those little corporals may have control over the house but it's a spiritual battle.

> It's a spiritual battle and we'll never win until we understand that.[141]

Reading the Scripture in context reveals that David Barton is wrong to declare the prayers of believers are sometimes delayed 21 days because "principalities are up there fighting in the Heavenlies." Daniel 10:12–14 does not say that Daniel's prayer was delayed reaching heaven for 21 days, but that his prayer was heard from the first day but the angel was delayed 21 days in coming to Daniel:

> Then he said to me, "Do not fear, Daniel, *for from the first day that you set your heart to understand, and to humble yourself before your God, your words were heard;* and I have come because of your words. But the prince of the kingdom of Persia withstood me twenty-one days; and behold, Michael, one of the chief princes, came to help me, for I had been left alone there with the kings of Persia. Now I have come to make you understand what will happen to your people in the latter days, for the vision refers to many days yet to come." (Emphasis mine.)

If Barton cannot read the Scripture in context and exegete an accurate meaning of the text, and if he cannot see from the doctrinal fruit of Glenn Beck that he is not a born-again Christian, we can hardly rely on Barton to accurately interpret the worldview of America's founding fathers.

In 2010, I too began to question many of David Barton's claims about America's founding fathers. After extensive research, I pulled all of Barton's books and DVDs from our website because I believe he is in error not only theologically but also historically. I work hard to educate my radio, television, and conference audiences about America's founders and will not see them misled. I plan to address this more fully in my next book. Meanwhile, you will find in our bookstore at worldviewweekend.com a nearly four-hour DVD in which Chris Pinto and I set the record straight with historical, verifiable facts about American history.

Jay Richards, a Catholic who co-wrote *Indivisible* with James Robison, is even concerned. Although Robison has worked extensively with Glenn Beck and Beck and Barton have worked together on numerous projects, Richards has "gone public" against Barton. In August 2012, *World* magazine reported Richards' concern:

Jay W. Richards, senior fellow at the Discovery Institute, and author with James Robison of *Indivisible: Restoring Faith, Family, and Freedom Before It's Too Late,* spoke alongside Barton at Christian conferences as recently as last month. Richards says in recent months he has grown increasingly troubled about Barton's writings, so he asked 10 conservative Christian professors to assess Barton's work.

Their response was negative. Some examples: Glenn Moots of Northwood University wrote that Barton in *The Jefferson Lies* is so eager to portray Jefferson as sympathetic to Christianity that he misses or omits obvious signs that Jefferson stood outside "orthodox, creedal, confessional Christianity." A second professor, Glenn Sunshine of Central Connecticut State University, said that Barton's characterization of Jefferson's religious views is "unsupportable." A third, Gregg Frazer of The Master's College, evaluated Barton's video *America's Godly Heritage* and found many of its factual claims dubious, such as a statement that "52 of the 55 delegates at the Constitutional Convention were 'orthodox, evangelical Christians.'"[142]

The article goes on to reflect the degree of Richards' dismay:

Richards emphasizes that he and the scholars he consulted about Barton are politically conservative evangelicals or Catholics. They largely agree with Barton's belief that Christian principles played a major role in America's founding, but Richards argues that *Barton's books and videos are full of "embarrassing factual errors, suspiciously selective quotes, and highly misleading claims."* (emphasis mine)[143]

On August 9, 2012, worldmag.com reported:

The Thomas Nelson publishing company has decided to cease publication and distribution of David Barton's controversial book, *The Jefferson Lies: Exposing the Myths You've Always Believed about Thomas Jefferson,* saying it has "lost confidence in the book's details." Casey Francis Harrell, Thomas Nelson's director of corporate communications, told me the publishing house "was contacted by a number of people expressing concerns about [The Jefferson Lies]." The company began to evaluate the criticisms, Harrell said, and "in the course of our review learned that there were some historical details included in the book that were not adequately supported. Because of these deficiencies we decided that it was in the best interest of our readers to stop the publication and distribution."[144]

It appears that some individuals and parts of the Christian media are getting up to speed. Many news outlets and organizations will never report the truth, though, simply because "ignorance is bliss" or because it does not fit their moralizing, political agenda, their dominion theology, or their patriotic ecumenicalism—all of which are unbiblical. When Christians try to make men who were not Christians out to be Christians, we all look foolish and dishonest to the unsaved historians who know the truth. I highly recommend *The Religious Beliefs of America's Founders,* a book by Gregg Frazer, The Master's College professor referenced in the World article. In it, Frazer examines the faith of eight key founders: John Adams, Thomas Jefferson, Benjamin Franklin, James Wilson, Gouverneur Morris, James Madison, Alexander Hamilton, and George Washington.

But let's dig even a little deeper. Additional NDP board of reference members include C. Peter Wagner and Rick Warren. The website also lists Harry Jackson as a member of the NDP's national advisory committee. In an August 29, 2011, article, "Bishop Harry Jackson, an NAR favorite," *The Christian Post* quotes Jackson: "He [Jackson] said many of the people and groups considered to be under the NAR umbrella are simply seeking to be 'light and salt' in their communities."[145] In addition, the National Day of Prayer lists GodTV, known for broadcasting popular Word of Faith false teachers, as a ministry partner. According to ABC News,[146] in 2008, GodTV broadcast NAR "prophet" Todd Bentley's Lakeland, Florida, revival. This is the same Todd Bentley who was installed as a "prophet" by C. Peter Wagner in a service that can still be viewed on the Internet.[147]

I have been concerned for several years with the theological leanings of both NDP chairperson Shirley Dobson and her husband, Dr. James Dobson. In 2008, Shirley Dobson, in her position as chairperson for the National Day of Prayer Task Force, appeared on *The Hour of Power* with Robert Schuller. She concluded her appearance by saying to him, "Thank you, thank you, Dr. Schuller. God bless you and the good work you're doing here."[148]

What "good work" is Dr. Schuller doing? Read and listen to him and you will quickly see that he is teaching a false gospel that is leading millions of people to hell. Do the Dobsons agree with the heretical theology of Pastor Schuller? In early 2008, H. B. London, Dr. Dobson's cousin and vice president of outreach/pastoral ministries for Focus on the Family at the time, spoke for the Re-think Conference hosted by the Crystal Cathedral, Dr. Schuller, and Emergent pastor Erwin McManus.

For NDP, such ecumenism is standard procedure. At the start of the 2008 National Day of Prayer, Rabbi Bruce Lustig prayed this broad-brush prayer:

> As we stand in this historic place, ready to begin our 57th National Day of Prayer, we turn to the Psalms and know that the Psalmist knew the power of prayer, the indispensable ability of humanity to humbly give thanks to God. When the Psalmist wrote the very words of 28:7, [reads in Hebrew], the eternal is my strength and my shield, my heart trusts in God and I am helped. No matter our creed, our color, our income or our status in life, whether Christian, Muslim, Jew, Sikh, Buddhist or Jain, before the Eternal, we are all equal in God's eyes, we are equal in prayer, for through prayer, God can and will be our strength, and our shield, and our help.[149]

My research reveals that no one at this service corrected the rabbi's unbiblical and ecumencial statement.

Besides involvement with the National Day of Prayer, there are other reasons to question the Dobsons's ongoing theological integrity. In 2012, for instance, Shirley Dobson appeared on Glenn Beck's radio show to talk about prayer and God. In the process, she praised Beck for his "great job" and "good work." Again, how can Beck's promotion of another Jesus and another gospel be a good work, and why do "evangelical" leaders seem eager to compromise the admonishments of 2 Corinthians 6:14, Romans 16:17, and 2 John 9–11?

In 2008, James and Shirley Dobson joined Lou Engle, New Apostolic Reformation personality and assistant pastor at the International House of Prayer, for "The Call" in San Diego.[150] While the events by Engle may seem like little more than a prayer service, Engle, IHOP, and the NAR are preaching another Jesus and, thus, another gospel. Therefore, such events are not only futile and unbiblical but spiritually dangerous.

In March 2012, James Dobson interviewed Lou Engle on his radio program and praised him for his "ministry." Does Dobson agree with IHOP? Does he accept contemplative prayer and all that is promoted within the New Apostolic Reformation? Is Dobson not greatly concerned that the NAR and groups like IHOP are blaspheming the Holy Ghost? I have spent countless hours of radio and television time, and now this entire book, warning the Church that we had better be very careful who we're listening to. Just because they're popular doesn't mean they're right.

Some of the world's most prominent "evangelical" and pro-family leaders have become some of the biggest potential threats to true Bible-believing churches simply because they're giving credibility to false teachers. You may wonder why I don't have any tolerance for this anymore. It is because I have personally warned many of these people about what is happening. Do they not have search engines on their computers? A quick web search reveals countless articles by credible and biblically based organizations detailing the heretical teachings of Engle, IHOP, Schuller, and the NAR. There is no excuse for aligning with such false teachers in today's information age. So the big question is: why do so many "Christian" leaders unite with false teachers?

One pro-family leader defended his organization's participation with false teachers by declaring that his is not a theological organization. This statement alone reveals the leader's degree of spiritual deception. A person's view of God makes up his or her theology. Individuals and organizations live out their theology whether they believe this is the case or not. Would this pro-family leader dare send out a letter to the thousands of Christians on his mailing list and declare that his organization is not interested in theology? It appears to me that many pro-family groups love to talk about God and getting

America back to Him, but if building a bigger mailing list, a bigger following, and more donors means uniting with the enemies of God and His Word, they quickly cease to be an organization interested in biblical theology and doctrine.

If embracing false teachers is how to reclaim the culture, I don't want to be a part of it. Besides, there is no reclaiming the culture apart from God. Romans 1 explains that compromise and union with those who embrace and promote pagan spirituality is how you destroy a culture and speed up God's judgment. When God finally brings judgment upon America, I believe you will be able to point to some of America's favorite "evangelical" and pro-family leaders and say, "You and your organizations are as responsible, if not more responsible, for the Divine judgment on our nation than any secular company or organization in America. By your actions you gave credibility and rise to Satan's number-one tool—false teachers—helping them to infiltrate and wage war against Satan's number-one earthly adversary, the true Church."

(2) The New Apostolic Reformation believes in the promotion of a social gospel and social justice instead of biblical evangelization of the lost.

As you recall, "social justice" is a buzz word of progressives, socialists, and Communists. And when social justice, dominion theology, universalism, and other religious terminology are intertwined, you end up with a social gospel. Wagner reflects just this sort of mixture: "Warfare prayer is not an end in itself, but a means of opening the way for the Kingdom of God to come, not only in evangelism, but also in social justice and material sufficiency."[151] When the NAR speaks about the Great Commission, it does not mean evangelizing the lost but rather awakening the Church to the need to take back the culture and establish God's Kingdom on earth.

(3) The New Apostolic Reformation promotes ecumenicalism.

The NAR and those committed to dominion theology are willing to work with any and all religions to bring about the implementation of "kingdom values." This is one reason I have a problem with people like Richard Land and Rick Warren engaging in interfaith dialogues and initiatives or building bridges of mutual respect and understanding with Mormons, Muslims, and other false religions on cultural issues. You cannot separate cultural issues from theology and doctrine.

(4) The New Apostolic Reformation is committed to a communitarian philosophy that seeks to bring the Church, the government, and corporations into an equal partnership in solving world problems and bringing about global peace and stability.

This communitarian philosophy is not only proclaimed by the NAR but also by Rick Warren, and the common thread here is Peter Wagner. He is not only the founder of the New Apostolic Reformation but also one of the founders of the megachurch or seeker-sensitive movement. Wagner is listed as Rick Warren's "advisor/mentor" for the doctoral thesis he wrote while at Fuller Theological Seminary. Warren has also been influenced by Peter Drucker as well as Wagner.

The three-legged stool of Peter Drucker, C. Peter Wagner, and Rick Warren is embraced by the NAR. The NAR believes God has and will give financially successful businesses to Christian men, not only so they can take over their specific fields for the establishment of God's earthly kingdom but also that they might use their wealth to fund the projects and initiatives of NAR. This helps explain why the NAR is so flush with cash. Are some businessmen giving to the NAR because they think this will move God to increase their financial bottom lines?

(5) The New Apostolic Reformation believes the Great Commission is not primarily about biblical evangelism and discipleship but about awakening Christians to their need to take back dominion over the earth and establish God's Kingdom on earth.

Dale Neill, as president of the International Christian Chamber of Commerce, put the message of the Gospel in NAR terms:

> The Church must grow past the "Gospel of Salvation" message and understand that it is only when we begin to implement the principles of the "Gospel of the kingdom" that we will really begin to see change in lives and cities and nations. The Church has no understanding of this realm....The Church must grow up.[152]

So we need to get "past the Gospel of Salvation" and go to the "Gospel of the kingdom"? Please understand what they mean by preaching the Gospel, or the Gospel of the kingdom, or by taking dominion, or by Great Commission. Their definitions of these terms would not fit with those of most evangelical Christians.

The NAR is not really interested in the preaching of the Gospel. I've heard many of these folks speak, and very rarely, if ever, have I heard them offer the biblical Gospel. What I have heard over and over is this emphasis on Christians getting involved in the culture war.

In January 1987, Robert Crabtree was a district superintendent in Ohio for the Assemblies of God. Pastor Crabtree put out a report to the pastors in his district that featured this warning about the dangers of dominion theology:

> Kingdom Now teachers have redefined the Gospel which requires *re-evangelizing* the church without an emphasis upon Jesus Christ. Salvation moves one from the kingdom of sin to the Kingdom Now of Christ on earth. This new kingdom is being built by waking up the professing Christians rather than reaching the lost. These renewed Christians are to seek control of the earth and assume stewardship responsibilities of the material world. (Emphasis mine.)[153]

(This quote is not meant as an endorsement of Robert Crabtree, because I don't know him or his biblical beliefs, but I do agree with what he says in this report. I also appreciate the fact that, at least in 1987, he warned the pastors under his organizational care to steer clear of dominion theology.)

Another key Assembly of God pastor, George Wood, has also cautioned against dominion theology. As of the writing of this book, he is the general secretary for the Assemblies of God, and as far back as the 1980s he had the foresight to put out a warning about the proponents of dominion theology (again, this is not an endorsement of Pastor Wood or whatever else he's written or said). He cautioned that dominion theology wrongly suggests that "The Church would have a larger mission than that of proclaiming personal salvation through Christ.... The political, social, and economic systems of nations and cultures would need to be 'Christianized.'"[154]

Peter Wagner demonstrates the rightness of Wood's caution elsewhere in Wagner's 2007 online letter about the need for the Church to shape the culture through what he calls the "Seven Mountain Mandate":

> In my view it is not possible to get an operational handle on how to initiate corporate action toward social transformation without taking into account the seven mountains or what I like to call "molders of culture." The seven are religion, family, business, arts & entertainment, government, education, and media. Which leads us to the second stage of the goal of transformation, namely corporate or social transformation. We want to see whole cities and regions and states and nations transformed to support the values of the kingdom of God.[155]

How about having the cities and towns transformed by the preaching of the Gospel, not just "values of the kingdom"? We should not be interested in people simply being moralized. It's not enough to "moralize" the unsaved world. It makes no sense to expect the unsaved, pagan world to act in any other manner than in an unsaved, pagan manner. John MacArthur has it right when he says:

> It makes no difference if an unsaved person is for or against abortion, a political liberal or a conservative, a prostitute or a police officer, he will spend eternity apart from God unless he repents and believes the gospel.[156]

Living a life of good works is not going to keep anyone from hell. Attempting to legislate a city, state, or nation into righteousness is a wasted effort that will yield no eternal rewards. That doesn't mean we should do away with laws against murder, rape, stealing, and fraud. Romans 13 tells us that the purpose of government is to reward the righteous and punish the wicked. God created civil government for the purpose of maintaining a stable and just society so the other two institutions God created—the family and the Church—could go about their respective biblical mandates. Cities, states, and nations need laws. Some Christians have, and I pray will continue to have, a godly impact in government as individuals. But collectively, the Church needs to realize how foolish it is to spend so much time and money trying to force our biblical values onto an unsaved culture.

The way to produce a change in any culture is to preach the Gospel. It is only as individuals place their faith and trust in Jesus Christ as Lord and Savior that people are changed, families are changed, values are changed, and thus communities and cultures are changed. You cannot change a culture simply by fighting the symptoms of a depraved and sinful culture. A culture reflects the values embraced by the people living in a city, state, or nation, and until you change an individual's values, you will not change a culture with legislation or moralizing. A person's actions are based on his or her values, those values are based on the person's worldview, and that worldview consists of his or her theology, philosophy, ethics, etc.

The unsaved humanist is not going to change his or her values until the worldview based on a theology that denies the God of the Bible is changed. That means the goal of the NAR to legislate "kingdom values" through the Seven Mountain Mandate is a waste of time and money. Preaching a biblical Gospel, on the other hand, is never a waste of time and money.

I believe many of the NAR members fail to preach the Gospel simply because they themselves are not saved. They are false teachers. They do not dare preach a biblical Gospel because they want to work with all the world's religions to establish their own version of the Kingdom of God on earth, and it is hard to get invited to speak at Mormon or Muslim conferences if you insist on preaching the Gospel of Christ.

This idea that the NAR can establish the Kingdom of God on earth reeks of arrogance. It also reeks of a power grab—that "we're gonna take control, gonna be in power, we're gonna tell 'em how to run the world." It reeks of a humanism that really believes it can control God, that God is dependent on them in order for Christ to return. This might be shocking except that the NAR has some strong New Age, cosmic humanist ideals.

The Seven Mountain Mandate is eerily similar to the goals laid out by occultist Alice Bailey. Bailey claimed that her personal demon, the Tibetan, was a member of a group of Ascended Masters which "each have a special contribution to make towards human progress in one of the seven major fields of world work: political, religious, educational, scientific, philosophical, psychological or economic."[157] Notice the similarity between those seven fields and Wagner's seven mountains of "religion, family, business, arts & entertainment, government, education, and media"?

(6) The New Apostolic Reformation has a radical commitment to electing so-called Christians to public office in order to establish a Christian government, or theocracy, for God's Kingdom on earth.

In the March 2000 issue of *Despatch Magazine,* W. Howard reported that "Wagner is awaiting a *'critical mass'* of Christians to arise to take over the political systems of the world."[158]

Do you see anywhere in the Bible that we're to rise and take over the political systems of the world, and that once we do this, Christ can return? No. Please understand that I am not saying people should not run for elected office. I am not saying people should not go vote. What I am saying is that the first priority of Christians is to proclaim the Gospel. Paul makes this clear in 1 Corinthians 15:3–4:

> For what I received I passed on to you as of first
> importance: that Christ died for our sins according to
> the Scriptures, that he was buried, that he was raised
> on the third day according to the Scriptures.

(7) Members and leaders of the New Apostolic Reformation promote pagan spirituality.

Another characteristic of the NAR crowd is the promotion of pagan spiritual practices, such as contemplative prayer. Members of the NAR claim that contemplative prayer allows them to access new revelations from God and that these revelations are equal to the Word of God. Many NAR members embrace the occultism of walking a prayer labyrinth, and many of them are actively talking to what I believe are demons, even though they claim the beings are angels. Whether it is called contemplative prayer, breath prayers, centering prayers, or soaking prayers, it is nothing less than transcendental meditation. Transcendental meditation or contemplative prayer is a form of self-hypnosis.

Again, Alice Bailey seems to understand how this will work:

> The spiritual Hierarchy [demons] of the planet, the ability of mankind to contact its Members and to work in cooperation with Them, and the existence of the greater Hierarchy of spiritual energies of which our tiny planetary sphere is a part—these are the three truths upon which the coming world religion may be based.[159]

C. Peter Wagner has openly spoken of the "new" revelation they claim NAR prophets and apostles are receiving from God:

> Pentecostal theologians have made the helpful suggestion of distinguishing the logos word of God from the rhema word of God.... The rhema is regarded as a more immediate word from God which we do not find in the 66 books of the Bible.[160]

As I will explain further in the next chapter, God does not give extra-biblical revelation. He is not audibly speaking to these false prophets and apostles. So that raises the question: just who are they hearing from? I believe many of these false teachers are fooling around with the occult whether they know it or not and are accepting the doctrines of demons. First Timothy 4:1 tells us that the increase in people following the doctrines of demons is a sign that we are living in the last days: "The Spirit clearly says that in later times some will abandon the faith and follow deceiving spirits and things taught by demons."

In his 1980s warning to the Church, George Wood picked up on this same dangerous direction in NAR teachings, pointing out the errant belief that:

> The Church could no longer rely solely on written Scripture for doctrine. It would have to develop the five-fold ministry of apostles, prophets, evangelists, pastors, and teachers, from whom the Church could learn rulership. These new "apostle's" and "prophet's" words would be obeyed and not judged or tested by the Church. The door would be open to ongoing rev-

elation through which God would reveal components of His will and ways not found in the Bible.[161]

(8) The New Apostolic Reformation believes prophets and apostles are for today.

The next chapter covers this topic in detail, and I will reveal from the Word of God why prophets and apostles are not for today, yet this is the position of the NAR:

> The New Apostolic Reformation is an extraordinary work of the Holy Spirit that is changing the shape of Christianity globally....The Lord is establishing the foundations of the Church for the new millennium. This foundation is built upon apostles and prophets. Apostles execute and establish God's plan on the earth. The time to convene a conference of the different apostolic prophetic streams across this nation is now! This conference will cause the Body to understand God's "new" order for this coming era. We look forward to having you with us in Brisbane in Feb. 2000.[162]

Notice the invitation says "this conference will cause the Body to understand God's new order for this coming era." The NAR promotes a new order, an idea compatible with globalists like the Rockefellers and their friends at the Council on Foreign Relations. I contend they are all working for the same order, for the same kingdom—a New World Order that will be Satan's kingdom based on humanism and his lies. But take hope: Daniel 2:44 assures us that God will crush Satan's kingdom.

Wagner and his NAR friends are not prophets or apostles, and they are not building God's Kingdom. Although I could quote many different Bible teachers, here is John MacArthur's explanation of why we do not have prophets today:

> They were a temporary group, as they were temporary earlier. You know the prophets were only around till the Old Testament Canon was closed and...bang... when it was closed they were gone. [There] aren't any prophets for the 400–year period after the Old Testament. As soon as the New Testament is to be written,

prophets appear again, and as soon as the New Testament is complete...bang...prophets are gone. There aren't any prophets today because the Word of God gives us all we need.[163]

MacArthur also explains why this makes sense:

We don't need apostles today. You know why? We already have doctrine. Is that right? Do we need new doctrine? Do we need new truth? Do we need a new pattern for the church? No.[163]

Nevertheless, Peter Wagner has been involved in commissioning "apostles." Here is a transcript from a portion of his installation service of Todd Bentley as a prophet:

My name is Peter Wagner, and I'm president of Global Harvest Ministries based in Colorado Springs, Colorado. I have served the body of Christ in apostolic ministry for many years, and currently I preside over the International Coalition of Apostles, which brings together over 500 recognized apostles. I have the honor of being assigned to preside over this momentous occasion, and I am humbled, as I approach the task with an enormous sense of awe.

Holy Spirit, I invite your presence, your power, and your direction. Amen? This is a ceremony celebrating the formal apostolic alignment of Todd Bentley. My first desire is to lay a biblical foundation for what we are about to do.[165]

Unfortunately, there is no biblical foundation for what he was about to do. And to underscore how effective these men are in living biblically: A few weeks after Bentley was installed as a "prophet," he left his wife and children for another woman. He eventually divorced his wife and married the other woman.

Todd Bentley, Rick Joyner, and the other NAR prophets and apostles are the very kind of false prophets and apostles Jesus warned about. In fact, in Matthew 24, the disciples ask Jesus to give them a sign of His imminent return. He mentions false teachers, prophets, and apostles *more than* war, rumors of wars, earthquakes, and famines.

(9) The New Apostolic Reformation believes that signs and wonders validate their authority.

Wagner said this about their experimentation with signs and wonders:

> One of our adjunct professors, John Wimber, who is a pastor of Vineyard Christian Fellowship of Yorba Linda, California, came to us recently with a suggestion that we offer a course in Signs, Wonders, and Church Growth. I agreed to cosponsor the course with him, and early in 1982 we experimented with it.[166]

John Wimber was a major leader in the growth of the Vineyard churches. Most Vineyard churches participate with the New Apostolic Reformation and its unbiblical theology and doctrine.

Rick Warren, upon the death of John Wimber, offered this on a Vineyard website:

> I will remember John Wimber as a man who truly loved Jesus more than anything else. I always enjoyed our conversations because that love for Christ produced an uncommon passion in his life that was contagious. I will miss that. A hundred years from today, people will still be singing "Spirit Song" because it verbalizes that deep love for Jesus.[167]

Many members of the NAR believe they have the power to raise the dead. For instance, Wagner has said:

> I too now believe that dead people are literally being raised in the world today. As soon as I say that, some ask if I believe if it is normative? I doubt if it would be normative in any local situation, but it probably is normative in terms of the universal Body of Christ. Even though it is an extremely uncommon event, I would not be surprised if it were happening several times a year.[168]

Why is it that whenever you hear these stories of an NAR member raising the dead, it is in some third-world country with no verifiable proof? I do not believe people who are clinically dead are being brought back to life. I do believe there will be an increase in demonic, counterfeit miracles, signs, and wonders that will deceive many. The Bible speaks of the antichrist performing such counterfeit miracles. Second Thessalonians 2:9 says: "The coming of the *lawless one* is according to the working of Satan, with all power, signs, and lying wonders." And in Matthew 24:24, Jesus warned that "false Christs and false prophets will rise and show great signs and wonders to deceive, if possible, even the elect."

(10) The New Apostolic Reformation believes in spiritual evolution.

Spiritual evolution is a common belief within Fabian socialism, the Emergent Church, the communitarian church growth movement, and the New Age movement. It will play a major role in bringing many of the world's religions together as one. In a CBN interview in 2000, Peter Wagner alluded to similar thinking when he declared, "We're going to new levels in the spiritual."[169]

The NAR teaches that certain individuals are becoming new spiritual beings. George Wood warned of this:

> The revived Church anticipated by the Kingdom Now proponents would demand a new breed of Christians: supermen and superwomen. Believers would be taught that they are more than human....Some Kingdom Now adherents go beyond being "little gods" to holding to the possibility that we are the "manifested sons of God," ...the race of Christians whose bodies will be transformed, not by the coming of the Lord, but by His inner secret coming from within themselves.[170]

This NAR teaching is consistent with the New Age movement or cosmic humanism, declaring that man needs to tap into his "Christ consciousness." Cosmic humanism (also known as the New Age movement or pagan spirituality) is a major foundation of the NAR.

Jewel Grewe has been researching the Latter Rain movement, the Kansas City Prophet movement, and the NAR since the early 1980s.

Jewel's husband was an Assemblies of God pastor, who like many within the Assemblies of God, became concerned when this heresy began to rise within more and more churches. In 1991, Jewel released a report—even more relevant today than when it was released—entitled "Joel's Army" in which she correctly indentifies four aspects of the "Manifested Sons of God" heresy:

1. The claim to perfection through progressive revelations beyond Scripture;
2. The written Word of God is held in low esteem and experiential knowledge very high;
3. The Word of God is perceived as a symbolic book;
4. The claim that the "god-man" dwells in every member and is waiting to be discovered and manifest by the believers.[171]

A man named Paul Cain was one of the original "prophets" of the New Apostolic Reformation. When he was popular, it was called the Kansas City Prophet movement. After his rise to prominence, Cain was discovered to be both an alcoholic and a homosexual—facts readily admitted by the NAR. On his website in 2004, Rick Joyner explained:

> In February 2004, we were made aware that Paul had become an alcoholic. In April 2004, we confronted Paul with evidence that he had been recently involved in homosexual activity. Paul admitted to these sinful practices and was placed under discipline, agreeing to a process of restoration....[172]

This public-relations nightmare seems to have been the catalyst behind the Kansas City Prophet movement dissolving and later morphing into Mike Bickel's International House of Prayer (IHOP) movement. Cain had been a promoter of the Joel's Army heresy, also known as Manifested Sons of God, Manchild Company, Omega Children, and Over-coming Bride heresy. Cain declared:

> Paul Cain tells it like it is. I don't know what the Second Coming means to you, there's so many different returns of the Lord, or comings of the Lord, I don't know, we have a cardinal doctrine like that, but

let me tell you he's coming to YOU. He's coming to his Church, he is coming to abide in you, to take up his abode in you.

I want you to know he's coming to the Church before he comes FOR the Church. He's gonna perfect the Church so the Church can be the Image, and be him, and be his representation.[173]

Bob Jones (no connection to Bob Jones University), also a major leader in the Kansas City Prophet movement of the 1980s, proclaimed:

And the Church that is raising up the government will be the head and the covering for them.... There is a ministry after the five-fold called the ministry of perfection—the Melchizedek Priesthood.... Your children will be moving into the ministries of Perfection... coming into that Divine Nature of Jesus Christ.... They themselves will be that generation that's raised up to put death itself underneath their feet...because the Lord Jesus is worthy to be lifted up by a church that has reached the full maturity of the GOD-MAN![174]

NAR proponent Bill Hamon has similarly declared:

Jesus will come back to earth and be given the Kingdom that has been won for Him by this "man-child company." The Manifested Sons of God doctrine teaches that these sons will be equal to Jesus Christ: immortal, sinless, perfected sons who have partaken of the divine nature. They will have every right to be called gods and will be called gods.[175]

Hamon has also written:

The Earth and all of creation is waiting for the manifestation of the sons of God, the time when they will come into their maturity and immortalization.... When the Church receives its full inheritance and redemption, then creation will be redeemed from its cursed condition of decay, change and death....The Church has a responsibility and ministry to the rest of creation. Earth and its natural creation is anxiously waiting for the Church to reach full maturity and come to full sonship. When the Church realizes its full sonship, its bodily redemption will cause a redemptive chain reaction throughout all of creation.[176]

The NAR teaches that Joel's Army will be doing the same things Christ did while here on earth and that this "army" will establish God's Kindgom here on earth. In an interview with *The Voice Magazine* Bill Hamon declared:

We are at the prophetic-apostolic. The prophetic movement of the 80s brought in the prophet. And in the 90s it was the apostle. Now we have all five ascension gifts fully restored. Now we can get busy, working, training, equipping, and activating the saints to demonstrate the Kingdom of God.... Now it's the whole Body of Christ arising and demonstrating the supernatural. We will see the Body of Christ coming forth in the Saints Movement. We've crossed over the Jordan. The moment you cross over Jordan you're going into warfare. As fanatical as it may sound to fundamental evangelical Christians, the Church is destined to subdue all things and put all things under Christ's feet before He actually literally returns from heaven.... The Church is being prepared now for the next moves of God. After the Saints Movement will be the Army of the Lord Movement. The next movement after that will be the Kingdom Establishment Movement.[177]

The International House of Prayer in Kansas City now has houses of prayer all over America. This heretical group includes leaders such as Lou Engle and Mike Bickle. Jewel Grewe and her team listened to hours of audio tapes of Mike Bickle teaching, and they documented heretical assertions like this:

We'll have the power to raise people from the dead; that even death won't stand before the power of the Church. We'll see those four days Lazarus kind of deals. The Lord's going to begin to give those in the days to come.[178]

Remember that pro-family leaders have worked with Engle and Bickle. The president of the American Family Association sent me a letter (which he also sent to five others, thus making it a public letter) criticizing me for publicly opposing The Response—a prayer rally that included some of the most egregious false teachers of the day. His organization had been a sponsor, along with other "evangelical" and pro-family leaders. The letter informed me that he believes "both the International House of Prayer and Cindy Jacobs ministries have statements of faith that are solid."

What many people don't seem to understand is that a group's doctrinal statement on its website is not the test of doctrinal purity. Biblical-sounding terms used by the NAR, for instance, do not have biblical definitions. When the NAR speaks of the "Day of the Lord," they are not referring to the biblical, literal second coming of Jesus Christ when He puts His foot on the earth. Those that embrace the heresy of the "Manifested Sons of God" have allegorized such scripture as Joel 2 to mean that the "Day of the Lord" is not when Christ comes *for* His Church but when He comes *in* His Church. Jewel Grewe offers this example:

> References in the book of Joel pertaining to Israel and the "Day of the Lord" are spiritualized to apply to the Church. Literal Israel becomes "the Church" and the "Day of the Lord" is seen as the manifestation or "incarnation of God" in this Joel's Army.[179]

So if you read the doctrinal statement of an NAR proponent or the "Manifested Sons of God" and it states that they believe God's Kingdom is not established on earth until after the second coming of Jesus Christ, you would believe the doctrine is sound—unless you know what these folks really mean by "the second coming of Christ" or the "Day of the Lord." It seems that uninformed evangelicals and New Religious Right leaders are easily duped when they tell you IHOP, C. Peter

Wagner, and the NAR have solid doctrinal statements. Almost all theological cults like the Mormons, New Apostolic Reformation, and Word of Faith proponents have different definitions of "Christian" terms.

The New Age movement does the same thing. It often refers to people discovering their God consciousness as the "Omega Point." Ironically, the Manifested Sons of God heresy often uses the terms "Omega Children" and "Omega sons and daughters" to describe the generation that is indwelt by this secret coming of Jesus. They suppose that these people will take on "the very divine nature of Christ Himself, as explained by "Prophet" Bob Jones:

> ... the Church is in no condition for the Lord to come today.... He's going to come for a church that is mature in righteousness... progressively going in this righteousness until you take on THE very divine nature of Christ Himself and you begin to see Christ in the Church. Christ won't come for The Church until you see Christ in The Church. Until the Church looks like Jesus. Papa [God] planted Jesus, He sowed Him down here in this earth to have a whole nation of brothers and sisters that looked just like Jesus and he will have it. His Son was ALPHA SON, your children are the OMEGA sons and daughters... (Mike Bickle interjects here, "Jesus was the beginning, but our children and us, we're included in this... we're the end of this thing [Manifested Sons of God].) The Church is asleep, but when she gets woke up, there's not any power...when she gets woke up and joins together in an army, there's not any power any place that can stop her, for she'll know nothing but victory when she joins hands and becomes one in purpose and that's to reveal the Kingdom on the face of the earth. [180]

One well-known proponent of the Manifested Sons of God was Earl Paulk. Paulk died in 2009 after pastoring a large Pentecostal church in Georgia. Paulk's church ran a public housing program that was honored by President George H. W. Bush as part of his Thousand Points of Light campaign. Yet numerous women accused Paulk of sexual misconduct.[181] Are you noticing a pattern here? Whether it is Earl

Paulk, Paul Cain, Ted Haggard, or Todd Bentley, doctrinal heresy and moral failure often go hand in hand.

Ted Haggard was connected to the work of C. Peter Wagner. When NPR asked Wagner how he felt upon "finding out that Ted Haggard, his World Prayer Center co-founder, had used drugs and had sex with men," Wagner replied:

> I don't think I've still recovered. Just by a matter of history, a few years before that happened, my wife, Doris, and I left the World Prayer Center, turned it back to Ted and went on a different route here in Colorado Springs, so we were not closely associated. But when his homosexuality was revealed, it was a devastating blow to me because not only was he pastor of this influential church, he was president of the National Association of Evangelicals.[182]

And here is Earl Paulk's take on the Manifested Sons of God:

> Jesus Christ has now done all He can do, and He waits at the right hand of His Father, until you and I as sons of God, become manifest and make this world His footstool. He is waiting for us to say "Jesus, we have made the kingdoms of this world the Kingdom of our God, and we are ruling and reigning in Your world. Even so, come Lord Jesus."[183]

It is a humanistic blasphemy to believe God is waiting in heaven, helpless until man reclaims the world and the culture, takes dominion like some Christian Taliban, and then hands it all over to God so He can send Jesus back to earth to accept the kingdom we have built for Him. The proponents of the "Manifested Sons of God" point to Romans 8:18–23 as justification for their heresy: "For the earnest expectation of the creation eagerly waits for the revealing of the sons of God."

Yet, like so many of their beliefs, this is also based on a misinterpretation of God's Word through spiritual allegorizing. Romans 8:18–23 is talking about believers returning with Jesus Christ at the Second Coming in their resurrected bodies. At that time, *Christ* restores creation as it was before the fall and sets up *His* millennial kingdom. The

Romans passage cannot be correctly interpreted to produce the belief that Christians on earth become the sinless sons of God who raise the dead and establish God's kingdom on earth. Yet Bill Hamon clearly teaches otherwise:

> Until we come into the unity of faith and exhibit perfection, Christlikeness, and maturity, there is no way that Jesus Christ can come again. The apostles, prophets, evangelists, pastors, and teachers were given for the perfecting of the saints, and unless that perfection is reached, the Kingdom of God cannot be established. The whole world groans, waiting for someone to demonstrate the principles of the Kingdom, waiting until "we all come in the unity of the faith, and of the knowledge of the Son of God, unto a perfect man, unto the measure of the stature of the fullness of Christ." This is the most important and critical issue in the world today. There is absolutely no way that the Kingdom of God can come to pass until the walls of division are broken down and we comprehend what is meant by "unity of faith."[184]

This quest for "unity" is why NAR proponents are interested in ecumenicalism. Earl Paulk describes his ecumenical strategy this way:

> What would a meeting be like which brought together liberal evangelicals, such as we are, conservative theologians, represented by Holiness groups and Southern Baptists, and Catholics. Seventh-Day Adventists, and members of the Church of Jesus Christ of Latter-Day Saints [Mormons]? Many of these groups have become so different that we almost regard them as enemies, rather than as brothers and sisters in the faith. How can we step over these walls that have been built so high?[185]

Notice that Paulk calls himself a liberal. Later, I will go into more detail about how the left and right are converging spiritually. It is also significant that Paulk includes Catholics and Mormons in this quest for the Kingdom of God on earth. Doubtless, Paulk would be pleased to see evangelical leaders embracing Mormon Glenn Beck and Catholic Jay Richards in their spiritual enterprises.

To justify such unbiblical ecumenicalism, Paulk and others like him must take the apostle Paul out of context. Paulk writes:

> It is my honest opinion that the Kingdom of God cannot come to pass until "we all come in the unity of the faith." He specifically does not say anything about doctrine, because he is not concerned about doctrinal points. As long as the world of religion continues to act as it is acting now, there will never be a Kingdom of God in reality. For so long as we have said, "Why don't the Seventh-Day Adventists change? Why don't the Mormons change?" Perhaps we should be the ones to change.[186]

Paulk clearly does not recognize any doctrinal distinction between Mormons, Catholics, Seventh-Day Adventists, and others, and what he hoped for is happening now. Shirley Dobson, James Dobson, Jim Garlow, Kirk Cameron, John Hagee, Richard Land, David Barton, James Robison, Tim LaHaye, and a host of others have either defended or praised Glenn Beck. They have either talked with him about God or joined him in one of his spiritual enterprises. And for what? The answer seems to be to reclaim America or to reclaim the culture, but regardless of the reason, such pragmatism fits much too nicely with the goals and agenda of dominion theology that embraces ecumencialism for the sake of building the Kingdom of God on earth.

Responding to Paulk, Tommy Ice writes:

> We have searched the Bible in vain for the passage which Paulk has in mind where Paul lays down the unity of the faith as a condition for the coming in of the Kingdom. He seems to have in mind Ephesians 4:13. But the Kingdom of God is not even found in this context....How can Paulk say that Paul is not talking about doctrine? The phrase "the faith" is a synonym for doctrine or teaching. Paul is using it in the objective sense—the content of what we believe. Paul

contrasts the faith in verse 13 with "every wind of doctrine" in verse 14. So it does have something to do with doctrine. The unity to be achieved is a unity of the faith. This is supposed to protect the Church from being tossed around by false doctrine (v. 14), like Mormonism. Apparently Paulk has not attained to a unity of the faith, or he would not be interested in merging with Mormons.[187]

Paulk is not alone, of course. Word of Faither Benny Hinn has long been teaching his own version of the "manifested sons of God" heresy. He believes Jesus Christ was not God incarnate but came to earth as a man and then became divine while here on earth. Hinn and other Word of Faith false teachers like Kenneth Copeland teach that Jesus set the pattern for man to follow and that we will become like Jesus through a special type of spiritual evolution. Consider the blasphemy of Hinn in these statements of his:

> When Jesus was on earth, the Bible says that first He disrobed Himself of the divine form. He, the limitless God, became man, that we men may become as He is.[188]

> The new creation is created after God in righteousness and true holiness. The new man is after God, like God, godlike, complete in Christ Jesus. The new creation is just like God. May I say it like this, "You are a little god on earth running around"?[189]

Word of Faith preacher Kenneth Copeland echoes Hinn's false teaching:

> If we ever wake up and realize who we are, we'll start doing the work that we're supposed to do. Because the church hasn't realized yet that they are Christ. That's who they are. They are Christ.[190]

A popular belief among Word of Faith and NAR heretics is that Jesus did not come to earth as God but as man. They teach that Jesus was somewhere between human and divine, and after the Spirit fell on Jesus at His baptism, He began to do great signs and wonders and became divine. Copeland says, "Why didn't Jesus openly proclaim Himself as God during His 33 years on earth? For one single reason. He hadn't come to earth as God, He'd come as a man."[191]

The belief that Jesus was not God incarnate but came to earth as a man is known as Arianism, (not to be confused with the Aryanism of Adolf Hitler.) The heresy is named after Arius who died in 336 AD. The belief that Jesus emptied Himself of His deity when He came to earth is known as Kenotic Theology. This false teaching is derived from a misinterpretation of Philippians 2:6–7, which reads: "who, being in the form of God, did not consider it robbery to be equal with God, but made Himself of no reputation, taking the form of a bondservant, and coming in the likeness of men."

By examining the Greek meaning of the word "emptied," John MacArthur explains what these verses actually mean:

> Jesus Christ emptied Himself completely of every vestige of advantage and privilege, refusing to assert any divine right on His own behalf. He who created and owned everything forsook everything. It must also be kept in mind that Jesus emptied Himself only of certain aspects of His prerogatives of deity, not of deity itself. He was never anything, and never will be anything, but fully and eternally God, as Paul was careful to state in the previous verse [v. 6 "being in the form of God"]. All four gospels make it clear that He did not forsake His divine power to perform miracles, to forgive sins, or to know the minds and hearts of people. Had He stopped being God (an impossibility), He could not have died for the sins of the world. He would have perished on the cross and remained in the grave, with no power to conquer sin or death.[192]

On the other hand, Copeland reveals his belief in Kenotic Theology when he writes:

> [Most Christians] mistakenly think Jesus was able to work wonders, perform miracles and live above sin because He had divine powers that we don't have. Thus, they've never really aspired to live like He lived....They

don't realize that when Jesus came to earth, He voluntarily gave up that advantage, living His life here not as God but as a man. He had no innate supernatural powers. He had no ability to perform miracles until after He was anointed by the Holy Spirit (see Luke 3:22).[193]

New Ager and author Barbara Marx Hubbard founded the Foundation for Conscious Evolution. Her group teaches spiritual evolution, and so do the New Age movement, the Word of Faith, the New Apostolic Reformation, Mormons, Hindus, Buddhists, and the Emergent Church. Note the similarity between the Manifested Sons of God teaching and Hubbard's paganism:

> Finally, you start the transition.... During the transition, millions of members of the body awaken to their power to be natural Christs, full humans in the model of the first person to manifest the next stage in the development of humanity.[194]

Like the New Apostolic Reformation belief that Christ must come "in the church" before He comes "for the church," Hubbard teaches that the Second Coming will be when man realizes that:

> the divisions of the religions would be over.... We would each know that God is within us.... If all who feel we are connected to each other, to nature and to God join in a planetary Pentecost, we shall be transformed in this lifetime. I believe in the peaceful Second Coming.[195]

Ms. Hubbard wrote a book entitled *Emergence*, and as we will learn in another chapter, the heresy of the Emergent Church, too, holds that man is beginning to realize his Christ-consciousness and that he is one with the universe. It is little wonder that the New Age movement, Mormons, the New Apostolic Reformation, Emergent Church proponents, the Word of Faith movement, Hindus, and Buddhists will come together and form the one-world religion described in Revelation 17.

Pastor Brian McLaren is one of the most popular authors and speakers within the Emergent Church, and on his website McLaren recounts a conversation with a college student about how the Emergent Church was formed: "Emergent grew out of the Young Leader Networks, which was launched in the mid-90's by Leadership Network, a Dallas-based foundation."[196] McLaren is saying here that Bob Buford and his organization, Leadership Network, helped form the Emergent Church. Buford's organization is also known for helping establish the seeker-sensitive church model of Peter Drucker and has also promoted the New Apostolic Reformation.

The January-March 1999 Leadership Network newsletter *Next* featured an article by C. Peter Wagner. Entitled "Another New Wineskin...The New Apostolic Reformation," the article claims that NAR "is changing the shape of Protestant Christianity around the world."[197] Wagner also says he and his friends expect opposition from Bible-believing Christians: "We are well into the early adoption phase of the New Apostolic Reformation, when we can expect fairly strong objections from traditionalists who are threatened by changes."[198]

That such a movement would appeal to the Leadership Network with its Emergent Church/seeker-sensitive church models is not surprising since much of what the Leadership Network, Emergent Church, and seeker-sensitive proponents call for is a "new kind of Christianity." In fact, *A New Kind of Christianity* is the title of a book written by Brian McLaren. The change threatening us is their desire to transform New Testament churches into their new breed of Christian and new Christianity that consists of pagan spirituality, a different Jesus, and a false gospel.

This theological aberration has implications for many core Christian beliefs as evidenced by a radio interview with Brian McLaren. He describes the fallacy of believing in hell:

> [T]his is one of the huge problems with the traditional understanding of hell, because if the Cross is in line with Jesus' teaching, then I won't say the only and I certainly won't say ... or even the primary but a primary meaning of the Cross ... is that the Kingdom of God doesn't come like the kingdoms of this world by inflicting violence and coercing people. But that the Kingdom of God comes through suffering and willing, voluntary sacrifice, right? But in an ironic way, the doc-

trine of hell basically says, "No, that's not really true. At the end God gets his way through coercion and violence and intimidation and domination just like every other kingdom does." The Cross isn't the center then. The Cross is almost a distraction and false advertising for God.[199]

And he is attracting many "evangelical" leaders, pastors, and pro-family organizations to align with him!

(11) The New Apostolic Reformation is blatantly hostile toward Christians who refuse to accept its esoteric revelations and self-appointed leadership.

"Esotericism" is hidden knowledge, and the proponents of the NAR believe they are obtaining hidden knowledge through communication with angels, hearing the audible voice of God while in a meditative state, and by receiving dreams or visions. NAR apostles or prophets quickly become hostile toward Christians who refuse to accept their revelations, self-appointed authority, and globalist agenda. As George Wood warned years ago:

> [T]he Church everywhere would be called to "unity." Since Kingdom Now teachers do not want their teaching to be challenged, they attempt to silence their critics by suggesting that Christians lay aside their differences and join in common witness.[200]

C. Peter Wagner substantiated this very point when he was asked what would be a stumbling block for him and his NAR disciples in accomplishing their goal. He said it would be Christians and pastors who stand on the authority of the Word of God and sound biblical doctrine. He argued that such people will be under demonic influence:

> "...a commitment to tradition amongst ministers." Wagner states: "I think that some are bound by religious forms and functions that are ineffective and I think in many cases it is demonic influence."[201]

Doesn't Satan always work that way? He and his followers accuse us of the very thing that is really true about them. We hear the false church saying: "You're divisive. You're mean. You're mean-spirited. You're intolerant. You're a bigot. You're a hatemonger. You're not interested in unity. You're not interested in truth." Yet throughout the Word of God, we read that Christians are the ones who will be persecuted. Jesus tells us that false teachers and false prophets will persecute true Christians. Jesus also makes it clear that Christians will not become so popular that they are elected to office worldwide as a means to usher in a Kingdom of God on earth. Rather, He says that all nations of the world will hate Christians: "Then they will deliver you to tribulation, and will kill you, and you will be hated by all nations because of My name" (Matthew 24:9).

What is particularly interesting is that in this very same chapter Jesus warns about false teachers and false prophets. I believe Jesus is speaking of the very kind of false prophets who make up the New Apostolic Reformation. In Matthew 24:3, 4, 11, 23, and 24 Jesus mentions the rise of false teachers and false prophets as the *leading indicator* of His imminent return.

Rick Joyner, one of the most visible and popular leaders in the NAR, oversaw the restoration of "prophet" Todd Bentley to ministry after he left his wife and children for another woman. Joyner also claims to have received visits from an angel. Like Wagner, Joyner has claimed that those who oppose the NAR are under demonic influence:

> Some pastors and leaders who continue to resist this tide of unity will be removed from their place. Some will become so hardened they will become opposers and resist God to the end.... Some that were used greatly of God in the past have become too rigid in doctrinal emphasis.... Some leaders will actually disband their organizations as they realize they are no longer relevant to what God is doing.... This harvest will be so great that no one will look back at the early church as a standard.... Those who have become vessels for this spirit and do not repent, will be displayed as so insane that even the most immature Christians will quickly discern their sickness.... The source of

witchcraft against us may not be the obvious satanic cults or New Age operatives. It can come from well meaning, though deceived, Christians who are praying against us instead of for us.[202]

How interesting that Joyner would speak of the New Age movement as an opponent when the NAR is filled with New Age teachings.

Notice also that Joyner says, "This harvest will be so great that no one will look back at the early church as a standard." That alone should tell you that what they are doing is unbiblical, because the standard for the Church is to be the doctrinal foundation once delivered to the saints, as instructed in Jude 3.

Joyner writes that "those who have become vessels for this spirit and do not repent, will be displayed as so insane that even the most immature Christians will quickly discern their sickness." Joyner is calling people like me insane for opposing their heresy. Yet he is the one claiming in his 158–page "prophecy" entitled *The Final Quest* that he has gone to heaven and visited with an angel in the form of a talking eagle.

The false dominant church is going to be the primary persecutor of the true Bride of Christ, that true remnant which perseveres even in the face of persecution. I recommend that you prepare yourself now for persecution from people who call themselves Christians and from false teachers, false apostles, and false prophets who carry the title of pastor and reverend. Joyner even calls for "The Great Christian Civil War," which will be used to drive out those who have "become too rigid in doctrinal emphasis."[203]

Pastor Bill Randles, an independent Pentecostal pastor who authored *Beware the New Prophets: A Caution Concerning the Modern Prophetic Movement,* says this about Rick Joyner:

> In the surreal world of the prophets, symbolism takes on a life of its own. The Blues in the army have been interpreted as those who are operating on revelation knowledge, blue being symbolic of heaven. The Grays are still operating out of their heads (gray matter, the brain, get it?). The Gray Army (of Christians) are seeking to hold the church in "spiritual slavery."[204]

This tracks with how Rick Joyner describes the situation in *The Final Quest:* "A great spiritual civil war now looms before the church....

The church will not be destroyed, but the institutions and doctrines that have kept men in spiritual slavery will be."[205]

And what doctrines are they that he finds so offensive, or that are keeping people in slavery? Could it be the biblical doctrine that reveals that false teachers are of their father, the devil?

(12) New Apostolic Reformation leaders use traditional terms deceptively by giving them new meanings as defined by their movement.

I am not the only one who has studied this movement and believes NAR is offbase. One of these is Rob Crabtree. While superintendent for the Ohio district Assemblies of God in 1987, he wrote a letter to pastors warning them to:

> Watch for the development of new terms and re-definition of old terms with new shades of meaning that will be utilized in an attempt to accommodate the various types of Kingdom Now theologies.[206]

(13) The NAR belief system is not based on studying the Bible in context through exegesis but rather on a commitment to interpreting the Bible through personal opinions, feelings, desires, and experiences—also known as the practice of isogesis.

Exegesis is the process of studying the Bible in context—using Scripture to interpret Scripture. Exegesis also includes hermeneutics, studying passages in the original Greek or Hebrew to see more clearly what the passage is stating.

The NAR, Name It and Claim It, and the Word of Faith movement—featuring personalities such as Kenneth Copeland, Kenneth Hagin, and Benny Hinn—are notorious for using verses that have nothing to do with money to teach that if you give them and their ministries money, you will reap a financial harvest. However, if you study most of the verses they use, they have absolutely nothing to do with money.

There are other misuses of Scripture as well. Psalm 46:10, for instance, reads, "Be still and know that I am God." Study this verse in context, and you will see that it is not referencing prayer. Yet people often say, "Oh, that's about praying, and I need to be still and hear the voice of God." Fox Faith has even produced a DVD called *Be Still* that uses this verse to promote contemplative prayer. Psalm 46:10, though, is referring to the sovereignty of God. That is clear when you pay attention to how the complete verse reads:

> Be still, and know that I *am* God;
> I will be exalted among the nations,
> I will be exalted in the earth!

The verse declares that God is in control. It says, in essence, "Stop fidgeting, stop fussing, and don't be so restless; God is in charge." The verse was not only assurance to the nation of Israel, but a warning to the enemies of God.

Correct *exegesis* reveals the true meaning of this verse. *Isogesis* uses presupposition, predetermined interpretation, and feelings to come up with the mistaken "personal" application. Again, Peter Wagner's thoughts reflect precisely what is wrong with this approach:

> Christianity began with 120 in the Upper Room; within three centuries it had become the predominant religion of the Roman Empire. What brought this about? The answer is deceptively simple: while Christianity was being presented to unbelievers in both Word and deed, it was the deed that far exceeded the Word in evangelistic effectiveness.[207]

So the deed is more important than the Word of God? Feelings are more important than God's Word? Now you see why they have so little concern for exegesis.

John MacArthur correctly observed:

> The sad truth is that the gospel proclaimed by the Word-Faith movement is not the gospel of the New Testament. Word-Faith doctrine is a mongrel system, a blend of mysticism, dualism, and gnosticism that borrows generously from the teachings of the metaphysical cults. The Word-Faith movement may be the most dangerous false system that has grown out of the char-

ismatic movement so far, because so many charismatics are unsure of the finality of Scripture.[208]

I am guessing that even the majority of noncharismatics are unsure of the finality of Scripture—its ultimate authority—which is why many noncharismatic churches embrace the NAR and dominion theology. Even Thomas Road Baptist Church, once pastored by Jerry Falwell, and Liberty University have embraced Rick Joyner, Cindy Jacobs, Lou Engle, and other "prophets" of the NAR at their conferences.

NAR Pragmatism

Christian pragmatism—is it possible? The answer is a resounding no, but Peter Wagner seems to think Christian pragmatism (the belief that the end justifies the means) is just fine:

> ...we ought to see clearly that the end *does* justify the means. What else possibly could justify the means? If the method I am using accomplishes the goal I am aiming at, it is for that reason a good method. If, on the other hand, my method is not accomplishing the goal, how can I be justified in continuing to use it?[209]

In Leadership Network's *Next* newsletter, C. Peter Wagner expands the pragmatic theme:

> No church can do everything. How do we choose? The new apostolic answer is simple—do whatever works.... Among new apostolic church leaders, whether denominational or otherwise, there is little aversion to pragmatism. They say, "If God has given us a job to do—let's get it done! If a methodology works, use it; if it doesn't work, scrap it!...New apostolic church leaders constantly seek ways to update and contexualize their outreach ministries."[210]

Why do the epistles not declare that the purpose of the Church is to establish a physical Kingdom of God on earth here and now? The word *kingdom* is used 129 times from Matthew through John in the King James, but it is only used 34 times from Acts through Revelation. If the main goal of the New Testament Church was to build the Kingdom of God on earth, we would expect to see the word *kingdom* used over and over in the epistles. The epistles deal with the establishment of the Church, the qualifications of church leaders, the job description of church leaders, and the goals and objectives of a biblical New Testament Church. The list does not include any mandate to build a physical Kingdom of God on earth or to take over political and cultural institutions.

The word *kingdom* in Matthew through John is used in relation to the Gospel of the Kingdom of God. For instance, Matthew 4:23 says, "And Jesus went about all Galilee, teaching in their synagogues and preaching the Gospel of the kingdom, and healing all manner of sickness and all manner of disease among the people."

Notice that Jesus was preaching the Gospel of the Kingdom. And what is the Gospel? It is the good news of salvation through Jesus Christ alone.

Mark 1:14–15 reflects a similar idea: "Now, after John was put in prison, Jesus came to Galilee, preaching the Gospel of the kingdom of God, and saying, 'The time is fulfilled and the kingdom of God is at hand. Repent and believe in the Gospel.'"

And in Luke 4:43: "Jesus said to them, 'I must preach the kingdom of God to the other cities also because for this purpose I have been sent.'"

Jesus did not say He was on earth to build a physical kingdom but that He was sent to preach the Kingdom of God. What does that mean? Luke 17:21 explains that "the kingdom of God is within you." In other words, the Kingdom of God is within the heart (soul) of those who have come to a saving knowledge of Jesus Christ through faith and repentance.

Luke 8:1 alludes to this ongoing reality: "Now it came to pass, afterward, that [Jesus] went through every city and village, preaching and bringing the glad tidings [gospel] of the kingdom of God."

God's Kingdom will come, but it's not something we build on this earth. We can be involved in spiritually building God's Kingdom as we preach the Gospel of the Kingdom and people are added to the Church as they are saved. Matthew 24:14 makes this clear: "And this gospel of the kingdom will be preached in all the world as a witness to all the nations, and then the end will come."

Notice that this verse does *not* say that after the Gospel of the Kingdom is preached then the Kingdom of God will be established on earth. God, not us, will establish His millennial Kingdom, and God is not dependent on us to establish His Kingdom on earth. The Bible is clear that there will not be a worldwide revival that sees Christians taking over the earth and taking over the seven mountains listed by the NAR. The Bible says the last days will be marked by an increase in false teachers (like the NAR) and that there will be a great falling away from biblical truth. This falling away is described in the Bible as the great apostasy. Second Thessalonians 2:9–12 reveals that the apostasy of the last days will not bring in God's Kingdom on earth but will be the precursor to the antichrist that will be under Satan's control:

> The coming of the *lawless one* is according to the working of Satan, with all power, signs, and lying wonders, and with all unrighteous deception among those who perish, because they did not receive the love of the truth, that they might be saved. And for this reason God will send them strong delusion, that they should believe the lie, that they all may be condemned who did not believe the truth but had pleasure in unrighteousness.

In keeping with this growing problem of apostasy, 2 Timothy 3:13 does says things are not going to get better and better until the Kingdom of God is established on earth but rather that the world situation will get worse: "But evil men and impostors will grow worse and worse, deceiving and being deceived."

Charles Spurgeon highlights this teaching:

> The kingdom of Christ is not a kingdom of this world. Otherwise would his servants fight. It rests on a spiritual basis and is to be advanced by spiritual means. Yet Christ's servants gradually slipped down into the notion that his kingdom was of this world and could be upheld by human power.[211]

The religious Trojan horse is already inside the Church. The New Apostolic Reformation and its dominion theology is not about preaching the Gospel but is about the things of this world such as arrogance, humanism, and occultism. Beware!

CHAPTER 4

Beware of False Apostles and Prophets

Given that the New Apostolic Reformation is growing so rapidly, even within mainstream evangelicalism, it is critical to understand the biblical basis on which I and others who recognize the problem take issue with the movement. NAR members claim that Christians must yield to their leadership because God has appointed them to be apostles and prophets to lead the Church in establishing the Kingdom of God here on earth.

Lest you think this is simply a squabble between Pentecostals and non-Pentecostals, please note that an August 6, 2001, report released by the General Presbytery of the Assemblies of God (a Pentecostal denomination) included the following statement:

> It is also clear that while the apostles (with the elders) were established leaders in the Early Church, there was no provision for their replacement or continuation.... It is instructive, however, that nowhere in the New Testament after the replacement of Judas is any attention given to a so-called apostolic succession. No attempt was made to replace James son of Zebedee (John's brother), executed by Herod (Acts 12:2). Other than the original appointments by Christ himself, there is nothing concerning the appointment of apostles. And apart from the criteria set for the selection of Matthias (Acts 1:21–26) and the criteria implied in the actions of Jesus and the account of Paul (1 Corinthians 15:3–11), there are no directions for making such an appointment. By contrast, there are clear qualifications and instructions for the appointment of elders/overseers and deacons (1 Timothy 3:1–13;

Titus 1:5–9). It seems strange that apostles of Jesus Christ, concerned about faithful preservation of their message (cf. 2 Timothy 2:2), would provide for the appointment of overseers/elders while ignoring their own succession if such were indeed to be maintained.... In fact, there are certain exegetical hints the apostles of Jesus Christ are not to have successors.[212]

You will notice in Scripture that there are three kinds of apostles (I'll discuss apostles first, then prophets): Apostles of the Lord Jesus Christ, apostles of the Church, and false apostles. I'll explain each in turn and then tell you why NAR leaders fall into the third category.

Apostles of the Lord Jesus Christ

First Thessalonians 2:6 says, "Nor of men sought we glory, neither of you, nor yet of others, when we might have been burdensome, as the apostles of Christ," (KJV). The crucial phrase "apostles of Christ" shows that the Apostles were not appointed by man but by God. Yet NAR leaders declare themselves and those they designate to be apostles.

Scripture is clear that there were 12 Apostles. Judas hung himself after betraying Jesus, and so another Apostle was added to bring the number back to 12 living at the time. To be very specific, Hebrews tells us that Jesus Christ was a messenger sent by God, so in that sense, you could even say Jesus Christ Himself was an Apostle, but we will focus on the thirteen, Paul being the special—and final—Apostle of the Lord Jesus Christ.

Apostles of the Church

The first apostles of the Church were the Apostles of the Lord Jesus Christ, but after them came the second tier apostles of the Church. Second Corinthians 8:23 references Titus in this regard: "He is my [Paul's] partner and fellowhelper concerning you: or our brethren be inquired of, they are the messengers of the churches, and the glory of Christ," (KJV).

Another word for (small "a") apostle is "messenger" or "sent one." So, do we have apostles of the Church today? Yes, within this meaning of the word, your missionary would be considered a messenger, a sent one, or an apostle. But it's important to understand that an Apostle of the Lord Jesus Christ is very different from an apostle of the Church. The office of the Apostle of the Lord Jesus Christ is closed. Today we have apostles of the Church by the more generic meaning of the word "apostle"—those who are sent. In fact, we are all to be messengers, sent ones proclaiming the Gospel, but none of us are Apostles of the Lord Jesus Christ or the equivalent. This is clearly a biblical notion as reflected in Philippians 2:25, which says, "Yet I supposed it necessary to send to you Epaphroditus, my brother, and companion in labour, and fellowsoldier, but your messenger, and he that ministered to my wants" (KJV).

John MacArthur offered an entire biblical series on this and points out:

> Messenger [as used in Philippians 2:25 and 2 Corinthians 8:23] comes from the same word that yields the English "apostle." He [Epaphroditus] was not an apostle of Christ, but an apostle ("sent one") in the broader sense that he was an apostle of the church in Philippi.[213]

MacArthur's view underscores the small "a" of church apostle versus the big "A" of an Apostle of the Lord Jesus Christ.

False Apostles

The third classification of an apostle is that of false apostle. The Scriptures tell us in 2 Corinthians 11:13 that "such are false apostles, deceitful workers, transforming themselves into the apostles of Christ."

Isn't it interesting that this passage says *they* transformed *themselves* into Apostles of Christ? It doesn't say they transfer themselves into the apostles of the Church. They don't transform themselves into being a messenger or a sent one from the Church but Apostles of Christ—the context showing that those who do such a thing are by definition *false* apostles. This is indeed what the Scriptures say will happen in the last days. Revelation 2:2 supports this understanding: "I know your works, your labor, your patience and that you cannot bear those who are evil. And you have tested those who say that they are apostles and are not, and have found them liars."

This is Jesus Himself speaking to that church and commending it for pointing out those who are false teachers or false apostles. So is it appropriate that we, too, point out false teachers and false apostles? The answer from this scripture is, "Absolutely!" Jesus commends the church for calling out false apostles. To make sure we know how to identify false apostles, the Bible is clear about the distinctives of the Apostles of the Lord Jesus Christ.

Distinctive #1: Apostles of Jesus Christ were appointed by God.

In Galatians 1:1 Paul, an Apostle, says he was appointed "not of men, neither by men, but by Jesus Christ and God the Father, who raised him from the dead" (KJV). So under what authority is Paul an Apostle of the Lord Jesus Christ? By the power and authority of the Lord Jesus Christ and God the Father. Luke 6:13 is also decisive about who qualifies: "And when it was day he [Jesus] called unto him his disciples: and of them he chose twelve, whom also he named apostles "(KJV).

So an Apostle of the Lord Jesus Christ is called by God—God the Father or Jesus, God incarnate. In 1 Corinthians 12:28 Paul elaborates: "And God hath set [appointed] some in the church, first apostles, secondarily prophets, thirdly teachers, after that miracles, then gifts of healings, helps, governments, diversities of tongues" (KJV).

Paul emphasizes that "God has set [appointed]" these specific offices. This should not be confused with the office of apostle or the office of prophet associated with the spiritual gifts mentioned later.

After apostles and prophets, 1 Corinthians 12:28 says, "thirdly, teachers." We have teachers today that we also call shepherds, pastors, or elders. There are people in the Church we would not classify as holding the *office* of shepherd, pastor, or elder, but they do have the spiritual gift of teaching. Such individuals can be found teaching Sunday school, writing books, speaking at Bible conferences (or at Worldview Weekends), or hosting a radio program.

Distinctive #2: Apostles of Jesus Christ had to have seen the risen Lord.

The Apostles of the Lord Jesus Christ at some point saw the risen Lord. Acts 1:22 articulates this requirement: "Beginning from the baptism of John, unto that same day that he was taken up from us, must one be ordained to be a witness with us of his resurrection" (KJV).

So to be an Apostle of the Lord Jesus Christ, you had to be appointed by God *and* you had to have seen the risen Lord. That makes it a little hard for people today who claim to be Apostles of the Lord Jesus Christ to qualify. They have not seen the risen Lord.

Distinctive #3: Apostles of Jesus Christ were used by God for a limited time to establish the doctrinal foundation of the Church.

Apostles laid the foundation, the correct doctrinal teachings of the Church. And, of course, a foundation is laid only one time. Ephesians 2:19–20 expounds on this idea of foundation:

> Now therefore ye are no more strangers and foreigners, but fellowcitizens with the saints, and of the household of God; And are built upon the foundation of the apostles and prophets, Jesus Christ himself being the chief corner stone. (KJV)

The foundation for the Church was built by the Apostles and the Prophets—once. That means we do not need foundation builders today.

Distinctive #4: Apostles of Jesus Christ received Scripture from the Holy Spirit and proclaimed God's Word.

The job of an Apostle of the Lord Jesus Christ was to receive the Word of God as the Holy Spirit moved. The Bible the Apostles authored is God-breathed and uniquely God-inspired. These men wrote the Scriptures as the Holy Spirit led them. It was a unique job of an Apostle of Jesus Christ.

Are we receiving new revelations from God today that are equal to the Bible? No! Jude 3 is clear that Scripture is "once for all" delivered to the saints. Scripture also says that we don't add to or take away from Scripture. Because the canon of the Bible is complete, we do not need Apostles today when it comes to receiving the Word of God or revelations from Him.

The false Apostles of the Lord Jesus Christ we looked at in the last chapter believe they receive new revelations equal to the Word of God, contrary to scriptures such as Ephesians 3:4–5:

> [B]y which, when you read, you may understand my knowledge in the mystery of Christ), which in other ages was not made known to the sons of men, as it has now been revealed by the Spirit to His holy apostles and prophets.

The mysteries of our faith have been revealed to us, therefore making them no longer mysteries through the ministry of the Prophets and the Apostles who received and wrote down the Word of God as the Holy Spirit moved upon them.

Distinctive #5: Apostles of the Lord Jesus Christ had the gifts of signs and wonders.

The Apostles of the Lord Jesus Christ had the gifts of signs and wonders for what purpose? To bring glory and honor to themselves? Was the purpose to pack an arena using signs and wonders and to take up huge offerings and sell books and handkerchiefs, as we see some false apostles doing today? No and no.

The true Apostles of the Lord Jesus Christ were given power from God to do signs and wonders in order to bring credibility to the message they proclaimed. It was not to glorify their own flesh or their own egos. It was simply to make the Gospel believable as they preached.

Today, the clowns, freaks, and charlatans who call themselves apostles and prophets are not performing signs and wonders. In fact, Scripture tells us that these false apostles will perform lying signs and wonders and will not preach a biblical Gospel. For instance, 2 Corinthians 12:12 says, "Truly the signs of an apostle were wrought among you in all patience, in signs, and wonders, and mighty deeds." One of the signs of an Apostle was that he could do incredible signs and wonders. And 2 Peter 2:2–3 warns of the danger from those who say they do but don't: "Many will follow their unrestrained ways, and because of them the way of truth will be blasphemed. In their greed they will exploit you with deceptive words."

So do we have people today who are apostles in a sense that they are messengers sent by God? Yes. Are there people today who have spiritual gifts of teaching or of being a pastor, shepherd, or elder? Yes again. But the offices of Apostle and Prophet are closed.

Why Is the Office of Apostle Closed?

There are several straightforward reasons why the office of Apostle is closed today, as I review below.

(1) No one sees the risen Lord today.

These guys who claim to be Apostles of the Lord Jesus Christ today are not, simply because they have not seen the risen Lord. In 1 Peter 1:7–8 we see why this is so:

> ...that the genuineness of your faith, *being* much more precious than gold that perishes, though it is tested by fire, may be found to praise, honor, and glory at the revelation of Jesus Christ, whom having not seen you love. Though now you do not see *Him,* yet believing, you rejoice with joy inexpressible and full of glory.

"Though now you do not see Him." People no longer see Him in the way the Apostles of Jesus Christ saw Him. Hebrews 11:6 proclaims that this "not seeing" is essential to our spiritual well-being: "Without faith it is impossible to please God." People do not see the risen Lord today, and you would have to see the risen Lord if you were going to be a true Apostle. You would also have to be called or appointed by God as an Apostle.

(2) The foundation was laid, and we don't lay a foundation twice.

Each of us lives in a structure that has a foundation. And how many times did the builder lay that foundation? Once. You do not lay the foundation of your house again next week. That only needed to happen one time, and the job was assigned to the biblical Apostles of Jesus Christ.

(3) We are commanded not to add to the Word of God.

The Word of God is complete. We don't add to it, so why would we need Apostles? Jude 3 speaks of this:

Beloved, when I gave all diligence to write unto you of the common salvation, it was needful for me to write unto you, and exhort you that ye should earnestly contend for the faith which was once delivered unto the saints.

Proverbs 30:5–6 also makes it clear we are not to be adding to the Word of God: "Every word of God is pure: he is a shield unto them that put their trust in him. Add thou not unto his words, lest he reprove thee, and thou be found a liar" (KJV).

Despite what people like C. Peter Wagner claim, no one is receiving new revelations from God. Deuteronomy echoes this truth in verse 12:32: "Whatever I command you be careful to observe it. You shall not add to it nor take away from it." Similarly, Deuteronomy 4:2 says, "You shall not add to the word, which I command you, nor take from it that you may keep the commandments of the Lord your God which I command you."

(4) There are no Apostles mentioned in the Epistles.

The Epistles give us the specific requirements and practices of a New Testament Church, and yet the topic of Apostles being for today's New Testament Church is never addressed. What comprises the function, authority, purpose, and duties of the Church? John MacArthur answers this way:

> In fact, if we need apostles today and we need prophets today, how come it never says anything about them in the epistles to the founding of the churches... In all of that about how the church is to be run, and how the church is to be governed, and how the church is to operate, and who is to lead the church, and who is to guide the church, and who is to serve the church, there's never a word about an apostle, never a word about a prophet. And we don't need apostles today. You know why? We already have doctrine. Is that right? Do we need new doctrine? Do we need new truth? Do we need a new pattern for the church? No![214]

Why Is the Office of Prophet Closed?

Similar to Apostles, the office of Prophet closed because there is no need for Prophets today. Please understand that this does not mean that we no longer have people in whom the gift of prophecy operates. The office of Prophet is different from the gift of prophecy. Do people still have the gift of prophecy? Yes, they do. And what does that mean? The word *prophet* means "one who speaks forth or speaks out." People with a prophetic gift speak the truth of God's Word. Many people confuse the office of Prophet that is closed with this spiritual gift that is active today.

As another helpful bit of background regarding Prophets: associating the term *prophet* with someone who predicts the future did not come about until medieval times. So it's a rather new concept to say that someone who is a Prophet is someone who foretells the future. Do Prophets warn about God's future judgment to nations? Yes, they do, because they know the Word of God. They can study Scripture and say, "Look, if we continue down this path, the Bible is clear about what will happen to a nation. Here is what we're doing when we go against the character and nature of God." We set ourselves up for judgment, and God always warns when He's getting ready to judge. He does that in order to give people a chance to repent. But the "gift of prophecy" referenced in Romans 12:6 means "speaking forth," not predicting the future.

Facts about Prophets

To understand the biblical nature of what constitutes Prophets and prophecy, it is helpful to outline nine basic facts about Prophets.

Fact #1—Prophets, like Apostles, were appointed by God.

Look again at Ephesians 4:11: "And he gave some apostles; and some, prophets; and some, evangelists; and some, pastors and teachers." In the Church today we still have the office of evangelist, pastor, and teacher, but we don't need the prior offices of Apostle and Prophet for the reasons I have outlined earlier.

Fact #2—Whatever the Prophets of the New Testament said had to be consistent with what was proclaimed by the Apostles.

Prophets proclaimed a message consistent with the foundational doctrine laid down by the Apostles. Prophets have to agree with the biblical foundation, the biblical theology, the biblical doctrine set by the Apostles.

One reason we know that the men and women of the New Apostolic Reformation are false prophets is that much of what they say does not line up with the foundational doctrine of the Apostles. They do not proclaim a message that accords with the Apostles' theology and doctrine. In fact, false prophets speak *against* the foundational doctrine laid down by the Apostles. As 1 Corinthians 14:37 notes: "If anyone thinks himself to be a prophet or spiritual, let him acknowledge that the things which I write to you are the commandments of the Lord."

Fact #3—Prophets, along with the Apostles, laid the foundation for the Church.

Again, you lay a foundation only once. Some of the same arguments we're using for why we don't have Apostles today are the same reasons we don't have Prophets today.

Fact #4—Prophets were God's spokesmen to reveal doctrinal truth about what we are to believe and the practical truth regarding how we are to live.

Fact #5—Prophets could perform miracles to confirm the authority and source of their revelation.

Fact #6—Prophets had to be 100 percent accurate, or they were killed.

Countless prophecies given by Cindy Jacobs, Rick Joyner, the New Apostolic Reformation, or the International House of Prayer have not come true. According to Scripture, a "prophet" only has to be wrong one time in order to be considered a false prophet. The Bible explains that a prophet who gives a false proclamation is to be executed.

I have read blogs and books by NAR people, and some argue that when a prophet is maturing, he or she makes mistakes. Rick Joyner, for instance, has written:

There is a prophet named Bob Jones who was told that the general level of prophetic revelation in the church was about 65% accurate at this time. Some are only about 10% accurate, a very few of the most mature prophets are approaching 85% to 95% accuracy. Prophecy is increasing in purity, but there is still a long way to go for those who walk in this ministry.[215]

Rick Joyner says that giving a wrong prophecy does not make someone a false prophet, even though the Bible says otherwise:

One of the greatest hazards affecting maturing prophets is the erroneous interpretation of the Old Testament exhortation that if a prophet ever predicted something which did not come to pass he was no longer to be considered a true prophet (see Deut. 18:20–22). The warning was that if this happened, the prophet had been presumptuous and the people were not to fear him. If one predicts something in the name of the Lord and it does not come to pass, he probably has spoken presumptuously and needs to be repented of, but that does not make him a false prophet. No one could step out in the faith required to walk in his calling if he knew that a single mistake would ruin him for life.[216]

In other words, today's false prophets are trying to justify their false prophecies by saying "Hey, we're going to give prophecies that don't come true, but that is part of the process of spiritually maturing."[217]

I suggest that the reason these contemporary "prophets" are not accurate is that the office of Prophet is closed. According to the Scriptures, you have to be 100 percent accurate, or you are not a Prophet. It was unhealthy, to say the least, for Old Testament Prophets to be wrong, as explained in Deuteronomy 18:20–22: "But the prophet, which shall presume to speak a word in My name, which I have not commanded him to speak, or that shall speak in the name of other gods, even that prophet shall die."

It is very serious to say you are a Prophet when you don't meet the biblical qualifications, and I believe today's false prophets will find themselves under severe eternal judgment for the souls they have mis-led and the heresies they have proclaimed.

Fact #7—Jesus warns about false prophets.

What did God say about false prophets? Jeremiah 23:16 reports: "Thus saith the LORD of hosts, Hearken not unto the words of the prophets that prophesy unto you: they make you vain: they speak a vision of their own heart, and not out of the mouth of the LORD" (KJV).

In other words, be aware of these people who set themselves up as prophets. They are false prophets and do not speak according to the Lord.

In Matthew 7, the disciples ask Jesus for a sign of His second coming, and Jesus warns again and again that one sign of His return will be an increase in false prophets and false teachers. More than war, rumors of wars, plagues, famines and pestilence, the number one thing He mentions is false teachers and false prophets. Matthew 24 also makes several references to this:

> Verses 3–4: "Now as He sat on the Mount of Olives, the disciples came to Him privately, saying, 'Tell us, when will these things be? And what *will be* the sign of Your coming, and of the end of the age?' And Jesus answered and said to them: 'Take heed that no one deceives you.'"

> Verse 11: "Then many false prophets will rise up and deceive many."

> Verses 23–24: "Then if anyone says to you, 'Look, here *is* the Christ!' or 'There!' do not believe *it.* For false christs and false prophets will rise and show great signs and wonders to deceive, if possible, even the elect."

Fact #8—False teachers and prophets proclaim unbiblical doctrine.

You don't have to spend too long watching Trinity Broadcasting Network (TBN) and similar networks to realize that these people are not teaching sound biblical theology and doctrine. I watched Benny

Hinn one night in his TV-audience costume and realized that he is a perfect example of the false teacher and false prophet Jesus warns of in Matthew 24.

Hinn and many Word of Faith, Name It and Claim It (what some have called "blab it and grab it"), other prosperity gospel proponents, and New Apostolic Reformation members are confirmation that we are living in the last days before the second coming of Jesus Christ. These false teachers are notorious for taking Scripture out of context for their own gain.

Matthew 7:16 offers another measure by which to judge false teachers: "Ye shall know them by their fruits. Do men gather grapes of thorns, or figs of thistles?" The fruit Jesus refers to is their doctrinal fruit.

Fact #9—False prophets and false teachers will grow worse until Christ returns.

This fact is clear from 2 Timothy 3:13: "But evil men and seducers shall wax worse and worse, deceiving, and being deceived."

Mathew 24:11 is similar: "And many false prophets shall rise, and shall deceive many."

These verses don't say *some* or *a few* false teachers will arise but *many* false prophets will rise. So what should our response be to this increase in false teachers?

Warn the Church and Warn the Unbeliever

One of our responses certainly should be to warn the Church of false teachers. To that end, I received an email one afternoon from a lady who wanted to encourage and thank me for exposing false teachers. She said someone had given her one of our *Worldview Weekend Digest* magazines. She opened it to an article in which I expose the false teachings of Rob Bell. A few days later, she attended her ladies Bible study and discovered they were preparing to read a book by Rob Bell. Because of my article, she was able to reveal Bell's falsehoods. As a result, the study agreed not to read Bell's book. The email thanked me for the Worldview Weekend ministry and encouraged me to continue exposing false teachers like Bell. She said if she had not read the article, she would not have been able to protect herself or her Christian friends from this instance of false teaching.

All Christians should be about this type of work and warning. Unfortunately, some people tell me, "Howse, you are divisive. Who has called you to do this?" My answer is simply that if we are people who follow the Lord Jesus Christ, then *He* has called *all of us* to do this. It is the job of a disciple to address falsehood in the Church. Ephesians 5:11 says, "Have nothing to do with the unfruitful works of darkness, but rather expose it."

If we don't, false teaching will lead many people astray. If we love the Gospel and biblical truth, we will not want people to follow another Jesus or believe another gospel.

We should also warn unbelievers about false teachers. If we have a heart for Jesus, we will have a heart for reaching the lost, and we will expose false teachers for what they are, because we are burdened by the fact that so many people are being deceived right into hell by false teachers.

Another sign that we are living in the last days is apostasy or a great falling away from traditionally held biblical truths. This apostasy will have a form of godliness but will deny the true God. Scripture is very clear that apostasy will come, and I believe it is here.

We are going to see more and more people claiming to be Prophets and Apostles. But we must go back to the Word of God and explain that the office of Apostle is closed. The office of Prophet is closed. I suggest using this book to reveal the importance of studying biblical theology and doctrine and studying the Word of God in context, because only doctrine can reveal the will of God for our lives. Doctrine brings discernment, and doctrine convicts those who contradict the truth.

The number-one reason people today cannot recognize false teaching is that they don't have biblical discernment. They haven't studied theology and doctrine—which is why we have baby Christians who are easily deceived. Others don't see the deceptions because they are false converts. They may attend church and hang their salvation on walking the aisle or praying a sinner's prayer, but they never truly understood what it means to repent of sins.

By contrast, 2 Corinthians 7:9–10 speaks of the godly sorrow necessary to produce repentance unto salvation:

> Now I rejoice, not that you were made sorry, but that
> your sorrow led to repentance. For you were made

sorry in a godly manner, that you might suffer loss
from us in nothing. For godly sorrow produces repentance *leading* to salvation, not to be regretted; but the
sorrow of the world produces death.

A key component of the religious Trojan horse is false apostles and
false prophets. They have and will continue to declare open war on
true believers of Jesus Christ.

Christians who are biblically minded and make the Word of God
their standard will be accused of being judgmental, for hindering unity, and for being harsh and unloving. Yet the most loving thing we can
do is to point out unbiblical doctrine which leads to an eternity of
God's judgment.

You will likely see the real Church, the real bride of Christ, persecuted and maligned by popular "Christian" authors, well-known
pastors, and "Christian" speakers who are a part of this false church.
It is all the more reason we must know the Bible, be steeped in biblical theology and doctrine, and understand the foundation laid by the
Apostles and Prophets. Only then will we be ready to contend for the
faith that was once for all delivered to the saints.

CHAPTER 5

Keep the Change (Agents)

The Church in America, and worldwide, is being co-opted by at least four groups.

#1 The Neo-Evangelicals

The first group calls themselves the "New Evangelicals," but I prefer to call them neo-evangelicals. If that sounds a little like *neo-Marxists*, there's a reason for that. Many of them embrace the economic philosophies of Karl Marx as well as all manner of heresy handed down by their forerunners who embraced "neo-orthodoxy."

As Iain Murray points out in his exceptional book *Evangelicalism Divided:*

> The "new evangelicalism" was the name first employed to describe what was proposed at Fuller. When its intended meaning was misrepresented by critics… the faculty [dropped] the term.[218]

By dropping "new evangelicalism," the terms *evangelicalism* or *evangelical* have been diluted by liberalism and have come to mean nothing.

The most noteworthy characteristic of neo-evangelicals is their commitment to postmodernism, the belief that truth and reality are created by man and not by God. According to postmodernism, each person defines his or her own version of truth. Truth is subjective, situational, and is known primarily through experiences—including occult practices such walking a labyrinth, yoga, and transcendental mediation.

Many neo-evangelicals also accept liberation theology, a mixture of Marxism and Christianity, which means it ceases to be real Christianity as defined by the Word of God. Others adopt dominion theology and falsely believe it is their job to establish God's Kingdom on earth. The liberation theology camp uses social justice as a primary tool, while the dominion theology group advances the cause through church culture that promotes their specific version of what the world should look like.

As noted earlier, Jesus refuted both approaches in John 18:36 when He said, "My kingdom is not of this world. If My kingdom were of this world, My servants would fight, so that I should not be delivered to the Jews; but now My kingdom is not from here."

Many within the neo-evangelical camp have little interest in the conservative movement and tend to be both political and theological liberals. They have historically opposed the Religious Right, because of their disagreement with the right's conservative political and theological worldview.

#2 The New Religious Right

The New Religious Right consists of some who believe in dominion theology and some who do not. The hallmark of the group is an obsession with politics at the expense of the Gospel. The New Religious Right rarely, if ever, publicly proclaims the biblical Gospel. When they do, it is often alongside false teachers of the New Apostolic Reformation, the Word of Faith Movement, and New Agers. The result is a public confused as to which gospel is true Gospel.

My firsthand experience with many New Religious Right leaders and my years of studying them lead me to believe that they are largely committed to pragmatism, power, popularity, and access to political leaders, and they will compromise the Gospel and biblical principles in order to form political and religious connections with known heretics (can you say, "Glenn Beck"?) if that is what it takes to be successful in their agenda.

I believe the New Religious Right is often driven by what will fill their fundraising coffers. They embrace projects and initiatives based on an assessment of what will increase donations as well as public visibility and likeability among "people of faith." Mainstream acceptance increases the size of honorariums they can charge for speeches at churches or "conservative" banquets. Yet their speeches rarely include the Gospel because the ultimate goal is not biblical preaching but winning another political battle, the next conflict in the culture war, or an upcoming election. That way, they can take credit in the next fundraising letter.

#3 Change Agents—a.k.a. Christian Impersonators

The third group consists of change agents who are really imposters posing as Christians, evangelicals, or neo-evangelicals in order to infiltrate from within. These "change agents" are rabid haters of Christians, the Gospel, and the Bible and know exactly how to manipulate the Church for their own ends. Many of them co-opt religious organizations and institutions in order to turn them toward pagan spirituality, ecumenicalism, liberation theology, dominion theology, and the creation of a New World Order. A significant goal of change agents and neo-evangelicals is to transform the Church so it is no longer an obstacle to the New World Order but an active participant and builder of it.

#4 Useful Idiots

By calling the fourth group "useful idiots," I am not name-calling but using a historic term created by Josef Stalin to describe those who gave him credibility. Useful idiots generally are so spiritually immature that they do not have the theological and doctrinal discernment to understand they are being used. They love having their egos fed by invitations from the "rich and famous" to sit on boards of directors, give speeches at conferences, or join high-profile organizations. Their Achille's heel is the pride which drives them to desire popularity, to be part of the in-crowd, to seem important, to be admired, and to be seen with celebrities of all sorts. Useful idiots can be found among neo-evangelicals, the New Religious Right, and change agents, but the separate tracks they all run on converge in one grand scheme.

Merging Tracks to Globalism

Globalism is being implemented along two tracks: political and spiritual. You can see this convergence as religious leaders implement political programs and give political speeches. But you will also see political leaders—such as Tony Blair and his Tony Blair Faith Foundation—speaking in blatantly religious ways as well. You will likely see more and more pastors, Christian leaders, Christian organizations, universities, and colleges accept the agenda of people such as Rick Warren and Tony Blair.

This compromise is happening in my own "backyard." I live about 75 minutes from Union University, a school supported by the Southern Baptist Convention (SBC), and although many SBC colleges, universities, and seminaries have long since been lost to liberalism, Union has consistently promoted itself as the university committed to integrating a biblical worldview into all subjects. Yet in a March 31, 2011, press release, Union boasted:

> Former British Prime Minister Tony Blair will be the keynote speaker for Union University's 14th annual Scholarship Banquet Oct. 3 at the Carl Perkins Civic Center in Jackson, Tenn. "In recent years Mr. Blair has become one of the most admired men in the world with his many efforts to promote good will through numerous means such as his faith foundation, his sports foundation, his charitable work and many other laudable efforts," Union University President David S. Dockery said. "The Union community will be pleased once again to bring a major world leader to West Tennessee."... He founded the Tony Blair Faith Foundation to promote respect and understanding between the major religions and makes the case for faith as a force for good in the modern world.[219]

Union's worldview now apparently includes the promotion of ecumenicalism and the willingness to host a Fabian socialist. There's good reason the rediscovered Fabian window depicts a wolf in sheep's clothing.

Receiving the Union press release did not shock me. I already knew that, in February 2006, David Dockery joined Rick Warren and other leaders in signing the *Evangelical Climate Initiative,* which was supported by the globalist Rockefeller Brothers Fund. In my estimation, that renders Dockery a useful idiot. He may really believe such projects and initiatives are pleasing to God, but in fact, friendship and partnership with the enemies of Christ are not.

The Union University press release also trumpeted that "previous speakers have included....Mikhail Gorbachev, Laura Bush, Rudolph Giuliani, and Colin Powell, among others." Gorbachev? Mikhail Gorbachev, the former leader of the Soviet Union, has used his foundation to promote globalism and pagan spirituality. He speaks openly of the need for a new world religion:

First of all, we must return to the well-known human values that are embodied in the ideals of the world religions and also in the socialist ideas that inherited much more from those values. Further, we need to search for a new paradigm of development that is based on those values and that is capable of leading us all toward a genuinely humanistic or, more precisely, humanistic-ecological culture of living.[220]

And in October 2011, Gorbachev spoke at Lafayette College in Easton, Pennsylvania. William F. Jasper reported on the speech by Gorbachev:

"Transformation," "transformational," and "transformative" are well-worn words in Mr. Gorbachev's globalist lexicon, always signifying a supposed urgent need to deconstruct the current political/economic system of sovereign, independent nation states and the market-based economy and restructure (transform) it into a globalized, centralized, socialized "new world order" (NWO).

In his address to the Lafayette students and faculty members, Gorbachev lamented that "the opportunities that existed after the end of the Cold War....were not used properly. At that same time, we saw that the entire world situation did not develop positively. We saw deterioration where there should have been positive movement toward a new world order…"

"But we still are facing the problem of building such a world order. We have crises: we are facing problems of the environment, of backwardness and poverty, of food shortages. All of these problems are because we do not have a system of global governance."[221]

Another example of the political and spiritual tracks merging is evident in the Global Faith Forum that was held November 11–12, 2010, at Northwood Church in Texas. The conference slogan is revealing: "Moving from a conversation *about* other faiths, to a conversation *with* other faiths" (emphasis mine).[222] Sponsors listed on the conference website included the Leadership Network, which Emergent pastor Brian McLaren says is responsible for the launch of the gnostic Emergent churches.

Another sponsor was the Council on Foreign Relations. The CFR apparently continues Rockefeller's objectives to use the Church for global governance as described on the Global Faith Forum:

> The Council on Foreign Relations (CFR)—an independent, nonpartisan membership organization, think tank, and publisher—spearheads a Religion and Foreign Policy Initiative to connect religious and congregational leaders, scholars, and thinkers with CFR's resources on U.S. foreign policy and provides a forum for this community to discuss a broad range of pressing international issues.[223]

Speaker and biographical sketches listed on the Global Forum website included:

> Ed Stetzer, Southern Baptist Convention's Lifeway Research;
>
> John Esposito, professor at the Jesuit-run Georgetown University;
>
> Shamil Idriss, who was appointed Deputy Director of the UN Alliance by Secretary-General Kofi Annan in 2005 and is a member of the Muslim Leaders of Tomorrow network;
>
> Le Cong Phung, Ambassador Extraordinary and Plenipotentiary of the Socialist Republic of Vietnam to the United States of America
>
> Eboo Patel, Founder and Executive Director of Interfaith Youth Core and named by *Islamica Magazine* as one of ten young Muslim visionaries shaping Islam in America;
>
> Prince Turki bin Faisal, who served as Saudi Arabia's ambassador to the United States from July 2005 until December 11, 2006;

Sami Awad, Executive Director of Holy Land Trust (HLT), a Palestinian nonprofit organization which he founded in 1998 in Bethlehem. HLT works with the Palestinian community at both the grassroots and leadership levels in developing nonviolent approaches that aim to end the Israeli occupation...[224]

This reads like a bad joke—"Did you hear the one about the Southern Baptist, Muslim, and Communist who got together for a conference on religion?" I wish it were a joke, but there's nothing humorous about "Christians" who think they can meet with Muslims and Communists under a common slogan such as "many distinct beliefs, one common respect."[225] And unfortunately, this sort of influence is far more widespread—and insidious—than a conference here and there.

Neo-Marxist Jim Wallis

David Noebel wrote an article for WorldviewWeekend.com that details the radical and antibiblical worldview of Jim Wallis. That Wallis has served as President Obama's spiritual adviser reveals a great deal about his belief system. Dr. Noebel exposes the following facts about radical change agent Jim Wallis:

> First, Jim Wallis has had relationships with the communist Committee in Solidarity with the People of El Salvador (CISPES).
>
> Second, his "Witness for Peace" was an attempt to defend the Nicaraguan Sandinistas! Wallis, together with the Rev. Jeremiah Wright (Obama's former pastor of 20 years) "rallied support for the communist Nicaraguan regime and protested actions by the United States which supported the anti-communist Contra rebels" (*Family World News*, February 2009, p. 7).
>
> Third, Wallis and his Sojourners community of fellow-travelers believe Fidel Castro's Cuba, Hugo Chavez's Venezuela, Daniel Ortega's Nicaragua, and the other revolutionary forces "restructuring socialist societies" are the Communist paradises the United States needs to emulate in order to establish "social justice." Writing in the November 1983 issue of *So-*

journers, Jacob Laksin notes, "Jim Wallis and Jim Rice drafted what would become the charter of leftist activists committed to the proliferation of Communist revolutions in Central America" (Laksin, "Sojourners: History, Activities and Agendas" in Discoverthenetworks.org, 2005).

The ugly truth is Wallis wishes to see the destruction of the United States as a nation and in its place "a radical nonconformist community" patterned after the progressive, socialist commune he established in Washington, D.C., in 1971 (Laksin, Ibid.).

"The Sojourners community," says Laksin, "actively embraced 'liberation theology,' rallying to the cause of communist regimes that had seized power with the promise of bringing about a revolutionary restructuring of society." Clark Pinnock, a disaffected former member of Sojourners, said that the community's members were "100 percent in favor of the Nicaraguan [communist] revolution" (Laksin, Ibid.).

And yes, Wallis portrays the evangelical right that happens to be pro-American and anti-Communist "as members of the forces of darkness" (Nash, p. 66, 71). For Wallis, a good Christian is someone who is pro-communist and socialist, while a bad Christian is someone who is anti-communist and pro-capitalist. The cry of the Sojourners crowd is "social justice" for the poor and downtrodden—social justice being code for socialism/communism.[226]

You would hope that a radical like Jim Wallis would be the last person embraced by people who call themselves Bible-believing conservatives. The problem is that many individuals, churches, and organizations *think* they are Bible-believing conservatives, but their actions, theology, doctrine, and associations say otherwise.

Legitimacy at Prestonwood

Prestonwood Baptist Church in West Plano, Texas, scheduled Wallis to speak for a church luncheon on March 9, 2010. I found this shocking because Prestonwood is considered by many to be a strongly conservative church, and the senior pastor at the time, Jack Graham, had served two terms as president of the Southern Baptist Convention.

I called the church to alert them that they had invited someone I believe is a neo-Marxist to speak at the church, but no one seemed interested in my warning—until I discussed their Wallis invitation on my radio program and distributed the program to our Worldview Weekend email list. Suddenly, a representative from Prestonwood wanted to talk to me. In an email and a phone call, he informed me that Wallis would not be speaking at the March 9 function after all. That was good news, of course, but the bad news is that upon further communication, I could not get the church to make a statement declaring that Prestonwood Baptist Church does not agree with the worldview of Jim Wallis.

One wonders if the church actually agrees with Wallis's radical worldview. He was, after all, originally invited to speak for a church luncheon, yet after withdrawing the invitation, the church would not denounce the man's radical worldview. Did the church cancel Wallis as a speaker simply because of the controversy or because the church really does not agree with Jim Wallis? Why wouldn't Jack Graham put out a statement saying he and his congregation denounce the social justice, Emergent Church, socialist worldview of Wallis and his friends? Such a statement would have put the issue to rest and would have been a real encouragement to hundreds of thousands of people and thousands of other pastors. Prestonwood's invitation to Wallis and the church's lack of willingness to denounce his radical worldview, I believe reveals just how far some churches have slid from their once biblically solid foundation.

(Some of our listeners and our email alert recipients, by the way, reported that when they called the church to voice concern, they were led to believe Wallis had never been booked to speak at the church. To demonstrate otherwise, we emailed our folks a screenshot of the luncheon announcement that had been removed from the church website.)

National Association of (Non-) Evangelicals

When the National Association of Evangelicals (NAE) was founded in 1942, it was organized in part to counter the liberalism of the Federal Council of Churches, which eventually became the National Council of Churches. The Federal Council had been organized by

Fabians Walter Rauschenbusch and Harry F. Ward, two revolutionaries we discussed in chapter 2.

Today, the NAE embraces many of the same radical ideas supported by the National Council of Churches. From radical environmentalism to redistribution of wealth to compromising on biblical theology and doctrine, the NAE is a major player in the religious Trojan horse.

An article in the April 28, 2011, *Christian Post* explains the NAE's participation in a socialist scheme called "The Circle of Protection":

> In a move that may be surprising to some, evangelicals have formed a coalition with progressive Christians as well as Catholics to oppose federal budget cuts that would hurt the poor.[227]

"Progressive" is another word for a socialist. So even the *Christian Post* writer admits this is an agenda of socialists. The article also reveals that the NAE is working with Jim Wallis and the radicals at the National Council of Churches to accomplish their goal of redistribution of wealth:

> Alongside the Rev. Jim Wallis of Sojourners, David Beckmann of Bread for the World and the Rev. Peg Chemberlin of the National Council of Churches USA, NAE President Leith Anderson is among the signatories to the "Circle of Protection."[228]

A progressive income tax is one of the ten planks of the *Communist Manifesto,* so it should come as no surprise—since socialism is the economic philosophy embraced by Karl Marx—that Leith Anderson, Jim Wallis, and the other members of this theological and economic cabal embrace taxing "wealthy" Americans in order to steal the private property of one group and give it to another. The *Christian Post* reported:

> In a Wednesday media call, coalition members also urged for increased taxes to the wealthy... The Circle of Protection's mission is a continuation of the "What Would Jesus Cut?" campaign launched by social justice group Sojourners and Evangelicals for Social Action's "Call for Intergenerational Justice." All three

proposals emphasize the biblical importance of helping the poor. They also all recommend that Congress explore other financial options rather than make cuts to programs that offer health, educational and food aid to the poor.[229]

I would guess that Leith "Robin Hood" Anderson and Jim "the Red" Wallis have never started a for-profit business from scratch and earned an appreciation of America's free-market system.

What's more, in talking about the poor, it is crucial that we understand the biblical definition of "poor." In the Bible, someone who was poor did not have a coat or a place to lay his or her head. The Bible also speaks at times of the unsaved as poor. This is a reference to being spiritually poor.

What we call "poor" in America today is not poor in the biblical sense. The facts noted below refer to people defined as poor by the Census Bureau, taken from various government reports:

- Forty-three percent of all poor households actually own their own homes. The average home owned by persons classified as poor by the Census Bureau is a three-bedroom house with one-and-a-half baths, a garage, and a porch or patio.
- Eighty percent of poor households have air conditioning. By contrast, in 1970, only 36 percent of the entire U.S. population enjoyed air conditioning.
- Only 6 percent of poor households are overcrowded. More than two-thirds have more than two rooms per person.
- The average poor American has more living space than the average individual living in Paris, London, Vienna, Athens, and other cities throughout Europe. (These comparisons are to the *average* citizens in foreign countries, not to those classified as poor.)
- Nearly three-quarters of poor households own a car; 31 percent own two or more cars.
- Ninety-seven percent of poor households have a color television; over half own two or more color televisions.

- Seventy-eight percent have a VCR or DVD player; 62 percent have cable or satellite TV reception.
- Eighty-nine percent own microwave ovens, more than half have a stereo, and more than a third have an automatic dishwasher.[230]

While I believe in bringing the gospel and material assistance to the truly needy, the reality is that most of today's neo-evangelicals are only interested in promoting their socialist agenda, not in helping those truly in need—and they are certainly not interested in sharing a biblical Gospel.

NAE's Third Way Proponent

Keep your eye on the NAE. I believe it is being driven by neo-evangelicals and change agents. For instance, one of the organization's board members, according to its website at the time of this writing, is Pastor Joel Hunter.

For several years, I've noticed that Hunter's name keeps appearing on lists of those who participate in one radical conference, initiative, or organization after another. He has a long history as a Methodist pastor but today is the founding pastor of Northland Church in central Florida. Northland boasts an attendance of 15,000 people in four locations.

Hunter is a proponent of the "Third Way," the Hegelian Dialectic Process I discussed in chapter 1 as well as in *Grave Influence*. Pastors such as Hunter want evangelicals and progressives to "dialogue" and find consensus on issues like global warming, abortion, stem cell research, and same-sex marriage. Yet 2 Corinthians 6:14 says this is impossible unless the "evangelicals" involved compromise on biblical truth: "Do not be unequally yoked together with unbelievers. For what fellowship has righteousness with lawlessness? And what communion has light with darkness?"

Author and columnist Aaron Klein revealed in a June 1, 2011, article that the NAE's board member, Pastor Joel Hunter

> is part of a group of evangelicals and progressives who organize under the auspices of the left-leaning "Third Way" organization. There, he helped draft a new position paper, "Come Let Us Reason Together: A

Fresh Look at Shared Cultural Values Between Progressives and Evangelicals."[231]

Klein reports that Hunter "has spoken at numerous interfaith forums, including a 2009 Georgetown University panel, 'A Common Word: Religious Pluralism in the 21st Century.'"[232]

Recall that President Bill Clinton, in his 1998 State of the Union Address, declared:

> We have moved past the sterile debate between those who say government is the enemy and those who say government is the answer. My fellow Americans, we have found a Third Way.

I say to you that the apostate church has also found the Third Way, and it wants you to compromise biblical truth in order to join a consensus supporting this way. When you and I do not compromise, we will be accused of hindering unity. We'll be castigated as "narrow-minded," "bigoted," "intolerant," "selfish," and "extremist." Hate-crime laws will be a likely tool to punish those of us who dissent from this consensus.

Pluralism holds that all religions are equal. So it is unconscionable that a pastor would take part in a panel that pushes the unbiblical philosophy of pluralism. It is worthwhile noting, though, that Georgetown University, where Hunter participated in the panel, is a Jesuit school. The Jesuits aggressively promote ecumenicalism, liberation theology, and dominion theology.

Klein also reports that Hunter, author of *Right Wing, Wrong Bird: Why the Tactics of the Religious Right Won't Fly with Most Conservative Christians* and *A New Kind of Conservative,* appeared at this Georgetown event with Ingrid Mattson of the Islamic Society of North America. This is the same Ingrid Mattson with whom Richard Land of the Southern Baptist Convention has served on the U.S. Muslim Engagement Initiative. Land has claimed that Christians need to build bridges to Muslims, but Klein explains why such a goal is absurd: "The ISNA is an unindicted co-conspirator in a scheme to raise money for Hamas, and has been listed by the Muslim Brotherhood as one of its 'like-minded' organizations."[233]

Hunter is even listed on the website of the Council for a Parliament of the World's Religions as a participant and also as part of the

United Nations' "Alliance of Civilizations" from 2008–2010. So is he part of the New Religious Right, a change agent working undercover as a neo-evangelical, or a neo-evangelical who has become a change agent? Whichever is the case, I believe Hunter is onboard the religious Trojan horse, hoping to convince evangelicals to accept a one-world religion.

I have warned the Church of people like Joel Hunter who want us to compromise with Third Way-think. In *Grave Influence,* I explained:

> The pastors and authors of one of America's fastest growing spiritual movements, the Emergent Church, sing the praises of socialism. As I'll explain in more detail later, the Emergent Church champions the neo-Marxist call for a utopian society through spiritual evolution where good and evil merge to form a "better" third option. This idea derives from the belief system of philosophers such as Georg Wilhelm Friedrich Hegel and finds its contemporary manifestation in the "Third Way" movement of Bill Clinton and Tony Blair. In the Third Way, capitalism, socialism, and communism merge to form a misanthropic combination of the three. This blending is now represented in the terms "the New World Order" and "the new enlightenment."

> The Third Way promotes Communitarianism, a toxic blend of communism, socialism, atheism, and Cosmic Humanism. Communitarians believe in universal health care, government-subsidized housing and education, radical environmentalism, Fabian socialism, and the like.[234]

Not to be hoodwinked by the window dressing of Third Way advocates, however, Vaclav Klaus, prime minister of the Czech Republic, warns against the real future it offers: "The Third Way is the fastest route to the Third World."[235] But that seems to be where communitarians (more about them in the next chapter) want to take us.

Dr. Amitai Etzioni, often referred to as the "guru" of the communitarian movement, founded the Communitarian Network in 1990. Etzioni received his PhD in sociology from the University of California,

Berkeley; served as professor of sociology at Columbia University, and then went to George Washington University as director of the Institute for Communitarian Policy Studies.

Etzioni characterizes President Obama as a communitarian in a February 4, 2009, *Jerusalem Post* article: "There is no philosophy that better describes Obama's position than Communitarianism," which Etzioni calls a philosophy "that would speak for community and the common good."

Prior to Obama, Dr. Etzioni even noted communitarianism at work in the Bush administration. In "Needed: Catchword for Bush Ideology; 'Communitarianism' Finds Favor," a February 1, 2001, *Washington Post* article, Etzioni described the inaugural address of President George W. Bush as "a Communitarian Text." The article also revealed that staffers inside the Bush White House were familiar with communitarianism and the Third Way:

> "This is the ultimate Third Way," said Don Eberly, an adviser in the Bush White House, using a favorite phrase of President Bill Clinton, who also sought, largely unsuccessfully, to redefine the debate with an alternative to the liberal-conservative conflict. "The debate in this town the last eight years was how to forge a compromise on the role of the state and the market. This is a new way to rethink social policy: a major reigniting of interest in the social sector."[236]

Some have pointed to Communist Mikhail Gorbachev's "perestroika"—which sought to merge socialism with capitalism when he was president of the USSR—as an example of the Third Way. Whatever you call it and no matter how it evolves, it is the foundation of tyranny and punishment of those who dissent and reject collectivism.

Communitarians have repackaged socialist ideas contrary to a biblical worldview and to the purpose and responsibility of civil government declared in America's founding documents. Christians must expose and fight all degrees of socialism, Communism, and Marxism/Leninism. Regardless of how it begins or the assurances given, the end will be infringement of parental authority and freedom of religion, the elimination of freedom of speech such as radio programs that speak out against the government's tyranny, the establishment of hate-crime laws that criminalize Christianity, and much more. But many Christians and pastors still just do not get it. Pastor Jim Belcher has written a book, *Deep Church: A Third Way Beyond Emerging and Traditional,* in which he calls for the Emergent Church (neo-evangelicals) and traditional evangelicals to blend their worldviews. This is yet another recipe for building the religious Trojan horse.

Joel Hunter's approach has found appreciation in some very high places. In 2009, he was appointed to President Obama's White House Advisory Council on Faith-Based and Neighborhood Partnership, and he has now served there with Lynne Hybels of Willow Creek.

Hunter writes for BioLogos, a pro-evolution organization for which Reformed pastor and "Gospel Coalition" member Tim Keller also writes. BioLogos received a large grant from the Templeton Foundation, which has been pushing evolution and ecumenicalism for years. Hunter, like Keller, is a major promoter of social justice.

It was Hunter's passion for social justice and fighting global warming that caused him to resign in 2006 as president-elect of the Christian Coalition. The *New York Times* reported that Hunter stepped down "saying the group resisted his efforts to broaden its agenda to include reducing poverty and fighting global warming."[237]

That Hunter could even become the president-elect of the Christian Coalition, I believe, reveals that the coalition is not interested in sound biblical theology and doctrine. At that point, it was already clear to me that Hunter is not a conservative evangelical. I believe the reason pro-family groups have been so unsuccessful in recent years is that they lack commitment to solid biblical theology and doctrine.

A person's theology and doctrine determine his or her worldview. The worldview determines values, and values determine that person's conduct. Christians cannot change an ungodly culture unless they preach the Gospel, change people's theology, and set right their errant worldviews. The culture war is a symptom of the spiritual battle described in Ephesians 6:12, yet most pro-family groups refuse to address theological issues because they do not want to offend their Catholic and Mormon donors. Once a pro-family or conservative organization abandons biblical theology and doctrine, though, it is left to fight only symptoms rather than the root problems of sin and apostasy.

Until these pro-family organizations take a strong stand on the Word of God and use the culture war as a platform to preach the Gospel, they will continue to spend millions of dollars with little to show for it. When James Dobson gave his retirement speech to the Focus on the Family board and employees, he all but admitted that there has been little success in the culture war:

> James Dobson, 72, who resigned recently as head of Focus on the Family—one of the largest Christian groups in the country—and who once denounced the Harry Potter books as witchcraft, acknowledged the dramatic reverse for the religious Right in a farewell speech to staff.

> "We tried to defend the unborn child, the dignity of the family, but it was a holding action. We are awash in evil and the battle is still to be waged. We are right now in the most discouraging period of that long conflict. Humanly speaking, we can say we have lost all those battles."[238]

In February 2006, I called Dr. Dobson's office and talked to his personal secretary. I asked her to convey to Dr. Dobson the need to use his radio program to expose the Emergent Church and its social justice agenda, its attack on the Word of God, and its embracing of pluralism and mysticism. At the time, few Christians had heard of the Emergent Church, and I believed Christian leaders needed to warn the Church of what I was already calling a religious Trojan horse in articles. I explained that the unbiblical theology and doctrine of the Emergent Church was not only going to take many of our young people spiritual prisoners, but it would also convince them that abortion and same-sex marriage are not biblical issues. To my knowledge, Focus on the Family never broadcast any such program, even though I think it can be said that the organization not only interviewed but helped foster the popularity of Tony Campolo many years earlier. There seemed to be no desire to name names or to warn the Church of false teaching, to apologize for promoting such men as Tony Campolo, or to explain why Campolo had become a threat to the Church—as I explain below.

Why did Dobson choose not to interview godly men regarding the problem of false converts in the Church? I am not aware of any programs that were committed to how to biblically share the Gospel with our children, extended family members, and community like Jesus did using the moral law. I believe if Dobson had worked with godly men to train Christians in biblical evangelism, countless lives and families would have been transformed because the father or mother or child would have become new creations in Jesus Christ. While I appreciate some of the strong stands Dobson has taken, I believe if he would have been less about "Christian" psychcology and more about biblical theology, he would have provided Focus on the Family far more of an eternal impact.

Regarding the status of the culture war, in 2001, *World* magazine asked the president of Focus on the Family, Jim Daley, if the battle against same-sex marriage could be won. Daley replied:

> We're losing on that one, especially among the 20– and 30–somethings: 65 to 70 percent of them favor same-sex marriage. I don't know if that's going to change with a little more age—demographers would say probably not. We've probably lost that.[239]

Pat Roberston has also expressed doubt on how much his culture-war activities have really accomplished:

> In a reflective mood for Easter, evangelical icon and onetime presidential candidate Pat Robertson echoes the Rev. Billy Graham's recent acknowledgment that he wished he had spent less time on politics and more time on the ministry and his family.

> "When you get it all said and done, what did my work accomplish in the political realm?" Robertson wondered rhetorically during an exclusive interview with Newsmax.TV in which he offers an inspirational Easter message.[240]

We need to follow the example of Paul in 1 Corinthians 15:3–5, where he declares that his first priority is the Gospel:

> For I delivered to you first of all that which I also received: that Christ died for our sins according to the Scriptures, and that He was buried, and that He rose again the third day according to the Scriptures.

Christian pro-family leaders would do well to examine every initiative, project, book, speech, broadcast, and conference in light of whether it will further the proclamation of the biblical Gospel or compromise scriptural principles clearly laid out in God's Word.

Tony Campolo and His Red-Letter Christians

David Noebel reveals that "today, *Sojourners'* Board of Directors includes Wallis, Ron Sider, Brian McLaren, and Bart Campolo."[241] Bart Campolo is the son of Tony Campolo, and as the saying goes, "birds of a feather flock together." Campolo and Wallis are comrades, and Campolo's son has served on the board of the organization run by Wallis.

Wallis endorsed Campolo's book *Letters to a Young Evangelical* by saying, "Tony Campolo is my favorite evangelical." By "evangelical," Campolo surely means a neo-evangelical who embraces socialism and is committed to waging war against Bible-believing, conservative Christians.

David Noebel, in another excellent article written for the Worldview Weekend website, pulls no punches when he describes Campolo's distaste for biblical truth and those who defend and proclaim it:

> The purpose of Campolo's letters to two young evangelicals (Timothy and Junia) is to convince them that the "Religious Right" in America is their sworn enemy, and if they wish to get serious about God's business, which is assisting the poor and oppressed to bring in the Kingdom of God, they must reject the... conservative wing of Evangelicalism and stake their claim with the true "progressives," namely the Sider, Wallis and Campolo camp. This camp will bring forth the Kingdom of God on earth in spite of the constant

foot dragging of their non-progressive, conservative, Evangelical counterparts.[242]

Campolo calls his followers "red-letter Christians." Why? I will let Campolo answer that question from an article he wrote for *Sojourners*:

> Who first suggested the label? A secular Jewish Country-and-Western disc jockey in Nashville, Tennessee. During a radio interview he was conducting with Jim Wallis, he happened to say, "So, you're one of those Red-Letter Christians—you know—who's really into those verses in the New Testament that are in red letters!"

> Jim answered, "That's right!" And with that answer, he spoke for all of us. By calling ourselves Red-Letter Christians, we are alluding to the fact that in several versions of the New Testament, the words of Jesus are printed in red. In adopting this name, we are saying that we are committed to living out the things that He said. Of course, the message in those red-lettered verses is radical, to say the least. If you don't believe me, read Jesus' Sermon on the Mount (Matthew 5–7).

> In those red letters, He calls us away from the consumerist values that dominate contemporary American consciousness. He calls us to be merciful, which has strong implications for how we think about capital punishment. When Jesus tells us to love our enemies, He probably means we shouldn't kill them. Most important, if we take Jesus seriously, we will realize that meeting the needs of the poor is a primary responsibility for His followers.[243]

The primary responsibility of Christians is to preach the Gospel—the good news of salvation through Jesus Christ alone. This is a biblical doctrine I believe Tony Campolo rejects. It is also interesting that Campolo apparently ignores the words of Jesus in the parable of the laborers in Matthew 20:8–15 in which Jesus says:

> So when evening had come, the owner of the vine-
> yard said to his steward, "Call the laborers and give
> them *their* wages, beginning with the last to the first."
> And when those came who *were hired* about the elev-
> enth hour, they each received a denarius. But when
> the first came, they supposed that they would receive
> more; and they likewise received each a denarius. And
> when they had received *it*, they complained against the
> landowner, saying, "These last *men* have worked *only*
> one hour, and you made them equal to us who have
> borne the burden and the heat of the day." But he an-
> swered one of them and said, "Friend, I am doing you
> no wrong. Did you not agree with me for a denarius?
> Take *what is* yours and go your way. I wish to give to
> this last man *the same* as to you. Is it not lawful for me
> to do what I wish with my own things? Or is your eye
> evil because I am good?"

As with all parables, Jesus is telling an earthly story with a spiritual meaning. The spiritual meaning is that those who serve Christ
for many years and those who come to salvation through Jesus Christ
in the later years of their lives will both receive the same reward of
heaven.

Jesus also clearly states that the landowner had kept his private
contract with the laborers who had toiled the entire day and was not
being dishonest to anyone by paying the same amount to the laborers who had only worked a portion of the day. Why? Because the
landowner *had the right to do what he wanted with his private property*.
Jesus assumed this as background for the story. He didn't dispute this
"common knowledge."

The same biblical concept of private property is affirmed in Acts
5:1–5:

> But a certain man named Ananias, with Sapphira
> his wife, sold a possession. And he kept back *part* of the
> proceeds, his wife also being aware *of it,* and brought
> a certain part and laid *it* at the apostles' feet. But Peter
> said, "Ananias, why has Satan filled your heart to lie to
> the Holy Spirit and keep back *part* of the price of the

land for yourself? While it remained, was it not your own? And after it was sold, was it not in your own control? Why have you conceived this thing in your heart? You have not lied to men but to God." Then Ananias, hearing these words, fell down and breathed his last. So great fear came upon all those who heard these things.

Annanias and Sapphira were struck dead by God for lying and for their hypocrisy of saying they had given more to God than they really had. But notice verse 4 in which Peter tells Ananias, "While it remained, was it not your own? And after it was sold, was it not in your own control?" Here again, we see the biblical concept of private property. They could have kept whatever portion of the proceeds from their sale they chose to, and Peter wouldn't have disputed them. Their dishonesty is what caused their personal calamity.

In Exodus 20—the chapter that introduces the Ten Commandments—verse 15 commands, "You shall not steal," clearly referring to a person's private property. The notes in the *MacArthur Study Bible* describe the meaning of the verse this way: "Any dishonest acquiring of another's goods or assets greatly disturbs the right to ownership of private property, which is an important principle for societal stability."[244]

Exodus 20:17 reflects yet another aspect of private ownership:

> You shall not covet your neighbor's house; you shall not covet your neighbor's wife, nor his male servant, nor his female servant, nor his ox, nor his donkey, nor anything that *is* your neighbor's.

The act of stealing always begins by coveting, and coveting and stealing are a violation of God's character and nature. Campolo, however, does not seem interested in biblical facts but rather in using Jesus as a prop for his predilection toward liberation theology. Neo-evangelicals like Campolo would like to convince people Jesus is in favor of the government stealing from one person in order to give to another, instead of cutting government entitlements to the "poor."

The "What Would Jesus Drive" campaign is another example of similar manipulations, trying to convince people of faith that Jesus would drive a car powered by some kind of a rubber band. These people could not care less what Jesus actually taught about sin, the exclusivity of Christ, the inerrancy of His Word, and the futility of building an earthly kingdom.

In 1989, Campolo wrote a 28–page paper entitled "The Road to Damascus." David Noebel explains not only the agenda behind this errant publication but how the National Association of Evangelicals has been involved in the promotion of its ideals:

> This publication was distributed in the United States primarily through the efforts of Jim Wallis and his Sojourners organization in Washington, D.C. The purpose of the document was to enlist Christians to help Marxist/Leninist efforts to consolidate Leftwing governments in at least seven nations. All signers of the document were Leftists from these nations—the Philippines, South Korea, Namibia, South Africa, El Salvador, Nicaragua and Guatemala.
>
> The thrust of the document was to paint communism as the true representative of a Christian theology that "sides with the poor and oppressed" and to condemn Christians who side with the rich and oppressors of the poor. The "good people" in this struggle are the proponents of liberation theology, while the bad people are the Christians who oppose Christian Marxism. To make certain that the point is not missed, the document identifies anti-communist evangelicals as "members of the forces of darkness." Good Christians are portrayed as pro-communist while anti-communists are Neanderthal, non-progressive, conservatives.
>
> Lest you think that this is just ancient history, I direct your attention to the National Association of Evangelicals' *Toward An Evangelical Public Policy*, published by Baker Books (2005) and copyrighted by Ron Sider and Diane Knippers. Its first chapter, entitled "Seeking a Place," makes it very clear that anti-communism "was largely an exercise of destruction" and that Jim Wallis of *Sojourners* is where the true Christian action consists. And this despite the fact that Wallis was

pro-Viet Cong during the Vietnam War. Wallis actually referred to those seeking to escape from the ravages of communist Vietnam after the war as persons bent on feeding "their consumer habits in other lands." Wallis' response to the Cambodian Communists' slaughter of two million men, women, and children was to deny the bloodbath. Compassion for the poor and oppressed brought on by communism does not enter into the leftist playbook. Leftists have compassion for the poor and oppressed only when they can, however implausibly, blame capitalist America. Shame on the NAE![245]

Pro-abortion Pastor?

Greg Boyd is founder and senior pastor of Woodland Hills Church in St. Paul, Minnesota, and some would say a leader in the Emergent Church movement. I track the beliefs and teachings of Boyd and his emerging cronies, and it appears that Boyd's "evangelicalism" attracts a predictable mix of endorsers for his book *The Myth of the Christian Nation*, including Tony Campolo and Brian McClaren. Boyd has convinced far too many people that he is an evangelical.

Although he first attracted national attention by promoting "open theism," which proclaims that God does not or at least chooses not to know the future, Boyd also holds the delusion that he can be pro-abortion and pro-life at the same time. I suppose if you buy the postmodern worldview that truth is created by each individual, then black and white can be the same color, but that doesn't alter the basic falsehood of the position.

In June 2005, as a guest on my friend Todd Friel's radio program, Boyd offered a rationalization of his views on abortion that so upset some of his congregation members, he later wrote a paper to defend his position. He explained:

> On June 11th I was interviewed on KKMS, and the host, Todd Friel, asked me about some of my personal political views... I was asked if I thought abortion should be legal... I told him I thought it would be best if second and third trimester abortions were outlawed while the decision during the first trimester was left up to the mother.

Perhaps you think I'm being too hard on such "nice" men. But Jesus himself called the hypocrites and heretics of His day some pretty harsh names: dogs, white-washed tombs, vipers. It underscores the fact that "niceness" is not a Christian virtue, despite what many Christians today want to think.

The word "nice" derives from the word "ignorant." According to "The Mavens' Word of the Day":

> Nice can be traced back to the Latin word *nescius* "ignorant" which is actually a combination of the prefix *ne* "no" and the word *scire* "know."... In other words, if you were nice, you did "not know." You were ignorant or foolish.[246]

Many nice people today are being deceived by other nice people such as Boyd, Wallis, McClaren, and Campolo. And there are even more nice people who lack the courage to expose the false teaching of these deviant teachers.

Tony Campolo's heretical pronouncements include the following:

- "I am saying that there is no salvation apart from Jesus, that's my evangelical mindset. However, I'm not convinced that Jesus only lives in Christians."

- In his book, *Partly Right*, Campolo says, "We affirm our DIVINITY by doing what is worthy of gods, and we affirm our humanity by taking risks only available to mortals. God has to become one of us before He could be heroic... (Robert) Schuller affirms our divinity, yet does not deny our humanity....isn't that what the gospel is?[247]

- We want to convince the whole human race that there is a God who established the infinite value of every person, who mystically dwells in each person....[248]

Boyd's other bedfellow, Brian McClaren, has spouted similarly crazy ideas like:

- ...many Hindus are willing to consider Jesus as a legitimate manifestation of the divine...many Buddhists see Jesus as one of humanity's most enlightened people...

A shared reappraisal of Jesus' message could provide a unique space or common ground for urgently needed religious dialogue—and it doesn't seem an exaggeration to say that the future of our planet may depend on such dialogue. This reappraisal of Jesus' message may be the only project capable of saving a number of religions.[249]

- ...to be truly inclusive, the kingdom must exclude exclusive people, to be truly reconciling, the kingdom must not reconcile with those who refuse reconciliation... Desmond Tutu and Nelson Mandela learned what happens when you try to expand the borders of who is considered 'in... And if critics see you as a transgressor and criticize you for opening the doors and expanding the boundaries, you go pursuing your purpose, making it clear that the kingdom of God is open to all, except those who want to ruin it by dividing it against itself.[250]

- [T]his is one of the huge problems with the traditional understanding of hell, because if the Cross is in line with Jesus' teaching, then I won't say the only and I certainly won't say... or even the primary but a primary meaning of the Cross... is that the Kingdom of God doesn't come like the kingdoms of this world by inflicting violence and coercing people. But that the kingdom of God comes thru suffering and willing, voluntary sacrifice, right? But in an ironic way, the doctrine of hell basically says, "No, that's not really true. At the end, God gets his way through coercion and violence and intimidation and domination just like every other kingdom does." The Cross isn't the center then. The Cross is almost a distraction and false advertising for God.[251]

Much of neo-evangelicalism seems committed to altering the meanings of words in order to convince people to embrace a humanistic, moral relativistic worldview that rejects absolute truth while still sporting the veneer of evangelicalism. Worse, they'd like you to believe that true evangelicals are the cause of the problems in America, the Church, and the world. They refer to them pejoratively as "fundamentalists." These men believe they and their Emergent Church, neo-evangelical friends are the real Christians with the real answers to the world's (very real) problems.

Infiltrating the Southern Baptist Convention

The Southern Baptist Convention's Ethics and Religious Liberty Commission, headed by Richard Land at the time this book went to press, is a woefully good example of the "useful idiot" strategy in operation. I believe Land has been used to push radically unbiblical, politically correct, and anti-American agendas. Land exhibits the characteristics of a New Religious Righter (more about that later). Please note that as a member of a solid, Bible teaching Southern Baptist Convention (SBC) church, I have a vested interest in Land's activities, and, frankly, I'm worried. But those who are not members of an SBC church should be just as concerned, since Land has an exceptionally strong voice on behalf of evangelicals. The Southern Baptist Convention is the nation's largest Protestant denomination, and Mr. Land's office was funded to the tune of more than $3.2 million dollars for just the 2010–2011 fiscal year. I believe Land is working largely *against* the biblical worldview held not only by most SBC church members but by most conservative, Bible-believing Christians as well.

In September 2010, the Anti-Defamation League formed an "interfaith coalition" to help Muslims build mosques in America. Land took the opportunity to involve himself in one more pluralistic, politically correct project. But why would any Christian, much less a Christian leader, help build mosques? Islam is a demonic, anti-Christian religion. Supporting the spread of that religion is a clear violation of the biblical mandate not to be involved in spiritual enterprises with nonbelievers. SBC members are not paying Mr. Land to help build Islamic houses of worship.

The names and mission statements of many organizations that make up the interfaith coalition clearly reveal that the League's ultimate goal is not just building mosques but pushing ecumenicalism. According to its website, members include the "Vicar for Ecumenical and Inter-Religious Affairs." This means, of course, not just Christian groups but all religions. Dr. Eboo Patel is also on the list. His organization, Interfaith Youth Core, has a goal "to introduce a new relationship, one that is about mutual respect and religious pluralism. Instead of focusing a dialogue on political or theological differences…."[252]

Religious pluralism, you'll recall, is the belief that all religions are equal in their truth claims. Yet while it is possible that all religions are wrong, they absolutely cannot all be true. Still, the Interfaith Youth Core wants to set aside "theological differences."

But should Christians set aside biblical theology just to obtain consensus with an amalgamated group of various religions? The answer is "No." Second John 9–11 says that if someone brings another doctrine other than the essential doctrines of Jesus Christ, then we are not to greet them or invite them into our homes, much less seek common ground with them or support their spiritual goals and objectives.

Richard Land apparently disagrees. He declared in an August 3, 2010, USA Today article that "mosque opponents are misguided."[253] Land pontificates that by allowing governments to limit mosques, we are setting up the government to limit other religions. What he fails to see is that the issue centers around local and state governments, which should have the right to limit the building of mosques. The federal government should never be involved in the approval of churches or mosques, but local governments regulate the construction of church buildings as a matter of local zoning laws all the time. The only reason the federal government should shut down a mosque is in the case of a national security threat. If a local government or a state wants to prohibit the building of a mosque, however, it is within its rights to do so—particulary when experts have revealed that a large percentage of the mosques in America are funded by Saudi Arabia and teach jihad against the United States.

If the FBI learns that a mosque is a training and education center for Wahhabi Islamic Jihadists with money from Saudi Arabia (the country from which most of the 9/11 hijackers came), then the mosque should be closed down. Islam is fighting for a religious theocracy based on Islamic Sharia Law. This faces us with a national security threat of the highest order, and Muslims use "religious liberty" as a weapon against us. Wahhabi Islam is more of a terrorist organization than a religion, but it is based in Muslim teachings. By contrast to its predilection for violence, when was the last time you saw a group of Baptists, Lutherans, or Presbyterians fly planes into skyscrapers?

I, among many who live in the Memphis area, are not misguided in this issue. We do not favor the Islamic Center, with its terrorist ties, being built in Memphis. It is, after all, a center that has hired Sheikh Yasir Qadhi. Foxnews.com reports on the background of this sheikh and one of his former students:

> The Memphis Islamic Center is gearing up to create "a multipurpose Islamic Center to serve the needs of Muslims in the Memphis area and beyond," according to its website. But critics wonder exactly what that means, especially given the center's newest hire: Sheikh Yasir Qadhi. Qadhi, the dean of academic affairs at the Al Maghrib Institute, a weekend seminary where instructors travel to teach advanced Islamic studies, made headlines in 2001 with a speech in which he referred to the Holocaust as "false propaganda" and pointed to Jewish people's "crooked nose and blond hair" as evidence that they "are not a Semitic people." In 2006, Qadhi admitted to being on a terror watch list, saying he had no idea why. His name has since been removed. Three years later, Qadhi was again thrust into the spotlight when it was discovered that his institute's list of alumni included accused "underwear bomber" Umar Farouk Abdulmutallab and reportedly includes convicted terrorist Daniel Maldonado, also known as Daniel Aljughaifi.[254]

In October 2010, I wrote an article discussing Land's involvement with the Interfaith Coalition, and I was invited as a guest on several national radio programs to talk about it. After being contacted by several SBC leaders who thanked me for bringing this information to their attention, Land resigned from the Interfaith Coalition. However, he made it known he was not resigning because he had seen the light but because he had felt the flames:

> A top leader of the Southern Baptist Convention has resigned from a new interfaith coalition, saying some fellow Southern Baptists felt it was inappropriate for him to support the building of mosques.

Richard Land, who heads the SBC's Ethics and Religious Liberty Commission, told organizers at the Anti-Defamation League that "many Southern Baptists share my deep commitment to religious freedom and the right of Muslims to have places of worship."

At the same time, "they also feel that a Southern Baptist denominational leader filing suit to allow individual mosques to be built is 'a bridge too far.'" Land told the ADL in a Jan. 14 letter that he had received a "spirited response" to his support of a disputed mosque project in Murfreesboro, Tenn., and some fellow Baptists viewed it as promotion of Islam.

"I do not agree with that perception, but Southern Baptists have the oft-expressed right to form their own perceptions as well as the right to expect their denominational servant to be cognizant of them and to respect them," he said.[255]

Land also has been part of the U.S. Muslim Engagement Project and has endorsed a report released by the group. Its goal is for Americans and Muslims to find common ground. Yet common ground is impossible when several Muslims associated with this organization have, according to credible news sources, ties to known terrorist organizations, and at least one has defended Sharia Law. Dalia Mogahed, Barack Obama's adviser on Muslim affairs, appeared on British television and declared, "Sharia is not well understood and Islam as a faith is not well understood."[256] As Robert Spencer writes in *Human Events* magazine, Mogahed:

...made her defense of Sharia on a TV show hosted by a member of Hizb-ut-Tahrir. This is an organization that is banned as a terrorist group in many nations, and which is openly dedicated to the worldwide imposition of Sharia and the destruction of all governments that are constituted according to any other political philosophy—including Constitutional republics that do not establish a state religion.[257]

Mogahed appeared on the program with two Hizb-ut-Tahrir members who attacked the "lethal cocktail of liberty and capitalism.... Mogahed, for her part, offered no contradiction to any of this."[258]

Imam Feisal Abdul Rauf, who has been pushing to build a mosque mere yards from Ground Zero, also served with Land on the Muslim Engagement Project. Another project member is Ingrid Mattson "whose group was founded in 1981 by the Saudi-funded Muslim Students' Association."[259] In 2010, a Muslim Students' Association member bragged of the organization's "Hitler Youth" week on the University of California San Diego campus.

What common ground does Richard Land possibly think American Christians have with such radicals? Yet he endorses the U.S.-Muslim Engagement report this way:

> This initiative is a serious, comprehensive, bipartisan effort that seeks to address a critical and dangerous problem: The world Muslim community misunderstands Americans and Americans misunderstand them. This initiative lays out a detailed and comprehensive plan to vastly decrease that misunderstanding through a multi-faceted approach that will build constructive bridges of mutual understanding between Americans and the Muslim world.[260]

No matter how much we seek to "understand" Islam, radical Muslims (like the Wahhabi sect) are not going to stop being radicals, since their approach is the very essence of the Islamic religion.

America was doing nothing to Muslims when on September 11, 2001, Islamic terrorists murdered nearly 3,000 of us. This problem is not with America or American Christians but with Muslims who view America as the "great Satan" and Israel as the "little Satan." Brainwashing Americans into being more "understanding" of Muslims is not going to stop the extremists. President Reagan was right when he declared that we cannot negotiate with terrorists.

The Richard Land and Barack Obama Amnesty Agendas

Land's troubling work doesn't end with Islam-related issues. An article in the *New York Times* demonstrates his enthusiastic support of Obama's amnesty for illegals agenda. The article refers to Land and other pro-amnesty evangelicals as "a secret weapon" for Obama, noting that Land has declared:

> I've had some older conservative leaders say: "Richard, stop this. You're going to split the conservative coalition," Dr. Land continued. "I say it might split the old conservative coalition, but it won't split the new one."[261]

To support Obama's amnesty agenda, Land and others have taken assorted scriptures out of context. For example, he has used Leviticus 19:34—"You must regard the foreigner who lives with you as the native-born among you. You are to love him as yourself, for you were foreigners in the land of Egypt" (HCSB)—to claim that the pro-amnesty position is biblical. This verse, however, has nothing to do with immigration law. It is part of the ceremonial and civic laws of Israel. It does not support acceptance of law-breaking, illegal immigrants. Rather, it addresses the issue of Jews being gracious and fair with non-Jews who are traveling with them or through their land.

The scripture also speaks to church practices. *Matthew Henry's Concise Commentary* describes the meaning this way: "Strangers shall be welcome to God's grace; we should do what we can to recommend religion to them."[262]

Does Land think it is biblical and moral to have millions of illegal immigrants in America when at the time he made these comments, the true unemployment rate for U.S. citizens stood at 22 percent? Most illegals in America painting houses, cutting grass, siding and roofing homes do not pay federal taxes, state income tax, or worker's compensation insurance. Most do not buy liability insurance, nor do they spend countless hours and thousands of dollars each year complying with government red tape. Illegal aliens can drastically underbid American small-business owners precisely because the latter do comply with all the laws of our land. As a result, American small-business owners cannot compete with illegal aliens.

Unfortunately, Land is not alone in promoting the amnesty agenda. In June 2012, the "Evangelicals' Immigration Table" was announced at a press conference. Those pushing for amnesty (that's what it is despite claims to the contrary) for illegal aliens included a mix of liberals, progressives, and "evangelicals." Richard Land was joined by Jim Wallis (what more did you need to know than that neo-Marxist Wallis is involved in this movement?), Tom Minnery of Focus on the Family, National Association of Evangelicals president Leith Anderson, and several others. To reveal how widespread the merging and converging of "evangelicals" and progressives goes, here is a small sampling of those listed as signatories of the Evangelicals' Immigration Table:

- Jerry D. Porter, General Superintendent, Church of the Nazarene;
- William J. Hamel, President, Evangelical Free Church of America;
- JoAnne Lyon, General Superintendent, The Wesleyan Church;
- Bryan Wright, President, Southern Baptist Convention;
- Gary Walter, President, The Evangelical Covenant Church;
- Ed Boschman, Executive Director, U.S. Mennonite Brethren;
- Gary Benedict, President, The Christian and Missionary Alliance, United States;
- Jim Daly, President and CEO of Focus on the Family;
- Ed Stetzer, President, Lifeway Research;
- Bill Brown, President, Cedarville University;
- Richard Mouw, President, Fuller Theological Seminary.[263]

Some Americans have gone out of business and lost their livelihoods because illegal immigrants underbid them by working for cash under the table, without the overhead of American business owners who comply with the law. Is that just and biblical? A serious problem with many of the "religious leaders" that were pushing Obama's amnesty plan is that many of them have never actually run a business.

Romans 13 declares the purpose of government is to reward the righteous and punish the wicked. Yet unenforced immigration law is rewarding those who break the law while they steal from law-abiding Americans.

Something is clearly wrong when so called evangelicals and the Communist Party USA are both pushing for amnesty. The CPUSA wants to turn millions of illegal residents into legal voters for the Communist agenda. As Worldview Weekend columnist Trevor Loudon writes:

> From a paper entitled "Special Convention Discussion: Mexican American Equality" submitted by Rosalio Munoz for discussion before the May 21–23, Communist Party USA National Convention in New York. *The pre-convention call for our 29th convention gives the right lead for our party, class and people and the Mexican American people and their struggles for equality and justice. It stresses:*
>
> *Mexican Americans are strong supporters of the Obama administration's efforts to move away from the right wing policies of the past and to move for progressive reform… Mexican Americans are a necessary force in the struggle to break through the right wing obstructionism and counteroffensive and win progressive changes in health care, jobs and income, immigration, civil rights, labor rights and a more reasonable foreign policy in ongoing electoral struggles and the coming elections.*[264]

Where are the leaders of the SBC? Why are they not stopping Land from using the denomination's credibility to send out press releases, give interviews, and testify before Congress in support of Obama's amnesty agenda?

In case I haven't yet convinced you that Richard Land has assisted the SBC in giving credibility to the Trojan horse, I've noted below several more reasons for concern.

(1) *Land endorses a book by radical Jim Wallis.* In 2008, neo-Marxist Jim Wallis released a book entitled *The Great Awakening.* This is Richard Land's endorsement: "Despite our significant public-policy differences, I commend Jim Wallis for advocating religious belief as an invaluable resource in addressing the urgent moral and social crisis of our time." So Land is more concerned

about the public-policy beliefs of Wallis than he is about his religious beliefs? Does Land even know of the religious beliefs that Wallis proclaims?

(2) *Land offers credibility to Mormonism.* Land enthusiastically endorsed Glenn Beck's 8–28 rally and literally locked arms with leaders of multiple religions there, including Muslim imams. In a clear violation of 2 Corinthians 6:14, Land added to the pluralistic propaganda and confusion when he declared: "I think perhaps the most charitable way for an evangelical Christian to look at Mormonism is to look at Mormonism as the fourth Abrahamic faith."[265] Mormonism does not believe in one God but millions of gods. It is a polytheistic religion. The other three religions are monotheistic, meaning they believe in only one god. So how does that make Mormonism a fourth Abrahamic religion?

(3) *Land gives credibility to global governance.* A few years ago Land joined the anti-Christian, anti-American, globalist organization known as the Council on Foreign Relations. He defends his membership by saying he wants to be salt and light and that the organization invited him because it wants the input of evangelicals. What they really want is to use the credibility of Christians—especially the good name of the Southern Baptist Convention—to make people believe their group is not anti-Christian even while promoting the CFR's anti-Christian, anti-American, globalist agenda. Land is clearly one of their useful idiots.

It is some comfort that on August 1, 2012, Richard Land announced that he would be retiring as head of the Southern Baptist Convention's Ethics and Religious Liberty Commission on October 23, 2013. The Associated Baptist Press reported:

> He [Land] also worked to repair Southern Baptists' checkered reputation with regard to race, joining others to draft a landmark 1995 SBC resolution apologiz-

ing to African-Americans for past racism and vowing to eradicate all forms of racial prejudice from Southern Baptist life.

Land's record on that front received a blemish in March, when he angered black Southern Baptists with comments on his weekly radio show defending George Zimmerman, later charged with second-degree murder in the shooting death of 17-year-old Trayvon Martin in an incident widely viewed as racial profiling. The ERLC trustee executive committee publicly reprimanded Land for "hurtful, irresponsible and racially charged words" and for failing to give proper on-air attribution for remarks read on his program that were written by others.

Land, in a letter published by Baptist Press, said while retiring from denominational work, he is not stepping away from the culture wars.[266]

I'm tempted to say of the trustees' action, "It's about time!" Were they not upset over Land's commending Jim Wallis for "advocating religious belief as an invaluable resource in addressing the urgent moral and social crisis of our time"? Did it not cause concern when Land called Mormonism the fourth Abrahamic religion? Were they not bothered by Land's membership on the Council on Foreign Relations, where he pushed for what can be described as nothing less than amnesty, regardless of what he and others called it? Were the trustees not upset about Land taking part in the "U.S. Muslim Engagement Project" and endorsing a report released by the project that calls for finding common ground with Muslims? Were they not worried over Land's involvement with Glenn Beck on at least two occasions? The trustees taking issue with Land's comments about the Zimmerman case or for reportedly not giving proper on-air attribution seems to me to be straining at gnats and swallowing camels.

Be a Biblical Berean, Not a Useful Idiot

Many self-professing Christians have become useful idiots without even knowing it. Far too many give money to organizations and churches that have ceased to proclaim the biblical Gospel but instead proclaim a social gospel. They give to organizations committed to building the kingdom of God on earth instead of building the Kingdom of God in the spiritual realm through the proclamation of God's Word.

This has happened because they lack biblical discernment. Most don't even know how to defend essential Christian doctrines and theology, and as a result, they cannot tell right from wrong. Hebrews 5:12–14 speaks of those who have been Christians for a long time but still lack the biblical knowledge to teach others correct beliefs. Verse 14 indicates that those who are spiritually mature *can* discern good from evil. Similarly, Ephesians 4:14 warns that spiritually immature believers are like children who lack discernment, who are blown here and there by every wind of doctrine and by the cunning and craftiness of men in their deceitful scheming. Matthew 7:15 says many will appear to be Christians—some will even be pastors—but they will be wolves in sheep's clothing.

The Church in America has been greatly weakened—and in some cases completely compromised—by false teaching and a false gospel. Many Christians and churches have been co-opted by neo-evangelicals, the New Religious Right, and change agents. It needs to stop.

CHAPTER 6

The Communion of Communitarians

As I noted in chapter 2, communitarianism and Fabian socialism are twin sisters, although we do not generally label communitarians as Fabian socialists because most do not or did not belong to the Fabian Socialist Society. Communitarians and Fabian socialists are united in the common goal of merging capitalism with socialism, promoting social justice, and establishing a new world order.

The hallmark of Fabians, of course, is their methodology for implementing socialism through gradual, surreptitious change rather than overt, revolutionary conversion. Today's communitarians have done a great job of employing the Fabian playbook and in many ways have taken surreptitious change (the Gramsci approach) to an even more insidious level. Some of today's most popular religious and business leaders are among the most active communitarians among us. In this chapter, we will look at several communitarians with massive public followings, such as Peter Drucker and Rick Warren.

Opposites Detract

One technique communitarians like to employ is especially effective at taking opponents off-guard. In debate, interview, sound bite, or any other communication platform, they encourage conflict between opposing ideas, develop a mixture of the thesis and the antithesis, move it toward the left, and work toward a predetermined outcome of their choosing.

I have quoted Julian Huxley many times over the years because he so clearly represents this deceptive formula. Huxley, a Fabian socialist, was also the first director of the United Nations Educational, Scientific and Cultural Organization (UNESCO). This is how he describes the "Hegelian Dialectic Process" originated by the German philosopher:

> ...at the moment, two opposing philosophies of life confront each other....You may categorize the two philosophies as super nationalism, or as individualism versus collectivism....or as capitalism versus communism, or as Christianity verses Marxism. Can these opposites be reconciled, this antithesis be resolved in a higher synthesis? I believe not only that this can happen, but that, through the inexorable dialectic of evolution, it must happen.[267]

Hegel has had a tremendous influence on the growth of communitarianism. While the term "communitarian" is thought to date back to the 1840s, "communitarianism" has been made popular in the twentieth century by Dorothy Day. Day, a Catholic, published the *Catholic Worker Newspaper*, promoting communitarianism and social justice.

If you grasp the Hegelian Dialectic Process,[268] you will understand much of what is happening in economics, law, and religion. The Hegelian process is a thoroughgoing manipulation of America and the world population. Karl Marx was a proponent of the dialectic process, and others have similarly influenced thought through outlets such as the Frankfurt School. (For more information, *Grave Influence* includes an entire chapter on Aldous Huxley, brother to Julian and author of *Brave New World*.)

But can the thesis, an idea, and the antithesis, an opposite idea, fight, conflict, synthesize, and merge together to produce a third option, or a mixture of both? That's certainly the intent. Huxley calls it the "the dialectic of evolution," but many of today's communitarians call it the "Third Way." Bill Clinton and Tony Blair are promoters of this way of talking about their system. Many globalists like them believe in societal evolution tied to spiritual evolution.

They believe we are all spiritually evolving, spiraling up toward some greater existence. In their worldview, nobody goes to hell. Emergent Church philosophers jump on this same bandwagon with their concept that "good and evil will merge to produce a better third option." They believe compromise—even between opposites—will produce an ultimate harmony among people. But, as the Gospel makes clear, spiritual evolution is a lie. People have never and will never evolve to the point of purifying themselves and their social systems.

Fabian socialist Walter Rauschenbusch was Richard Rorty's grandfather, and it is evident that Rauschenbusch passed on his worldview to his grandson. Instead of terms like Fabian socialism, statism, globalism, or communitarianism, Rorty called his approach welfare-capitalism. He explains the development of welfare-capitalism this way:

> Most people on my side of this....cultural war have given up on socialism in light of the history of nationalization enterprises and central planning in Central and Eastern Europe. We are willing to grant that the welfare-state capitalism is the best we can hope for. Most of us who were brought up Trotskyite now feel forced to admit that Lenin and Trotsky did more harm than good.[269]

Globalists and their useful idiots promote the idea that through the dialectic process, both socialism and capitalism can merge, and the end result will be "welfare-state capitalism." However, the dialectic is not only applied to economics but also to law, society, spirituality, and ecclesiology.

Church in Process

The area that concerns me the most is how the Hegelian Dialectic Process is being applied to the Church to produce what I call the communitarian church growth movement. Most people know this as the seeker-sensitive church growth movement, but a more accurate name would be the "sinner-sensitive church growth movement," since the real goal is to transform the church from a place where the saints are equipped for the work of ministry to a place where the world is made comfortable and consensus is achieved.

Robert Klenck summarizes the dangers of the seeker-sensitive church growth movement:

> ...in this movement, it is imperative that unbelievers are brought into the church; otherwise, the process of continual change cannot begin. There must be an antithesis (unbelievers) present to oppose the thesis (believers), in order to move towards *consensus* (compromise), and move the believers *away from their*

moral absolutism (resistance to change). If all members of the church stand firm on the Word of God, and its final authority in all doctrine and tradition, then the church cannot and will not change. This is common faith. Soon, we will see why these "change agents" are pushing so hard for change to occur in the church.[270]

Klenck is saying that the movement is dangerous because "change agents" who implement the Hegelian Dialectic Process know exactly how to alter people's behavior. They build on the work of behavioral psychologist B. F. Skinner (also covered in more detail in *Grave Influence*). Twentieth-century socialist Saul Alinsky also promoted the idea that change comes through conflict.

Change agents have deliberately brought this philosophy into the Church in order to set up conflict. They know that to be effective in church, they need discord so people will tire of disagreeing and be willing to compromise biblical truth so as to attain consensus.

Many pastors read books by change agents and run to church-growth conferences hosted by change agents who tell them how to grow their churches by attracting unbelievers through seeker-sensitive church programs. Yet most of these change agents are not Christians. Often, they do not believe in absolutes. They are Fabian socialists, globalists, pagan spiritualists, and communitarians. Many church-growth conferences are sponsored by people and organizations such as the Rockefellers and the Council on Foreign Relations.

The public face on what these people do is always calculated to sound and look good. Take the popular "Co-exist " bumper sticker, for instance. With letters created from various recognizable religious symbols, it is crafted to encourage everyone to "get along." Yet the communitarians, that this so well represents, are not interested in co-existing with Christianity. They want to co-opt Christianity for their own ends, expressing a supposed form of godliness but denying God Himself. The Bible warns of such a sign of the apostasy of the last days, and we are seeing disguises like this emerge as a major characteristic of the religious Trojan horse.

Far from biblical principles, the communitarian church-growth movement (CCGM) is built on points like these:

- Societal evolution;
- Spiritual evolution;
- The social gospel is proclaimed instead of the biblical Gospel;
- The end justifies the means;
- Pastors are not shepherds but managers;
- Church members are customers;
- Pastors are community organizers;
- Marketing and managing is emphasized instead of preaching and praying;
- Felt needs should determine church programming.

Some common phrases used by the communitarians include:

- Shared opportunity,
- Shared community,
- Shared experience,
- Shared values,
- Common good,
- Social justice,
- Healthy society,
- Third Way,
- Group consensus,
- New World Order,
- Global governance.

For the communitarian church-growth movement, it does not matter what you do to attract an audience in order to get customers into your church. In the CCGM world, the end justifies the means—do whatever it takes to grow a church. Some have had "clown communion," pastors dressed up as Elvis or superheroes. Some CCGM churches have a circus. Do a quick video search on the Internet, and you can see some of this bizarreness for yourself.

Many pastors fall for the communitarian church-growth movement because they believe their churches can have a major impact on the community. They see themselves feeding the hungry and providing clothes to those who need assistance, painting an elderly person's home, mowing lawns, or raking leaves. And if any of this is used to bring people the Gospel, I am, of course, fine with it. But these pastors and their congregations try to impact the community and be a force for "change," even though everything they're doing is the social gospel, social activism, and social justice. The truth, of course, is that the Gospel is the only thing that changes lives. Yet most of these ministers will not preach the Gospel. Instead, they take part in "interfaith dialogues" with other religions in their community. So should we be shocked when someone they emulate, such as Rick Warren, sits on the advisory board of Tony Blair's Faith Foundation? Should we be surprised when people like Leith Anderson, Bill Hybels, Rick Warren, and nearly 130 others sign onto "A Common Word at Yale," published as a full-page advertisement in *The New York Times* on November 13, 2007? These "Christian" leaders were responding to an open letter written by Muslim leaders and released on October 13, 2007. The Christians who signed the "Yale document" agreed that:

> What is common between us lies not in something marginal nor in something merely important to each. It lies, rather, in something absolutely central to both: love of God and love of neighbor... We applaud that A Common Word Between Us and You stresses so insistently the unique devotion to one God....We find it equally heartening that the God whom we should love above all things is described as being Love. In the Muslim tradition, God, "the Lord of the worlds," is "The Infinitely Good and All-Merciful"...."Let this common ground"—the dual common ground of love of God and of neighbor—"be the basis of all future interfaith dialogue between us," your courageous letter urges. Indeed, in the generosity with which the letter is written you embody what you call for. We most heartily agree. Abandoning all "hatred and strife," we must engage in interfaith dialogue as those who seek each other's good, for the one God unceasingly seeks our good. Indeed, together with you we believe that we need to move beyond "a polite ecumenical dialogue between selected religious leaders" and work diligently together to reshape relations between our communities and our nations so that they genuinely reflect our

common love for God and for one another... We are persuaded that our next step should be for our leaders at every level to meet together and begin the earnest work of determining how God would have us fulfill the requirement that we love God and one another.[271]

What are the problems with this statement? First of all, Christians do not serve the same God as the Muslims. Allah is not the God of the Bible. In fact, Allah, in the Koran, fits the definition and the characteristics that we find of Satan in the Bible. We don't worship the same God, and clearly, Muslims don't love their neighbors as themselves. Islam teaches its followers to be nice until they have the upper hand, and then they will slay or enslave any "infidel." Rick Warren, Leith Anderson, and Bill Hybels are some of America's leading false teachers—and, tragically, its most effective "useful idiots."

Call One Man "Father"—of the CCGM

Peter Drucker is best known as the "father of modern management." But I believe he could just as well be known as the father of the communitarian church-growth movement. Although he died on November 11, 2005, his worldview lives on through his disciples Bill Hybels, Rick Warren, and perhaps hundreds of thousands of pastors, elders, and deacons who have consumed his spiritual poison.

In a *U.S. News and World Report* article entitled "Preacher with a Purpose," Jeffery Sheler reveals that Rick Warren has called Peter Drucker one of his mentors:

> His [Warren's] most important role models he says, have been Billy Graham ("a model of great integrity"), Drucker ("a personal mentor on managing rapidly growing organizations"), and his late father, a Baptist minister.[272]

The article also outlines Drucker's admiration for Warren:

> Peter Drucker, the management guru, has described Saddleback's organizational model as "the most significant sociological [phenomenon] of the second half of the [20th] century."[273]

Warren has boasted many times about his being mentored by Peter Drucker:

> The most significant sociological phenomenon of the first half of the twentieth century was the rise of the corporation. The most significant sociological phenomenon of the second half of the twentieth century has been the development of the large pastoral church—of the megachurch. It is the only organization that is actually working in society. Now Drucker has said that at least six times. I happen to know because he's my mentor. I've spent twenty years under his tutelage learning about leadership from him, and he's written it in two or three books, and he says he thinks it's the only thing that really works in society.[274]

Warren seems to be saying that unless a church follows his megachurch model, it is not having an impact on society. But I contend that if your church follows Rick Warren's model, you are not having a biblical impact on society. You may be having an impact, but it is a negative one based on social justice, the social gospel, and communitarianism.

Rick Warren's website claims astounding success in connecting churches with his *Purpose Driven Church* model. In an interview with ABC News reporter Jake Tapper, Warren glowed:

> We've trained now almost 500,000 church leaders around the world in 162 countries. I've been training leaders for twenty-eight years, business leaders, government leaders, church leaders.[275]

To understand the unbiblical nature of Rick Warren's worldview of church, government, and corporations, we must grasp the worldview of Drucker, the communitarian. The December 24, 2002, issue of *Business Week* featured an article on Peter Drucker entitled "Peter Drucker's Search for Community" in which Ken Witty explains the foundation of Drucker's thinking:

> He brings a communitarian philosophy to his consulting... He said that what he's all about is this search

for community, the search for where people and organizations find community for non-economic satisfaction.[276]

Since communitarians and Fabian socialists share the same philosophies and desire the same outcome of welfare-state capitalism and global governance, it should be of no surprise that in 1983, Peter Drucker praised Fabian socialist and economist, John Maynard Keynes. Peter Drucker wrote an article entitled, "Modern Prophets: Schumpeter and Keynes?" in which he exclaimed, "The two greatest economists of this century, Joseph A. Shumpeter and John Maynard Keynes.... No one in the interwar years was more brilliant, more clever than Keynes."[277]

The Drucker Foundation held conferences with other globalists and communitarians in a quest to merge government, corporations, and community organizations (such as churches) into an equal partnership for global governance. "Emerging Partnerships: New Ways in a New World" was a symposium organized by the Peter F. Drucker Foundation and sponsored by the Rockefeller Brothers Fund in December 1996. Its purpose is as follows:

> The Drucker Foundation believes that a healthy society requires three vital sectors: a public sector of effective governments; a private sector of effective businesses; and a social sector [churches] of effective community organizations.[278]

A merging of churches, corporations, and government is also known as the "three-legged stool," a favorite term used by Drucker disciple Rick Warren. The three-legged stool is an aspect of communitarianism. As explained earlier, the Rockefellers have been working to co-opt the Church for their globalist and ecumenical goals for generations. Similarly, Peter Drucker was a globalist, universalist, and pragmatist who did not believe in absolutes for society. The October 5, 1998, issue of *Forbes* magazine quotes Drucker's attitude towards absolutes:

> But a social discipline, such as management, deals with the behavior of people and human institutions.

The social universe has no natural laws as the physical sciences do. It is thus subject to continuous change. This means that assumptions that were valid yesterday can become invalid and, indeed, totally misleading in no time at all.[279]

Drucker was a perfect partner for the Rockefellers.

If we keep peeling back the layers, we discover that Drucker himself was influenced by questionable sources. The *New York Times* published "A Man's Spiritual Journey from Kierkegaard to General Motors," an article about Peter Drucker. In this tribute to Drucker the week after his death, the *Times* notes that "at age 19, Mr. Drucker came across the works of the theologian and philosopher Søren Kierkegaard—and was bowled over. He studied Danish in order to read Kierkegaard's yet-untranslated writings."[280]

Understanding Drucker's admiration for Kierkegaard helps explain Drucker's proclaiming that there is no such thing as absolutes for society. In his book *Landmarks of Tomorrow*, Drucker expands this point:

> Society needs a return to spiritual values—not to offset the material but to make it fully productive… Mankind needs the return to spiritual values, for it needs compassion. It needs the deep experience that the Thou and the I are one, which all higher religions share.[281]

The Thou and the I are one? That is nothing more than Eastern mysticism. The belief that we are all one is monism. The belief that God is all is pantheism, and the belief that God is in all is panentheism.

The Bible is very clear: God is in heaven, and we are on earth. The only people who can say we are empowered by God are those who are indwelt by the Holy Spirit. The Holy Spirit resides only in the life of the believer after he or she places faith and trust in Jesus Christ with repentance and turning from sin. God is not in all people.

When Drucker says "society needs a return to spiritual values," the spirituality of which he is speaking is paganism. In a *Journal of Management History* article entitled "The Unfashionable Drucker: Ethical and Quality Chic," authors James S. Bowman and Dennis L. Wittmer explain another of Drucker's dubious influences:

> Convinced of the overall importance of Confucian ethics, he claims that "if ever there is a viable 'ethics of organization,' it will almost certainly have to adopt the key concepts of Confucian theory: clear definitions of relationships, universal rules, focus on behavior rather than motives, and behavior that optimizes each parties' benefits."[282]

The philosophy of Confucius emphasized personal and governmental morality, correctness of social relationships, justice, and sincerity.[283]

Peter Drucker admitted he was not a Christian, yet this is the man who influenced Rick Warren and the man whom hundreds of thousands of pastors have followed by following Warren. Drucker could hardly have been more clear on his spiritual standing:

> I'm not a born again Christian; no. I've been going to church and conducted tithing all my life but I do not claim to be...if you read one thing of mine read my essay on Kierkegaard...it is the best thing I ever wrote easily but it's also the only thing I ever wrote about religion.[284]

In "Management's New Paradigms," published in the October 5, 1998, issue of *Forbes* magazine, Drucker declared:

> So the nonprofit social sector [churches] is where management is today most needed and where systematic, principled, theory-based management can yield the greatest results fastest. Just think of the enormous problems facing the world—poverty, health care, education, international tension—and the need for managed solutions becomes loud and clear.[285]

You will notice that Drucker left out the one most important issue that faces mankind: his sinfulness, depravity, and need to repent of sin and accept Jesus Christ as Lord and Savior. Drucker, on the other hand, promotes social justice or a social gospel. He and his disciples address the material problems of man but not the ultimate spiritual condition addressed by Jesus Christ and the atonement provided through His death, burial, and resurrection.

Drucker also said, "The most important thing in communication is to hear what isn't being said."[286] And what is it that Drucker and his disciples are not saying? They're not saying anything about the Gospel.

The great management guru was expressing the goals of today's communitarians and Fabian socialists. And as we saw in the 1953 Congressional hearings, the Communists wanted to move the Church away from spiritual things and make it more about materialism. This emphasis on the material matches perfectly with Communism and the redistribution of wealth.

Drucker's Founding Follower

The Leadership Network is a major church consultation organization that specializes in helping churches apply growth strategies. Businessman Bob Buford founded the organization after being greatly influenced by Peter Drucker. In his book *Halftime,* in fact, Buford claims that "Drucker is the man who formed my mind."[287] And in the November 14, 2005, *Leadership Network-Advance,* Buford describes Drucker's impact on Leadership Network this way: "Peter Drucker is the 'intellectual father' of most all that guides my approach to philanthropy. I've long since ceased trying to determine what thoughts are mine and which come from Peter."[288]

So how does Leadership Network teach pastors to grow their churches? Do Buford and his staff of consultants pull guidance from the Bible and show, for example, the New Testament characteristics of a church, including preaching, praying, and picking godly men full of wisdom and empowered by the Holy Spirit? Does Buford tell his pastor clients that they need to follow Ephesians 4:12, which describes the job of a pastor as being "for the equipping of the saints for the work of ministry, for the edifying of the body of Christ"?

The answers are no, no, and no. In fact, the Leadership Network website once declared that these ideas are not what they tell their pastor/church clients because theology is not their focus for growing a church:

The mission of the Leadership Network is to accelerate the emergence of the 21st century church. This new paradigm is not centered in theology, but rather it is focused on structure, organization, and the transition from an institutionally-based church to a mission-driven church.[289]

If Buford's company and its clients are not basing their paradigm or worldview on biblical theology, then what is their worldview centered on? Given that Buford is a disciple of Drucker, it's a good guess that the focus is on social justice, the social gospel, and felt needs. If your philosophy for growing a church is not based on biblical theology, then it should not be used in a Bible-based, New Testament church.

Author Chris Rosebrough reveals that Bill Hybels, Rick Warren, and Bob Buford were all greatly influenced by Peter Drucker. Rosebrough, in fact, suggests a special designation for this trio of Drucker devotees:

Rick Warren, Bob Buford and Bill Hybels are the Druckerite "trinity." All three of these men were personally mentored by the late business guru Peter Drucker and these three men more than any others are responsible for innovating the church by purposely changing congregations from a pastoral leadership model to a CEO / Innovative Change Agent leadership model. All of these innovations were strategically crafted under the careful eye of Peter Drucker. And all of these innovations were incubated, introduced and injected into the church through the coordinated efforts of Drucker's disciples through their different but intimately connected organizations; Leadership Network, the Purpose Driven Network and the Willow Creek Association.

What many people don't realize is that the Emerging Church is a product created by and promoted by the Druckerites.

...without the Druckerites there may have never been an "emerging church." The Druckerites formed, bank-rolled and promoted the Emerging Church much the same way a music marketing company might form and promote a boy band like the Backstreet Boys or 'N Sync.

Take a look at who endorsed Dan Kimball's 2003 book *The Emerging Church*. In that list you will see both Druckerites as well as outright Emergent Heretics all singing the praises of Kimball's book. In fact, Rick Warren AND Emergent apostate Brian McLaren both wrote the foreword to the book.

Why would a supposedly conservative evangelical pastor like Rick Warren want to lend his credibility to the Emergent Church and have his name be direct-ly associated with men like Tony Jones, Doug Pagitt and Brian McLaren? Rick Warren is a Druckerite and the Emerging Church is a product developed by the Druckerites. Rick Warren is in fact one of the Fathers of the Emerging Church. That's why he lent his name and credibility to the product....

Rick Warren lent his credibility and endorsement to the Emerging Church movement without even so much as a hint that he had any concerns about the troubling doctrine and theology of its leaders. Bill Hy-bels has invited Emergent Leaders like McLaren to speak at Willow Creek Conferences and Youth Leader Conferences, and Bob Buford's Leadership Network has been promoting and selling McLaren's books for years on the Leadership Network website....

It's time for Rick Warren, Bob Buford and Bill Hy-bels to do the right thing and admit they've endan-gered the body of Christ by releasing a doctrinally de-fective and theologically dangerous product. For the sake of the body of Christ they MUST issue a safety re-call for their entire "Emerging Church" product line.[290]

To see more about what's behind this sort of thinking: the Leader to Leader website, originally established in 1990 as the Peter F. Drucker Foundation for nonprofit management, declares:

> The Leader to Leader Institute will chart the future path for the social sector as the equal partner of business and government in developing responsible leaders, caring citizens, and a healthy, inclusive society.[291]

What is that all about? I am not interested in my church being an equal partner with the government, and neither should you be.

The government would like to become an "equal partner" by using hate-crime laws to tell us what we can and cannot say from the pulpit. The government would like to tell churches that they cannot deny employment to homosexuals or transgender individuals. Merging the social sector—which means churches with the government—is what Hitler did when he picked the Reich Bishop. And how did that work out? Hitler's fascism was based on coercing and at times outright forcing the churches and corporations of Germany to exist for the advancement of the Nazi state.

When Communitarians Commune

Pastor Brian McLaren is one of the most popular authors and speakers within the Emergent Church movement. On his website, McLaren recounts a conversation with a college student about how the Emergent Church was formed: "Emergent grew out of the Young Leader Networks, which was launched in the mid-90s by Leadership Network, a Dallas-based foundation."[292]

I include a chapter on the Emergent Church in *Grave Influence*, but in case you're not familiar with it: it is a church philosophy and movement based on embracing mysticism, uncritical tolerance, and postmodernism. Please note that this is not my definition. It is a summary according to my friend Jason Carlson, who was part of the founding of the Emergent Church. When Tony Jones, Brian McLaren, and some of the other Emergent founders began to embrace heretical teachings, Carlson left and became a nationally recognized EC critic. In fact, Worldview Weekend has produced a one-hour DVD featuring a keynote presentation by Jason entitled "My Journey Into and Out of the Emergent Church." (It can be purchased through the online bookstore at worldviewweekend.com.)

Jason outlines the tenets of the Emergent Church this way:

- A highly ambiguous handling of truth;
- A desire to be so inclusive and tolerant that there is virtually no sense of biblical discernment in terms of recognizing and labeling false beliefs, practices, or lifestyles;
- A quasi-universalistic view of salvation;
- A lack of a proper appreciation for biblical authority over and against personal experience or revelation;
- Openness to pagan religious practices like Hindu yoga and incorporating them into the Christian life and Christian worship;
- Openly questioning the relevance of key historical biblical doctrines such as the Trinity;
- An uncritically open embrace of the Catholic and Orthodox churches;
- An unbridled cynicism towards conservative evangelicalism and fundamentalism;
- A reading of Scripture that is heavily prejudiced towards a social gospel understanding;
- Little or no talk of evangelism or saving lost souls.[293]

Christians who have not "studied to show themselves approved" unto God and who are not committed to the Word of God are at great risk for spiritual deception as the Emerging Church has mixed Christianity with pagan spirituality and thereby embraced the apostasy warned about in 2 Timothy 3:1–5:

> But know this, that in the last days perilous times will come: For men will be lovers of themselves, lovers of money, boasters, proud, blasphemers, disobedient to parents, unthankful, unholy, unloving, unforgiving, slanderers, without self-control, brutal, despisers of good, traitors, headstrong, haughty, lovers of pleasure rather than lovers of God, having a form of godliness

but denying its power. And from such people turn away!

Merging Church and Culture

As with many corrupting philosophies, Emergent Church ideas have been sparked by schools of higher education. One of the seminaries that has done the most harm to America's churches is Fuller Theological Seminary, where New Apostolic Reformation and church-growth leader C. Peter Wagner taught for many years. Rick Warren also attended Fuller and listed Wagner on his doctoral thesis as being his "advisor/mentor."

In 1998, the *Baptist Press* article "Church Growth Scholar Advocates Radical Change in New Millennium" detailed the agenda of Fuller Theological Seminary professor Eddie Gibbs:

> Eddie Gibbs, professor of church growth at Fuller Theological Seminary, Pasadena, California, speaking during the annual meeting of the American Society for Church Growth at Golden Gate Seminary's Mill Valley, Calif., campus Nov. 12–14. Gibbs warned churches must embrace transitions or "forfeit the possibility of exercising a transformational ministry within changing cultures."[294]

Transformational? The traditional terminology has been the thesis and antithesis of the Hegelian Dialectic Process. The communitarian church-growth movement has adopted the code words "traditional, transitional, and transformational," and now many conference speakers and Emerging authors tout the importance of a transformational church.

The CCGM is transitioning traditional churches by bringing in unbelievers to conflict with the believers. The church gradually moves from being a traditional church to a transitional church to finally becoming a transformed church. In the end, the church has been completely transformed and has become a totally different organization with a totally different purpose and goal. I believe the goal is to take a traditional church, transition it into a seeker-sensitive church, and then transform it into a church that embraces Emergent Church theology.

In April 2011, I spoke on this topic to more than 1,500 people at one of our Worldview Weekends, and I asked the audience how many of them, after having this process explained, could say they attend or have attended a church that has gone from being a solid, Bible-teaching, traditional church to being completely transformed. More than 60 percent of the people in the auditorium raised their hands!

Emergent Church proponent Jim Belcher wrote a book in 2009 titled *Deep Church: A Third Way Beyond Emerging and Traditional*. His book is a perfect example of the Hegelian Dialectic Process in action. Belcher calls for traditional evangelicals and the Emergent Church to come together in dialogue, find what is good about each other, and then blend their ideas.

The truth is that it is impossible to blend biblical truth with heresy, yet that is exactly what you would be trying to accomplish if you followed Belcher's "Third Way." Belcher, of course, sees things differently:

> Yet the two sides can't get along? They are hostile to each other, using their writings and conferences to denounce the other side. The vast majority of people are confused by the debate. Many have read emerging authors, agreeing with their assessment of the problem and aspects of what they are proposing. But they also have read traditional authors and are drawn to parts of their vision of the church as well. The majority want to learn from both sides.... This book is written for those caught in between. They are unhappy with the present state of the evangelical church but are not sure where to turn for an answer. They like some of what the emerging and traditional camps offer, but they are not completely at ease with either. The public conflicts make this anxiety worse, and these people don't know who to trust or believe. What if both are off target? Is there a third option, a via media? I believe there is a third way.... I will demonstrate the strengths and weaknesses of both groups, and move beyond them to a third way, the deep church.[295]

The foreword for Belcher's book was written by Fuller Seminary president Richard Mouw. Mouw was a signer of the 1994 Evangelicals and Catholics Together document declaring that Catholics and Christians are both Christian groups, and thus evangelicals need to stop trying to convert Catholics. The ECT document proclaimed:

> In the exercise of these public responsibilities there has been in recent years a growing convergence and cooperation between Evangelicals and Catholics. We thank God for the discovery of one another in contending for a common cause. Much more important, we thank God for the discovery of one another as brothers and sisters in Christ. Our cooperation as citizens is animated by our convergence as Christians. We promise one another that we will work to deepen, build upon, and expand this pattern of convergence and cooperation.... [I]n view of the large number of non-Christians in the world and the enormous challenge of our common evangelistic task, it is neither theologically legitimate nor a prudent use of resources for one Christian community to proselytize among active adherents of another Christian community.[296]

In *Deep Church*, Belcher speaks highly of Mouw's influence, referring to him as "my mentor at Fuller Seminary, President Richard Mouw."[297]

Mouw also defended Emergent Church pastor and author Rob Bell's heretical book on universalism when he wrote on his blog, "I told the *USA Today* reporter that Rob Bell's newly released *Love Wins* is a fine book and that I basically agree with his theology."[298]

Mouw even reveals his theological liberalism when he says, "Did Mother Teresa go to hell? My guess is that she was a little confused about justification by faith alone. If you think that means she went to hell, I have only one response: shame on you."[299]

While I do not know what Mother Teresa believed on her death bed, all previous doctrinal fruit suggests that Mother Teresa did not reject pagan spirituality and cling to Jesus Christ alone. Numerous statements, such as this one, reveal Mother Teresa's rejection of biblical truth: "If in coming face to face with God we accept Him in our lives, then we . . . become a better Hindu, a better Muslim, a better Catholic, a better whatever we are.... What God is in your mind you must accept."[300]

Belcher's book is endorsed by Tim Keller, an extremely popular author in the Reformed theology movement. Some friends who speak at conferences with Keller were shocked when I pointed out the errors in Keller's theology. Although I will have more to say about that in a later chapter, for now let me say that what makes the religious Trojan horse so dangerous is that pastors who are thought to be theologically sound embrace false teaching and thereby give false doctrines credibility which would otherwise be rejected if presented by known theological liberals such as Rob Bell, Brian McLaren, or Tony Campolo. That's why I believe pastors like Tim Keller can be more dangerous than Bell and the like. Keller's endorsement of Belcher exclaims:

> Jim Belcher shows that we don't have to choose between orthodox evangelical doctrine on the one hand, and cultural engagement, creativity and commitment to social justice on the other. This is an important book.[301]

You know you have a problem when Tim Keller, together with one of the founders of the Emergent Church, Tony Jones, endorse Belcher's book!

Belcher is not the only one calling for a synthesis of the traditional church with the culture. Eddie Gibbs has declared:

> The church itself will need to go through a metamorphosis in order to find its new identity in the dialectic of gospel and culture. This new situation is requiring churches to approach their context as a missional encounter.[302]

Excuse me, but the Church does not need to find a "new identity." It needs to return to the prescription, the formula, the biblical requirements of a New Testament Church. We do not need to merge the Church and culture. Christians are called to be in the world, but not of the world. According to *Baptist Press*, though, this is not good enough for Gibbs, who says:

> "For the church to become a missional church, a new kind of leader will be required," Gibbs argued. "It will not simply be a matter of people with traditional

mind-sets acquiring new ministry skills to supplement what they already know."[303]

Gibbs' new breed is a pastor/leader who more closely resembles a community organizer promoting social justice than a biblical shepherd of the flock. Behind this thinking is a commitment on the part of most of these authors to dominion theology, which promotes the building of God's Kingdom through our own efforts here and now on earth.

We are co-workers with God to build His Kingdom in the spiritual realm by preaching the Gospel without compromise. Preaching a social gospel, on the other hand, is nothing more than what a friend of mine calls "giving water bottles to people on their way to hell." Social justice is the redistribution of wealth through socialism, and the social gospel is social justice embraced by the Church and given a Christian veneer by twisting and distorting the Word of God. These men should repent of their double-minded thinking and preach faith and repentance through the teaching of God's Word.

Leadership (Communitarian) Network

In a Drucker Foundation book, *The Community of the Future*, Bob Buford contributed a chapter on the Leadership Network. Entitled "How Boomers, Churches, and Entrepreneurs Can Transform Society," Buford's chapter explains:

> There are three major sectors in American society: the government, which ensures compliance with laws and allocates resources; the business sector, which provides jobs and fosters economic development; and the social sector, [churches and nonprofits] which addresses social and existential needs. All three sectors must do their part if we wish to create…healthy, socially functioning communities in the twenty-first century.

Where have we heard that before? This is the same message we hear from Bob's mentor, communitarian Peter Drucker, and his disciple Rick Warren.

The Community of the Future introduced Bob Buford as

> …founder of Leadership Network, a non-profit organization that encourages innovation and entre-

preneurship among leaders of large churches and parent church organizations. He has held leadership roles with the Young President's Organization, and the World President's Organization, and has been a moderator of executive seminars at the Aspen Institute.

That Bob Buford has moderated executive seminars with the Aspen Institute is incredibly significant. The Aspen Institute is a radical group trained in Fabianesque techniques for how to bring about changes within a community. They are skilled at changing people's behavior.

As background: in 1977, *The Third Try at World Order* was written by Harlan Cleveland of the Aspen Institute (the full name of the group, by the way, is Aspen Institute for Humanistic Studies). Cleveland explained that the institute calls for "changing Americans' attitudes and institutions...complete disarmament (except for international soldiers)...for individual entitlement to food, health and education."[304] This means disarming the populace—taking away the Second Amendment rights of Americans—along with a redistribution of wealth.

The list of honorary trustees for the Aspen Institute for Humanistic Studies includes communitarian Maurice Strong, who hosted the Earth Summit in Rio de Janeiro in 1992 and helped write the summit's *Agenda 21*. Strong also helped write the *Earth Charter*.

In reaction, since the early 1990s, my friend Tom DeWeese has exposed the truth about this group:

> Maurice Strong, Secretary General of the U.N.'s Earth Summit, which produced the Biodiversity Treaty and Agenda 21....Strong owns a ranch in Colorado, where he has built a Babylonian sun god temple. Strong told the Earth Summit, "Isn't the only hope for the planet that the industrial civilizations collapse? Isn't our responsibility to bring that about?"

Someone who worships a Babylonian sun god seems like a strange bedfellow for the head of a "Christian" leadership organization.

Worship Service or Customer Service?

Following Peter Drucker's model, the people who go to church can now be viewed as customers. In a 1998 *Forbes* magazine interview, Drucker bridges business and church strategies when he says, "Non-customers are as important as customers, if not more important: because they are potential customers.... Yet it is with the noncustomers that changes always start."[305]

This suggests that nonchurch attendees are potential customers, so noncustomers are more important than the church's customers. There are also more noncustomers than customers, and if you can find out why noncustomers aren't yet customers, you can turn them into customers by doing the right things to attract them.

What market research can help you discover this necessary non-customer information? You go around your town or city and take a survey of neighborhoods, asking unbelievers how they would program a church so they would want to attend (this has really been done). The unsaved, not surprisingly, want a church that looks like the world and makes them feel comfortable. They want a pastor who is a life coach to assist them in having their "best life now."

This is the same model Bill Hybels of Willow Creek Church has promoted for years. Hybels also signed the Yale document and has hosted Rob Bell, Brian McLaren, Tony Blair, and rock star Bono at his church or conferences. (His family aids in perpetuating the agenda as well: Bill Hybels's wife writes for neo-Marxist Jim Wallis in *Sojourner* magazine.) Hybels seems especially comfortable with the Drucker model as he declares:

> Unchurched people today are the ultimate con-sumers. We may not like it, but for every sermon we preach, they're asking, "Am I interested in that subject or not?" If they aren't, it doesn't matter how effective our delivery is; their minds will check out.[306]

The unbeliever who attends a church where the Gospel is being preached might laugh and discount the message because the cross is foolishness to those who are perishing (1 Corinthians 1:18). The un-believer may hear the Gospel and decide that he or she wants to hear more. Or he or she may hear, believe, repent, and come to faith. These are the three responses Paul received when he preached the Gospel to skeptics and critics on Mars Hill as recounted in Acts 17. That's the way it is supposed to work.

Yes, the unsaved may hear the Gospel and reject it, but the solution is not to water down the Gospel to make it more appealing, but to preach the Gospel and pray the Holy Spirit convicts unbelievers of sin and that they respond by repenting and placing their faith and trust in Jesus Christ. It is not our job to get people saved. It is simply our calling as disciples of Jesus Christ to present the biblical truth of the Gospel without compromise.

The Communitarian-Driven Church

Even a cursory study of Rick Warren's church philosophy reveals that Warren embraces the communitarian worldview of his mentor Peter Drucker. For instance:

> In his speech, Warren argued that the solution of the world's greatest problems lies in what he called the "third partnership." The third partnership involves a relationship between faith communities, the government and the business sector.... "If business and government were able to solve the world's problems by themselves, they would have done it by now. A combination of the public, profit and parish sector is needed."[307]

Warren has repeated this theme in interview after interview, book after book, and conference after conference:

> The government has the administrative power to form agendas and set goals, the business sector can provide the expertise, the capital and the managerial skills, and the church can provide the distributive network and the local credibility.[308]

That Rick Warren can call all religious faiths to join him in this global plan reveals that he is not presenting the biblical Gospel but social justice. Social justice is even a major tenet of Islam, which is why Warren was welcomed to speak to the Islamic Society of North America. He also invited them to join him in working for the "common good" through his global PEACE plan.

The *U.S. News & World Report* article "Preacher with a Purpose" said of Rick Warren, "Today, what began in Warren's teeny living room has 82,000 on its rolls. A realization of Warren's vision for 'a church for people who hate church.'"[309]

Nowhere in the Scriptures do we see that our calling is to create a church for those who hate church. On the contrary, the New Testament Church is not about unbelievers but about "equipping" those who do believe. William Still wrote about this very issue in a serious yet humorous article:

> The pastor is called upon to feed the sheep. (Now that may seem quite obvious.) He is called upon to feed the sheep even if the sheep do not want to be fed. He is certainly not to become an entertainer of goats. Let goats entertain goats, and let them do it in Goatland. You will certainly not turn goats into sheep by pandering to their goatishness.[310]

It's important to connect the dots when tracing the progression of various philosophies, and many of today's dots connect back to the midtwentieth-century socialist radical named Saul Alinsky. Alinsky used the word "change" over and over in his book *Rules for Radicals*, and by change he meant "revolution." Fabian socialists, communitarians, globalists, statists, and internationalists are co-opting the Church in support of an Alinsky-style revolution. How do we know that? Rick Warren, for one, plays the theme when he says, "I think pastors are the most underrated change agents in America."[311]

The book of Revelation makes it clear that this will happen and that there will be a false church working with the anti-Christ to help him build the New World Order. The image in Scripture is the great whore or the woman that rides the beast in Revelation 17 and 18.

Peter Drucker in "Business of the Kingdom," a November 15, 1999, article in *Christianity Today*, describes "the pastor as manager."[312] But does the Bible describe a pastor that way? Ephesians 4:11–12 offers an answer: "And He, Himself, gave some to be apostles, some prophets"—now we come to the offices of today—"some evangelists, and some pastors and teachers." Then we read, "some to be managers and CEOs." Oh, I'm sorry. That's not what it says at all. In fact, nowhere in the description of a pastor/teacher/shepherd do we see that he is called to be a chief executive officer.

A pastor/teacher/shepherd is to be a godly man exercising his God-given spiritual gift for the purpose of the edification and equipping of the saints for the work of ministry. The pastor's job is to feed the sheep, not to entertain goats. Scripture commands, "Go ye therefore into the world," not, "Hey, world, come ye therefore into here." The model for the biblical New Testament Church is to be a place to equip and train believers and then send them out. "Out there" they evangelize and preach the Gospel. They explain to people the need for salvation through Christ alone with faith and repentance. If an individual becomes a follower of Jesus Christ through faith and repentance, then we disciple him or her in biblical truth. That's how we fulfill the Great Commission for evangelism and discipleship—not by meeting the "felt needs" of the unsaved world.

In *The Purpose Driven Church*, Rick Warren says, "Small groups are the most effective way of closing the back door of your church."[313] Warren writes this because he understands the power of the small-group setting. It's where the dialectic process works best. In a large church meeting, it is more difficult to manipulate, intimidate, and co-opt dissenters. The dialectic process (also called the Delphi Technique) is most effective in a small or cell group in which the goal is to divide and conquer.

Small-group discussions and forums keep dissenters apart and keep them from identifying each other and joining up in a larger group. Once dissenters have been spread through the network of small groups, an individual or married couple who expresses dismay at the unbiblical transformation of their church can be manipulated by being told they are the only ones who have expressed such a view. They can be subdued by being told they are harsh, judgmental, arrogant, and a detriment to church unity and fellowship. This divide-and-conquer strategy either causes dissenters to conform to the group consensus or to leave the church, thinking they were the only ones that noticed and disagreed with the unbiblical transformation of the church.

People who lead small groups that implement the Delphi Technique or the Dialectic Process are often called facilitators. Pre-trained facilitators know the outcome the church leadership desires.

To be sure, small groups can be a great benefit to Bible-based churches. They enhance fellowship and disseminate biblical teaching when structured properly under qualified Bible teachers who teach in context rather than simply share opinions or inject hidden agendas. But this is not the Rick Warren model.

Change agents see the small group as a prime way to manipulate people. Very few people want to be put on the spot, to be ostracized, to be made to feel like they're not part of the group. Those who go against the group consensus are challenged, and thus the conflict between thesis and antithesis begins. Wanting to be part of the group or to avoid being embarrassed or criticized, most individuals will compromise their convictions and accept the group consensus. When that happens, the facilitator has been successful in closing the door on "the wrong type of people." This is nothing less than the psychological process of behavior management a la B. F. Skinner.

Occultists Come to Church

Although what I'm about to share flies in the face of Rick Warren's immense popularity, it is important to be clear that Rick Warren is a false teacher. I believe he has no real commitment to biblical theology and doctrine but is above all committed to the communitarian church-growth movement. His goal is to add numbers to his church and convert the congregation to his brand of communitarianism and pagan spirituality. (Since his mentor Peter Drucker was committed to pagan spirituality, should we be shocked that Warren has also promoted pagan spirituality and the occult?)

Even many who now doubt Warren's commitment to biblical Christianity believe he remained biblically sound until after the release of his blockbuster book, *The Purpose Driven Life*. However, this book itself was filled with unbiblical material. In *The Purpose Driven Life*, Warren positively quotes no less than nine individuals who promote mysticism:

> Thomas Carlyle (page 27),
> Bernie Siegel (page 31),
> Henry David Thoreau (page 32),
> Brother Lawrence and Benedictine monks (pages 88–89),
> Gary Thomas (pages 102–103),
> St. John of the Cross (page 108),
> Henry Nouwen (pages 108, 269),
> Madame Guyon (page193),
> William James (page 285).

On page 88, Warren writes, "The classic book on learning how to develop a constant conversation with God is *Practicing the Presence of God*." Yet Brother Lawrence, the author of that book, was a monk who lived from 1614 to 1691 and believed God is in all things. This is panentheism, and it is a major doctrine of spiritual evolution, foundational for the globalist and communitarian worldview. So Warren believes a book that promotes the mysticism of contemplative prayer is a Christian classic.

Warren has revealed his commitment to the "do whatever it takes to bring in new customers" agenda. For pastors committed to Warrenology, this includes carrying out a marketing strategy that will bring goats into the sheepfold. The plan might include raffling flat-screen TVs or automobiles on any given Sunday morning. In Warren's case, his 2011 scheme to attract more goats was to create a diet and exercise program featuring three doctors known for promoting the occult. The Daniel Plan, as it is called, was discussed in an article in *The Orange County Register*:

> Pastor Rick Warren will host three health experts—including the star of the "Dr. Oz Show" —at Saddleback Church on Saturday to launch a yearlong, church-wide fitness plan. Dr. Mehmet Oz, a cardiac surgeon and TV show host, Dr. Mark Hyman, an expert in metabolism, and Dr. Daniel Amen, a bestselling author and clinical professor of psychiatry at UC Irvine, will help Warren kick off "The Daniel Plan." The effort is part of Saddleback's Decade of Destiny— a 10–year plan to expand the ministry.... The plan will include a 52–week customized program, a curriculum for small groups, an interactive website with a meal menu, exercise and shopping tips. There will also be monthly conference calls for encouragement. Warren also encouraged his congregation to get the word out to friends and neighbors.... "This is the greatest opportunity for you to introduce friends to Saddleback Church through a non-threatening event." Medical professionals will also be on hand to take measurements, conduct weigh-ins and take before and after photos.[314]

Do we see anywhere in the biblical model of the New Testament Church that we are to turn our church into the local health club, to provide exercise and shopping tips, or host weight-loss programs hosted by doctors who promote the occult? Obviously not.

Note that *The Orange County Register* quoted Warren as saying, "This is the greatest opportunity for you to introduce friends to Saddleback Church through a non-threatening event." I would contend, though, that you could bring any unsaved friends to any Saddleback church service led by Rick Warren, and it won't be threatening. I do not believe Warren would be giving a solid, clear Gospel.

So how does a pastor grow a church biblically? Acts 2:47 says, "And the Lord added to the church daily such as should be saved." How do you grow the Church? You preach the Gospel; the Holy Spirit convicts hearers of their sin; and they repent, are saved, and are then brought into the church to be discipled. You don't add to your church by marketing schemes to bring in unbelievers. You certainly do not bring in speakers who embrace the occult.

The November/December 2007 issue of *Spirituality and Health* featured an article written in part by Dr. Oz, one of Rick Warren's Daniel Plan fitness experts. In the article, Dr. Oz reveals why he follows the cult of Dr. Emanuel Swedenborg:

> Swedish mystic Emanuel Swedenborg...I later learned, was a scientist and theologian.... In his mid-fifties he came into an altered state of awareness in which he experienced a simultaneous dual consciousness of this life and the afterlife. His emphasis on overcoming the delusion of the self and on the profound interdependence of all things in both the spiritual and natural worlds aligns so closely with Buddhist thought that the Zen master D. T. Suzuki referred to him as "the Buddha of the North." According to Swedenborg, heaven and hell are not merely places but spiritual states. We do not "go there" when we die. We are already there. By choosing a life of good will and devotion, we build heaven in our hearts. This place within us then becomes our eternal home. After death, the veil that separates the spiritual from the material world is lifted, and we continue as our true selves—either

angels or evil spirits, depending on whether we have internally made a heaven or a hell for ourselves while living here. I have always had trouble with the idea of selective redemption. How could a compassionate God condemn his children for nothing more than being born into the "wrong faith"? How could an all-loving God choose to extend that love to only a select few? Swedenborg taught that God loves us all, and the various religions allow us to approach him in the way best suited to our needs. He argued that we are all born for heaven, and that it is what we love that determines our fate, not what we profess to believe.... Further, Swedenborg claimed that God never judges us.... Angels as described by Swedenborg aren't a separate species but people who are regenerate—literally, reborn humans. Swedenborg saw the Bible as...a detailed metaphor for the human condition.[315]

Swedenborg was a cult leader who mocked the Word of God and the exclusivity of Jesus Christ. He dismissed the idea of God's judgment on those who do not repent and place their faith and trust in Jesus Christ. Why would Rick Warren allow such a false teacher onto his church platform to deceive both the saved and unsaved at his church?

As for others on Warren's platform: Dr. Daniel Amen is author of *Change Your Brain, Change Your Body,* in which he has stated:

> In my book *The Brain in Love,* I wrote about tantric sexual practices. I was fascinated by the concept. I wanted to experience it for myself, and thought it would be a wonderful way to embrace my relationship with my wife Hannah. Tj Bartel became our teacher. I felt as if I had to share his knowledge with everyone I knew.[316]

When I read this, I had no idea what tantric sex was, so it wouldn't surprise me if you don't either. Christian author and New Age expert Ray Yungen explains this strange practice:

> Tantra is the name of the ancient Hindu sacred texts that contain certain rituals and secrets. Some deal

with taking the energies brought forth in meditation through the chakras and combining them with love-making to enhance sexual experiences.[317]

In another of his books, *Making a Good Brain Great*, Dr. Amen recommends "an active form of yoga meditation called Kriya Kirtan. It is based on the five primal sounds saa, taa, naa, maa, aa." Dr. Amen suggests doing this for 12 minutes, but make no mistake: this is nothing less than a mantra for the purpose of entering into an altered state of consciousness.

Yoga is a form of meditation and self-hypnosis by which one can indeed encounter a spirit or master guide, but these guides are actually demons. The word *yoga* means "yoke or union" with a Hindu god in Sanskrit. So "Christian yoga" is an oxymoron, like saying someone is a Christian Satanist or that there is such a thing as a Christian Ouija Board. For a more detailed explanation of the dangers of yoga and the difference between Eastern meditation and biblical meditation, Worldview Weekend offers a one-hour DVD by Ron Carlson. (The DVD, entitled "Confronting the Spiritual Confusion in the Church," is available in our bookstore at worldviewweekend.com.)

Yoga has taken hold in this country largely through the Maharishi Mahesh Yogi, who is credited with being the founder of the transcendental movement in America. Through meditation and other means, New Age followers are encouraged to get in touch with "the masters," better known to Christians as demons.

In his book *Change Your Brain, Change Your Body*, Dr. Amen calls Ekhart Tolle's book *The Power of Now* "extraordinary."[318] Ekhart Tolle has been a guest on *The Oprah Winfrey Show* many times and, with Oprah, taught an online course in which a million people reportedly took part. Eckhart, like many New Age spiritualists, quotes the Bible completely out of context. In *The Power of Now* he explains his version of Jesus:

> Christ is your God-essence or the Self, as it is sometimes called in the East. The only difference between Christ and presence is that Christ refers to your indwelling divinity regardless of whether you are conscious of it or not, whereas presence means your awakened divinity or God-essence.[319]

237

Eckhart is telling people that they are god, Dr. Amen calls Eckhart's book extraordinary, and Rick Warren brings him to his church anyway.

You'll recall that Dr. Mehmet Oz was there too. For more about what he stands for, take note of this excerpt from a press release distributed by the public relations firm PR Web on January 9, 2010:

> Reiki Masters across America and the world had cause for celebration on January 6 when Dr. Mehmet Oz revealed his Ultimate Alternative Medicine Secrets for 2010 during his nationally broadcast afternoon talk show. He ranked Reiki #1. Dr. Oz said, "Reiki is one of my favorites, we've been using it for years in the Oz family, and we swear by it."

What is Reiki? A pro-Reiki book entitled *The Everything Reiki Book* reveals:

> During the Reiki attunement process, the avenue that is opened within the body to allow Reiki to flow through also opens up the psychic communication centers. This is why many Reiki practitioners report having verbalized channeled communications with the spirit world.[320]

Yes, the spirit world—demons again. And who is promoting this? Dr. Oz. And who had Dr. Oz at his church as a part of the 52–week Daniel Plan? Rick Warren.

But wait, as they say, there's more! The book *The Instruction: Living the Life Your Soul Intended*, written by Ainslie MacLeod, is endorsed by Dr. Oz: "I recommend this book to those who seek greater spiritual well-being and a better understanding of their life's purpose."[321]

What is it that Dr. Oz is recommending when he recommends *The Instruction*? The book's Amazon.com product description explains:

> Have you ever sensed that your life has a deeper, more meaningful purpose—but don't know what it is? If so, you're not alone. To help you and the millions like you, psychic Ainslie MacLeod's spirit guides have given him a systematic approach to uncovering who

you really are—and the life your soul has planned for. They call it *The Instruction*. Now, for the first time, this unique teaching is offered as a step-by-step program for realizing personal fulfillment.

The Instruction will take you through 10 "doorways" to unveil the life plan your soul created before you were even born, including:

Your Soul Age: Determining how it shapes your beliefs and behaviors

Your Soul Type: Are you a Hunter? Thinker? Creator? What your Soul Type reveals about your true self

Your Powers: Connecting fully and permanently with your spirit guides to create your destiny

Your Talents: Using your past lives to enhance the present[322]

Connecting with your spirit guides? This author is teaching how to connect to a demon. "Using your past lives to enhance the present" is a reference to reincarnation. Is not Dr. Oz's appearance at Rick Warren's church a religious Trojan horse for the New Age movement? Although Warren has been dubbed "America's pastor," I submit that a more accurate title would be "America's false teacher."

Remember the declaration on Bob Buford's Leadership Network website that "the mission of the Leadership Network is to accelerate the emergence of the 21st-century church.... This new paradigm is not centered in theology"? Well, Rick Warren's promotion of Oz and the like is what you get when you do not center on biblical theology in a church. The church ends up promoting whatever it takes to appeal to the unsaved world and to attract more customers—even if it means promoting the doctrines of demons!

The Biblical Model for the New Testament Church

We've seen that the communitarian church-growth model is built on man-centered theology, pagan spirituality, and pragmatism. The

CCGM is all about numbers and seeing the pastor as CEO or manager. People sitting in the pews are customers, and there is really no concern as to whether the customers are sheep or goats. The CCGM emphasizes the social gospel rather than the biblical Gospel, which simply means applying religious terminology to social justice. The CCGM is also committed to dominion theology and globalism.

But what is the biblical model for the New Testament church? I've outlined below some characteristics of a biblical New Testament church.

Number One: A biblical New Testament church is about equipping the saints for the work of ministry. We've already seen this characteristic in Ephesians 4:11–12.

In addition, Romans 10:13–17 declares:

> How then shall they call on Him in whom they have not believed? And how shall they believe in Him of whom they have not heard? And how shall they hear without a preacher? And how shall they preach unless they are sent?

A New Testament church equips the saints for the work of ministry, which includes sending people out to preach the Gospel to the world, not bringing the world into the Church and catering to them.

I'm not suggesting that we don't want unbelievers in our churches. What I'm saying is that if an unbeliever comes into our church, he or she should hear the Word of God preached. We don't cater to unbelievers by dumbing down the message of Christ and by avoiding such topics as sin, the judgment of God, the wrath of God, dying to self, picking up our crosses, and being willing to suffer for the Gospel. Our goal should not be to deliver a message that makes the unbeliever feel comfortable, but to deliver a message that makes an unbeliever feel uncomfortable in his or her lost and sinful state. If the Gospel is being preached, the unsaved should be uncomfortable and under conviction, as we see in 2 Corinthians 7:9–11:

> Now I rejoice, not that you were made sorry, but that your sorrow led to repentance. For you were made sorry in a godly manner, that you might suffer

loss from us in nothing. For godly sorrow produces repentance *leading* to salvation, not to be regretted; but
the sorrow of the world produces death. For observe
this very thing, that you sorrowed in a godly manner:
What diligence it produced in you, *what* clearing *of
yourselves, what* indignation, *what* fear, *what* vehement
desire, *what* zeal, *what* vindication! In all *things* you
proved yourselves to be clear in this matter.

Today's seeker-sensitive church-growth model has given us churches filled with false converts who have not heard the true and complete
Gospel preached in their churches. And without the Gospel, no one
can repent and follow Christ.

By contrast, Acts 6:7 shows what happens when people hear the
truth: "Then the word of God spread, and the number of the disciples
multiplied greatly in Jerusalem, and a great many of the priests were
obedient to the faith."

How did the disciples or followers of Jesus Christ multiply?
Through gimmicks, entertainment, a fitness or weight-loss plan?
No! The disciples multiplied because of church members speaking,
preaching, and teaching. The Word of God spread, people were saved,
and God added to the Church. That is what we should be doing,
equipping saints for the work of ministry, sending them out to preach
the Gospel.

You'll recognize that this is not what Rick Warren is equipping and
training his congregation to do—or the 500,000 churches he claims
have been following his leadership. Warren has said, "the Pulpit is the
ultimate tool for church growth."[323]

But pastors or teachers are not to use the pulpit as a marketing
tool. More than 50 years ago, Merrill Unger warned of what we're seeing today:

> To an alarming extent the glory is departing from
> the pulpit of the twentieth century. The basic reason
> for this gloomy condition is obvious. That which im-
> parts the glory has been taken away from the center
> of so much of our modern preaching and placed on
> the periphery. The Word of God has been denied the
> throne and given a subordinate place.[324]

Number Two: A biblical church has godly leadership that feeds as well as protects the flock while exercising discernment and church discipline.

Number Three: A biblical church faithfully preaches the whole counsel of the Word of God.

Number Four: A biblical church follows Christ's blueprint for building His Church and prays for God to provide the increase.

These characteristics are all made clear in Acts 6:3–4:

> Therefore, brethren, seek out from among you seven men of *good* reputation, full of the Holy Spirit and wisdom, whom we may appoint over this business; but we will give ourselves continually to prayer and to the ministry of the word.

"The ministry of the word" is a reference to preaching and teaching Scripture. So, how is a New Testament church to be conducted, and how does a New Testament church grow? By picking godly men with godly reputations as leaders, full of the Holy Spirit, full of wisdom, who will preach and pray. The Scriptures are clear that God adds to His Church as people are being saved.

And how is the unbeliever saved? By hearing the Word of God and being convicted by the Holy Spirit of sin. This results in godly sorrow that produces repentance unto salvation.

Communitarian church-growth books and conferences do not train and equip pastors and church leaders in the biblical model of evangelism to create true converts. David Eby, writing in *Power Preaching for Church Growth,* reveals this from his research of typical church-growth resources:

> ...of the forty-eight books, besides many brief passing references, only twenty pages were devoted to preaching, and only twenty-eight to prayer. Granted, this may not be a scientific survey, but the message is obvious. Think of it. Over 10,000 pages on church growth and under 50 on preaching and prayer. Something is out of balance. Then I dove into ten books

on church renewal, all of which have been influenced by the Church Growth Movement. And the finding? Over 2,000 pages of print, and besides the now-expected passing references, only seven pages devoted to preaching and sixteen to prayer.

Clearly the communitarian church-growth movement is not interested in theology. Its proponents are not interested in doctrine. They're not interested in preaching the whole counsel of God. What they do want is not friendly toward God's purposes. James 4:4 says: "Do you not know that friendship of the world is enmity with God? Whoever, therefore, wants to be a friend to the world, makes himself an enemy of God." It is obvious that when you bring people who embrace the occult into church, you're embracing the world and are at enmity with God. The bad news is clear: Such people are under God's wrath.

Number Five: A biblical church loves the Lord and not the world.

First John 2:15 says, "Do not love the world, or the things in the world. If anyone loves the world, the love of the Father is not in him."

Number Six: A biblical church is not ashamed of the Gospel.

A Bible-based church does not water down the Gospel or avoid preaching the Gospel in order to make sinners feel comfortable. A Bible-based church is not ashamed of the Gospel. We preach the Gospel, pray that the Holy Spirit convicts unbelievers, reveals their sin to them, and that they come to faith in Christ.

Many CCGM pastors and authors call for the "contextualizing" of the Gospel. What they really mean is that the Church needs to dilute the Gospel so it is more appealing to the culture. Such influencers believe we need to make the Gospel more relevant, but let me make this really clear: Either the Holy Spirit reveals sin to unbelievers and they are convicted, repent, and are saved, or they harden their hearts and are lost for eternity. We can't make the Gospel any more (or less) relevant. All we can do is be faithful to preach the Gospel.

Contextualization, as practiced by the false church, is not preaching the biblical Gospel that transforms people living in the culture but is, rather, the preaching of a social gospel by people who were transformed by the culture. Yet Romans 1:16 says, "For I am not ashamed of the Gospel of Christ, for it is the power of God to salvation for everyone who believes, for the Jew first, and also for the Greek." And 2 Timothy 4:1–4 picks up the theme:

> I solemnly charge you in the presence of God and of Christ Jesus, who is to judge the living and the dead, and by His appearing and His kingdom: preach the word; be ready in season and out of season; reprove, rebuke, exhort, with great patience and instruction. For the time will come when they will not endure sound doctrine; but wanting to have their ears tickled, they will accumulate for themselves [false] teachers in accordance to their own desires; and will turn away their ears from the truth, and will turn aside to myths.

Such "myths" and pagan spirituality are taught by false teachers like Rick Warren, Bill Hybels, and Drs. Amen, Hyman, and Oz.

Number Seven: A biblical church will suffer persecution. Second Timothy 3:12 cautions, "Yes, and all who desire to live godly in Christ Jesus will suffer persecution."

Neutralizing the Opposition

I believe the communitarian church-growth movement is a deliberate strategy to infiltrate the Church and transform it from being an opponent of the demonic New World Order to being a willing participant and promoter of its goals. Whether you call them communitarians, Fabians, globalists, statists, internationals, New Agers, or progressives, the goal is global governance. Whether they know it or not, these people are building Satan's kingdom, but I have news for them: Daniel 2:44 promises that God will crush Satan's kingdom and that God's Kingdom will have no end.

Until that glorious day, we are to assist in building God's Kingdom in the spiritual realm as we fulfill the Great Commission. We are not to build an earthly kingdom of God on earth, as Jesus explained in John 18:36. Christians who preach the Gospel and teach according to God's Word are ultimately the greatest obstacle to Satan building his temporary kingdom.

Globalists seek to neutralize, infiltrate, compromise, and co-opt the opposition and create a religious Trojan horse.

Too many pastors and Christian authors have endorsed the books and conferences of men like Rick Warren. Christian leaders and Christians are being deceived because they are not familiar with the philosophies of the day, such as Fabian socialism, communitarianism, internationalism, globalism, the Hegelian Dialectic Process, postmodernism, New Age spirituality, dominion theology, the New Apostolic Reformation, social justice, and religious syncretism. Colossians 2:8 warns, "Beware lest anyone cheat you through philosophy and empty deceit, according to the tradition of men, according to the basic principles of the world, and not according to Christ."

The reason many Christians are so easily deceived is that they lack discernment. Yet discernment comes from the study of doctrine. Doctrine is truth; it reveals the will of God for our lives. In John 17:17, Jesus prayed, "Sanctify [make them holy] by Your word; Your word is truth."

God's Word has given us a clear description of what a New Testament church should be. May we have a commitment to the model God has laid out. The Church is not a building; it is the people of God. Christ died for the Church, so let's live to defend His Church and add to it as we preach the Gospel without compromise.

CHAPTER 7

The Watermelon Church:
Environmental Green and Socialist Red

An ever-increasing number of New Religious Right members, neo-evangelical leaders, useful idiots, and their organizations, churches, and denominations are cultivating the "watermelon plan." The center-piece of this strategy involves giving credibility to or outright jumping on the bandwagon of radical environmentalism to promote the green movement and its related Communist (red) socialism.

A few years ago, for example, the International Church of the Naz-arene released its "Creation Care" document, which declared:

> In this most critical moment in Earth's history, we are convinced that *the central moral imperative* of our time is the care for Earth as God's creation. Church-es, as communities of God's people in the world, are called to exist as representatives of the loving Creator, Sustainer, and Restorer of all creation. We are called to worship God with all our being and actions, and to treat creation as sacred. We must engage our political leaders in supporting the very future of this planet. We are called to cling to the true Gospel—for "God so loved the world" (John 3:16).[325]

"The central moral imperative of our time is the care for Earth as God's creation"? Really? What about the millions of people who die each day and go to hell for eternity? How sad that the central moral imperative of the day for the Church of the Nazarene is not the fulfill-ment of the Great Commission.

This misappropriation of priorities is not limited to the Church of the Nazarene, though. In May 2011, Lynne Hybels, wife of founding pastor Bill Hybels of Willow Creek Church in Chicago, was appointed to President Obama's faith council. Lynne, who also writes for the magazine and website of Jim Wallis, wants her husband's church to focus on the imperative of global warming and care for the environment. Concerned about the Hybels's emphasis on such an agenda, David Noebel wrote an article for worldviewweekend.com entitled, "Pastor Bill Hybels' Wife and Willow Creek Are Proud of the 'Social Justice' of Rev. Jim Wallis." In it, Noebel quotes one of Lynne Hybels's blog posts:

> I look forward to the day when we as a church will be known for being the greenest church on the planet, not just because we enjoy the beauty of God's creation, but because we know that climate change is a justice issue.[326]

Lynne's job title at Willow Creek Church is "Advocate for Global Engagement." Apparently, she's more interested in engaging the globe itself than the people who live on it.

David Noebel also reveals that Lynn Hybels's friend and co-laborer for the advancement of socialism, Jim Wallis, is a "defender of Fidel Castro and a party to the proliferation of Communist revolutions throughout Central America, moving amongst the evangelicals and deceiving them left and left."[327]

The Hybels have embraced an assortment of radicals. Speakers at their church services and conferences include Bill Clinton, Bono, Tony Blair, Rob Bell, and Brian McLaren, among others. Hybels admits he is a progressive—yet another name for "socialist"—in his endorsement of Jim Wallis's book *The Great Awakening*:

> Progressive and centrist evangelicals are one stirring away from a real awakening. We are interested in the poor, in racial reconciliation, in global poverty and AIDS, in the plight of women in the developing world. What Wallis has been talking about is coming to fruition.[328]

Sojourners, the organization run by Jim Wallis, has received funding from George Soros, a graduate of the Fabian socialist London School of Economics. In a column at worldviewweekend.com, Noebel explains how Wallis and the Hybels are emerging as the new leaders of the religious left Trojan horse:

According to *Newsweek*'s Educational Site, on November 30, 2010, Wallis was among a dozen "moderate" Christian leaders who gathered in Washington to discuss ways to "articulate a vision of Christianity that will counter a new—and newly powerful—religious-right rhetoric in advance of the 2012 election." In other words, they were plotting ways to make conservative evangelicals think of Obama as one of them. How this pro-abortion, pro-homosexual, pro-socialist president could be "one of them" is difficult to fathom. But Joel Hunter, pastor of the Northland Church in Orlando, and Tony Campolo, sociologist and advisor to former President Clinton, were among the Christian leaders at the meeting.

Campolo set the tone for the meeting by denouncing the religious right's "vision of America as God's own country, and free-market capitalism as crucial to the nation's flourishing." He went on to elaborate that what motivates religious conservatives is this distorted vision of God and country and that anyone who disagrees with them "is a socialist or a communist."

To this group and others of like mind, the "radical right" (i.e., conservative Christians) must be demeaned if not destroyed so the new guard of evangelicals, led by the Rev. Wallis and his loyal sidekicks Bill and Lynne Hybels (Lynne writes for *Sojourners* magazine) of Willow Creek Church in Chicago, must emerge as the new leaders.

The truth is that Jim Wallis and Tony Campolo have been part of the religious left for years (see Ron Nash's *Why the Left Is Not Right*), and Wallis has been swimming in Marxist waters ever since his college days at Michigan State University when he was involved with Students for a Democratic Society.

Wallis recently showed his dialectical morality when challenged by Marvin Olasky, editor of *World* magazine. When Olasky asked Wallis to finally admit he was "a man of the left," Wallis insisted he was a man of the center. When Olasky insisted that men of the center don't take financial help from the radical leftist George Soros and his Open Society Institute, Wallis insisted his organization (Sojourners) never took funds from Soros. When Olasky produced evidence that Sojourners has taken tens of thousands of dollars from Soros, Wallis finally had to say "uncle." Indeed, Wallis actually apologized to Olasky for calling him "a liar" (see *World* magazine, August 18, 2010.)[329]

Noebel thinks the Hybelses and their neo-evangelical friends should put their money where their mouth is and go live in the socialist "heaven" of Cuba or Venezuela:

> The progressive evangelicals who are helping to bring about this descent into a socialistic hell need to live in Cuba or Venezuela for a year before they entice any more naïve evangelicals into such a quagmire of hopelessness and despair.[330]

In a February 13, 2006, article at worldviewweekend.com, I explained what some of these progressive "evangelical" leaders were up to:

> During a press conference at the National Press Club in Washington, organized by the Evangelical Environmental Network, a newly formed coalition called the Evangelical Climate Initiative, released a statement signed by more than 85 "evangelical" leaders.
>
> Some of the global warming gad flies that signed the *Climate Change: An Evangelical Call to Action* include Rick Warren, author of *Purpose-Driven Life* and pastor at Saddleback Church; Senior Pastor of Wooddale Church in Eden Prairie, MN, and former [now president again at the time I am writing this book in Fall 2011] National Association of Evangelicals (NAE) president Leith Anderson; World Vision president Rich Stearns; Salvation Army national commander Todd Bassett; *Christianity Today* editor David Neff and

executive editor Timothy George; and Wheaton College president Duane Litfin, Rob Bell of Mars Hill, Bill Hybels of Willow Creek, Dan Kimball, Vintage Faith Church, Brian McLaren, Emergent Church leader, Richard Mouw, President of Fuller Theological Seminary, Joel Hunter, Northland Church and former president elect of the Christian Coalition, Richard Stearns, President of World Vision.

It is bad enough that so many "evangelical" environmental extremists have infected our churches, colleges, universities and evangelicalism with their liberal brand of Christianity, but now they want to damage America's free enterprise system by making it difficult for business to compete in the world marketplace?

According to the *New York Times*, the group's efforts are being funded by such liberal organizations as the Rockefeller Brothers Fund and the Hewlett Foundation. The Rockefeller Brother's Fund has given grants to such radical environmental groups as Greenpeace. Let's not forget that it was the Rockefellers that donated the land and formed the United Nations.

According to a press release by the pro-life group Human Life International, the Rockefeller Brothers Fund supports many anti-Christian ideals and organizations including the United Nations Millennium Peace Summit:

The United Nations Millennium Peace Summit called for organized religions to support the United Nations' world peace aims. Among the items for consideration is the Charter for Global Democracy, which has been described as the new "Ten Commandments" for the world. The summit is a project of the United Religions Initiative (URI), along with other groups. The URI favors abortion, sex education, same-sex marriage, and population control. The event is being funded, among other private entities, by the United Nations Foundation and the Rockefeller Brothers Fund.

According to the website of lifesite.net, in 2001, The William and Flora Hewlett Foundation approved a grant of $600,000 to International Planned Parenthood Foundation (IPPF) to provide "sexual and reproductive health services to adolescents in Brazil, Ecuador and Peru."

Behold my friends, the discernment, brain-trust and leadership behind some of today's leading churches, colleges, Christian publications and Christian organizations.

This is an emerging brand of Christianity that is assisting in and giving credibility and cover to groups in favor of globalism, the end of national sovereignty, tyranny and eventually the persecution of Christians. Let's face it; the environmental initiative of many of today's popular Christian leaders is being funded by some of the most anti-Christian, anti-American, globalist organizations. Follow the money trail.

The group of 85 is nothing less than the secular left's Trojan horse that has been placed inside evangelical circles. The question is, does the group of 85 know they are being used? If so, what does that say about the group of 85? If they don't know they are being used what does that tell you about their discernment? Can you really follow any of these "evangelical" leaders that are either complicit or ignorant in their involvement with such anti-Christian, globalist organizations?[331]

As far back as February 2006, I warned about the religious Trojan horse that had infiltrated evangelicalism. Remember that Rick Warren and Leith Anderson also signed onto the "Yale document," which declares that Christians and Muslims worship the "one God." Do you see the pattern here? NAE board member and "Third Way" proponent Pastor Joel Hunter also signed the Evangelical Climate Initiative.

As religious leaders become more political and political leaders become more religious, they facilitate the creation of the woman riding the beast—the harlot church. I predict you will soon be shocked to see individuals you never thought would betray Jesus Christ falling in with this unholy alliance.

SBC Connections to the National Council of Churches

You'll recall that the National Council of Churches was started by Fabian socialists. So it is shocking that America's largest Protestant denomination, the Southern Baptist Convention, would allow one of its leaders to sign a declaration in concert with the NCC and other religious radicals. Why has Richard Land worked with so many politically correct organizations—the National Religious Partnership for the Environment (NRPE), for example? Land is strangely unpredictable. On the one hand, he will sign declarations written by the radically liberal NRPE, and then he will say something I agree with, such as:

> The question is whether or not evangelicals allow themselves to be manipulated, allow themselves to be duped, and what we are to do is to judge everything by the plumb line of the Word of God. And the Word of God in the first nine chapters of Genesis gives us the foundational planks of a biblical environmental ethic. And if you look at those you will find that they're considerably at odds with the modern radical environmental movement.[332]

Land, like many Christian leaders, appears to allow himself to be manipulated and/or duped by the ecumenical and environmental globalists. If Land had actually done as he recommends and used the Bible as his plumb line, he would know that 2 Corinthians 6:14 and 2 John 9–11 clearly forbid him from signing a document such as the NRPE's "Declaration of the Mission to Washington," which is part of the organization's "Interfaith Environmental Engagement." The Southern Baptist Convention, through Richard Land's participation, partnered with the National Council of Churches, the US Conference of Catholic Bishops, and the Coalition on the Environment and Jewish Life. He signed the radical environmental declaration under the title "Executive Director, Christian Life Commission of the Southern Baptist Convention."

Despite the complaints of many SBC pastors and members (including me), the trustees of Land's office have not been willing to publicly demand that Land cease from his radical, pluralistic, ecumenical activities. They have had plenty of time to figure out his leanings. Land's history of such work goes back at least to 1994 when he signed the "Evangelicals and Catholics" document that called for evangelicals and Catholics to stop evangelizing each other since both groups "are Christian."

The Deception Spreads

The "evangelicals" fell for the trap, and now many leaders no longer seek to share the Gospel with Catholics. Meanwhile, the Church of Rome continues its evangelistic efforts. Other signers of the Interfaith Environmental Engagement Declaration include:

- Reverend Joan Campbell, General-Secretary, National Council of Churches of Christ
- Mr. Warren Eisenberg, Ecumenical Officer, Greek Orthodox Archdiocese of North and South America
- The Most Reverend William B. Friend, Chair Committee on Science and Human Values, National Conference of Catholic Bishops
- Reverend Dr. William Gardiner, Director of Social Justice, Unitarian Universalists Association
- Sally Grover Bingham, California Diocese: Environmental Commission, Episcopal Church
- Dr. Elizabeth Bowen, Representative, National Spiritual Assembly of the Baha'is of the United States
- The Most Reverend Edmond L. Browning, Presiding Bishop, Episcopal Church of America
- Mr. John Carr, Secretary for Department of Social Development and World Peace, United States Catholic Conference
- Father Drew Christiansen, Director, Office of International Justice and Peace, United States Catholic Conference
- Mr. Robert H. Cory, Quaker United Nations Office
- Mr. Herman Daly, Senior Economist, World Bank
- Reverend Thomas Berry, Director, Riverside Center for Religious Research

- Dr. Henry Kendall, Stratton Professor of Physics, Massachusetts Institute of Technology, and Chairman of the Board, Union of Concerned Scientists
- Mr. Alden Meyer, Director, Climate Change and Energy Program, Union of Concerned Scientists

As you can see, the list is ripe with groups associated with the United Nations, ecumenicalism, and the promotion of socialism. Regarding the last two signers and their membership in the Union of Concerned Scientists, you may want to note that Helen Caldicott, in speaking for the Union of Concerned Scientists, has said, "Capitalism is destroying the earth."[333]

Tom DeWeese, in 2008, wrote an article posted at worldviewweekend.com in which he detailed the history of the Union of Concerned Scientists:

> Please note that the UCS was started in the late 1980s as a part of the Nuclear Freeze movement, which was proven to be funded in part by the Soviet KGB. The membership of the UCS has always consisted of less than 10 percent scientists and more than 90 percent generic America-bashers.[334]

These associations alone should be enough reason for Richard Land *not* to sign his name to the Declaration of the "Mission to Washington." But wait, as they say, there's more! One of the other signers is the Reverend Thomas Berry, and Tom DeWeese reveals that Berry is not only an environmental extremist but also an advocate of anti-Bible and pro-pagan spirituality:

> Father Thomas Berry, a dissident Catholic Priest, is a prime spokesman for Gaia. Father Berry contends that Christianity promotes a "deep cultural pathology of human greed and addiction." He advocates that the earth is disintegrating and that Christianity is to blame. In his book *Dream of the Earth* (published by Sierra Club Books), Berry never uses the word "God" but speaks of a supernatural force in the universe. He says that "we should place less emphasis on Christ as a person and

a redeemer. We should put the Bible away for twenty years while we radically rethink our religious ideas."

So just what does the Declaration of the "Mission to Washington" proclaim? Here's an example:

> We are thinning the ozone layer and creating holes in it. We are poisoning the air, the land and the water. We are destroying the forests, grasslands and other ecosystems. We are causing the extinction of species at a pace not seen since the end of the age of the dinosaurs.... Our own country is the leading polluter on Earth, generating more greenhouse gases, especially CO2, than any other country.[335]

The only problem is that there is no evidence for these end-of-the-world scenarios. America is not the "leading polluter on earth." Based on twenty-five factors, in fact, the Environmental Performance Index in 2010 listed America as the 61st Cleanest Country in the world out of 163 that were ranked.[336] Nevertheless, the declaration stated:

> We reaffirm here, in the strongest possible terms, the indivisibility of social justice and the preservation of the environment. We also affirm and support the indigenous peoples in the protection and integrity of their cultures and lands. We believe the wealthy nations of the North, which have historically exploited the natural and human resources of the Southern nations, have a moral obligation to make available additional financial resources and appropriate technology to strengthen their capacity for their own development. We believe the poor and vulnerable workers in our own land should not be asked to bear disproportionate burdens. And we must end the dumping of toxic waste materials disproportionately in communities of low income and of people of color.[337]

Did you notice the words "social justice" in the first sentence of that quote? This is a phrase common to those who embrace socialism.

The document is clearly referring to redistribution of wealth as it calls for "the wealthy nations of the North...making available additional financial resources" to poorer nations. The declaration continues:

> Collectively, the nations of the world spend one trillion dollars a year on military programs. If even a modest portion of this money were spent on environmental programs and sustainable economic development, we could take a major step toward environmental security.[338]

Sustainable development is the goal (to get a detailed understanding of "sustainable development," read *Grave Influence*) in advocating these left-wing causes:

> Abortion on demand
> Population control
> Gun control
> Social justice
> Global governance
> The New World Order
> Socialized medicine
> Social welfare programs
> Elimination of property rights
> Elimination of national sovereignty
> Elimination of parental authority
> Elimination of free-market capitalism
> Education to serve the masses
> Public housing
> Redistribution of wealth
> Legal positivism and judicial activism
> Hate-crime laws that criminalize Christianity

A key milestone in the sustainable development movement, the 1992 United Nations Earth Summit in Rio de Janeiro, unveiled *Agenda 21*. The nearly 400–page document details how sustainable development is to be implemented in every country of the world. Its proponents admit that sustainable development is the framework for global governance.

And still more, the "Mission to Washington" declaration also calls for:

> ...phasing out all significant ozone-depleting chemicals, in halting deforestation and slowing the decline in species diversity, in planting forests and restoring other habitats and in realizing worldwide social justice. We believe there is a need for concerted efforts to stabilize world population by humane, responsible and voluntary means consistent with our differing values. For these and other reasons, we believe that special attention must be paid to education and to enhancing the roles and the status of women.[339]

Worldwide social justice is another term for global socialism. Stabilizing world population for the environmental globalists means abortion on demand, population control, eugenics, and active euthanasia through socialized medicine that allows for rationing of healthcare. In order for these radical ideas to be implemented, the state needs to target the educational system with social justice curriculum—also known as environmental justice.

I wonder how many members of America's Southern Baptist churches know that their association is tied to such an anti-biblical agenda. And what is it called when the enemy moves inside the camp unnoticed? Trojan horse again!

The roots of this involvement are deeper than you might imagine. A 1992 article in the *Directory of Environmental Activities and Resources in the North American Religious Community,* prepared by an SBC office, listed Richard Land as the contact person. The report was a project of "The Joint Appeal by Religion and Science for the Environment." The inside cover of the report noted that "support for the work of the Joint Appeal has also come from...The William and Flora Hewlett Foundation...Mr. Steven C. Rockefeller, The Rockefeller Brothers Fund... The Tides Foundation." These are troublesome bedfellows for Bible-believing Southern Baptists.

Steven Rockefeller assisted in writing the "Earth Charter," a document now elevated as the New Ten Commandments and brought to the United Nations in the Ark of Hope. The ark is a replica of the Ark of the Covenant adorned with New Age, environmental, and ecumenical artwork.

The Tides Foundation is another wolf-in-sheep's-clothing organization. Discover the Network reveals this about it:

> Established in 1976 by California-based activist Drummond Pike.... Among the crusades to which Tides contributes are: radical environmentalism; the "exclusion of humans from public and private wildlands"; the anti-war movement; anti-free trade campaigns; the banning of firearms ownership; abolition of the death penalty; access to government-funded abortion-on-demand; and radical gay, lesbian, bisexual, and transgender advocacy. The Foundation is also a member organization of the International Human Rights Funders Group, a network of more than six-dozen grantmakers dedicated to financing leftwing groups and causes.[340]

And then there's the National Religious Partnership for the Environment. Discover the Network reveals the following about this progressive group:

> Laying its junk science aside, the National Religious Partnership for the Environment renders two invaluable services to the political left. These partisan clerics intone the proof-texts of the Green movement in the language of brimstone and redemption, conferring an air of sanctity to the left's agenda.[341]

I'm thankful the SBC church I attend has a senior pastor who is equally disgusted by these alignments and has had the courage to call out Richard Land by name in a sermon broadcast on the radio. Because the SBC allows some of its leaders to be involved in such ecumenical and unbiblical endeavors, I personally give only to my church in ways that are guaranteed not to benefit the SBC headquarters. Whether an SBC church or not, I have urged my radio listeners to consider giving only to their local church in a way that assures the funds stay under the control of their church, instead of to a denominational headquarters that may be participating in questionable activities.

I have also explained on my radio program that almost every denomination in America is involved in some sort of unbiblical political correctness or doctrinal compromise, and I am not talking about just mainline churches (it is a given that they are now completely apostate). I am referring to such "evangelical" churches as the Southern Baptist Convention, Evangelical Free Churches of America, Assemblies of God, Church of the Nazarene, and Christian and Missionary Alliance, to name just a few.

The SBC-authored article in *A Directory of Environmental Activities and Resources in the North American Religious Community* boasted that the Southern Baptist Convention's Christian Life Commission hosted an environmental conference that "offered participants guidance in starting recycling programs at their own churches." The article also lauded the SBC for producing a brochure on "the need for...social justice in making energy choices."[342]

There were far more important issues facing the church in 1992 (as there are today) than to waste time and resources teaching churches how to start a recycling program. Perhaps when and if the church in America actually learns how to biblically evangelize the lost and how to train students and adults in a comprehensive biblical worldview, then we can talk about recycling. Besides, studies have shown that recycling can be a waste of money and actually produce dangerous byproducts:

> "People in New York and other places are tilting at recycling windmills," says Porter, who left the E.P.A. in 1989 and is now president of a consulting firm, the Waste Policy Center in Leesburg, Va. "There aren't many more materials in garbage that are worth recycling." Porter has been advising cities and states to abandon their unrealistic goals, but politicians are terrified of coming out against recycling. How could they explain it to the voters? How could they explain it to their children?[343]

A detailed report in the *New York Times*, written by John Tierney and entitled "Recycling Is Garbage," revealed that "recycling newsprint actually creates more water pollution than making new paper: for each ton of recycled newsprint that's produced, an extra 5,000 gallons of waste water are discharged."[344]

An article in the *Bismarck Tribune* summed up the lengthy *Times* article this way:

> Few people know that almost all the virgin pulp that goes into making paper is produced on tree farms that wouldn't exist if we didn't use these trees to make paper. Secondly, it's a fact that we have three times more trees than we did in 1920. Recycling paper is a manufacturing process that can save landfill space but produces a harmful chemical sludge that must be disposed of properly. It would be safer to allow these products to biodegrade naturally.
>
> According to the New York Department of Sanitation, it costs $50 to $60 a ton to pick up the regular garbage and take it to a landfill. It then costs $150 a ton to deal with the recyclables, and at least 40 percent of what is separated to be recycled ends up in the same landfill as the regular trash anyway.[345]

Rather than being preoccupied with recycling, church and denominational leaders would be wiser to worry about the huge number of their students who walk away from the faith before and after high school graduation. It is precisely because parents and church leaders have not addressed from a biblical perspective issues such as radical environmentalism and the rise of earth worship that so many churched youth buy into philosophies that are not truly Christian. Colossians 2:8 warns of this:

> Beware lest anyone cheat you through philosophy and empty deceit, according to the tradition of men, according to the basic principles of the world, and not according to Christ.

God's Global Warming

Christian parents need to make sure they explain from the Bible that manmade global warming is *not* going to destroy the earth. God-made global warming *will*—but it won't be gradual. That may come as a surprise to you, but 2 Peter 3:7 clearly states that God is going to preserve the earth until He judges it with *fire*: "But the heavens and the earth *which* are now preserved by the same word, are reserved for fire until the day of judgment and perdition of ungodly men."

As Christians, we should take what is common to the culture and turn it into a pulpit. Christians should look for opportunities to steer conversations from the natural into the spiritual realm. The topic of global warming provides just that kind of opportunity. Explain to your unsaved friends that God is a just God Who must judge sin, and one day He will judge each individual who has ever lived. Those who have placed their faith and trust in Jesus Christ and repented of their sins will pass from judgment into life.

We now live in a sinful and fallen world, but when God created the world and placed Adam and Eve in the Garden of Eden, it was perfect. God Himself said it was "good" (Genesis 1:31). However, because of one man, Adam, sin entered the world, and the consequences are that the world is going from a state of order to a state of disorder. In Isaiah 51:6, the Bible says the earth will grow old and worn out like an old shirt:

> Lift up your eyes to the heavens,
> And look on the earth beneath.
> For the heavens will vanish away like smoke,
> The earth will grow old like a garment,
> And those who dwell in it will die in like manner;
> But My salvation will be forever,
> And My righteousness will not be abolished.

Sin wears down the earth and our bodies. Because of sin, death, disease, and dying entered the world. Genesis 3:17–19 recounts the consequences that God explained to Adam and Eve because of their sin:

> Then to Adam He said, "Because you have heeded the voice of your wife, and have eaten from the tree of which I commanded you, saying, 'You shall not eat of it':
>
> "Cursed *is* the ground for your sake; In toil you shall eat *of* it All the days of your life. Both thorns and

thistles it shall bring forth for you, And you shall eat the herb of the field. In the sweat of your face you shall eat bread Till you return to the ground, For out of it you were taken; For dust you *are*, And to dust you shall return."

The Myth of Manmade Global Warning

Global warming is a hot issue (so to speak), not because it's a real problem, but because many would like to scare you into thinking it is. Consider this report:

> Mayor Bloomberg yesterday compared the scourge of global warming to the threat of terrorism and the proliferation of weapons of mass destruction. Although it is a "long-term" fight, he said, reducing gas emissions may save the life of "everybody" on the planet, the same way that fighting terrorism and its proliferation saves lives in shorter terms.[346]

The New York mayor believes this even though more than 10,000 scientists don't. For example, Michael Griffin, head of NASA, has said he does not see global warming as a threat.[347]

Global warming proponents base their belief on the alleged fact that temperatures are rising. But are they? Here are the facts:

- Professor Bob Carter, a geologist at James Cook University, Queensland, Australia, says the global warming theory is neither environmental nor scientific, but rather, "a self-created political fiasco." Carter explains that "climate changes occur naturally all the time, partly in predictable cycles and partly in unpredictable cycles."[348]

- According to Robert Essenhigh, professor of energy conservation at Ohio State University, the ice sheets at the poles have been melting since the early 1900s, and the earth's warming had begun about the middle 1600s.[349]

Some studies show that the earth's temperature has risen, and others indicate it has fallen. Why can't experts agree on the temperature? For starters, the earth's temperatures are taken in two different ways, and one method is not as reliable as the other. Dr. S. Fred Singer, an atmospheric physicist at George Mason University explains:

> You have to be very careful with the surface record. It is taken with thermometers that are mostly located in or near cities. And as cities expand, they get warmer. And therefore they affect the readings. And it's very difficult to eliminate this—what's called the urban heat island effect. So I personally prefer to trust in weather satellites.... And if you look through the summary [of the United Nations Intergovernmental Panel on Climate Change (IPCC)], you will find no mention of the fact that the weather satellite observations of the last twenty years show no global warming. In fact, a slight cooling. In fact, you will not even find satellites mentioned in the summary. These are the only global observations we have. They are the best observations we have. They cover the whole globe. They don't cover the oceans very well, which is 70% of the globe. So you see, the [U.N.] summary uses data selectively, or at least it suppresses data that are inconvenient, that disagree with the paradigm, with what they're trying to prove.[350]

But regardless of temperature issues, we know the rise in sea level threatens much of civilization, don't we? That would be "No." In the April 16, 2007, issue of *Newsweek International*, Richard S. Lindzen of the Massachusetts Institute of Technology, wrote "Why So Gloomy" in which he pointed out that:

> the ill effects of warming are overblown. Sea levels, for example, have been increasing since the end of the last ice age. When you look at recent centuries in perspective, ignoring short-term fluctuations, the rate of sea-level rise has been relatively uniform (less than a couple of millimeters a year). There's even some evidence that the rate was higher in the first half of the twentieth century than in the second half. Overall, the

risk of sea-level rise from global warming is less at almost any given location than that from other causes, such as tectonic motions of the earth's surface. There is no compelling evidence that the warming trend we've seen will amount to anything close to catastrophe.[351]

Not exactly a compelling reason to start building another ark.

If you're beginning to get the idea that manmade global warming as we know it is a myth, congratulations. But have you stopped to wonder who's behind all this myth-mongering? There are three primary players:

1. *Cosmic Humanists* (*New Agers*). These folks believe in pantheism, that all is god and god is all and that mother earth should be worshipped. Radical environmentalists and animal rights extremists—many of whom come from this group—place more value on the earth and animals than on humans.

2. *Globalists and socialists.* Globalists—many of whom haunt the United Nations—intend to erode America's national sovereignty and create a one-world government. The United Nations' Global Warming treaty—the Kyoto Protocol—would seriously damage America's free enterprise system, and yet it does not even apply to some of the world's biggest polluters, such as China and India.

3. *Scientists and think-tanks.* You've heard the old saying "follow the money"? When you follow the trail behind the global warming myth, it leads you to "scientists" who are willing to say anything to keep government grant money flowing their way. Some studies place U.S. government spending on climate change as high as $4 billion a year. Tom DeWeese, president of the American Policy Center, explains how this works:

> Simply put, scientists know where the grants will come from to pay their salaries. Dr. Patrick Michaels, a leading opponent to the global warming scaremongers, calls it the federal/science paradigm. He describes it this way: Tax $ = Grants = Positive Feedback Loop to Get more Grants.
>
> Says Dr. Michaels, "What worker bee scientist is going to write a proposal saying that global warming is

exaggerated and he doesn't need the money? Certainly no one wanting advancement in the agency! There is no alternative to this process when paradigms compete with each other for finite funding." The only ones who can openly oppose the party line of the day are those who don't need the grants or who have some other source of funding. There aren't many.[352]

DeWeese goes on to detail why there is so much money in the global-warming racket:

> The money is in global warming because it's being pushed by a political agenda that wants power. They want power in Washington, power on the international stage, power over economic development, power over international monetary decisions, and power over energy. In short, power over the motor of the world. It's driven by literally thousands of large and small non-governmental organizations (NGOs) sanctioned by the United Nations, and implemented by a horde of bureaucrats, university academics and an ignorant but pliable news media.[353]

The GW crowd has told us that manmade carbon dioxide is the reason for the supposed rise in global temperatures. However, Robert Essenhigh, professor of energy conservation at Ohio State University, gives the lie to their claim:

> The two principled thermal-absorbing and thermal-emitting compounds in the atmosphere are water and carbon dioxide. However—and this point is continually missed—the ratio of water to carbon dioxide is something like 30–to-1 as an average value. At the top it is something like 100–to-1. This means that the carbon dioxide is simply 'noise' in the water concentration, and anything carbon dioxide could do, water has already done. So, if the carbon dioxide is increasing, is it the carbon dioxide driving the temperature or is the rising temperature driving up the carbon dioxide? In

other words, *the carbon dioxide issue is irrelevant to the debate over global warming.*[354] (Emphasis mine.)

As I've pointed out, the temperature of the earth goes up and down in cycles. And the cause of the up-cycle is the sun. Perhaps we need legislation to control our solar neighbor in the sky? You might note, too, that—according to *Access to Energy*—Mars, Jupiter, and Pluto are also warming up. It's doubtful U.S. companies have caused that.

Dr. Sallie Baliunas, an astrophysicist who serves as senior scientist at the George C. Marshall Institute in Washington, D.C., and who chairs the Institute's Science Advisory Board, gave a lecture on February 12, 2008, at the University of Texas entitled, "Warming Up to the Truth: The Real Story about Climate Change." Dr. Baliunas believes the warming and cooling of the earth is more related to solar variability than it is carbon dioxide in the atmosphere. In other words, the increase and decrease in *solar output* has led to the cyclical warming and cooling of the earth.[355]

So if you think the variation of temperature by a degree or two in one way or another is worthy of destroying America, free enterprise, and our national sovereignty, then hop on the band wagon. Otherwise, keep your cool, and don't move your membership to the Watermelon Church.

CHAPTER 8

Compromising the Gospel
for the Sake of Liberty

I have repeatedly noted that Satan is the ultimate conspirator be-hind much compromise in the Church. Clearly, a Hegelian dialectic process has been set up. President Obama and his administration scared many self-professing Christians right into the arms of Glenn Beck, the Church of Rome, and ecumenicalism. Many evangelicals be-lieve this is acceptable in order to make sure our freedoms are secured and that America doesn't fall into tyranny.

Yet governmental tyranny is not the worst that could befall us. God has used oppression many times to call a people back to Himself. In fact, I so much want my kids (and yours!) to come to know Christ as their personal Lord and Savior that if it takes tyranny to do that, as has happened with various revivals and in the church in Cuba or China, then fine. Bring it on.

I believe our country's political Christian activism and the ec-umenicalism it entails has become another of Satan's tools. In the summer of 2012, for example, the Family Research Council pro-moted an event entitled "Two Weeks of Freedom, Catholics and Evangelicals Together for Freedom." The event website boasted that "Christians from across denominational lines join together for a special newscast program that will mark the beginning of a two week period of nationwide prayer and action in support of religious liberty."[356] Self-professing evangelicals were involved as well as Catholics and, in particular, Catholic priest Frank Pavone. But this is not a wholly new concept. In 1994, Chuck Colson was among those who promoted the document "Evangelicals and Catholics Together," declaring that Catholics and evangelicals are both Christian groups, and thus, evangelicals need to stop trying to convert Catholics.

Today, it appears to me that Satan's strategy of using political ac-tivism and the fear of losing freedoms is working. More and more self-professing Christians compromise biblical admonishments to the contrary and declare Catholics as Christians. John MacArthur has a great deal to say about this problem. On June 20, 2012, he was a guest on my radio program, and when I asked about his concern over this, he replied:

> Well, I agree with you 100 percent. That's a really astute observation. I think Obama or whoever brings about the dramatic alteration in the America that we've known in the past, is a force chasing people into the arms of Rome, into the arms of the Mormon Church. There's no question. You're absolutely correct about that. We don't have enough sense to get it. We don't know when we're being suckered, again because of the abysmal lack of discernment.
>
> You know, when I was involved with that evangelicals and Catholics together, that wasn't hard for me. That wasn't some kind of challenge to my understanding of the Word of God to embrace or not embrace Catholics. Catholics aren't Christians. Unless they don't believe what the Catholic Church teaches. They believe in salvation by works. A combination of grace and works. That is a damning belief.
>
> The Roman Catholic system is a false church. It hasn't changed. It has always been a false church. It continues to be a false church. There is no fellowship between light and darkness. There's no concord between Christ and Belial. It is ludicrous to have a prayer meeting with Roman Catholics and to assume that they are communicating with God when the fact is they are not communicating with God. Their prayers are not heard by God. That's kind of a sad thing about being Roman Catholic. The saints don't hear their prayers because no saint hears anybody's prayers. And God doesn't hear their prayers because they have no access to Him, which comes only through faith in Jesus Christ, and by grace.

So they don't pray to anybody other than, as the Scripture says, the things that the gentiles offered. They offered to demons. They sacrificed to demons. So a false form of religion.

But again, Brannon, we come back to this same issue. The church is so ignorant and so indifferent towards sound doctrine that it is really shocking. Before that series we did with John Ankerberg, we had just had a seven-hour meeting locked up in a room in Kennedy's church, and it was with Bill Bright and Jim Packer, J. I. Packer, and myself, and R.C. Sproul, and Chuck Colson.

And you know, we were talking about whether evangelicals and Catholics could get together based upon a common salvation. And it was maybe the seven most interesting hours of my life, because we kept saying, R. C. Sproul and I, we kept saying this is about whether you are saved or not. And we couldn't even get that point across. That they have a false form of salvation.

One of the things that came out of that was a crazy statement that what we decide in this room is going to determine whether millions of people are going to go to heaven or not. Well, we almost fell off our chairs when that statement was made, as if by some decision we made in a room, somebody's eternal destiny was determined. But that's how strange the thinking was there.

But again, Rome always wants to be accepted. The false church wants to be seen as the true church. We need to run from Christianity and all its false forms, and any kind of an alliance with those false forms betrays our calling, betrays our Lord, and gives the illusion to the lost that they're saved. And that is a tragic thing to convey. [357]

Partners with Mormons Too?

On March 31, 2011, I received a letter from a well-known evangelical leader, rebuking me for a stand I had taken in opposition to several other influential Christians. In what I believe was an appropriately loving and Christ-honoring way, I had pointed out that men such as David Barton, Jim Garlow, John Hagee, and James Robison should not be speaking at conferences associated with members of the New Apostolic Reformation. Neither should they be partnering with New Age Mormon Glenn Beck in any spiritual or Body of Christ undertaking. Yet they were doing just that. This is not a gray issue. The Bible is completely clear about partnering with false teachers in spiritual enterprises.

Despite confirmation that he had received my response to his letter, I never received any further feedback from him, although I had requested it. I (as well as some of his friends) believe the reason is that he could not refute the clear scriptural and doctrinal case as to why it violates Scripture to unite with false teachers in a spiritual enterprise. In Acts 20:28–31, for instance, Paul warned elders from the church in Ephesus:

> Therefore take heed to yourselves and to all the flock, among which the Holy Spirit has made you overseers, to shepherd the church of God which He purchased with His own blood. For I know this, that after my departure savage wolves will come in among you, not sparing the flock. Also from among yourselves men will rise up, speaking perverse things, to draw away the disciples after themselves. Therefore watch, and remember that for three years I did not cease to warn everyone night and day with tears.

The American Church has entered into what is likely the most dangerous time ever in our nation's spiritual history, and I will continue to plead with Christians to join me in warning the Church about the great threat we face. Many think they are upholding American values, but Christians who partner with false teachers and think they are defending liberty for the sake of the Gospel are actually doing the opposite. They're compromising the Gospel for the sake of liberty. The imminent and most serious threat to the Church in America is coming from a religious Trojan horse rather than from the government.

The stakes are high, which makes the issue for which I was "called to task" all the more urgent. I appreciate the fact that the gentleman who sent me the email chose not to blast me publicly. Therefore, it would not be right to name him. Besides, I want to keep the focus of this issue on biblical principles and not on personalities. My goal in sharing my interchange with him is to make you aware of the issues to which the Church in America needs to awaken. Our first calling is to preach the Gospel.

Bear in mind that I recognize I am not immune to this difficult problem. A few years ago, I had to repent for being guilty of Americanism, for having a greater commitment to liberty and freedom than I did to proclaiming the Gospel and making disciples of Jesus Christ. I pray this book causes you to repent of the same sin, if necessary. So, for the cause of keeping the Church on track in its primary mission, I share below the email challenging my stance, followed by my response.

Dear Brannon,

I have watched him [Glenn Beck] carefully for years, and while he doesn't do things and say things the way you and I would, remember he is not a preacher. But he does say more gospel at times (and a few way out things) that many gospel preachers don't even say in their churches or on TV or radio. And in my judgment, he is the best thing that has happened to TV in my lifetime. Not because I agree with everything he says, but like others on Fox, right now they are doing more to promote getting America back to the basic Christian values this nation was founded on than anyone in my lifetime. Certainly more than the five prominent secular networks.

When I heard Dr. Francis Schaffer say part of the reason we were losing our country to the secular socialists was because the church bought into the pietistic philosophy that "politics was a dirty business, we Christians should never get involved in politics but leave that to the nice civic-minded people while we preach the gospel." He condemned that idea and said to save our nation and its unique religious freedom principles we should get heavily involved in educating Christians and others who share our moral values, getting them registered and out to vote on Election Day. That it is no compromise when working with people of other faiths as "cobelligerents" (his term), people we could not work with in the spreading of the Gospel but as fellow citizens we can work with them to save the country.

...I took this to heart...to save religious freedom for the preaching of the gospel and the freedom to teach our own children by activating Americans who share our concern for returning this country through the ballot box to the traditional values of our basically Christian Founding Fathers and adherence to our U.S. Constitution. I can assure you, when the time comes to oppose a religious union (like the Harlot of Babylon in Revelation) of people regardless what they think about Jesus Christ and His Word, Pastor Jim Garlow and I will be right there with you.

God bless you my friend,

Here is a portion of my response:

You know my great respect for you, so I appreciate your emailing me today with your concerns and for the opportunity to explain the biblical reasons for my recent radio programs.

Today, I play audio clips of Cindy Jacobs speaking of having Jim Garlow and David Barton with her at a conference. Websites report that Jim was actually at her 2009 and 2010 Convergence Conference. Cindy Jacobs is part of the New Apostolic Reformation and sees herself as a prophet. C. Peter Wagner years ago wrote that she is "the U.S. national apostle." I also play clips of Jim on the platform with Lou Engle. Lou, according to his website, is with the International House of Prayer. The New Apostolic Reformation movement believes in extra-biblical revelation, prophets, apostles, and a host of other heresies.

The mixing of evangelicals with false prophets for the sake of the culture war is really an offense to the Gospel. God is not dependent on us to violate biblical principles in order to be successful at restoring righteousness. How can we restore righteousness through an unrighteous manner? How can we hope to restore biblical principles within government when we have willingly violated biblical principles within the Church? The end does not justify the means.

The culture war is really the byproduct of a spiritual battle and the spiritual condition of America. The Church cannot confront the cultural and spiritual problems by compromising on biblical and spiritual issues.

God is watching, and I contend that our efforts are being thwarted by God as Divine judgment for setting aside Scriptural warnings and uniting with false teachers in spiritual enterprises intertwined with our Christian activism. If biblically sound Christians stand together for righteousness in the public square and yet we lose, we still win because we were able to lift up the Gospel in our godly efforts. However, if Christians compromise the Gospel and unite with false teachers in spiritual and political enterprises, regardless of the political outcome, we will have lost because we gave credibility to false teachers and their false gospel. I believe this is Satan's strategy. Satan has moved his false teachers into our camp as a religious Trojan horse, and Christian leaders have embraced the Trojan horse of false teachers.

Our willingness to lose our liberty and freedom—and to even be enslaved before we compromise the Gospel—is how we can win, and win for eternity. Such reckless abandonment for Christ is what God can choose to bless. I guarantee you that God is not going to bless with greater freedom and liberty an American Church and its leaders that are embracing religious syncretism, compromise, and apostasy.

Christians uniting with the NAR crowd and false teachers not only keeps God from blessing our efforts, but it damages our testimony to the unsaved world that is watching. I have been reading numerous secular websites over the past few days, and many of the unsaved are openly writing that they cannot believe that evangelicals are uniting with what even they know are false teachers. How sad that the unsaved world is stunned by our compromise.

You speak of being co-belligerents with unbelievers on social issues. However, this is not working with unbelievers on fighting abortion, same-sex marriage, or even defending marriage between one man and one woman. Christian leaders joining Glenn Beck in what Beck referred to as uniting all faiths and looking to one God is not being a co-belligerent on political or civic issues. This is deliberately joining in spiritual enterprises with unbelievers and false teachers.

Liberty University through Awakening 2010 had Cindy Jacobs and Rick Joyner with them. This is becoming a real problem, and we are watching evangelicals give credibility to what I believe is the formation of the false church. Can you imagine what Vance Havner, Donald Barnhouse, and J. Vernon McGee would say to this? They would be on my program shouting "Amen."

Second John 9–11 speaks of not greeting or inviting into your house one that does not bring the essential Christian doctrines lest you partake in their evil deeds. The NAR crowd is all about pushing a false Jesus, a false gospel and an unclean spirit. This issue is also addressed in 2 Corinthians 6:14, where we are told not to be unequally yoked with unbelievers. I believe the fruit of the doctrine of some of the NAR leaders reveals they are false converts, false prophets, and thus false brethren. This is so black and white. I am stunned that I must make this case to you.

The late Vance Havner was correct when he declared: "The devil is not fighting religion; he is too smart for that. He is producing a counterfeit Christianity so much like the real one that good Christians are afraid to speak out against it."

I pray that America's Christians and pastors will understand that there is an unbiblical and dangerous spiritual convergence taking place throughout the nation and the world, and today is the day to choose whether you will uncompromisingly stand for the living God or give credibility to pagan spirituality.

In 1 Kings 18:20–21 Elijah declared to the Children of Israel, who were seeking to follow God while also mixing their worship of God with pagan spirituality, that they must choose to whom they would pledge their allegiance. Elijah asked the Israelites "How long will you falter between two opinions? If the Lord is God, follow Him; but if Baal, follow him."

Yes, I would like to see the progressives/socialists, collectivists/Fabians/Communists defeated and the original intent of America's founding fathers restored, but that certainly will not happen if the true Bride of Christ compromises on biblical truth. This is no time to be committed to pragmatism, because the end does not justify the means. The means simply declare our priorities—and reveal in whom (or what) we really trust and serve.

Now we see the Religious Right, the GOP, Glenn Beck, the NAR, the Tea Party, and the dominion theology crowd converging for the sake of political spoils.

Christians that partner with false teachers in spiritual enterprises and think they are defending liberty for the sake of the Gospel are actually compromising the Gospel for the sake of liberty.

America needs men like William Tyndale and John Wycliffe that have the courage to speak the truth even if it is not popular with the religious leaders of the day. Spurgeon said "to pursue unity at the expense of truth is treason to Jesus."

The prophecy "expert" confirmed by email that he received my return letter but otherwise never replied. As one of his friends said to me, "How could he respond when you laid it out from the Scriptures as you did?"

An Amazon search also reveals that Jim Garlow wrote a chapter in *The Reformer's Pledge*. The book's contributors include New Apostolic Reformation proponents Bill Johnson, Lance Wallnau, Chuck Pierce, C. Peter Wagner, John Arnott, Cindy Jacobs, James W. Goll, and Lou Engle.

Because of this historic realignment among some evangelical leaders to lock arms with "all faiths" for political gain, I am going to use the rest of this chapter to detail chronologically how this seismic shift occurred and how my warnings and those of other talk-show hosts and columnists have gone unheeded.

Divine Destiny or God's Word?

Would you approve or disapprove if some of America's evangelical pastors and religious leaders announced they were going to show up at "Oprah's Divine Destiny" meeting at the Kennedy Center for an evening that would include uplifting music and nationally known religious figures from all faiths as they unite in prayer and recite historical speeches? Would it concern you if you knew that on her radio program Oprah has taught the book *A Course in Miracles* written by Helen Schucman? This book and the associated workbook include such quotes as:

"A slain Christ has no meaning."

"The recognition of God is the recognition of yourself."

"Do not make the pathetic error of 'clinging to the old rugged cross.'"

"My salvation comes from me."[358]

Bible-believing Christians would not approve of evangelical pastors and leaders uniting with Oprah in a self-described religious and spiritual meeting. Why? Because most biblically thinking Christians do not agree with Oprah's liberal politics, and they know that God's Word and Oprah's pagan spirituality do not mix.

Strangely, many of these same Christians have no problem when some of America's evangelical pastors join Glenn Beck for a spiritual program. Unlike Oprah, they reason, they share Beck's conservative political views. To many it makes no difference that Beck is a Mormon. His agreeable political views trump his religious views, and for this reason many felt justified taking part in "Glenn Beck's Divine Destiny" August 27, 2010, program at the Kennedy Center.

"Be ye not unequally yoked together with unbelievers: for what fellowship hath righteousness with unrighteousness? And what communion hath light with darkness?" In verse 16, Paul further declares that Christians must be spiritually separate from nonbelievers.

"Glenn Beck's Divine Destiny" program was not a political gathering but "a unique spiritual event," as described by organizers. The operative word being "spiritual," biblical Christians should have stayed away.

While I do agree with some of Beck's conservative and constitutional views, that does not give me or any other Bible-believing Christian justification to compromise biblical truth by joining Beck in such an event. Beck's website clearly advertised that this was a one-world religion friendly event:

- "...nationally-known religious figures from all faiths will unite..."
- "The audience for the event will be overwhelmingly made up of pastors, ministers and clergy..."
- The event "will help heal your soul."[359]

The problem begins with Beck's Mormon faith. His definition of God the Father is not the same as that described by Jesus in the Bible.

Glenn articulates his willingness to bend points of doctrine for the sake of unification:

> I have been reaching out to the biggest names in faith for the last year.... I have met with the biggest leaders of faith in the country privately and I have asked them to help me put differences aside and to reach out with one another so we can remind people to get down on their knees for our brethren's shield in our dangerous hour.[360]

Christians who want to be committed to biblical truth cannot "put aside" the cross and Gospel of Jesus Christ nor the supremacy of Scripture by uniting with those who proclaim another Jesus, another gospel, and declare the cross foolishness. Many American Christians allow their commitment to reclaiming the country, reining in Congress, lowering taxes, and defeating progressives override their commitment to the biblical mandate declared in 2 Corinthians 6, as well as the mandate of 2 Corinthians 10:3–5, which commands Christians to expose every "high and lofty" thing lifted up against the principles of the Lord.

American Christians should not and cannot rate our success on whether or not we return our country and culture to political and social conservatism. Our success or failure must be based on whether or not we have been faithful servants of the one and only true God and have earnestly contended for the faith which was once for all delivered to the saints (Jude 3).

While Christians could join an unsaved national talk-show host or unsaved politician in opposing tyranny, socialism, cultural Marxism, and the like, we cannot join unbelievers in spiritual enterprises. We can be co-belligerents on many moral issues with non-Christians, but we cannot find common ground theologically, doctrinally, and spiritually. This is not according to me, but according to the Word of God. Christians must understand that the Jesus of the cults is not the Jesus of the Bible. Just because unsaved people talk about Jesus—on the radio, TV, or person-to-person—does not mean it is the Jesus of the Bible.

Several years ago, I supported Glenn Beck in the face of advertisers who threatened to withhold advertising as leverage against some of his political views. I launched the website www.keepglennbeck.com, but at the time Glenn was not promoting spirituality. He was simply providing excellent information about what was happening in the arena of civil government and law. However, when Glenn moved into proclaiming New Age Mormonism, I had to draw a clear line theologically, doctrinally, and spiritually. I hit the "unsupport" button.

Some Christians have argued from Mark 9:38–41 that partnering with Glenn Beck for a "unique spiritual event" is acceptable biblically even if Glenn Beck is not a Christian. They cite verse 40 in which Jesus says, "For he who is not against us is on our side." But Mark 9 is not addressing a non-Christian doing something good. It is clearly speaking of a true follower of Jesus Christ—in this case, one that was successful in casting out a demon.

If it is not acceptable for a biblically committed Christian to unite in a spiritual event with Oprah Winfrey, then it is not acceptable to unite with Glenn Beck or any other religious leaders who do not adhere to biblical orthodoxy. The religious beliefs of Oprah and the Mormons are not decidedly different. Ed Decker was a Mormon for 20 years of his adult life, a member of the Melchizedek priesthood, a Temple Mormon, and active in many Mormon Church positions before becoming a Christian. Out of his vast experience in Mormonism, he has revealed to me such facts as:

- Mormons believe the cross of Christ is foolishness, and thus you will not find a cross in or on top of a Mormon temple. Like Oprah, a Mormon could say, "Do not make the pathetic error of 'clinging to the old rugged cross.'"[361]

- Mormons believe the blood Jesus Christ shed on the cross is not what saves. As a result, Mormons will not use red wine or red juice for communion. They use water instead. Thus a Mormon could say, "A slain Christ has no meaning."[362]

- Mormons believe salvation is not found by placing your faith and trust in Jesus Christ alone but in good works. A Mormon could say, "My salvation comes from me."[363]

- Mormons believe God is one of many gods and that every good Mormon man can become a god himself. This belief is called the law of eternal progression and is best described in the popular Mormon saying, "As man is, God once was, and as God is, man may become." A Mormon could say, "The recognition of God is the recognition of yourself."[364]

Do these pastors and Christian leaders not understand that by appearing on stage at this "unique spiritual event" they were sending the message that biblical Christianity and Mormonism (and any other unbiblical worldview represented) can find spiritual common ground? This was a public relations victory not only for Mormonism but also for universalism.

According to the LDS General Authority and President of the Council of the Twelve, Ezra Taft Benson, LDS doctrine holds that the living prophet is above the Scripture.[365] After I wrote several articles and hosted radio and television programs on this topic, many Christians emailed me to say that Glenn Beck uses Christian terms, and so he must be a Christian. While it is true that Mormons, as well as New Agers, use many of the same terms Bible-believing Christians use, their definitions of terms are in direct opposition to biblical definitions.

I have also received emails from people who claim to have heard Glenn Beck give the Gospel on his television program. I've watched the program they cite, and on it, Glenn states that he had called Richard Land of the Southern Baptist Convention so Land could explain to Glenn the Gospel message according to evangelicals. Glenn's explicit purpose was to contrast it with the collective salvation of President Obama. Glenn provided the valid contrast but did not indicate that he had personally rejected Mormonism for the truth of the biblical Gospel. (Despite my aggressive opposition to what they stand for, I do urge all Christians to pray for Oprah Winfrey and Glenn Beck that they may truly come to know the Jesus Christ of the Bible as their personal Lord and Savior.)

Millions of Christian families are watching for someone who will have the discernment and courage to obey God and His Word in which He has clearly revealed His will for us concerning this matter. My heart grieves for the teenagers, college students, and spiritually immature Christians who are confused and led astray by the incessant co-mingling of spiritual worldviews. Pastors and Christian leaders should not be shocked to see that their endorsement of spiritually pluralistic events increases the already rising numbers of young people leaving evangelical churches to join the Mormon Church. Neither should they be surprised when discerning Christians are leery of their future work because of the betrayal of clear biblical instruction regarding these things.

Former Mormons understand the seriousness of this issue. Here, for example, is an email I received from one concerned convert:

> I was a tenured professor at Brigham Young University from 1999–2008, a dug-in Mormon for 30 years. Christ drew me and I went face down in surrender to the biblical Christ, now a strong Christian. As former Mormon leaders, my husband and I have been speaking to Christians about Glenn Beck for some time and are shocked at the resistance we hear from Christians who don't seem to understand the gravity of this false and slippery "christ" of Mormonism.

As long ago as 1898, Abraham Kuyper warned in the Stone Lectures at Princeton: "Do not forget that the fundamental contrast has always been, is still and always will be until the end; Christianity and Paganism, the idols and the living God."

I pray that America's Christians will understand there is an unbiblical and dangerous spiritual convergence taking place throughout the nation and the world. Today is the day to choose whether you will stand uncompromisingly for the living God or give credibility to pagan spirituality.

In 1 Kings 18:20–21, Elijah confronted the Children of Israel who were seeking to follow God while mixing their worship of God with pagan spirituality. He declared that they must choose to whom they would pledge their allegiance. "How long," Elijah challenged, "will you falter between two opinions? If the Lord is God, follow Him; but if Baal, follow him."

As Beck's August 2010 rally approached, I was encouraged that Dr. Erwin Lutzer of Moody Church, while a guest on my radio program, was willing to explain to our listeners, from the Scriptures, why pastors who stand with Beck at his rally would be involved in heresy. I was also thankful to receive a voice mail of support from Kirk Cameron. He had been asked to take part in Beck's Kennedy Center event, but after reading one of my articles in which I explained why Christians should not join Beck in a spiritual enterprise, Kirk declined the invitation. Kirk also was a guest on my national radio program and explained how he had come to his decision after much prayer and searching the Scriptures.

Sadly, Kirk's convictions apparently changed between August 2010 and March 2012 when he released the movie *Monumental*. Many believe the film is historically flawed, at best. Kirk's featured expert in the film is Marshall Foster, who by all accounts seems to believe in a form of Reconstructionism. The most troubling aspect of this development is that, despite my personal warnings to Kirk, he proceeded with the production, which even includes an appearance by David Barton, whose historical facts have been proven inaccurate by numerous scholars. (Barton also has claimed that New Age Mormon Glenn Beck is a Christian.)

A few weeks before the film's release, Kirk appeared in Dallas as a guest on Glenn Beck's television program. And when *Monumental* debuted live in some 500 movie theaters on March 27, 2012, the preshow commentary featured Kirk sitting in his home, visiting with Beck (who was in Dallas at the time) on a large-screen television in Cameron's living room. In the interview, Glenn talked about God, yet Kirk never distinguished the God of the Bible from the god of Mormonism. (Mormons teach god was a man of flesh and bone who evolved to become God.)

Engaging in spiritual conversation with a New Age Mormon can clearly be called unbiblical according to 2 John 9–11:

> Whoever transgresses and does not abide in the doctrine of Christ does not have God. He who abides in the doctrine of Christ has both the Father and the Son. If anyone comes to you and does not bring this doctrine, do not receive him into your house nor greet him; for he who greets him shares in his evil deeds.

One national talk-show host reported that, a day or two after the March 27 film debut, he had a lengthy phone conversation with Kirk in which he explained that what Kirk had done violated 2 John 9–11.

The talk show host reported that Kirk did not agree that he had done anything wrong. Although disappointed, I am not shocked, since Kirk has seemingly had no problem with hosting a program for Trinity Broadcasting Network several times over the years. TBN, of course, features almost exclusively false teachers.

The Mormon Church, the Constitution, America, and the Last Days

Understanding the end-time beliefs of the Mormon Church, its view of America, and its beliefs about the Constitution may help you understand the ultimate goal of Beck's "Divine Destiny" event. To give my radio listeners a grasp of the Mormon perspective on the United States, I played sound bites of a speech called "Our Divine Constitution," delivered on October 3, 1987, by Mormon president Ezra Taft Benson. I've recounted below selections from that broadcast with my comments noted on each.

> BENSON: *I reverence the Constitution of the United States as a sacred document. To me its words are akin to the revelations of God, for God has placed His stamp of approval upon it.*

> MY COMMENTARY: This claim is outright heresy. Deuteronomy 4:2 warns not to "add to the word which I commanded you, nor take from it." Proclaiming the Constitution is "akin to the revelation of God" is not only adding to the Bible but is also lowering the supremacy of the Word of God. If the Constitution is akin to the Word of God, why has it been changed so many times?

> BENSON: *I have faith that the Constitution will be saved as prophesied by Joseph Smith.... It will be saved by enlightened members of this church, among others, men and women who understand and abide by the principles of the Constitution.*

> MY COMMENTARY: Will the Mormon Church and other "enlightened" Mormons save America?

If America is to be saved, it will not be by the errant gospel and false Jesus of the Mormons following the principles of the Constitution that they have elevated to equality with the words of God. Second Chronicles 7:14 says that "If my people, which are called by my name, shall humble themselves, and pray, and seek my face, and turn from their wicked ways; then will I hear from heaven, and will forgive their sin, and will heal their land." Part of the wickedness from which America needs to repent is following the Jesus of the cults or the Jesus of Oprah's New Age movement. The very thing Mormons are doing—and many Christian Americans are following—will not reclaim America but will actually bring God's judgment.

BENSON: *Have we read* The Federalist Papers? *Are we reading the Constitution and pondering it? Are we aware of its principles? Are we abiding by these principles and teaching them to others? Could we defend the Constitution? Can we recognize when a law is constitutionally unsound? Do we know what the prophets have said about the Constitution and the threats to it?*

MY COMMENTARY: The cross is higher than the flag, and the Word of God is above the Constitution. If we really want to defend a Constitutional Republic, we must get back to the Word of God—not the Mormon Bible and related teachings on end-time beliefs and on building God's Kingdom on earth or the New Jerusalem in Independence, Missouri (yes, they really believe that).

BENSON: *We are fast approaching that moment prophesied by Joseph Smith when he said: "Even this nation will be on the very verge of crumbling to pieces and tumbling to the ground, and when the Constitution is upon the brink of ruin, this people will be the staff upon which the nation shall lean, and they shall bear the Constitution away from the very verge of destruction"* (19 July 1840, as recorded by Martha Jane Knowlton Coray; manuscript in church historian's office, Salt Lake City).

MY COMMENTARY: This "prophecy" by Joseph Smith is known as the "White Horse Prophecy." The Mormon Church, in recent years, has developed a public-relations problem on this issue and has backed away from this belief. However, all Mormons know of this prophecy by Joseph Smith and believe the Mormon Church and its "enlightened members of this Church" will restore America's honor. Sound familiar? Was this the goal of Glenn Beck's "Restoring America's Honor Rally"?

BENSON: *Only in this foreordained land, under its God-inspired Constitution and the resulting environment of freedom, was it possible to have established the restored church. It is our responsibility to see that this freedom is perpetuated so that the church may more easily flourish in the future. The Lord said, "Therefore, I, the Lord, justify you, and your brethren of my church, in befriending that law which is the constitutional law of the land."*

MY COMMENTARY: So in the end, the big push for returning to the founding principles of America is to support the flourishing of the Mormon Church. How many people are aware of this ultimate goal? How many Americans want to live in a Mormon theocracy? Before you say they are not for a theocracy, you had better read the "Law of Consecration" that Mormons swear to in the LDS temple ritual. Among other things, the officiator requires that Mormons swear to "consecrate yourselves, your time, talents, and everything with which the Lord has blessed you, or with which he may bless you, to the Church of Jesus Christ of Latter-day Saints, for the building up of the Kingdom of God on the earth and for the establishment of Zion."

> BENSON: *Our Father in Heaven planned the coming forth of the Founding Fathers and their form of government as the necessary great prologue leading to the restoration of the gospel. Recall what our Savior Jesus Christ said nearly two thousand years ago when He visited this promised land: "For it is wisdom in the Father that they should be established in this land, and be set up as a free people by the power of the Father, that these things might come forth" (3 Ne. 21:4). America, the land of liberty, was to be the Lord's latter-day base of operations for His restored church.*

> MY COMMENTARY: The god of the Mormons (who was once a man of flesh and bone) planned America so the gospel of the Mormon Church could be restored. The Mormon Church proclaims that Jesus visited the promised land, which they call America, but you will only find that in the Mormon Bible. Notice Taft is quoting from the Mormon Bible, which claims that Jesus declared America would become the "Lord's latter-day base of operations for His restored church."

If Glenn Beck had promoted his events as a way to learn more about the Constitution of the United States that is equal to the inspired Word of God, he would have had more difficulty attracting a conservative Christian market. Even so, I'm afraid many American Christians have precious little discernment, and even if Beck were to publicly position the Constitution as "akin to the revelations of God," many would still follow simply because they are so hungry for a conservative leader and so eager to reclaim lost liberty and freedom. I believe some self-professing Christians are ready to betray God's ordained Word in exchange for the promise of security and protection. This, though, will *guarantee* that we do not reclaim America and instead will insure that our destiny is divine judgment. Beck's "Divine Destiny" was nothing more than a divine deception in which many Christians and Christian leaders took part.

Beck's Biblical Bigots

On his August 27, 2010, radio program, Glenn Beck referenced a CNN article that quoted an article from my website in which I explained from Scripture why biblically obedient Christians cannot unite with Beck on spiritual issues. Beck commented that "looking to one God is the theme" of the 8–28 event, and referring to the CNN article said, "...so now the religious bigotry is there, too." Here is what CNN reported:

> Brannon Howse, a conservative writer and founder of Worldview Weekend, which organizes Christian conferences, criticized evangelical participation in that event in a column this week. "The Apostle Paul warns Christians against uniting with unbelievers in spiritual endeavors...," Howse wrote. "While I applaud and agree with many of Glenn Beck's conservative and constitutional views, that does not give me or any other Bible-believing Christian justification to compromise Biblical truth by spiritually joining Beck."[366]

I have said repeatedly that Glenn has the right to practice his religion, but it does not mean Bible-minded Christians are bigots if they do not unite with his religious worldview and spiritual agenda.

A Mormon Christian?

The same CNN piece about which Glenn Beck attacked me quoted Jim Garlow offering an "apology" for Beck's spiritual views:

> I have interviewed persons who have talked specifically with Glenn about his personal salvation—persons extremely well known in Christianity—and they have affirmed (using language evangelicals understand), "Glenn is saved," Garlow said in his memo, which was dated Wednesday. "He understands receiving Christ as Savior."[367]

On April 22, 2012, Garlow actually went so far as to have Glenn Beck speak at his church in San Diego for two services. Beck spoke, along with James Robison and Jay Richards. A Mormon, a Catholic, and two "evangelicals" walk into a church (it sounds like a joke, but it is anything but funny), stand up, and talk about spiritual issues, and yet those concerned about this clear violation of 2 John 9–11, Romans 16:17, and 2 Corinthians 6:14 are the ones considered extreme.

At one point in the meeting, Richards declared that "we have to work together as a unified body of Christ" and Robison can be heard saying, "Yep."[368] So Mormons, Catholics, and ecumenical "evangelicals" are going to make up the body of Christ or the Church? Hardly. A combination like that will make up the Harlot church of Revelation 17 but certainly not the New Testment church.

During the program, Beck announced, "I'm a Mormon; I am a proud member of the Church of Jesus Christ of Latter-Day Saints,"[369] and the audience sitting in the church applauded. Beck went on to say that Garlow and Robison were heroes of his "because they follow the God of Abraham, Isaac, and Jacob just as I do."[370] Mormons do not serve the God of the Bible but a man who evolved to become a god. Garlow never corrected or refuted what Beck said to the people sitting in his church that day, and as a result, I believe Garlow encouraged the belief that Christians and Mormons worship the same God.

Beck also declared:

> I have this theory, and this is just kinda the gospel according to Glenn...Thou shall not take the Lord thy God's name in vain. What's his name? It ain't God; it's I AM. So when you say, "I am worthless, I am incapable," you are taking his name in vain."[371]

The entire time Beck was spouting this New Age, Law of Attraction heresy, James Robison was saying, "That's right." Beck went on to say, "Use the power of I AM; recognize the power within each of us."[372]

Even though Pastor Garlow did not refute this New Age teaching, prominent "evangelical" leaders have emailed me to say how much they respect Jim Garlow and that I should not publicly critize this "man of God."

Some support Beck whenever they can. On the Christian TV program *Life Today*, for instance, David Barton (who told me in a phone conversation in August 2010 that he had helped organize Beck's Black Robe regiment for Beck's Restoring Honor Rally), declared:

> Here is a guy that was raised as a Catholic. He found Jesus in Alcoholics Anonymous when he really screwed up his life, and he's now going to a Mormon

church, but that doesn't say anything about his personal relationship with Jesus, and that's what people need to look at.[373]

The interviewer asked David Barton, "So you believe that he is a Christian in every sense of the word?" Barton replied, "I do."[374]

So a practicing Mormon can be a Christian even though he has said 80 percent of his faith revolves around the Mormon Temple?[375] Would Barton believe a "Christian" could also attend a Unitarian Church or an Islamic Mosque? The Bible is very clear that a true follower of Jesus Christ will break from false teaching. Yet even after Barton and Garlow announced their opinions concerning Beck's salvation, Beck continued to say things completely hostile to biblical doctrine, which clearly reveal him to be a New Age Mormon. Yet Barton and Garlow, despite my email exchanges with them, refuse to acknowledge that Beck is publicly proclaiming heresy.

On August 27, 2010, Glenn also made a telling comment to a group of evangelical pastors and leaders appearing on his national television program. "I am a Mormon," he stated clearly, as he has said many times before. I have friends that were once practicing Mormons, and every one of them reports that the first thing they did when they placed their faith and trust in the Jesus of the Bible was to leave the Mormon Church. They recognized that the Jesus of the Mormon cult was not the Jesus of the Bible.

Beck continued on August 27, saying that, "The spirit is going to teach tomorrow, and you are going to feel things you have never felt before 8–28 rally." I would ask, "What spirit?" since Glenn is a Mormon who has said, "Looking to one God is the theme." It clearly was not the Holy Spirit of the Bible, because God's Spirit cannot teach that which is unbiblical.

What makes Beck's popularity so dangerous is that many Christians know so little about the Jesus of the cults; they do not realize the cults use the same terms as evangelicals but with completely different meanings. A pastor from Pennsylvania called my radio program a few days before Beck's 8–28 rally and described how he was grieved that his own son-in-law had organized a bus load to attend the event. This pastor said when he spoke to his son-in-law about this biblical perspective on attending, his son-in-law laughed. These are the perilous times 1 Timothy 3 tells us about—times that will even cause division in families.

Social Justice and an Earthly Kingdom

As I watched the Glenn Beck 8–28 rally, "red flags" popped up nonstop. The Mormon theology wrapped in Christian terms, combined with Christian speakers, made me very uncomfortable. The patriotic ecumenicalism was grossly unbiblical. The dominion theology affirmed by some Christians, combined with the "Kingdom of God" theology of Mormonism, and all faiths united and wrapped in the flag demonstrated to me how easily a one-world religion and one-world leader could be accepted, even by people who call themselves Christians.

Beck's rallies furthered the acceptance of ecumenicalism among evangelicals as well as less conservative Christians. The pastors and Christian leaders standing behind Glenn Beck at the end of the rally with their arms locked together looked silly, not at all like Christian statesmen. I truly believe they sold out. Not one of them seems to realize how severely they compromised the true Gospel of Jesus Christ and damaged their own testimony. Not only that, they greatly accelerated the acceptance of pluralism and ecumenicalism.

Whether they know it or not, Christians who took part in these rallies have endorsed an overwhelmingly humanistic message, no matter how bathed in patriotic and Christian trappings it may have been. While a few speakers gave a genuinely biblical message, it was so diluted by the soup of unbiblical messages that their presence served only to give credibility to Beck in the minds of unbelievers and undiscerning Christians. The overall message was that "we must save ourselves" and that "man can make a difference." But the Bible says even our righteous deeds look like wickedness to God. It makes no difference that many of the speakers used the name of God over and over because, for most of them, it was not the God of the Bible but of their own making, just as surely as if they had crafted an idol with wood or wax.

A similar agenda is pressing in from other directions as well. While Beck pushes a *conservative, right-wing,* godless, man-centered, good works version of social justice, Jim Wallis promotes a *liberal, leftist,* man-centered, godless, good works version.[376] Social justice is simply a man-centered attempt to create heaven on earth. Both Wallis and Beck want a revolution in America. They both promote an earthly kingdom based on humanism and paganism mixed with their individual versions of social justice. The two reject the God of the Bible and salvation found only in Jesus Christ. In the end, Beck and Wallis are on the losing team Jesus describes in John 8:42–47:

> If God were your Father, you would love Me, for I proceeded forth and came from God. …You are of your father the devil, and the desires of your father you want to do. He was a murderer from the beginning, and does not stand in the truth, because there is no truth in him. When he speaks a lie, he speaks from his own resources, for he is a liar and the father of it. … He who is of God hears God's words; therefore you do not hear, because you are not of God.

Man serves either God or Satan, and every issue at its very foundation is theological and spiritual. Beck's spirituality, theology, and doctrine cannot be separated from his public policy. Through Mormonism, Beck is seeking to build a kingdom that biblically committed Christians must not take part in helping him build. Years ago, LDS president John Taylor boasted of the goal of building a Mormon kingdom on earth:

> Let us now notice our political positions in the world. What are we going to do? We are going to possess the earth…and reign over it for ever and ever. Now, ye Kings and Emperors help yourselves if you can. This is the truth and it may as well be told at this time as at any other. There's a good time coming, Saints, a good time coming.[377]

Former Mormon Ed Decker reveals that this Mormon "Kingdom of God" is based on a socialistic theocracy:

> Joseph Smith implemented a program called the United Order in the church…. It was a plan of sharing…everything in common, all properties and wealth turned over and owned by the church and dispersed by the Brethren to the people on an as-needed basis with a requirement for good stewardship or loss of use. It was later determined that it could only work when both the secular and ecclesiastic functions operated

under one authority.... An LDS prophet ruling over a theocratic government where eternal commandments like the United Order...would function within the "Kingdom of God."[378]

The Mormon view of the U.S. Constitution is that it is god-breathed by the Mormon god and that America's founding fathers were specially chosen to write the U.S. Constitution and found "America, the land of liberty...to be the Lord's latter-day base of operations for His restored [Mormon] church."[379]

God's Church is not so weak that we have to partner with the theocratic agenda of a cult in order to accomplish His will—if indeed it is God's will that we reclaim America. Based on biblical descriptions, I believe God is beginning to judge America because of our national rebellion, which includes pastors and "Christian" leaders compromising on the supremacy of Scripture for political and social gain.

Pastors at Beck's rally would have been better off if they were back at home studying their Bibles and preparing Sunday sermons that call for their congregations to reject the pagan spirituality and pluralism endorsed by their standing with Glenn Beck. A June 26, 2008, article in the *Denver Post* revealed that pagan spirituality is doubling in America every eighteen months—a rate that is sure to increase as "evangelical" leaders give it credibility.

I have personally heard testimonies of numerous people who have lost friends over their stance for biblical truth. Jesus warned in Matthew 10:34–35 that it would be this way:

> Do not think that I came to bring peace on earth. I did not come to bring peace but a sword. For I have come to set a man against his father, a daughter against her mother, and a daughter-in-law against her mother-in-law; and a man's enemies will be those of his own household.

Change Agents Set the Stage for Paganism and Ecumenicalism

Although I warned evangelical leaders about Glenn Beck's rallies, most laughed at me. Yet, Greg West in the Mormon *LDS Examiner* validated my pre-Beck rally warnings. I told them that partnering with

Beck in a spiritual enterprise would send the message that Mormons are Christians, and here's what West writes about what happened:

> As a Mormon, I have to consider an unintended message throughout Beck's work, which has culminated in this event. That message is: "Mormons are Christian believers." Despite nearly two centuries of misrepresentation and religious envy by sectarian Christianity, Beck has achieved the visibility, prominence, and has had the time day after day, week after week, to speak openly and truly about his core beliefs. Those statements of faith have disoriented and confused those who had previously believed the lies about Mormons.
>
> Jim Garlow, a popular and influential pastor who partnered with the Mormon faithful in California to defend traditional marriage, was quoted recently in *CNN's Belief Blog*, saying, "I have interviewed persons who have talked specifically with Glenn about his personal salvation—persons extremely well known in Christianity—and they have affirmed (using language evangelicals understand), 'Glenn is saved....' He understands receiving Christ as Savior."
>
> Hallelujah! The light bulb has been switched on after nearly two centuries! Every single member of the Church of Jesus Christ of Latter-day Saints believes that a person must be "born again" and receive Jesus Christ as his Savior and Redeemer. Our holy books teach that salvation comes only in and through the atonement of Christ and that there is no other way a person can be saved.... Glenn Beck's beliefs are mainstream Mormon beliefs. Joseph Smith, the Church's founder, was a Christian prophet. He was an apostolic witness of the resurrection of Jesus Christ.[380]

Notice that West points out that Beck's broadcasts about his faith have "disoriented and confused" people who thought Mormonism was not consistent with Christianity. However, Beck, with the help of America's Christian leaders, has now convinced them that Mormonism and Christianity are compatible.

Beck's August 2010 events represented a seismic shift within evangelicalism that will go unnoticed by most Christian leaders. Too many Christian leaders and pastors are deficient in understanding the ideas and philosophies that have, and continue to be, the force behind the rushing cultural stream. As a result, members of their own congregations hear no advanced warning of the spiritual undertow nor do they acquire the needed biblical knowledge to keep from being children, tossed to and fro and carried about with every wind of doctrine, by the trickery of men, in the cunning craftiness of deceitful plotting (see Ephesians 4:14).

The compromise by evangelical leaders and pastors of uniting with "all faiths" has laid the foundation for untold numbers of self-professing Christians to embrace pluralism and pagan spirituality. The Mormon Church is now rejoicing over the public-relations success these undiscerning evangelical leaders have handed them. These pastors should remind themselves of Luke 17:2: "It would be better for him if a millstone were hung around his neck, and he were thrown into the sea, than that he should offend one of these little ones."

The New Old News

Glenn Beck not only embraces the pagan spirituality of Mormonism but also cosmic humanism. Mormonism says man can *become* god, a New Age concept. In this regard, notice what Glenn Beck said on *Fox News Sunday* with Chris Wallace: "There's nothing that we can do that will solve the problems that we have and keep the peace unless we solve it through God, unless we solve it in being our highest self. Be your higher self."[381]

Beck used the phrase "higher self" three times in the Chris Wallace interview, and I assure you, no one talks that way unless he or she knows exactly what it means. One New Age website explains:

> There are many great words to describe Who or What your highest identity or self truly is. Below are just a few: Higher Self, I am Presence, I Am That I Am…Cosmic Consciousness, God, Christ, Holy Spirit. And the list goes on….[382]

Notice that "I AM that I AM" is another term here for "higher self." Picking up the terminology, Beck said, "I Am That I Am is the most powerful phrase in any language as it is the name of god, never use it in vain; use it to create who you want to be. I AM blank."[383]

I AM is a title that should be reserved for God alone. In Exodus 3:13, God told Moses that when the people of Israel ask for His name he was to tell them, "I AM WHO I AM." And He said, "Thus you shall say to the Children of Israel, 'I AM has sent me to you.'" In John 8:58 we read, "Jesus said to them, 'Most assuredly, I say to you, before Abraham was, I AM.'" Used any other way, I AM is blasphemy.

New Age thinking displaces God as the true I AM and replaces Him with people. In the pagan practice of what is called "the law of attraction," this is clearly implied. In her book *The Secret* (promoted by Oprah Winfrey), Rhonda Byrne writes:

> The law of attraction is the law of creation.... You create your life through your thoughts. (p. 15)

> There isn't a single thing that you cannot do with this knowledge. It doesn't matter who you are or where you are, The Secret can give you whatever you want. (p. xi)

> With this powerful knowledge, you can complete-ly change every circumstance and event in your entire life." (p. 17)

That people like Beck on the right and Oprah on the left are pro-claiming the "I AM" message is a sign that we are living in the last days. According to Jesus:

> And they asked Him, saying, "Master, but when shall these things be? and what sign will there be when these things shall come to pass?" And he said, "Take heed that ye be not deceived: for many will come in my name, saying, I am *Christ*; and the time draweth near; go ye not therefore after them." (Luke 21:7–8 KJV)

Former New Ager and now biblical Christian Ray Yungen points out:

Notice, "Christ" is italicized in verse 8, meaning that it was not in the original manuscript. The translators of the King James Bible probably thought it awkward that it said "Many shall come saying, I am." Probably for the sake of clarity and to be consistent with Matthew 24, the translators added the word "Christ."[384]

Did you catch that? Jesus referred to people who say they are God by using the title "I AM." It is a sign that we are living in the end times. We are also told to run away from the people who say "I AM," but many of our pastors and Christian leaders did not run *from* Glenn Beck but ran to *join him* in a spiritual service and enterprise.

Beck has made unbiblical pronouncements on a variety of points. On one program, for instance, he declared, "Hell is an eternity of regret, not being able to forgive yourself." Nowhere in the Bible do we see an instruction to "forgive yourself." That is impossible. Forgiveness comes through the work of Christ as explained in 2 Corinthians 5:15: "He died for all, that those who live should live no longer for themselves, but for Him who died for them and rose again." Verse 17 then describes what brings peace through repentance of sins and placing faith and trust in the Jesus of the Bible: "Therefore, if anyone is in Christ, he is a new creation; old things have passed away; behold, all things have become new." Grace and forgiveness is provided to those who repent, so there is no need to believe the lie that you can "forgive yourself" of sins.

Glenn Beck accomplished what neither Oprah Winfrey nor Shirley McClain could. He used his conservative veneer and doublespeak to co-opt leaders of the religious right. As a result, perhaps sooner rather than later, the world will wind up in massive economic, political, and spiritual chaos, and an anti-Christ will call for the religions of the world to unite and embrace his version of spirituality. He will declare that he is not fixated on politics but wants only to bring about peace, unity, faith, hope, charity, stability, freedom, and prosperity under the common god of all religions. This world leader will perform counterfeit miracles, signs, and wonders, and those who reject biblical truth will follow him (2 Thessalonians 2:9–12) and embrace his plan.

If I had told you ten years ago that a "conservative" radio and TV personality would have millions of viewers, talk about the spiritual battle being waged in America, be a self-confessed member of a cult, quote New Age phrases, call for Christians and conservatives to look to the "one god," seek to unite all faiths, and convince dozens of evangelical pastors and leaders to support him in a spiritual service, you would have said I was writing fiction. Does the fact that this has now happened help clarify the magnitude of the spiritual shift that has occurred through Glenn Beck's success? The millions who see nothing wrong with the messages of Beck's August 2010 events reveal that the religious left and the religious right will readily be merged into the coming one-world religion under the one-world spiritual leader as prophesied in Revelation 17:8.

Embracing Beck's Blasphemies

In following up his rallies, Glenn Beck shows further why America's Christian leaders should not have offered their credibility to Beck. On his September 2, 2010, television program he claimed:

> America's religion. This is it gang; this is all you need to know. There is a God, He's going to judge us. We should be good to each other, 'cause Daddy's gonna be pissed in the end if we're not. That's it. That's called a big principle.

This is America's modern-day Moses? Glenn's plan for judgment is not what I read in my Bible. Then again, my God is not, as Mormonism teaches, a man of flesh and bone who evolved to become God and to eternally have sex with his goddess wives.[385] My God is a Spirit (John 4:24) and does not appreciate being described in such a vulgar way or being the punch line of a joke. On September 2, 2010, Beck also noted, "We need a Jesus or a Buddha."

Where is biblical repentance, the depravity of man, the biblical Gospel? Beck's religion is one of good works based on a false Jesus. If Christian leaders continue endorsing Glenn, then more people are going to follow his "spirituality." And they will die and go to hell. These Christian leaders need to reconsider their position on Glenn Beck. Even reclaiming America is not more important than the people who are dying and entering eternity unsaved.

Glenn's New Book of Old Lies

In January 2011, Glenn Beck released his book *The Seven Wonders That Will Change Your Life,* co-authored by psychiatrist Keith Ablow. It is a thoroughgoing promotion of universalism, postmodernism, and pagan spirituality—i.e., the New Age movement. It could just as well have been written by Oprah Winfrey, and I'm not the only one who sees the similarity. A January 4, 2011, article in *The Business Insider* featured a title that says it all: "Glenn Beck's New Year's Plan Sounds a Lot Like Oprah's New Network."

The excuses from various Christian leaders on behalf of Beck for his theology are quite remarkable. Some have said Beck was a "new Christian," "a baby Christian," "new brother," a "little lamb," or "very close to becoming a Christian." A friend of mine even emailed a megachurch pastor who publicly supported Glenn Beck's 8–28 rally to ask him to be careful about embracing Beck and his Black Robe Regiment because of the false theology espoused by Glenn. The pastor replied:

> Glenn Beck is a new brother and he is learning and growing and coming to the light day by day as he is being discipled by [name of Christian leader removed]. There was once a day when you and I were in the same place he is now. Be careful that you don't place a yoke on a little lamb rather than an ox.[386]

Would this pastor say Oprah Winfrey, too, is a baby Christian?

How confusing to the unsaved world and to baby Christians it must be to have Christian leaders make such claims about being a Christian, in light of Beck's latest book. Many now believe Mormon Glenn Beck promotes Christianity because Christian leaders have announced that "Glenn is saved." Teenagers have emailed me and some have talked to me privately at our conferences to say how confused they are by what Christian leaders have said about Beck being saved when they recognize that Beck promotes New Age heresy.

In light of the religious and spiritual proclamations in Beck's book, you would think Christian leaders would have issued press releases or posted statements on their websites disagreeing with Beck's pagan spirituality. Not only did that not happen, but many signed up to take part in Beck's August 2011 rally in Israel in which he again called for all faiths to unite.

Beck and Ablow promote the worldviews of Sigmund Freud, Carl Jung, New Age authors Robert Pirsig and James Redfied, Buddha, Buddhist teacher Sogyal Rinpoche, Gandhi, and the Gnostic "Gospel of Thomas." Beck recounts that he read *A Course in Miracles* by Helen Schucman. Her book is the "Bible" of the New Age movement (*Grave Influence* includes a complete chapter on Helen Schucman and the demon she channeled to help her write the book).

To those who know Mormonism, this is not surprising. Tracy, for instance, was a Mormon for 26 years and sent me an email to explain why many Mormons are open to New Age spirituality:

> It's not surprising how easy it is for many LDS to get involved in occult practices based on the "power of the priesthood." For example, energy healing (*chakras*), cloud-busting, and other mind-power things. My LDS friends and I were always interested in books like *The Magic of Believing*, *Embraced by the Light*, and other New Agey kinds of books. I remember seeing *Star Wars* when I was Mormon and how many of us in the ward (LDS congregation) were comparing the Force to the priesthood power.
>
> Since we believed we were on the godhood track, using the phrase "I AM" in the context Glenn uses it fits in neatly with the power of the priesthood through which worlds are created (according to Mormon doctrine). In fact, Mormonism teaches that God did NOT create the universe *ex nihilo*, because God can only manipulate and arrange existing matter; he cannot create it. Thus we see, from the LDS perspective, we too can become I AM, through the divine nature within us.

On page 79 of their book, Beck and Ablow promote transcendental meditation and Eastern mysticism. And on page 85, we read:

> As you commit to unlocking and bringing forth the truth inside you, don't be afraid to pray for help. Don't be reticent to sit with yourself in silence and meditate.

Connect with the miracle of spirit, of God, that has lived inside you from long before you were born.[387]

Christian meditation is not about "bringing forth the truth inside of you," nor is it about contacting the god who has "lived inside you from long before you were born." This is not biblical, and any Christian who thinks otherwise is at the least biblically illiterate or, worse, a false convert.

On page 132, Beck and Ablow proclaim:

Pray to whatever higher power you believe in.... Praying that God or Nature or the Cosmos or your own internal, immeasurable reservoir of spirit allows you the courage and faith to find and then face the truth....

In several places, the authors tell readers it really does not matter what religion or religious leader they follow. Beck writes on page 157 that "finding what worked for me made all the difference. Finding what works for you will do the same."

On page 74, the reader is instructed to "just be sure you visit with a minister or therapist from a religion or healing discipline you actually have affinity for, or suspect you might." On page 236, reincarnation is promoted through the writings of Robert Pirsig's book *Zen and the Art of Motorcycle Maintenance*: "...the 'spirit' of Chris or the "ghost' of Chris, then you can say without further translation that the spirit or ghost of Chris is looking for a new body to enter."

Committed and Knowledgeable

Several Christians have told me Beck does not really know "all that much" about the Mormon faith. But that is not what Beck says. On pages 149–150, his book leaves little doubt that Beck knows exactly what he is into:

I questioned everything I could think to question about the faith. I went over my doubts again and again with the church bishop. I read everything there was to read on their website and every word of Mormon Doctrine.... I went to anti-Mormon literature for hints, but I found most of it to be unfair or just plain wrong. I tried every trick I could think of to find a contradiction. The problem was that I couldn't. Mormonism seemed to explain the world and my place in it better than any other faith I had looked at.

Beck does not believe in hell, original sin, or that Jesus is the only way:

> Page 149—Latter-day Saints do not believe that your chances ever cease, even with death. They end only with the full understanding and denial of truth by your own exercise of real free will. And even then there is no "lake of fire."

> Page 154—As Keith likes to say, "There's no original sin left in the world. Everyone's just recycling pain now."

> Page 162—There is no infant delivered evil, out of the womb. There never has been. Not even one.... Charles Manson was not born evil. Ted Bundy wasn't. The BTK killer wasn't. Hitler wasn't.

Strange. The Bible says all have sinned and fallen short of the glory of God (Romans 3:23). The Bible says even babies are born with a sin nature and that we are all conceived in sin: "Behold, I was shapen in iniquity; and in sin did my mother conceive me" (Psalm 51:5 KJV). Although Glenn would have us believe "People are inherently good" (page 165), Scripture says: "The heart [is] deceitful above all [things], and desperately wicked: who can know it?" (Jeremiah 17:9).

Beck also uses the phrases "your truth," "your true path," or "my truth" at least 23 times. Here are a few examples:

> Page 124—"It is never too late to embrace your truth."

> Page 130—"What is your truth whispering?"

Page 161—"Use compassion to stay on the path to your own truth...."

Page 215—"...determination to unearth and embrace my truth."

Page 216—"The fact that I am always attempting to honor my truth...."

Page 220—"There is only your truth."

Page 288—"You must use courage and faith to empty the hard drive of your soul and then fill it with your truth."

Beck promotes the New Age idea that God dwells within all:

Page 57—"The third chapter of Exodus helped me start to understand how crucial it was that my focus be on finding God not just in the seas or the cosmos, but in myself."

Page 58—"If God is everything and everywhere and inside everyone, then I figured He had to be inside me, too...."

He promotes pantheism and panentheism:

Page 71—"Divine power is still inside you."

Page 283—"Reach out to people to steady them and enrich them and reflect back to them the light that comes from God inside them."

Page 254—"You won't doubt your ability to achieve what you want to achieve in this life because you won't doubt that God is not only by your side, but inside you."

Beck and Ablow promote the New Age idea that you need to tap into a positive energy for a successful and happy life:

> Page 79—"You have a polestar inside you. It is connected with all the energy in the universe. When you begin to follow that star you align yourself with immeasurable, inexplicable forces that will actually help you manifest your best intentions."

> Page 113—"The current energy that flows in your favor when you stop denying what you have lived through and how it has shaped you and how you must change is the immeasurable force that you can tap into to dramatically improve your existence."

> Page 117—"...you will elicit the same positive energy from others. When you stop pretending to be just fine and start admitting that you have struggled, just as we all have, then spiritual energy will fill you."

Hear this: Christians need to be watchmen (Ezekiel 33:6) who warn their family and friends about the spiritual deception of people like Glenn Beck, Oprah Winfrey, and a host of others who promote another Jesus and another gospel. Christians also need to be ready to explain to unsaved family and friends why Glenn Beck's worldview will not lead them to God as their Savior but only as their Judge. Nowhere in Beck's book does he mention the biblical Gospel. What he promotes is the same lie foisted on Adam and Eve by Satan in Genesis 3:1–5. Glenn Beck's seven wonders are lies that will condemn for eternity the souls of millions who believe them.

On numerous occasions, Beck has attacked the Word of God and Christians who seek to be faithful to the Word of God. He revealed his deviant ecumenicalism and disdain for the Word of God when he attacked the governor of Alabama for making this biblically solid proclamation: "Anybody here today who has not accepted Jesus Christ as their savior, I'm telling you, you're not my brother and you're not my sister, and I want to be your brother."[388] According to the *Alabama Local News*:

305

Beck said the problem was with the sentiment, not the wording. "A true messenger of Jesus Christ," he said, "must consider every person a brother or sister. Even Luke Skywalker recognized that Darth Vader was his father," Beck said. Later, he added, "Governor, you are sadly mistaken about your Christianity."[389]

On his radio program and on his website Beck clearly stated that he wants to have a debate on ecumenicalism:

Now he knows he can't say those things and so he says I will choose my words more carefully next time. Well, no. No, don't choose your words more carefully. Let's have the dialogue. I don't want you to live with that idea as being true. Let's not live in silence. Convince me or I'll convince you. Let's have the debate.[390]

I hear people say that we are all God's children, but that's only wishful thinking. In John 8:42, Jesus says, "If God were your Father, you would love Me, for I proceeded forth and came from God." In verse 44, He continues, "You are of your father the devil, and the desires of your father you want to do. He was a murderer from the beginning, and does not stand in the truth, because there is no truth in him. When he speaks a lie, he speaks from his own resources, for he is a liar and the father of it." Then in verse 47: "He who is of God hears God's words; therefore you do not hear, because you are not of God."

So when and how can one come to be called a child of God? John 1:12–13 tells us:

But as many as received Him, to them He gave the right to become children of God, to those who believe in His name: who were born, not of blood, nor of the will of the flesh, nor of the will of man, but of God.

Jesus Christ declared in John 14:6 that He is truth, and thus truth is that which is consistent with the character and nature of God. The Bible reflects God's character and nature, and so it is true. Jesus prayed this in John 17:17 when He said, "Sanctify them by Your truth. Your word is truth."

The Bible makes it clear we are in a spiritual, worldview war, and the leader of the opposition is Satan himself. Man serves either God or Satan, and every issue is theological and spiritual. The apostle Paul calls Satan "the god of this world" (2 Corinthians 4:4), and John states in 1 John 5:19 that "the whole world lies under the sway of the wicked one." First Peter 5:8 warns, "Be sober, be vigilant; because your adversary the devil walks about like a roaring lion, seeking whom he may devour."

Many people today, though, are being spiritually devoured by the lies of patriotic ecumenicalism that proclaims the falsehood of universalism. Ephesians 5:11 commands all Christians to "have no fellowship with the unfruitful works of darkness, but rather expose them." Please think of this chapter as a call to do just that, lest Paul's question in Galatians 4:16 apply: "Have I become your enemy because I tell you the truth?"

CHAPTER 9

Emerging and Converging:
The New Religious Right and Religious Left

In 2009, 2010, 2011, and 2012, I researched numerous examples of projects in which members of the New Religious Right (NRR) were working with the New Apostolic Reformation, the Word of Faith movement, the Church of Rome, and selected Emergent Church leaders. I call it the "emergence" of the New Religious Right because many Emergent Church ideas have found their way into the New Religious Right, and many in the New Religious Right openly join forces with members of the Emergent Church, the Church of Rome, the New Apostolic Reformation, and the Word of Faith movement.

I also call this new generation of pro-family leaders the "New Religious Right" because I do not believe that some of the now-deceased leaders of the religious right from the 1970s and 1980s would agree with the theological and doctrinal compromises made by many of today's NRR leaders.

On my radio program of August 3, 2011, Tommy Ice explained how the religious right was formed during the presidency of Jimmy Carter by leaders such as Jerry Falwell, Adrian Rogers, Pat Robertson, Ralph Reed, Cal Thomas, and D. James Kennedy. Tommy also revealed that his friend Jerry Falwell preached a sermon one month before his death on the dangers of the Emergent Church. At the conclusion of Falwell's sermon, Ice approached Falwell to thank him for the message. Falwell confided in Tommy and his wife that he was planning to break ties with Rick Warren since he believed Warren was embracing many errant ideas of the Emergent Church. This revelation by Tommy Ice is one reason I believe that if D. James Kennedy, Jerry Falwell, and Adrian Rogers were alive today, they would not enter into spiritual enterprises with members of the Emergent Church, the Word of Faith, and the New Apostolic Reformation.

Some of you may be aware that Adrian Rogers also endorsed Rick Warren's book *The Purpose Driven Life*. And perhaps you, as I, found that troubling. If so, I have some good news. A reliable source in Memphis, Tennessee, where I live and where Dr. Rogers pastored for many years, informed me that Dr. Rogers had personally explained in the last few weeks of his life that if he had to do it over again, he would not endorse Warren's book. I believe Falwell and Rogers had both figured out what Warren's vision for the Church was, and they could not agree with it.

Even the secular media is noticing the emergence of a New Religious Right. On July 21, 2011, *Business Insider* reported:

> As mainstream evangelical influence wanes, however, the New Apostolic Reformation is gaining broader acceptance among conservative Christians. The Response [Texas Governor Rick Perry's prayer rally], whose endorsers also include more mainstream fundamentalists, is evidence of the New Apostles' emerging influence—and of its leaders' growing appetite for political power. Here's what you need to know about the fastest-growing religious movement you've never heard of.[391]

While there are many examples of convergence among the religious right, the New Apostolic Reformation, the Word of Faith, and the Emergent Church with members of the Church of Rome, what may shock you most is the rat's nest in a woodpile I found while researching this problem. All the compatriots in this convergence seem to be embracing progressives. While running around the country holding conferences to fight socialism and the culture war, "conservative" and "religious" leaders can be found to include "evangelical progressives," globalists, and ecumenical proponents in their events, proclamations, and initiatives.

In this chapter, I will reveal that there is a convergence (to use the word of the New Apostolic Reformation, New Agers, and communitarians) occurring between the political left and political right as well as the theological left and theological right. Don't confuse the theological right with biblical theology. If those of the New Religious

Right were truly committed first and foremost to sound biblical theology and doctrine, they would not be involved in spiritual enterprises with those who participate in the New Age movement, the New Apostolic Reformation, ecumenicalism, globalism, communitarianism, the Church of Rome, the Word of Faith movement, social justice, and the social gospel.

Before I explain how the New Religious Right has been infiltrated by a Trojan horse, let me remind you that in U.S. Congressional hearings in July 1953, former Communists who had turned against Communism warned that Communists were infiltrating religious organizations and institutions in America. So we should not be shocked that today's progressives, globalists, and statists are still employing this Trojan horse strategy. Indeed, the Gramsci effect of marching through the institutions would obviously include evangelical churches and colleges.

On August 6, 2011, Texas governor Rick Perry, along with several pro-family organizations and "evangelical" leaders, hosted a prayer rally in Houston called "The Response." The New Apostolic Reformation, International House of Prayer, and Word of Faith false teachers were involved in the event, and that is what made it so unbiblical (2 Corinthians 6:14, 2 John 9–11). People can claim Jesus was exalted, but Jesus is never glorified when people disobey His Word and give credibility to false teachers.

Respected Bible teachers did not attend the Response rally because they understood that uniting with false teachers is a clear violation of Scripture, as noted in Romans 16:17–18:

> Now I urge you, brethren, note those who cause divisions and offenses, contrary to the doctrine which you learned, and avoid them. For those who are such do not serve our Lord Jesus Christ, but their own belly, and by smooth words and flattering speech deceive the hearts of the simple.

I believe many pro-family and "evangelical" leaders are deceived by the "smooth words and flattering speech" of the New Apostolic Reformation and Word of Faith leaders. Allowing such deception is the mark of simplemindedness, as described by John MacArthur:

The little word *simple* of the Hebrew language is real concrete, not abstract like Greek. Simple comes from a root word that means an open door. And a simple-minded person was somebody whose mind was always open… the simpleton was the person who had not enough discernment or discrimination or knowledge or understanding or wisdom to know what to accept and what to reject. And the Word of God will teach you how to close the door. It will teach you how to be wise. Wise is *chakam* in Hebrew, it means skilled in all aspects of living.[392]

Many within the New Religious Right willingly embrace false teachers because they either agree with them or because they are not offended by their heresy. According to 1 John 2:22–25, a true follower of Jesus Christ rejects false teaching and false teachers. Yet the New Religious Right has openly embraced the false teachers of the Word of Faith movement and the New Apostolic Reformation.

Even after the January 2011 release of Beck's book, *Seven Wonders That Will Change Your Life*—which clearly revealed Beck's New Age Mormonism—the religious community just could not get enough. Even a Christian school in the Bible-belt city of Jackson, Tennessee, featured Beck as a keynote speaker for its October 29, 2011, banquet at the Carl Perkins Civic Center.

The next day Beck spoke at John Hagee's church on Sunday, October 30, 2011. And on the Friday and Saturday before Beck's Sunday sermon, Hagee's church had featured Word of Faith false teachers Creflo Dollar and Jesse Duplantis.[393] (Chapter 10 on "Christian shamanism" will bring you up to speed on Creflo and Jesse if you are not familiar with their heresies.) The Word of Faith teaches that Christians are "little gods," so it stands to reason they would be at home with Mormon Glenn Beck since Mormons, too, believe they will become gods.

ChristianPost.com offers further proof of the theological convergence occurring among us. On October 10, 2011, the website reported that the president of Fuller Theological Seminary, Richard J. Mouw, believes that many Mormons worship the same Jesus that he does:

> "While I am not prepared to reclassify Mormonism as possessing undeniably Christian theology, I do

312

accept many of my Mormon friends as genuine followers of the Jesus whom I worship as the divine Savior,"
Mouw, head of the Pasadena, Calif., seminary wrote in
an article on CNN Sunday.[394]

Fuller, of course, is a super-liberal seminary, and Mouw, in addition
to signing the Evangelicals and Catholics Together document, believes
Catholics are Christians. Fuller's president is also hammering out a
similar document with the Mormons, according to the *Christian Post*:

> Mouw said he had been co-chairing, with Prof.
> Robert Millet of the Mormon Brigham Young Univer-
> sity, a behind-closed-doors dialogue between evangeli-
> cals and Mormons for over a decade. "We evangelicals
> and our Mormon counterparts disagree about some
> important theological questions," he admitted. "But
> we have also found that on some matters we are not as
> far apart as we thought we were," he added.[395]

The article also reported:

> ...Fuller president said Mormons "talk admiringly
> of the evangelical Billy Graham and the Catholic Moth-
> er Teresa, and they enjoy reading the evangelical C. S.
> Lewis and Father Henri Nouwen, a Catholic. That is
> not the kind of thing you run into in anti-Christian
> cults."[396]

But of course they do. As far as I can determine, Billy Graham never called Mormons out publicly as a cult, perhaps because of his own
"ecumenical strategy."[397] Mother Teresa was a Universalist by her own
admission, and Henri Nouwen is a Catholic mystic *and* Universalist.
In his book *Sabbatical Journey*, for instance, Nouwen writes:

> Today I personally believe that while Jesus came
> to open the door to God's house, all human beings
> can walk through that door, whether they know about
> Jesus or not. Today I see it as my call to help every per-
> son claim his or her own way to God.[398]

A year after Glenn Beck released his *Seven Wonders* book, my prediction that a greater convergence would occur between the religious right and the religious left was confirmed as Christians from both camps jumped on board the next spiritual bandwagon—the Texas prayer event. And why would such a rally be necessary? The website for The Response declared:

> America is in the midst of a historic crisis. We have been besieged by financial debt, terrorism, and a multitude of natural disasters. The youth of America are in grave peril economically, socially, and, most of all, morally. There are threats emerging within our nation and beyond our borders beyond our power to solve.[399]

The "youth of America are in grave peril economically, socially, and most of all, morally" because they are in peril spiritually, and giving credibility to and introducing youth and adults to false teachers and their unbiblical spirituality is only going to put people in even greater eternal, spiritual peril.

Governor Perry's event did not help reclaim the country, restore liberty or prosperity, and it certainly did not prompt God to bless America. As I said of the Glenn Beck rally, I believe events like this will actually hasten God's judgment on our country if He isn't already judging our land. Our nation has made it nearly impossible to mention God in our schools, entertainment industry (except as a swear word), and government.

A few days before the governor's rally, news reports revealed that Governor Perry said he has no problem with gay marriage in New York since he sees it as a state's rights issue. Did pro-family leaders who agreed to boycott secular companies for their support of gay marriage remain consistent and boycott Perry's prayer event? Not at all. To the contrary, the New Religious Right went into political spin-and-damage control. I guess it is easier to gore the ox of others over the issue of same-sex marriage than it is your own.

In what seemed like an attempt to repair the damage, one pro-family leader interviewed Perry. However, journalist Joseph Farah of *WND.com* saw through the smoke and mirrors and declared that Perry had fooled him:

...you can forget....the nice things I said and wrote about Rick Perry. I'm afraid I've wasted my time and your time. In fact, I was just dead wrong in all of my conclusions about the governor of Texas. I no longer want him to run and no longer believe he is a viable candidate. In fact, I will do all I can to warn the American people away from him.[400]

The Response was promoted as a time of prayer and repentance. But how can Christians and Christian leaders gather in a spiritual enterprise with individuals who embrace a theology and doctrine that teach a different Jesus and a different gospel? I and thousands of pastors and theologians believe the Word of God reveals that the teachings like those of the New Apostolic Reformation, the Word of Faith movement, and the prosperity gospel are completely unbiblical.

I am thankful for the pastors who are biblical shepherds and are protecting their flocks. The pastor of a large church in Houston, who is also a columnist at WorldviewWeekend.com, sent me the following email after studying the resources on our website concerning The Response:

> I'm praying for you. Thank you for bringing this out. I had planned on promoting the event until your stuff came out... Thank you for doing your homework... Stay committed to being the "voice crying in the wilderness."

Even before becoming one of our columnists, Tommy Ice wrote a book in 1988 on the unbiblical teachings of dominion theology. He has also written numerous articles on the dangers of the Latter Rain Movement, an aberrant group that has given rise to the Kansas City Prophet Movement and now the New Apostolic Reformation.

Since the early 1980s, Dr. Ice has been exposing the fallacies of dominion theology and reconstructionism, and this is how he defines reconstructionism:

> The belief that it is the moral obiligation of Christians to recapture every institution for Jesus Christ, both individual and social....Since God's kingdom

was established at Christ's first coming, godly dominion will be mediated through the church before the return of Christ. The victory of God's kingdom on earth
will be during and continuous with this present era.[401]

In 1986, reconstructionist Gary North described how the Word
of Faith camps united to lay the foundation for the synthesis we see
today among the New Apostolic Reformation, Word of Faith, and New
Religious Right:

> ...bringing together the postmillennial Christian
> reconstructionists and the "positive confession [Word
> of Faith] charismatics.... It began when Robert Til-
> ton's wife read Gary DeMar's *God and Government* in
> late 1983, and then persuaded her husband to invite
> a group of reconstructionists to speak before 1,000
> "positive confession" pastors and their wives at a Janu-
> ary 1984 rally sponsored by Rev. Tilton's church. The
> all day panel was very well received...[402]

As Dr. Ice accurately points out, "Reconstructionists get people
excited, not about Christ returning for us, rather about taking over the
world for Christ."[403]

Gary North also wrote a book in 1984 in which he predicted that
he and his movement would transform American religious life (indeed
they did—by aligning with heretics):

> A new Puritanism is developing—a Puritanism
> which offers men the hope of God honoring social
> transformation... We are now in a position to fuse
> together in a working activist movement the three
> major legs of the Reconstructionist movement: the
> Presbyterian-oriented educators [like North], the Bap-
> tist school headmasters and pastors [the Jerry Falwell
> types with their schools and colleges], and the charis-
> matic tele-communications system [Trinity Broadcast-
> ing Network, DayStar, GodTV, etc.]. When this takes
> place, the whole shape of American religious life will
> be transformed.[404]

How has that "new Puritanism" and "reclaiming the culture" worked out since 1984? It is not working, and things are not going to get better but worse, as described in Scripture.

Tommy sent me an email he had received from Robby Dean of West Houston Bible Church in which Dean shared a letter he had sent to the members of his church and to 50 other pastors. The purpose was to warn churches of what he believes to be doctrinal and theological problems with The Response. Dr. Dean cautioned:

> ...the delegation of the administration of this event, called "The Response," is to a Christian group with ties to what is, in my opinion, one of the most radical, fringe, quasi-cultic groups I have ever investigated. In my view, Response organizers have been exceptionally foolish in designating this a "Christian" event. The most distressing fact is that this event is being run by people from the International House of Prayer (IHOP), which has its roots in a movement called the Kansas City Prophets, which in turn was associated with the Vineyard churches founded by the late John Wimber. In the late 1980s I conducted more than two thousand hours of research and personal interviews with key leaders in the Vineyard movement as part of independent studies courses in my doctoral studies at Dallas Theological Seminary. In January of 1989 I attended a "Spiritual Warfare Conference" at the home Vineyard church in southern California. I was there when Paul Cain, one of the most extreme, cult-like leaders of this movement and one who himself taught his own brand of heresy, was first introduced to the Vineyard congregation. Cain became very influential in the life of Mike Bickle, who was then pastor of the Kansas City Fellowship. In October of 1990 Dr. Thomas Ice and I interviewed the pastoral leadership of the Kansas City Vineyard, the so-called Kansas City Prophets, a now defunct ministry. Bickle went on to become one of the founders of the International House of Prayer. Our critique of this movement was published in *Biblical Perspectives,* a bi-monthly news-

letter Dr. Ice and I published at that time. The Director and Program Coordinators for "The Response" are Luis and Jill Cataldo, both on the staff of the International House of Prayer.

One of the key heresies of the Kansas City prophets, which is also at the core of the thinking of the IHOP movement, is based on a misuse and abuse of a passage in the Hebrew Scriptures, Joel 2:15–16. This passage is at the core of a heresy which calls upon present day Christians to fulfill a passage that has nothing whatsoever to do with modern events. In their view this passage is twisted to be a call for spiritual elites, the so-called "Joel's Army," to take over the United States and then to purge it and bring in a Christian kingdom. Unfortunately, in a display of theological naiveté, Governor Perry was duped into using this passage as the rationale for his call to a Day of Prayer: "In the spirit of the Book of Joel, Chapter 2, Verses 15–16, I urge a solemn gathering of prayer and fasting. As those verses admonish: 'Blow the trumpet in Zion, declare a holy fast, call a sacred assembly... Gather the people, consecrate the assembly....' This is what happens when theologically uninformed politicians get duped by advisors whose religious agendas are not obvious. Few Christians are even aware of this movement, its heretical theology, and its political agenda. Governor Perry is not the only one who has been taken in by their pious duplicity.

On the basis of all my research into IHOP, I cannot, on the basis of the Word of God, endorse this event. Further, I must strongly encourage my congregation, and indeed all Bible believing Christians, to not participate in this event... Prayer is important, prayer for a nation is important, political leaders who recognize this are vital to our national health. But a right thing done in a wrong way is wrong. The end never justifies the means!! The way the Texas Day of Prayer is being administered is wrong and foolish, therefore the entire event is tainted. Rick Perry has let the wolves disguised as sheep into the hen house.[405]

Those involved in The Response and other such events are not just guilty by association but guilty by participation. They give undue credibility to false teachers by uniting with them. Ephesians 5:11 directs us to "have no fellowship with the unfruitful works of darkness, but rather expose them." Similarly, 2 Timothy 3:5 tells us "from such people turn away."

It appears the New Religious Right has on numerous occasions openly embraced, for the sake of political pragmatism, the New Apostolic Reformation, the Word of Faith movement, and proponents of the prosperity gospel. In 2011, James Robison wrote on his website about "supernatural gatherings" and listed "those who attended one or both Leadership Summits along with those who encouraged and assisted in bringing about the gatherings."[406] The list included both men whose ministries I have respected and also Word of Faith and New Apostolic Reformation teachers I have refuted.

I am not shocked that Robison would host an event that included false teachers since Robison appeared on Glenn Beck's television program and praised him. On his own television program, Robison has featured Word of Faith false teacher Creflo Dollar as a guest.[407] And in 2011, Robison had Catholic priest Jonathan Morris on his television program. During that show, Robison declared:

> And I'm just telling you straight on as an evangelical, as a protestant, every time you talk, every time I see you, I see Jesus. When you open your mouth that what you say is so consistent with the word of God, with the heart of God, with the spirit of God, and the spirit of Christ, that I marvel. And I've often said I wish most protestant preachers had the sensitivity and discernment and gift to communicate that you have. Don't you agree that you see Jesus when this wonderful man of God shares?[408]

Does James Robison not understand what the Church of Rome teaches about Mary, Jesus Christ, atonement, purgatory, tradition above

Scripture, the pope above the Word of God, and more than 100 anathemas the Council of Trent declared against Bible-believing Christians? Robison wishes Protestant preachers had discernment, but it appears Robison is the one lacking biblical discretion. He went on to call for the Catholic Church and Protestant churches to come together as one:

> And you know, here's the thing. God and really Billy Graham is the one that asked me, do you know these people you're talking about and telling me to stay away from? And I didn't. And I've said this and if you watch me you've heard me say this many times. We don't know Him as well as we should because we refuse to know them. And as a result of us not knowing one another and even being an answer to the prayer of Jesus that we be one, we've not learned as well as we should. And Father, listen, I have developed such wonderful relationships. I've got to be honest with you. If Catholics, evangelicals, protestants, if we would just come together on common ground, you talk about a city set on a hill that cannot be hidden. You talk about a city set on a hill that could light up the way the world should walk and reveal the way not to walk as well as to walk. I think it's going to happen.[409]

God has not called His disciples to be part of a false, pagan church but has called Christians to reject false teachers. Consider how far off that mark this dialog is between Robison and Morris:

> ROBISON—That I believe that I'm going to get to see and be a part of Jesus' prayer for us to have a oneness with the Father and to see a perfected, perfectingness and perfection coming from a supernatural unity. And the world will know we're His disciples because of our love that I think I'm going to get to see that. And just knowing the little exchanges that you and I have had really in the last weeks has been really quite remarkable and I'm thankful. Now you said in our conversations that you've seen some things in what you hear in my expression that encourage you.

MORRIS—You know, on the plane here today I read from cover to cover the manuscript that you sent to me of your new book, *Indivisible*, and I'm reading it and I'm blown away. I'm saying, you know what? Here we have and I think you wrote it with a Catholic, Jay Richards, and I'm reading. You know here we are, evangelical, well-known pastor writing about things that I would write about. Here I am reading a Catholic who helped you writing out evangelical things that I need to learn.[410]

Robison and his wife Betty declare that God and Jesus Christ are rejoicing over the coming together of Catholics and Protestants:

BETTY ROBISON—I believe God is happy when he sees his children fellowshipping together and getting along together.

JAMES ROBISON—I believe angels rejoice. I believe the Father rejoices. I know Jesus who's daily making intercession for us, I believe he's turned to his Father and said, "Father, my prayers are getting answered." We're getting together. I know – don't you like what you see and don't you know God likes us to come together? Let me just ask you to share something that I think is, it's really remarkable because this just shows that religion isn't the answer. Relationship with the Jesus you talked about right up front.[411]

Robison refers to the Jesus the priest mentioned at the beginning of the interview, but Robison and all Christians need to understand that Jesus of the Church of Rome is not the Jesus of the Bible. The Jesus of the Church of Rome appears in the communion wafer and is sacrificed each week in mass for sins. This is not the Jesus of the Bible.

Newt Gingrich, the Tofflers, Ecumenicalism, and the New Religious Right

The merging we're talking about extends into the political realm as well, and while there is no perfect candidate, that does not mean evangelicals should compromise biblical truth and embrace politicians with worldviews hostile to biblical truth. Newt Gingrich is just another in a long line of political candidates many of the New Religious Right have hooked their wagons to in political and spiritual endeavors. While the story of the New Religious Right and Newt will soon fade, it is important history to document and remember. Why? The Newt Gingrich and New Religious Right relationship is a great example of the compromise in which the New Religious Right will participate to achieve their largely self-serving and often unbiblical, unachievable goals and objectives—all to the detriment of the Gospel.

The Newt Gingrich/New Religious Right story reveals several problems. On a small scale, it is a preview of how a future group of global "Christian" leaders will assist in leading a false church into following not just a local, state, or presidential candidate, but a one-world leader. In other words, if today's New Religious Right can be convinced that a man like Gingrich is a Christian and is good for the country, American families, and the Church, then how much easier will it be for the antichrist to deceive the religious leaders of his day?

Newt may have been honey-tongued and tickled the ears of NRR leaders, but it did not come close to the deception that will come from the hand of the antichrist. What Gingrich did with the NRR will occur again on a global scale. Then it will be the antichrist the religious leaders help ascend to world power.

Occurrences like this are further evidence that God is judging America. The infiltration of the religious and political left into the New Religious Right is part of God's judgment as our nation and institutions are led by vain, foolish, and futile-thinking men (see Romans 1:21–22). America's national judgment includes God giving America leaders whose practices oppose the righteous judgments of God, while encouraging others to do the same (Romans 1:32). Romans 1:25 adds that national judgment involves God giving a people over to pagan spirituality. The New Religious Right has openly embraced the NAR, Word of Faith, and other groups that practice pagan spirituality.

To further understand how God is judging America, you must understand that leading political candidates on local, state, and national levels are almost always hostile to biblical truth. If not hostile in their words, they are hostile in their personal lives and public policy. The final leading presidential candidates in America's recent presidential races have shown that God is turning America over. Look at the worldviews of the final US presidential candidates in 2012—a Mormon, Mitt Romney, and two Roman Catholics, Newt Gingrich and Rick Santorum.

Gingrich offers a particularly important example because of the basis of his worldview. The modernist thinking of Heidi and Alvin Toffler was embraced and promoted by the former Congressman. He was so inspired by the futurist vision of the Tofflers that he wrote the foreword to their book *Creating a New Civilization: The Politics of the Third Wave*. And what did the Tofflers promote? What did Newt promote in his book *A Contract with the Earth*? It gets complicated.

Renewing America or Reinventing America?

The organization Renewing American Leadership—started by Newt Gingrich—posted a list of participating evangelical pastors, leaders of the New Religious Right, and leaders of the New Apostolic Reformation and Word of Faith movements, all uniting in a call to America for prayer and fasting. The list includes: Kenneth Copeland, Creflo Dollar, Mike Bickle, Che Ahn, Lou Engle, Cindy Jacobs, and Rick Joyner.[412]

Charismamag.com reported on an event sponsored by Gingrich's organization:

> Organized by California pastor Jim Garlow and Prison Fellowship founder Chuck Colson, Pray & Act has gained support from a cross-section of Christians, including Bible teacher Kenneth Copeland, former Arkansas Gov. Mike Huckabee, Generals International co-founder Cindy Jacobs, Southern Baptist Convention leader Richard Land, Atlanta pastor Creflo Dollar and Campus Crusade for Christ co-founder Vonette Bright.[413]

(There are many things I would call Kenneth Copeland, but "Bible teacher" is not one of them.) The article continued:

> The Pray & Act kickoff, to be broadcast on the American Family Association (AFA) website Sunday at 8 p.m. Eastern, will feature leaders attending the AFA's Values Voters summit this weekend. The speakers—

ranging from conservative politicians to pastors—will be interviewed by Garlow and will join him in calling Christians to 40 days of prayer and fasting.[414]

Do you really think God is going to bless a prayer-and-fasting event with false teachers like Creflo Dollar, Cindy Jacobs, and Kenneth Copeland? As John MacArthur has correctly said, many of these false teachers are blaspheming the Holy Spirit, and uniting with them in a prayer enterprise surely will not yield God's blessing. MacArthur explains:

> ...attributing to the Holy Spirit the work of Satan. Satan is alive and at work in deception, false miracles, bad theology, lying visions, lying dreams, lying revelations, deceptive teachers who are in it for the money and power and influence. Satan is alive and well and the work of Satan being attributed to the Holy Spirit is a serious blasphemy just as attributing to Satan the work of the Holy Spirit is a serious blasphemy...

> I couldn't even begin to give you all the illustrations; you have enough of them in your own mind. You can turn on your television and see any litany of them that you would choose. And in order to give credibility to all these things, all these lies, they attach them to the Holy Spirit as if it's a freebie, as if there's no price to pay for that kind of blasphemy.

> The latest wave of this, I'll just give you one illustration, the latest wave of this that is gaining traction and has entered into the sort of national news is a new form of Charismania, bringing reproach on the Holy Spirit called the New Apostolic Reformation, NAR, the New Apostolic Reformation. It is not new, it is not apostolic, and it is not a reformation, by the way. It is like Grape Nuts—it's not grapes and it's not nuts. It's like Christian Science—it's not Christian and it's not scientific. Well, the New Apostolic Reformation isn't

new, it isn't apostolic, and it isn't a reformation. But it is a rapidly expanding movement being generated by some of the same old troubling false teachers and false leaders that have been around in Charismania for decades, always dishonoring the Holy Spirit, always dishonoring the Scripture, always claiming miracle signs, wonders, visions, dreams. Peter Wagner, the Kansas City prophets, Mike Bickle, Cindy Jacobs, Lou Engle, and on and on and on it goes. In fact, this is exploding so fast that they have a 50–state network that are now involved in this…[415]

The website of the Pray & Act event included pro-family and evangelical leaders such as:

- Richard Land of the Southern Baptist Convention,
- Tony Perkins of the Family Research Council,
- Tim and Don Wildmon of the American Family Association,
- Jerry Falwell Jr. of Liberty University,
- David Barton of Wallbuilders,
- Chuck Colson, founder and president of Prison Fellowship,
- Tony Evans of Oak Cliff Bible Fellowship, and many more.[416]

If you think Newt Gingrich is someone America's evangelical and New Religious Right leaders should be uniting with, then I suspect you don't fully understand his worldview. Yet several pro-family leaders enthusiastically and publicly endorsed and campaigned for Newt Gingrich when he ran for president of the United States in 2011 and 2012. Don Wildmon actually declared:

Gingrich recognizes the threat to our country posed by judges and lawyers imposing values upon the country inconsistent with our religious heritage, and has proposed constitutional steps to bring the courts back in balance under the constitution. We need someone in the White House who can balance the budget and get the economy moving again. Newt is the only candidate who has done it before and I believe he can do it again. I am proud to endorse Newt Gingrich for president.[417]

I personally don't think most evangelical pro-family leaders really understand what has influenced Gingrich over the years—influence that includes a man who has actually called for replacing the governmental system installed by the Founding Fathers. As researcher Steve Farrell explains, Newt Gingrich promoted and embraced the worldview of Alvin Toffler:

> On November 11, 1994, still bubbling and cocksure over the Republican takeover of both houses of Congress, his coming coronation as speaker of the House, and his anointing as king of the Republican Revolution, Congressman Newt Gingrich couldn't resist taking advantage of the moment to put in a free plug for something he so devoutly believed in.[418]

> "The core of our Contract" and the solution for those "trying to figure out how to put me in a box," he said, could be found in a book by futurist Alvin Toffler called *The Third Way*, to which he added, "I am a conservative futurist."[419]

Farrell continues:

> ...futurism is a head-in-the-clouds political philosophy complete with theories and forecasts which envisions the use of force to insure that those theories and forecasts come to pass.

> I'm sure my Republican friends won't like this: but it would not be a stretch on futurism to sum it up thus: communism with economic vision. That is certainly how the futurists of the Third Way describe it. If so, what, then, is a conservative futurist? Well, if Mr. Gingrich was being honest about his agenda (which

became the agenda of the Party), it is individually: a post-1994 Republican; and in policy: the Contract with America, the go-along, get-along policies of a party that for the next six years caved under Clinton. It is, also, the faith-based subsidies, public-private partnerships, fast-track hopes, and the bipartisan spirit of the 2000–2008 Compassionate Conservative movement—the latter movement having its start in the already in place proposals, legislation, and underlying principles of the Gingrich-inspired Contract with America.

As fictitious as this may have sounded to the average pre-Tea Party party partisan who presumes his party is as conservative as the talk-show hosts who promote it, confirmation of it all comes in spades as we consider the sincerity and depth of Gingrich's relationship with the same center/left of center Third Wave/Third Way that pummeled our country under Clinton and Gore.[420]

In his foreword to Heidi and Alvin Toffler's *Creating a New Civilization*, Gingrich wrote:

The gap between objective changes in the world at large and the stagnation of politics and government is undermining the very fabric of our political system… This book is a key effort in the direction of empowering citizens….to truly take the leap and begin to invent a (new) civilization.[421]

The third wave of the Tofflers is also referred to as Third Way. (For quick review: Third Way is another word for the Hegelian Dialectic Process that involves bringing about change through conflict between opposites. This process is done in many areas, including economics, law, government, and religion. Karl Marx embraced the Third Way he learned from German philosopher George Hegel.)

Steve Farrell explains that the Third Way of the Tofflers is not a rejection of the philosophy embraced by Marx but a rebranding and renaming. After reviewing *Creating a New Civilization*, Farrell reveals some of its third-wave vision:

> Some will argue that Toffler's Wave 3 significantly departs, free-market-like, from Marx's centralized imperialistic model, because Toffler calls for decentralization. But Toffler's supposed decentralization, or what he and Congressman Gingrich call "decision division," shifts power not just downward to the states, but upward to the United Nations, to subsidiary international organizations like NAFTA, the WTO and NATO, and to totally unaccountable NGOs. Nothing could be more centralized and anti-free market than these. Toffler, apparently not one to miss throwing in a few hints of what he really means, a few caveats for his leftist readers to cherish, confirms this suspicion by his incessant insistence that national sovereignty is "a myth" and that these regional and global arrangements he desires to shift power upward need to assume nation-like powers, including enforcement mechanisms.[422]

The phrases that are often used by those who embrace the third wave or Third Way (communitarianism) include common good, shared community, shared values, shared principles, and shared opportunity. Farrell reveals some additional code words often used by Third Way-ers:

> While it's sure as shootin' that Toffler's Three Waves are but a remake of Marx's, it is equally revelatory that the whole wave thesis is built around another communist principle: the dialectical view of history. On this point, a reviewer would have to be hell bent on looking the other way not to notice the all too frequent cover-to-cover use of the communist dialectic's unique vocabulary. Words like: clash, collision, convergence, inevitable, compelled, quantum leap, and transformation appear over and over again and are applied precisely as Marx applied them.[423]

Most people don't see the Trojan horse inside our government, political, religious, and educational institutions, because politicians, pro-family leaders, and religious leaders alike have been hoodwinked by the "philosophies of men" (Colossians 2:8) that are not of Christ. Sadly, most evangelical pro-family leaders are misguided, and very few people in evangelical churches have the ability to discern the false ways of these leaders. Therefore, much damage is done in the name of pro-family causes.

The New Religious Right doesn't recognize the wolf-in-sheep's-clothing because they have never heard of the Third Way, third wave, communitarianism, or the Hegelian Dialectic Process. Hence, they are easily controlled and manipulated by doublespeak and newspeak.

So just why have the globalists targeted the Republican Party? Farrell explains:

> Surprisingly, leftist Alvin Toffler singled out the Republican Party, not the Democratic Party, as the preferred Third Way party. Why? Because the Republican Party had the largest contingency of centrists and moderates—perfect fodder for a scheme which thrives on compromising politicians, rather than dedicated ideologues to the left or the right.[424]

In two of his books, Toffler writes an imaginary letter to the Founding Fathers that reads as follows:

> For what I now must write can all too easily be misunderstood by my contemporaries. Some will no doubt regard it as seditious. Yet it is a painful truth I believe you would have quickly grasped. For the system of government you fashioned, including the very principles on which you based it, is increasingly obsolete, and hence increasingly, if inadvertently, oppressive and dangerous to our welfare. It must be radically changed and a new system of government invented—a democracy for the 21st century.[425]

If you think Gingrich was not basing his "Republican revolution" on the philosophies of Toffler, then consider the following:

Mr. Gingrich told his fellow congressmen in his Republican Revolution Victory Speech in November 1994 that "The Third Way [The Third Wave]" represented the key to figuring out where he and the new Republicans were coming from, and that this futurism-based book was "one of the seminal works of our time." It isn't. At best, the work represents a compilation of glaring contradictions, hasty generalizations, and shamefully shallow analysis of U.S. constitutional foundations, topped off with foolish, risky, naive solutions that discard the political past and leap blindly into a radically different political future for no better reason than "we must!" That's the kind appraisal. At worst, the work is intentionally deceptive, possibly treasonous, and clearly Marxist in its political, historical, and sociological philosophy. Either way, it is not seminal. It is one of the most embarrassing and revelatory documents on just how far the Republican Party has strayed since 1994 from the old hypothetical platform and from the promise of the Contract tith America to "return to the wisdom and brilliance of the Founding Fathers." The party simply did not then, and does not now, seek the wisdom of the Founding Fathers, but in its new gutless political outlook grovels in the gutter of the gulags in search of gangrenous Information Age answers.[426]

Why would so many pro-family leaders unite with Gingrich in spiritual events such as "One Nation Under God"? Numerous pro-family leaders promoted this webcast that included speakers such as Newt Gingrich and Samuel Rodriquez. "Prophet" Rick Joyner even hosted a "One Nation Under God" event with David Barton, Newt Gingrich, Samuel Rodriquez, and five other speakers.

Steve Farrell also documents that Toffler, in his book *The Third Wave*, wrote that "he wants divorce, hot affairs, bisexuality and immorality without guilt; he hopes that schools, churches and other institutions will cooperate in promoting this message to avoid the bloodbath."[427] Does that sound like family values to you? In 2009, columnist Rebecca Terrell documented what many other conservative writers and research have also seen:

> In 1994, Gingrich described himself as "a conservative futurist." He said that those who were trying to define him should look no further than *The Third Wave*, a 1980 book written by Alvin Toffler. The book describes our society as entering a post-industrial phase in which abortion, homosexuality, promiscuity, and divorce are perfectly normal, even virtuous. Toffler penned a letter to America's "founding parents," in which...[h]e went on to describe our constitutional system as one that "served us so well for so long, and that now must, in its turn, die and be replaced."[428]

Terrell also described the congressman's commitment to globalism:

> Another explanation for Gingrich's liberal voting record is that he has been a member, since 1990, of the Council on Foreign Relations (CFR), a group founded in 1921 as a think tank of influential politicians and policymakers dedicated to sacrificing national independence to create a global government. He showed his fidelity to internationalism in a speech at the Center for Strategic and International Affairs in July of 1995 when he brazenly admitted his disdain for our founding document.

> "The American challenge in leading the world is compounded by our Constitution," he said. "Under our [constitutional system]—either we're going to have to rethink our Constitution, or we're going to have to rethink our process of decision-making." He went on to profess an oxymoronic belief in "very strong but limited federal government," and pledged, "I am for the United Nations." That is certainly no surprise since his mentor is none other than former Secretary of State and National Security Advisor Henry

Kissinger (also a CFR member and one-world interna-
tionalist).[429]

Perhaps you think Gingrich has changed, and these are the views
of the young Newt. But to the contrary, Rebecca Terrell's research confirms my own when she explains:

> In front of a Tea Party crowd, he expounds the vir-
> tues of limited government, but elsewhere he is still
> the futurist conservative devoted to internationalism.
> His blog biography brags about his work as Speaker
> of the House and then boasts of such unconstitution-
> al credentials as serving on the CFR's terrorism task
> force, co-chairing the UN task force to "reform" (i.e.,
> strengthen) the United Nations, and receiving credit
> for the DHS being his brainchild. "Newt Gingrich is a
> leading advocate of increased federal funding for basic
> science research," reads the bio. Gingrich's ASWF en-
> dorses federal involvement in areas such as energy, ed-
> ucation, labor and the environment. He also founded
> the Center for Health Transformation, which advocates
> its own version of socialized medicine.[430]

Aside from promoting the Tofflers and their books, when Gingrich
ran for president in 2012, a pro-Gingrich Political Action Committee
(PAC) was given millions of dollars by a casino mogul. That is a bit
ironic, since some of the pro-family guys who supported or endorsed
Gingrich had previously spoken out aggressively against gambling,
casinos, and state lotteries. Why would pro-family advocates back a
presidential candidate whose campaign was benefiting from a political
action committee funded by a casino mogul?[431]

I am never surprised by the spiritual and political coalitions in
which self-professing evangelicals are willing to engage just to "win the
culture war" or to win the White House, even if it means supporting
a candidate whose worldview is backed by people hostile to the Bible
and the Gospel. In "Newt Gingrich and the Tofflers," a January 11,
2012, article for *American Thinker*, Sam Blumenfeld observes:

Yet, Newt considers himself a Reagan conservative. He claims to adhere to the U.S. Constitution, but his record—both in and out of Congress—has demonstrated many deviations from constitutionalism and conservatism...[T]he Tofflers also believe that our Constitutional system needs to be changed. In fact, they say it must "die and be replaced." They thank Thomas Jefferson for a system of government that has served us so well all these years, "and that now must, in its turn, die and be replaced."[432]

A pro-United Nations website praised Newt Gingrich because he "co-authored a lengthy treatise about the value of the United Nations to American interests"[433] in 2005. And Newt's 2007 book, *Contract with the Earth,* calls for strengthening the United Nations.[434]

Do the members of the New Religious Right not own computers that would enable them to research a candidate, or did they not care about Newt's worldview as long as they thought he could win the White House and give them a place at the table? Are today's New Religious Right leaders really committed to a biblical worldview, the defense, protection, and proclamation of a biblical Gospel, or are they more interested in power, political access, a big tent, bragging rights, and a seat at the table? Even at the table of those who promote a worldview hostile to biblical truth? Even if it is a seat inside the religious Trojan horse?

Yet Another Spiritual Enterprise Brings Together Left and Right

Another example of this strange convergence of conservatives, evangelicals, neo-evangelicals, the New Religious Right, Word of Faith, and the New Apostolic Reformation is the Freedom Federation. This coalition includes people involved in—among other things—ecumenicalism, the Third Way, common good, and social justice on both the political and theological right and left. It is a dream come true for those committed to the Hegelian process. The Freedom Federation website describes this coalition and its goal as not only political but also spiritual:

Today a federation of some of the largest faith-based organizations in the country gathered in the Nation's capital to plan, strategize, and work together on common interests within the Judeo-Christian tradition to mobilize their grassroots constituencies and to communicate faith and values to the religious, social, cultural, and policymaking institutions. The constituents of these organizations are concerned about the spiritual, moral, cultural, and economic condition of the Nation.

The Freedom Federation is a federation of individual, national, multi-ethnic and transgenerational organizations and leaders. The Freedom Federation is not a separate organization. It is a federation of organizations with large and unique constituencies that share common core values.[435]

The Freedom Federation website further explains:

These organizations represent some of the Nation's largest constituents of youth, Hispanics, African-Americans, women, clergy, and churches. The common shared interests include faith, moral values, and freedom. The Freedom Federation is committed to core values expressed in the Declaration of American Values, a document which sets forth foundational values. Based on these shared core values, the leaders of these national organizations will work together on common interests to plan, strategize, coordinate, message and mobilize their various constituents to mobilize a movement to advance these shared core values.

Freedom Federation Member Directory:

- American Association of Christian Counselors—www.aacc.net
- American Family Association—www.afa.net

- Americans for Prosperity—www.americansforprosperity.org
- American Values—www.ouramericanvalues.org
- Bott Radio Network—www.bottradionetwork.com
- Brotherhood Organization of a New Destiny (BOND)—www.bondinfo.org
- Burning Media Group—www.burningmediagroup.com
- Catholic Online—www.catholic.org
- Church of God in Christ—www.cogic.org
- Concerned Women for America—www.cwfa.org
- Eagle Forum—www.eagleforum.org
- Exodus International—www.exodus-international.org
- Extraordinary Women—www.ewomen.net
- Family Research Council Action—www.frcaction.org
- Generals International—www.generals.org
- Harvest International Ministries—www.harvestim.org
- High Impact Leadership Coalition—www.thetruthinblack andwhite.com
- Liberty Alliance Action—www.libertyalliance.org
- Liberty Counsel—www.lc.org
- Liberty University—www.liberty.edu
- Life Education and Resource Network (LEARN)—www.blackgenocide.org
- Lifenews.com—www.lifenews.com
- Morning Star Ministries—www.morningstarministries.org
- National Clergy Council—www.nationalclergycouncil.org
- National Hispanic Christian Leadership Conference—www.nhclc.org
- Renewing American Leadership—www.torenewamerica.com
- Strang Communications—www.strang.com
- Teen Mania—www.teenmania.com
- Teen Pact—www.teenpact.com
- The Call—www.thecall.com
- The Conservative Action Project—www.conservativeaction-project.org
- The Ethics and Religious Liberty Commission—www.erlc.com

- Traditional Values Coalition—www.traditionalvalues.org
- Vision America—www.visionamerica.us
- WallBuilders—www.wallbuilders.com

Did you notice the organizations listed such as Cindy Jacobs's General International, Rick Joyner's Morning Star, Samuel Rodriquez's National Hispanic Christian Leadership Conference, and Lou Engle's The Call? These are all individuals and organizations associated with the New Apostolic Reformation movement.

The Freedom Federation held their 2010 and 2011 conferences at Liberty University. Did you ever think you would see the day when Liberty University and Thomas Road Baptist Church would work in conjunction with those associated with the New Apostolic Reformation? Then, in 2012, the Freedom Federation conference was held at a church in Florida that embraces the Word of Faith movement. The Freedom Federation website listed as invited and/or confirmed the speakers for video presentations. Here is a partial list of those:

- Chuck Colson
- Vonette Bright (wife of the late Bill Bright, who founded Campus Crusade)
- Lou Engle
- Frank Gaffney (Deputy Assistant Secretary of Defense for Nuclear Forces and Arms Control Policy for the Reagan Administration.)
- Mike Huckabee
- Tony Perkins
- Samuel Rodriguez
- Tim Wildmon
- Cindy Jacobs
- Rick Joyner
- Richard Land
- Apostle Guillermo Maldonado[436]

The website also listed as a potential speaker Keith Fournier, who is described as "a deacon in the Roman Catholic Church..."[437] The bio also describes Fournier as "a human rights lawyer, author, scholar, broadcaster, activist, ecumenist and academic."[438] An ecumenist is someone who works to bring religious groups together. It is related to the words "ecumenical" and "ecumenicalism," ideas the Church of Rome has been promoting since Vatican II in 1962–1965.

Mr. Fournier is also founder and president of Common Good.[439] The Common Good website says their objectives include working "for the advancement of true social justice..."[440] Not only that, the name of the organization is itself significant. "Common good" is a phrase used by the pope and the Vatican ever since "the term and modern concept of 'social justice' was coined by the Jesuit Luigi Taparelli in 1840."[441]

These spiritual enterprises of the New Religious Right seem to be a regular occurrence. On January 3, 2012, for instance, the website of Cindy Jacobs reported that representatives of the Family Research Council would be joining Mike and Cindy Jacobs, along with NAR "prophet" Dutch Sheets, for "a night of intercessory prayer."[442] Unfortunately, this did not surprise me. As far back as 2008, the president of the Family Research Council, Tony Perkins, wrote on the FRC blog about taking part in "prophet" Lou Engle's rally on the mall in Washington, D.C. Perkins reported that "I was able to join Lou Engle for about half of the 12–hour event."[443]

A Covenant of Civility or Covenant of Compromise?

Then there is "A Covenant of Civility," which, according to the website of Jim Wallis, was signed by neo-evangelicals, members of the New Religious Right, New Apostolic Reformation associates, and Emergent Church leaders, such as:

- Leith Anderson, president of the National Association of Evangelicals;
- Chuck Colson, founder, Chuck Colson Center for Christian Worldview;
- Paul Cedar, chairman, Mission America Coalition;
- William Hamel, President, Evangelical Free Church of America;
- Jim Wallis, president and CEO, Sojourners;
- Rev. Samuel Rodriguez, president, Hispanic Christian Leadership Conference;
- Lynne Hybels, author and advocate for Global Engagement;

- Tony Campolo, founder and president, Evangelical Association for the Promotion of Education;
- Bart Campolo, minister, The Walnut Hills Fellowship; and
- Joel Hunter, senior pastor, Northland—A Church Distributed.[444]

I fear the American Church is following in the steps of "German Christians" who eliminated their denominations and abandoned doctrinal purity in order to unite under the "Reich Bishop" in order to "save" their country. Nationalism, ecumenical patriotism, mysticism, and a lack of biblical discernment—all of which leads to tolerance of false teaching—are growing at an alarming rate in America.

In April 2011, I wrote an article entitled "Christians that Partner with False Teachers and Think They Are Defending Liberty for the Sake of the Gospel Are Compromising the Gospel for the Sake of Liberty." I warned then, as I do now, that the mixing of evangelicals with false prophets for the sake of the culture war is an offense to the Gospel. God does not need us to violate biblical principles in order to restore righteousness. How can we hope to restore biblical principles in government when we have violated biblical principles within the Church? How can God bless the Church in America and our nation when Christians and Christian leaders are in direct disobedience to God's Word? How can Christians and Christian leaders repent of sin while participating in events that are themselves something for which to repent? The end absolutely does not justify the means. When Christians compromise the Gospel and unite with false teachers in spiritual and political enterprises, regardless of the political outcome, we have lost.

A Questionable Response to "The Response"

Among the endorsers of Governor Perry's rally are C. Peter Wagner. This is the same Wagner, of course, who installed Todd Bentley as a "Prophet." Evidently at some point this connection became a concern even to the promoters of The Response, and Wagner's name and picture were removed from The Response website. I have a printout, though, of the website when it included his name and picture.

In the video of Todd Bentley's installation service, a man is introduced as Che Ahn, who was also listed on the endorser page for The Response. Another friend of Mr. Bentley's is Rick Joyner. A written statement and video clips on Rick Joyner's website reveal Joyner discussing his efforts to restore Todd Bentley to ministry after Bentley divorced his wife and married another woman. Sadly, pro-family leaders like Tony Perkins of the Family Research Council also appeared on Joyner's Morning Star program. Ironically, Perkins once sat on the couch across from Joyner and declared, "We need men who rightly discern the times and can rightly divide the Word of God..."[445]

I believe if Tony were rightly dividing the Word of God, he would not be participating in the online TV program of Rick Joyner and speaking at a function for Rick Joyner's Oak Initiative.[446]

Months before Governor Perry's "Response" was even announced, I reached out privately to leaders of some organizations that ended up participating in the event. I pleaded with them not to join in a spiritual enterprise with anyone participating in the New Apostolic Reformation and the Word of Faith movement. I documented for them the unbiblical teachings of the NAR and Word of Faith movements. Some of them returned my calls, and some did not. A few did their own research and agreed not to participate in The Response or promote it, but others continued to make excuses that they are not in agreement with the theology or doctrine of all involved but are "just uniting for prayer." Yet 2 Corinthians 6:14 does not offer a loophole to make it acceptable to unite for the purpose of "just praying" with false teachers or those who embrace unbiblical theology: "Do not be unequally yoked together with unbelievers. For what fellowship has righteousness with lawlessness? And what communion has light with darkness?"

Likewise, 2 John 9–11 does not give us an "out" to partner with false teachers if we are "just praying":

> Whoever transgresses and does not abide in the doctrine of Christ does not have God. He who abides in the doctrine of Christ has both the Father and the Son. If anyone comes to you and does not bring this doctrine, do not receive him into your house nor greet him; for he who greets him shares in his evil deeds.

Were those who participated in The Response and the like aware of the unbiblical reasons members of the NAR pray? Such reasons include the desire to receive extrabiblical revelations, to see Jesus literally manifested in the Church so Christians become a super-spiritual breed, able to defeat death and the curse of sin.

Another reason their prayers are unbiblical is the desire to bind Satan so a spiritual awakening can occur and permit them to successfully implement public-policy initiatives. They believe the implementation of "kingdom values" will allow them to take over towns, cities, states, and nations and to ultimately establish a global Christian theocracy. But *nowhere* in Scripture are Christians called to "bind Satan," much less to usher in the physical kingdom of God on earth.

Do not be shocked at the excuses and justification that supporters and participants in these events and projects circulate in order to avoid obeying the clear mandate of Scripture not to unite with false teachers. A lack of biblical discernment, research, knowledge, and commitment to the authority of the Word of God has created church leaders who are theologically and doctrinally weak. As a result, they embrace anyone's call for revival, hoping that *some* kind of revival is better than no revival at all and that it will produce greater liberty and prosperity. I contend that what the Church needs to go through is a *decrease* in liberty and prosperity and an *increase* in persecution in order to see biblical revival. Our Christian brothers and sisters in China know this well.

We dare not settle for a false revival. The late Vance Havner put it best when he said:

> I am more afraid of false revival than of no revival—a false revival with a false gospel, false evangelists, false converts, false joy. It will seem so genuine that it would deceive, if possible, the very elect. Many church leaders will endorse it. Other good people will be afraid to oppose it for fear that they might be fighting against God.[447]

The Church in America has been infiltrated by false teachers who use Christian leaders to raise their own credibility and gain acceptance by Christians who would otherwise reject their false teachings. I believe many American Christians will allow their commitment to reclaiming the country, reclaiming Congress, lowering taxes, and defeating progressives trump their commitment to the biblical mandate declared in 2 Corinthians 6:14 that I noted earlier.

The majority of professing Christians in America have succumbed to a form of Christianity that is anything but biblical. I recognize that much of what I am writing and warning about will be met with hostility, and I also know some will marginalize and caricature me because they cannot argue against my message, which is deeply grounded in the Word of God. Charles Spurgeon referred to this kind of situation when he preached:

> We shall not get back a strong race of Christians till we get back such a sturdy band of outspoken men as dare their reputation, if not their lives, upon the unvarnished testimony they give to the Truth they know, the Truth as it is in Jesus, the Truth as it burns in their own hearts and fires their tongues, the Truth as it commends itself to every man's conscience in the sight of God! (1903, Sermon #2854)

Progressives, Evangelicals, and the Third Way

One of the honorary chairmen listed on The Response website was Samuel Rodriquez. And according to another website, one for Come Let Us Reason, Rodriquez was also part of the "Third Way's" leadership team that drafted the "agenda" to bring "evangelicals and progressives" together. The report was called, "Come Let Us Reason Together: A Fresh Look at Shared Cultural Values Between Evangelicals and Progressives."

I wonder if the leadership of the New Religious Right has even heard of the Hegelian Dialectic Process. Do you think they know that as far back as 1953 socialists had infiltrated churches and religious organizations in order to transform America from within? This tactic was taken straight from the teachings of Saul "the Red" Alinsky.

Pastors and authors of the Emergent Church sing the praises of socialism. As I explained in *Grave Influence*, the Emergent Church champions the neo-Marxist call for a utopian society through spiritual evolution where good and evil merge to form a "better" third option. So would you be surprised to discover that the Third Way document which calls for evangelicals and progressives to merge includes "statements of support" by neo-evangelicals, members of the New Religious Right, New Apostolic Reformation, and Emergent Church leaders? The endorsers include:

- Rev. Brian McLaren, author of *Everything Must Change*;
- Johnathan Merritt, founder, Southern Baptist Environment and Climate Initiative;
- Rev. Tony Jones, author of *The New Christians* and *Dispatches from the Emergent Frontier*;
- Dr. Richard Mouw, president, Fuller Theological Seminary;
- Richard Foster, author of *Celebration of Discipline* and other books;
- Dr. Tony Campolo, professor emeritus, Eastern University;
- Rev. Samuel Rodriquez,president, National Hispanic Christian Leadership Conference;
- Rev. Jim Wallis, president, Sojourners;
- Dr. Ronald Sider, president, Evangelicals for Social Action; and
- Rev. Bob Roberts, pastor, Northwood Church.

Ironically, the Come Let Us Reason Together Governing Agenda website includes statements from NARAL Pro-Choice America and People For the American Way. Concerning NARAL, an online encyclopedia, states:

> ...formerly the National Association for the Repeal of Abortion Laws, then National Abortion Rights Action League, and later National Abortion and Reproductive Rights Action League, is an organization in the United States that engages in political action to oppose restrictions on abortion and expand access to abortion. NARAL is often used as a short form of the name.[448]

NARAL Pro-Choice America's statement reads:

> As new leadership emerges in Washington and across the country, we have a unique opportunity to change the tone of the debate over reproductive rights. To that end, Third Way's proposals are a welcome

addition to this process. As our movement for common ground continues to gain steam among Americans across the political spectrum, we are watching with interest to see if anti-choice politicians will put aside their divisive old habits and join us in working for practical, commonsense solutions to help prevent unintended pregnancy.[449]

An online encyclopedia also says this about People For the American Way: "People For the American Way (People For) is a progressive advocacy group in the United States."[450] The organization's purpose statement reads:

Third Way has taken on a daunting challenge in reaching across culture war battle lines to build momentum for policies to move the nation forward. People For the American Way will continue to advocate energetically for full legal equality for LGBT Americans and for women's right to reproductive choice. Nonetheless, we recognize the significance of broadening evangelical support for these core principles including efforts to reduce unintended pregnancy and prevent job discrimination on the basis of sexual orientation. Just as passionate advocates for religious liberty sometimes disagree on the application of that core constitutional principle to specific policy questions, we know that there will never be unanimity on these difficult questions. But there is great value in conversation that seeks to find shared support for ways to move the nation toward the ideals of freedom, equality, and opportunity for all.[451]

What makes this call to cooperation especially ironic is that People For the American Way operates a website called Rightwingwatch. org. This site tracks activities of the religious right and spent months talking about Governor Perry's prayer event that was sponsored, supported, and promoted by pro-family and evangelical leaders. Yet the New Religious Right is so undiscerning and nonjudgmental about their partnerships with theologically and doctrinally erring groups that they chose as one of their honorary co-chairmen a minister who assisted in developing a report supported by NARAL and People For the American Way, a large progressive organization.

On almost a weekly basis I am finding more evidence that reveals that the political and theological left and right are converging. Many of the members of the New Religious Right are so undiscerning and so poorly read and informed on the philosophies ruling the day, and they are so ignorant of basic biblical doctrine, that they don't even know they are welcoming a Trojan horse.

The New Religious Right leaders I have warned are so theologically challenged that some of them could not even keep up with the most basic of terms I used in our conversations. One major New Religious Right leader told me he did not even know what the word *pantheism* means. This same New Religious Right leader told me he believes that people who do not believe Jesus is the only way can still go to heaven. In another conversation, I asked this New Religious Right leader what his eschatology was in regards to the rapture of the Church. This very public and long-standing member of the New Religious Right had to turn to someone inside his own organization and ask them what he believes as he did not know the answer to my question.

The Third Way holds a variety of nonbiblical positions as revealed in its document entitled "The Governing Agenda," which states that their goals include "making it illegal to fire, refuse to hire, or refuse to promote employees simply based on their sexual orientation."[452] Although "Come Let Us Reason" calls for an "exemption for faith-based employers," it is worth wondering how long such an exception would last. What about all the Christian families running their own small businesses? I believe this goal of "making it illegal to fire, refuse to hire, or refuse to promote employees simply based on their sexual orientation" will eventually include transgender, transsexual, and other such groups. If the stated goal of Come Let Us Reason ever becomes a full-blown reality and your family business hires a man in a suit who shows up the next day in a dress, it would be illegal for you to terminate his employment.

What must the executives at Home Depot think of many "pro-family" leaders? At one time, pro-family leaders criticized them for embracing the same-sex agenda, and yet some of the same New Religious Right can be observed in projects or initiatives with those who embrace Come Let Us Reason. Other aspects of the document's "Governing Agenda" which I find troubling include:

> Prevention policies include grants for sex education (age-appropriate, medically accurate and complete contraceptive information with an abstinence emphasis) and support for teen pregnancy prevention programs, including after-school programs and resources to help parents better communicate with teens, and increased access to contraception for low-income women.[453]

Do you want to see more tax dollars going into our schools with a mixed message of abstinence along with "complete contraceptive information"? Why then were members of the New Religious Right honoring as a co-chair of The Response Samuel Rodriquez, who was part of the leadership team that composed the Come Let Us Reason Governing Agenda? Rev. Rodriquez reportedly is also an apostle of the New Apostolic Reformation. His name was included in the 2009 membership directory of the "International Coalition of Apostles." Rev. Rodriquez is also listed, at the time this book is being written, on the executive committee of the National Association of Evangelicals (NAE). Have you kept up with what this radical organization has been involved with over the past few years? Let me give you just one example. The NAE is promoting what is called "The Circle of Protection," which states:

> Funding focused on reducing poverty should not be cut. It should be made as effective as possible, but not cut... National leaders must review and consider tax revenues, military spending, and entitlements in the search for ways to share sacrifice and cut deficits...[454]

In other words, the National Association of Evangelicals wants to continue the failed "war on poverty" in order to redistribute more income of working Americans to the slothful and lazy among us. Where in the Bible—or in the U.S. Constitution—is it the job of the government to fund the poor?

In 2005, David Noebel wrote a letter to the leaders of the National Association of Evangelicals warning that the organization (through its publication *Toward an Evangelical Public Policy*) seemed to be embracing Jim Wallis and his pro-Communist agenda. He cautioned, "If the NAE is going to follow the 'evangelical progressives' (translation: leftists, socialists, communists, statists, etc.) they will be making the biggest mistake of the 21st century." Unlike the New Religious Right leaders of today, Dr. Noebel understands that another word for progressive is "socialist." John Dewey, for example, was the father of progressive education, but he was also an atheist, socialist, and signatory to the 1933 Humanist Manifesto. He also headed the Fabian organization, League for Industrial Democracy.

This drift toward socialism is certainly welcomed by those with a one-world agenda. The list of federal programs focused on assisting hungry and poor people mentioned on the website of the Circle of Protection include numerous programs that promote the goals of the United Nations and its quest for global governance and sustainable development.

The Circle of Protection website lists Reverend Rodriquez as one of its "primary signatories," along with Jim Wallis of Sojourners. David Noebel has written an excellent piece on Jim Wallis that you can read in its entirety on our website at WorldviewWeekend.com, but here is an eye-opening excerpt:

> First, Jim Wallis has had relationships with the communist Committee in Solidarity with the People of El Salvador (CISPES).

> Second, his "Witness for Peace" was an attempt to defend the Nicaraguan Sandinistas! Wallis, together with the Rev. Jeremiah Wright (Obama's former pastor of 20 years) "rallied support for the communist Nicaraguan regime and protested actions by the United States which supported the anti-communist Contra rebels" (*Family World News*, February 2009, p. 7).

> Third, Wallis and his Sojourners community of fellow-travelers believe Fidel Castro's Cuba, Hugo Chavez's Venezuela, Daniel Ortega's Nicaragua, and

the other revolutionary forces "restructuring social-ist societies" are the communist paradises the United States needs to emulate in order to establish "social justice." Writing in the November 1983 issue of *So-journers*, Jacob Laksin notes, "Jim Wallis and Jim Rice drafted what would become the charter of leftist ac-tivists committed to the proliferation of Communist revolutions in Central America" (Laksin, "Sojourners: History, Activities and Agendas" in *Discoverthenet-works.org.*, 2005).

The ugly truth is Wallis wishes to see the destruc-tion of the United States as a nation and in its place "a radical nonconformist community" patterned after the progressive, socialist commune he established in Washington, D.C., in 1971 (Laksin, Ibid.).

The New Religious Right is fast becoming a company of the con-fused. Progressives base their liberal social action on theological lib-eralism. And today's New Religious Right leaders are becoming theo-logically liberal or ignorant. Either way, New Religious Right leaders are an easy mark for infiltration. Their philosophical and theological ignorance make them easy dupes for the progressives.

Bear in mind that progressives do not care if the Church in Amer-ica specifically promotes socialism by name as long as the Church is so weak theologically and doctrinally that it accepts socialism in principle. Ironically, many of the NRR believe they are fighting social-ism even as they give credibility and an audience to "evangelical" pro-gressives. Willow Creek Community Church is cozy with Jim Wallis's Sojourners organization—the senior pastor's wife is a writer for the organization.

Evangelical progressives and theological liberals must be laughing at how easy it has been for them to lead today's New Religious Right leaders around by the nose. Did you ever think the NRR could fall into a trap such as The Response, even after being warned? Do these men not own computers with a search engine? Did they never think of Googling the names of their new comrades before hooking their wagons to theirs? Did the New Religious Right think they would save the country from Obama's socialism while embracing evangelical progressives? The New Religious Right cannot even save themselves from useful-idiot status!

If today's pro-family and Christian leaders had taken time to read *Grave Influence* when it came out in November 2009 and if they had heeded my detailed warning on how socialists were attempting to infiltrate them, they would not be in the mess they are in today. I believe the next generation of pro-family leaders is extremely ignorant when it comes to the worldviews and philosophies of the day, and as a result, it is being taken captive by the philosophies of men that are not according to Christ as warned in Colossians 2:8.

Evidently some pro-family groups have no problem accepting the policies with which Samuel Rodriguez is associated. On January 19, 2011, Focus on the Family released a press release announcing that they would be working with the organization Rodriguez heads in order "to reach US Hispanics, the nation's largest and fastest growing demographic, with faith and family help resources tailored specifically for this audience."[455] In February 2012, Focus on the Family featured Rodriquez for a webcast to churches for a date night.[456] The American Family Association also advertised that Rodriquez would be a featured speaker at an AFA marriage conference in 2012.[457]

Pentecostal Pastor Warns the Church about the NAR

Independent Pentecostal pastor Bill Randles was a guest on my radio program on August 2, 2011. Bill has been warning about the Gnosticism of the New Apostolic Reformation for years, starting with his book *Beware of False Prophets*. Pastor Randles explained that Christians united with NAR members at the The Response were praying with people who do not describe the Jesus of the Bible in their teachings.

While I am sorry The Response was ever organized, I am thankful the event allowed Christians to see that if the Church in America follows the New Religious Right and their leaders, she does so at her own peril. The Church in America cannot say God has not been gracious by giving us such a clear example of who and what we must *not* follow.

What is sad is that while some self-professing Christians could not seem to grasp that this situation is about compromising the Gospel for political and pragmatic reasons, the left clearly figured it out. They recognize the compromise one must accept in order to unite with false teachers:

In my coverage of The Response, I talked to a woman whose blog post critical of the NAR from this perspective was taken off the American Family Association website. The AFA and other big religious right political operatives are not interested in the heresy hunters, though; they're interested in the bodies that NAR types bring to events like Perry's and ultimately to the voting booth. That's been a longstanding strategy of GOP candidates, as I reported in my book. There, even though Word of Faith (also known as the prosperity gospel) is, like the NAR and other neo-Pentecostal movements, considered problematic and even heretical by many conservative Christians, what the candidates look at is not intra-conservative theological disputes, or even the questionable ethics of some of the leading preachers, but at how many followers they have.

No doubt both the AFA and Perry's political team, as well as the group assembled by televangelist James Robison last September and more recently in June, were making those sorts of calculations.[458]

The New Religious Right did not take kindly to my talking about this on my radio program and writing about it in my columns. But again, the secular press picked up on the story:

The American Family Association has taken aim at fellow religious conservative Brannon Howse over his criticism of the AFA's recent sponsorship of GOP presidential candidate Rick Perry's The Response prayer meeting. Earlier this week, Jim Stanley, program director of AFA's radio network, American Family Radio, sent notices to two talk show hosts who are associated with Howse, informing them that continued presence on the AFA's radio network was conditioned on severing ties with Howse....

Howse heads Worldview Weekend, a socially conservative ministry which espouses similar conservative views as the AFA on culture war issues as abortion and homosexuality. However, Howse charges that religious right leaders have formed improper religious alliances with leaders in the New Apostolic Reformation such as Cindy Jacobs in order to promote a conservative political agenda. About his stance, Howse said, "Christians must defend the gospel when we believe Christian leaders are giving credibility to what the Bible describes as false teaching." About Wildmon's concerns, Howse added, "I have avoided naming this radio network or pro-family group and I have avoided naming several of the pro-family groups hoping they would repent."...

One of the targeted talk show hosts, John Loeffler, has decided not to continue with the AFA. Loeffler said, "I told Tim [Wildmon], 'you may remove my show based on your ultimatum since I will not stop speaking for Brannon Howse.'"[459]

Now please understand, I am not complaining; I knew up front that my stand for biblical truth would cost me in many ways, and it did. I also want you to know, though, that as 2011 and 2012 unfolded, our organization grew dramatically. Yet even if it had not, that would be acceptable. God is in control, and all promotion comes from Him (James 4:10).

Throughout those two challenging years, I came to understand just how many Christians and non-Christians are watching, and make no mistake, they are aware of who is being faithful and who is compromising. My job is not to be the conscience of those who have compromised. My job is to keep studying God's Word and do what He wants me to do.

I must be gracious to others as God has been gracious to me, but that does not mean I should not lovingly speak truth. Romans 8:18 is one of my favorite verses: "I consider that our present sufferings are not worth comparing with the glory that will be revealed in us."

The "soft persecution" you and I go through is nothing compared to what our brothers and sisters in Christ have endured for years in China, Cuba, and behind the former Iron Curtain. In fact, this "soft persecution" may be preparing you and me for what is to come. I believe persecution may indeed come most from a false church and that those now living in America are living in a nation under God's judgment—a judgment that will mean an increase in false teachers and those who follow them.

The infiltration of the religious left into the New Religious Right happens because God is judging America. I believe part of this judgment includes God giving America a new generation of leaders who do *not* understand the worldviews and philosophies that rule the day. Why else would these pro-family leaders willfully ignore the private warnings given to them in April 2011 about partnering with the progressives, the New Apostolic Reformation, and the Word of Faith movement? Even after all the evidence and Scripture has been produced to reveal the false teachers and their equally false teachings, NRR leaders and their followers continue to justify unbiblical projects, initiatives, and relationships.

Proverbs 15:32 sums up this situation: "He who disdains instruction despises his own soul, But he who heeds rebuke gets understanding." Evangelicals lose their souls when they lose sight of their first biblical priority and immerse themselves in political and cultural entanglements that cause them to partner with people who are not biblically sound. As 2 Timothy 2:4 notes: "No one engaged in warfare entangles himself with the affairs of this life, that he may please him who enlisted him as a soldier."

An individual's worldview is the foundation of his or her values, and those values are the foundation of the person's conduct. If the New Religious Right had a commitment first and foremost to biblical truth, it would have never put itself in this position. One pro-family leader informed me that it was acceptable to embrace those with unbiblical theologies because the organization was not a theological organization, per se. But *everyone* who is not committed first and foremost to biblical truth will find themselves deceived by a religious Trojan horse filled with progressives on the attack.

CHAPTER 10

Christian Shamanism
and the Law of Attraction

"Two weeks ago I experienced a great moment in my Christian journey. Seventy-two leaders joined together in supernatural spiritual unity..."[460]—James Robison, July 8, 2011 (posted at jamesrobison. net)

Well-known Baptist turned Word-of-Faither James Robison effervesced about a collection of evangelical leaders who should have known better than to "join together in spiritual unity" with him. The assembly listed on this website was rather lengthy, but the list included a few of the more recognizable evangelical or pro-family leaders such as:

- Tony Perkins, Family Research Council;
- Don Wildmon, American Family Association;
- Richard Land, SBC Ethics & Religious Liberty Commission;
- Tony Evans, Oak Cliff Bible Fellowship; and
- Vonette Bright, Campus Crusade for Christ.

Robison also listed a number of well-known teachers within the Word of Faith movement, but some of the most recognizable names include:

- Kenneth Copeland, Kenneth Copeland Ministries;
- Creflo Dollar, World Changers Church International; and
- Joyce Meyer, Joyce Meyer Ministries.

In his online article, Robison declared that:

...[I]t is imperative that those chosen to lead have enough wisdom to understand the importance of sit-

ting in the counsel of the godly, not the ungodly…
I am convinced God is going to use these national
leaders to help inspire a spiritual awakening…[461]

His statement presupposes that these leaders are "sitting in the counsel of the godly"—a contention which I say is wrong. How about Christian leaders who have enough wisdom not to unite with and give credibility to false teachers? What kind of spiritual awakening can occur when Christian and pro-family leaders unite with false teachers of the Word of Faith movement and the New Apostolic Reformation? Not the biblical kind, I'm afraid.

In his article, Robison also lauded several other questionable gatherings of "godly counsel":

I have been so blessed to host two national Leadership Summits in September 2010 and June 2011 attended by leaders who understand the importance of faith, family and freedom. They recognize that God and truth are under assault and that we must boldly proclaim liberty throughout the land… In these two leadership gatherings, I witnessed the spiritual unity that Jesus prayed for in John 17.[462]

While I agree that God and truth are under assault, I believe it is under assault largely because many of America's Christian leaders do not understand or obey the biblical directive that forbids uniting with false teachers. God's Word is being compromised because Christian leaders have placed Christian activism and reclaiming America over biblical theology and defending the Church from false teaching.

Mainstreaming the Word of Faith Movement

To further reveal how Word of Faith preachers are going more and more mainstream, consider this disturbing information. The website dfw.undergodindivisible.org promoted a July 27, 2012 event that included Word of Faith preacher Kenneth Copeland, "apostle" Samuel Rodriquez, Catholic priest Jonathan Morris, and Robert Sirico. Cohosted by James Robison, the event included Catholic Jay Richards, Robison's co-author of the book *Indivisible*. David Barton, also a featured speaker, has declared that Glenn Beck can be a Mormon and a

Christian at the same time. Other confirmed speakers were Richard Land and Jim Garlow, who had also hosted Glenn Beck, James Robison, and Jay Richards at his church for two events on April 22, 2012.

But now for the truly disturbing part: the speakers list also included Ravi Zacharias, Tony Evans, and David Jeremiah. Why would these three men participate in an event with Word of Faithers? Why would *any* Bible teacher want to speak at the same event with Kenneth Copeland? What's more, the website declared, "This meeting will be held separate from but in conjunction with, The Glenn Beck 'Restoring Love' gathering on July 28 in Cowboy Stadium."[463]

Again, why would a Bible teacher appear at an event "separate from but in conjunction with" New Age Mormon Glenn Beck? The website explained:

> This evening event begins at 6:30 PM and is an "Under God: INDIVISIBLE" call for spiritual awakening. This event is for leaders, pastors, businessmen and other concerned citizens and will include messages from a renowned group of national speakers who will encourage and challenge us to find common ground for common concerns. This will NOT be a political meeting, rather, it will be a call for a necessary spiritual awakening![464]

Do not be shocked at how people will defend Christian "celebrities" who unite in spiritual enterprises with Glenn Beck. Some excuse participation by pastors who should know better by declaring, "Well, they were there to preach the Gospel." The track record shows, though, that such proclamation of the Gospel rarely occurs. Yet, even if participants were to give the Gospel, it would be confused with the gospel of Glenn Beck unless the speaker were to specifically call out the false gospel, the false Jesus, the false god, the heretical cult of Mormonism, and the futility and blasphemy of a spiritual enterprise seeking to mix Christianity with pagan spirituality.

In addition, 2 John 9-11, 2 Corinthians 6:14, Romans 16:17, and Ephesians 5:11 close any loophole by which Christians might biblically unite in spiritual enterprises with unbelievers and false teachers in order to "present the Gospel." God does not need Christians to violate His Word so as to reach the lost. The problem is that many hearers will be spiritually confused when the true Jesus of the Bible is just another "Jesus" referenced in an ecumenical meeting by self-professing Christians. The true Gospel cannot be intermingled with a false gospel without undermining its essence, purity, and clarity. For this reason, we are strictly admonished in God's Word not to enter into spiritual enterprises with unbelievers and false teachers but to "avoid them" (Romans 16:17) and "from such people turn away" (2 Timothy 3:5). At the July 27, 2012 event Glenn Beck thanked the pastors assembled on stage for standing with him, a Mormon. Beck then spoke of the rapture: "the Lord is coming, and He is our Father in heaven."

Do these pastors follow the same God as Glenn Beck? That would be the impression given by many in attendance because, to my knowledge, no one refuted Beck's "our father in heaven" statement. As we have already learned, the LDS church teaches that the Mormon God was a man of flesh and bone that evolved to become God. Beck spoke of his accepting Jesus and "the atonement." Former Mormon Ed Decker and my friend Ron Carlson in their book *Fast Facts on False Teachings* explain what "atonement" means to a Mormon:

> To the Mormon, Jesus was our elder brother who pointed the way, but he isn't The Way as we Christians understand it. To the Mormon, Jesus was the god of the Old Testament, but once he took his physical form, he had to justify or earn his own spiritual salvation through his works while in the flesh, just as each of us must.

> Mormonism teaches that Jesus suffered for our sins in the Garden of Gethsemane, providing personal salvation (which may mean exaltation to godhood) conditional upon our obedience to the laws and ordinances of the LDS gospel. His death on the cross provided a general salvation, whereby all of us will be resurrected to be judged for our own works.

> It is no wonder that you will never see a cross on a Mormon Church—not when you see that Mormons cannot deal with its gift of grace. This is the same reason they use water for communion. They call it The

Sacrament, but that water washes away the reality of the blood shed for us at the cross of Christ.

> Jesus is the LDS savior only in the sense that his death gives the Mormon the means of returning to the god of this world, using the secret keys, handgrips, and passwords learned only in the Mormon Temple, secrets that will ensure safe passage through the doorway to personal godhood.[465]

In his speech at High Point Church before the pastors and priests assembled on stage and several thousand in the auditorium, Beck declared, "America is necessary for his [God's] work to be done." I read nowhere in the Bible that God *needs* America. However, Mormon eschatology teaches that the Mormon Church will be the outpost for the global LDS church and that Jesus will return to Independence, Missouri to set up his kingdom there in the "New Jerusalem." In fact, on August 3, 1831 Joseph Smith dedicated a plot of ground in Independence, Missouri where the temple is to be built just before the return of Christ. Mormon eschatology teaches that Jesus will sit in this temple and rule his earthly kingdom.[466]

I believe this Mormon eschatology explains why Beck thinks God needs him and his followers to save America. In addition, the "Joseph Smith White Horse Prophecy" predicted the Mormon Church would save America.[467]

After Beck's 8-28 rally in Washington DC, I stated that a seismic shift had occurred in evangelicalism and now the groundwork was laid for many "evangelicals" to unite with Beck and others who hold to heretical teachings for the purpose of "reclaiming America." I believe the July 27, 2012 event is proof of what I warned about two years earlier. However, this time it was not just the expected New Religious Right leaders who united with Beck but men who have been respected as conservative Bible teachers. I believe yet another seismic shift has occurred with the participation by Zacharias, Evans, and Jeremiah in such a clearly unbiblical and ecumenical spiritual event. Time will tell how their participation will be used by others to justify subsequent involvement in more ecumenical events that give credibility to "another" Jesus and another gospel.

The calling of Christians is not to guard the culture but to guard the Church and the Gospel. Our calling as Christians is not to rescue the culture through conservative politics but to rescue individuals through biblical truth.

Because Satan will proclaim truth in order to draw a crowd and then undermine the Gospel, I believe one of the best Scripture passages we can examine to understand the dangers of the spiritual enterprises of folks like Glenn Beck and his "evangelical" participants is Acts 16:16-18:

> Now it happened, as we went to prayer, that a certain slave girl possessed with a spirit of divination met us, who brought her masters much profit by fortune-telling. This girl followed Paul and us, and cried out, saying, "These men are the servants of the Most High God, who proclaim to us the way of salvation." And this she did for many days.
>
> But Paul, greatly annoyed, turned and said to the spirit, "I command you in the name of Jesus Christ to come out of her." And he came out that very hour.

The girl was possessed by demons, and Paul knew it. The apostle did not want the endorsement of the demons even if they were speaking truth by announcing, "These men are the servants of the Most High God, who proclaim to us the way of salvation." Why? Because Paul knew that Satan will use truth in order to attract a crowd and to gain credibility, but then he will manipulate the people and undermine the Gospel.

This is exactly what Glenn Beck has done with his religious talk that appeals to Christians and undiscerning evangelicals. As a Mormon, Beck mixes truth with error—Satan's strategy for infiltrating the church with a religious Trojan horse. John MacArthur explains the approach:

> Even praise of the gospel can be deceitful and misleading. When Paul and Silas began to minister in Philippi, Luke reports that "a certain slave-girl having a spirit of divination met us, who was bringing her masters much profit by fortunetelling. Following after Paul and us, she kept crying out, saying, 'These men are

bond-servants of the Most High God, who are proclaiming to you the way of salvation'" (Acts 16:16-17). What the girl said not only was true but seemed to be favorable to the gospel and to those who were proclaiming it.

But the purpose and motivation of what she said was exactly the opposite. The demons who controlled her meant to attract the people and, gaining their trust, then ridicule and undercut God's Word and the work of His ministers. In that case Paul could not judge by what was said, because the girl's words were true. He knew she was a demonic instrument only because the Holy Spirit revealed the false spirit that controlled her. [468]

Matthew Henry's Biblical Commentary on Acts 16:16-24 similarly declares:

Satan, though the father of lies, will declare the most important truths, when he can thereby serve his purposes. But much mischief is done to the real servants of Christ, by unholy and false preachers of the gospel, who are confounded with them by careless observers. Those who do good by drawing men from sin, may expect to be reviled as troublers of the city. [469]

When we point out the demonic nature of such spiritual enterprises, it will not be received well by many within the religious establishment. But make no mistake, there are only two kingdoms: the kingdom of God and the kingdom of Satan, and these two camps cannot merge. When this is attempted, you can be sure it is not of God.

When religious leaders are called out for giving a platform to those serving Satan and preaching another Jesus and another gospel, they often turn on those speaking biblical truth and bring persecution on the very ones trying to guard the Church as we are commanded to in Acts 20:28-31. Paul and Silas were persecuted and taken to jail because they were preaching the Gospel and exposing the plan of Satan to co-opt God's truth in order to undermine God's work. MacArthur notes:

Satan was quick to react, first attempting to infiltrate the young fellowship with a demon-possessed medium. When Paul's miraculous power thwarted that attempt, Satan tried to destroy the church through persecution. Those are always his two avenues of attack: infiltration—attacking the church from within; and persecution, attacking it from without.[470]

The Church is in great need of Christians who will warn of false teachers, false prophets, false apostles, and "evangelical celebrities" who compromise and in many cases wage war on God's Word. Of this, MacArthur says:

> I believe God still empowers some of His people to unmask false prophets and carnal hypocrites. He gives them insight to expose imitations and deceptions that most Christians would take as genuine.[471]

Great Awakening or Great Falling Away?

Glenn Beck has become the Joel Osteen of political activism. On July 28, 2012, when Beck hosted his "Restoring Love Rally" in Dallas, I watched his speech before a packed house (people were even sitting on the football field). His mixed message of New Age philosophy, Mormon theology, and self-help tickled the ears of many, as described in 2 Timothy 4:3-4:

> For the time will come when they will not endure sound doctrine, but according to their own desires, because they have itching ears, they will heap up for themselves teachers; and they will turn their ears away from the truth, and be turned aside to fables.

With a live orchestra playing behind him, Beck shouted, "Witness the Third Great Awakening! It's here; it's here!"[472]

On his radio program the Monday after his rally, Beck declared:

> As a guy who has been bringing you the bad news for I don't know how long now, let me bring you the good news: That is true. And if you don't know what the Third Great Awakening means, look it up. Look it up. People have been praying for it since before Martin

Luther King was born. People have been praying for it, and it's here. It's here. It's why we have, I really believe we—don't you feel it? Don't you feel that there's been a turning point in the country?"[473]

If you know anything about the first two Great Awakenings, they were not movements of political activism. They were not sparked by "all faiths uniting" to "look to one God." They were not sparked by evangelical leaders compromising the Word of God in ecumenical and pagan enterprises. The Great Awakenings were the result of the proclamation of a biblical Gospel and of men and women repenting of their sins and placing their faith and trust in the Jesus depicted in God's Word.

What Beck calls a "Great Awakening" would be more accurately called "A Great Falling Away." The Bible calls it apostasy, a turning from traditionally held biblical truths. Indeed there is a spiritual awakening. An October 2010 report revealed that 72 percent of young people between the ages of 18 and 29 now refer to themselves as more spiritual than religious.[474]

In 1 Timothy 4:1, Paul warns that in the period between the first coming of Jesus Christ and His Second Coming, there will be an increase in apostasy: "In the latter times, some will depart from the faith, giving heed to deceiving spirits and the doctrines of demons." Through Glenn Beck, many have been introduced to the doctrines of demons. To wit, Joseph Smith, the founder of Mormonism, testified that he received his special revelation from the angel Moroni. The claims of Smith and the Mormon Church notwithstanding, if Smith did receive such a visit and revelation, it was not from a messenger of God but from a demon or Satan himself. Ed Decker and Ron Carlson explain Smith's occult background:

> Michael Quinn, onetime professor of history at Brigham Young University, wrote a book entitled *Early Mormonism in the Magic World View*. It clearly documents the fact that Joseph Smith was heavily involved in the occult before he ever began to receive revelations from his messengers of light. Mr. Quinn is no longer with BYU or the LDS church. While the LDS church cannot refute his scholarship, they have nevertheless repudiated him personally.[475]

Today, "evangelical" leaders and pastors are giving credibility to Glenn Beck and assisting in the increase of apostasy—an apostasy that Jesus spoke of in Matthew 24 as a major sign of His approaching Second Coming. These folks should be cautious of any spiritual event that includes false teachers and calls for a "spiritual awakening." I agree with the late Vance Havner who said:

> I am more afraid of false revival than of no revival—a false revival with a false gospel, false evangelists, false converts, false joy. It will seem so genuine that it would deceive, if possible, the very elect. Many church leaders will endorse it. Other good people will be afraid to oppose it for fear that they might be fighting against God.[476]

A quick search of YouTube reveals numerous leaders of the New Religious Right appearing on programs of some of America's leading Word of Faith proponents. And Glenn Beck's frequent guest, David Barton, has appeared on Kenneth Copeland's television program as well.

Yet, as Robison's report demonstrates, Barton is not the only member of the New Religious Right who has cooperated with members of the Word of Faith movement. The "spiritual unity" Robison describes is not anywhere close to what Jesus spoke of in John 17 when He prayed for His disciples. In fact, I believe people like Creflo Dollar and Kenneth Copeland are not followers of Jesus Christ at all but are the very kind of false teachers Jesus warned would be prevalent in the last days.

A more accurate biblical reference would be 1 Kings 18 where we see the Children of Israel mixing their worship of God with pagan spirituality. I believe this is what we are seeing today as Christian and pro-family leaders unite with false teachers who openly promote pagan spirituality.

Christianizing Shamanism

Much of what we see in the Word of Faith movement and New Apostolic Reformation is "Christianized" shamanism. Dave Hunt warned about this growing trend in his 1985 best-selling book, *The Seduction of Christianity*, when he wrote:

Shamanism promises power to heal and transform through contact with a parallel universe of the spirit, from which this mysterious energy is allegedly drawn. That contact is said to be made in our minds: The thoughts we think and the words we speak become the vehicles of spiritual power. Those who accept this concept become victims of the great delusion that displaces God with self. In seeking power for self, they have become susceptible to the power of Satan. Nevertheless, even as the irrefutable evidence mounts documenting its destructive and evil power, shamanism's popularity and general acceptance is exploding in the secular world, and in "Christianized" forms is gaining increasing acceptance within the church.[477]

Hunt warns of the occult foundation upon which a vast majority of the Word of Faith movement is based:

The mental images that one is able to picture or visualize are no longer looked upon as mere figments of the mind, but as reality created by the mind that can even impact the physical world. The intimate relationship between thinking, speaking, and seeing (and the power thereby produced) has formed the basis of occult theory for thousands of years. The metaphysical philosophy underlying Positive Thinking and Possibility Thinking as well as major aspects of the Positive Confession movement is founded upon the alleged power inherent within thoughts and words.[478]

Please understand that I am not saying the individuals and groups discussed in this chapter are deliberately practicing shamanism or sorcery. Many believe they are practicing something biblical, but clearly it is not. Dave Hunt also saw this coming:

...the terminology, while sounding biblical, promotes concepts that cannot be found in the Bible, but are found in occult literature and practice. Moreover, some of the Positive Confession leaders not only admit but teach that the methods, laws, and principles they use are also used successfully by occultists. Nowhere in the Bible does it indicate or even imply that the people of God are to use the same methods or powers as the pagans.[479]

As we will examine later in this chapter, self-professing Christians and even pastors attribute to God the New Age "law of attraction" that is elsewhere promoted by people like Oprah Winfrey.

If you're not acquainted with some of these teachers, you'll be amazed at what passes from their lips as Christian teaching. Take, for example, this transcript of Gloria Copeland teaching:

> COPELAND—You know, you're the—you're supposed to control the weather. I mean, Ken's the primary weatherman at our house, but when he's not there I do it. And you can see what's happening out there. It shows just like they have on—at the weather—like on the news. I mean, he's got the computer that's got the current weather on it and all that for flying. So sometimes I'll hear something, I'll hear the thunder start, and maybe he'll still be asleep, and I'll say, "Ken, you need to do something about this." [Laughter]
>
> And knowing that—but you are the one that has authority over the weather. One day Ken and Pat Boone, when we were at Hawaii at their house, and we were—they were setting outside, and there was a weather spout out over the ocean.
>
> And that's like a tornado, except it hits the water. And so they were sitting there and they just watched it, rebuked it, and it never did anything. One day, I was in the airplane, in the back, and my little brother was in the back with me, and Ken was up front flying. And we were not in the weather, because we don't fly bad weather, but we could see the weather over here. And I looked out the window and that tornado came down just like this, down toward the ground. And Ken said, "I rebuke you in the name of Jesus. You get back up there!"

So this is how I learned how to talk to tornados. I saw this. And that tornado went [*makes repeated whooping noise*], even while I was watching. And my little brother was not a devout Christian at that time, and that was really good for him to see.

So you're the weatherman. You get out there—or the weatherwoman, whichever it is, and you talk to that thing, and you tell it, "You're not coming here. I command you to dissipate! And you get back up there in Jesus' name!" Glory to God. That—I won't charge you extra.[480]

My friend Justin Peters is one of the leading experts (if not *the* leading expert) in America on the unbiblical teachings of the Word of Faith movement). As a guest on my radio program, he responded this way to Gloria Copeland's weatherman episode:

If this is true that Gloria Copeland and others in the Word-Faith movement can control the weather, then might we ask where she was when hurricane Katrina came into town? Might we ask why she doesn't, right now, talk up some rain to the people in drought-stricken countries in eastern Africa? It's just, it's absurd on its face, but this [W-F theology], unfortunately, is the face of Christianity in much of the world today.

Gloria Copeland saying that we can control the weather, and what I teach in my seminar is, "Who else does this remind you of? Does it remind you of Someone Who, one day, was in a boat with His disciples and a storm came up, and He spoke to the storm and calmed it?" The Word-Faith proponents denigrate God's deity. They demote God to make Him look more human than what He is, and then in return they deify man to make us look more like God than what we really are. They ascribe to man attributes and powers that reside solely with God, and so they blur that distinction between God the Creator, and us, His created. That is a very, very dangerous line to blur.[481]

Another popular Word of Faith teacher is Benny Hinn, who, like many Word of Faith teachers, seems to believe that instead of man serving God, God is to serve man. Note this interchange between Hinn and Myles Munroe:

> BENNY HINN—We get the mind of God about His will, we pray it. When we pray it, we give Him legal right to perform it.

> MYLES MUNROE—Yes. Let me define prayer for you in this show. Prayer is man giving God permission, or license, to interfere in earth's affairs. In other words, prayer is earthly license for heavenly interference...God can do nothing on earth, nothing has God ever done on earth without a human giving Him access...Always looking for a human to give Him power of permission. In other words, God has the power, but you got the permission. God got the authority and the power, but you got the license. So even though God can do anything, He can only do what you permit Him to do.[482]

God does not need our permission to do anything. Psalm 115:3 declares, "But our God *is* in heaven; He does whatever He pleases." In Psalm 135:6, we read, "Whatever the Lord pleases He does, in heaven and in earth." And Psalm 103:19 announces, "The Lord has established His throne in heaven, and His kingdom rules over all."

Jessie Duplantis is another popular Word of Faith teacher who describes a similarly impotent God:

> I'm gonna say something, gonna knock your lights out. God has the power to take life, but He can't. He got the power to do it, but He won't. He's bound. He can't. He says death and life is in the power of whose son? Yours. You ready for this? You want something that'll knock your lights out? You choose when you live. You choose when you die.[483]

When I played this sound clip on my radio program, Justin Peters had this to say in response to Duplantis's blasphemy:

> Jessie says that "God has the power to take life, but He can't, He's bound, He won't." Well, I think that would come as a real surprise to King Herod. I think that would come as a real surprise to Uzzah, who reached up to steady the ark, and God struck him dead. I think that would come as a real surprise to everyone who was alive on the face of the earth, except for eight people, in that whole flood thing. But God is the One Who gives life. God is the One Who takes life. And it's just the height of arrogance to say that God can or cannot do anything. God can do whatever He wants to do... it's the height of arrogance to say God can't do things, and we have the power to do things that only God can do. So it's profoundly unbiblical. If people knew the Word of God, if they would just pick up their Bible and read it and study it, so much of this would go away.[484]

But wait, as they say, there's more. John Hagee appeared with numerous members of the New Religious Right at Glenn Beck's 8-28 rally in Washington, D.C. Hagee was also listed on the website of The Response, along with numerous pro-family and Christian leaders. In August 2011, Hagee spoke for Glenn Beck's Restoring Courage Rally in Israel. Perhaps he was returning the favor since Hagee had featured Beck as the keynote speaker at Hagee's July 2011 Christians United for Israel banquet in Washington, D.C.

After studying Pastor Hagee for years—including attending his church service several times—Justin Peters points out that Hagee clearly embraces Word of Faith theology. For example, Hagee declared:

> When you walk into a hospital room and your friend is there, a member of your family is there, you have the power to say, "In the name of Jesus, I rebuke that disease," and the God of heaven will heal that disease, when you are right with God in heaven.[485]

Kenneth Copeland holds similar views:

> People that get all upset at preachers who preach prosperity never have taken the time to pray and see if God wanted them to prosper financially, for some reason or another. God needs you saved. He needs you full of the Holy Ghost. He needs you well. And He needs you strong. And He needs you rich.[486]

Justin Peters's response to Copeland's assertion zeroes in on the problem:

> God could vaporize all of us right now, and He would be just fine. He doesn't need us at all. And does He need us rich? No, He doesn't need us rich. If you— one thing I say in my seminar—if you have to add an adjective to the Gospel, whether it's the prosperity or the social gospel, then you've automatically got a different gospel. There are no adjectives to the Gospel. It's just the Gospel. And if the gospel that you're preaching works in the United States of America but it doesn't work in Zimbabwe, or if it doesn't work in North Korea, or if it doesn't work in Sudan, then there's something wrong with your gospel, because the true Gospel works for all people in all places at all times, in every economic status.[487]

Benny Hinn's version of the false gospel perverts God's use of signs and wonders: "If the gospel doesn't have—if the gospel lacks— if the preaching of the gospel lacks signs and wonders, it's an empty shell."[488]

Justin Peters explains why this statement is so completely un-biblical:

> And you heard right from the horse's own mouth. Benny Hinn says that unless miracles, signs, and wonders accompany the Gospel, then the Gospel in and of itself has no power. And that is heresy. We could cite a number of verses, but just one, Romans 1:16, Paul

said, "For I am not ashamed of the gospel of Christ, for it is the power of God unto salvation."

What's the power of God unto salvation? The Gospel is. You know, a lot of people who hear me, or they were just made aware of me, think, "Oh, Justin doesn't believe that God heals people today." And, in fact, I got an email this morning from someone saying that I teach a dead gospel. Nothing could be further from the truth. I do believe God still physically heals people today when it is His will to do so. But, that having been said, is that the power of God? No, no, the Gospel is. That's the power of God unto salvation.

If God were to heal me of my cerebral palsy—and He could do it without breaking a sweat—that miracle would pale in comparison to what He did for me when He saved me from Himself, when He saved me from His own wrath. The greatest miracle of all is that of salvation.

I've come in contact with several over the last years of traveling. People who suffer far, far worse than I've ever even dreamed of suffering—I mean, terrible suffering—and yet they love the Lord. They remain faithful to Him. They praise Him. That's the power of God on display. Not somebody getting up on stage and saying they've been healed of a ringing in their ears, or as I saw just a few weeks ago at Copeland's meeting, being healed of athlete's foot. That's not the power of God. The power of God is the Gospel. That's the power of God.[489]

Benny Hinn's false gospel becomes even more apparent when he declares that healing *and salvation* go hand in hand:

It's as easy to get healed as it is to get forgiven. It's as easy to receive physical healing as it is to receive forgiveness for sin. It's just as easy to get healed. Healing is as easy as salvation. Do not complicate what is simple. Say it with me: It's as easy to get healed as it is to get forgiven. Healing should never be separate from salvation.[490]

Justin Peters was born with cerebral palsy, and God has chosen not to heal him. Is Justin's lack of healing a sign of his lack of salvation? Absolutely not! I believe God has used Justin's affliction to give him a platform by which to expose the false gospel of the Word of Faith movement. Joni Erickson Tada is another example of someone whom the Lord has mightily used to proclaim the Gospel as she sits in her wheelchair, paralyzed from the neck down.

The Word of Faith movement is a sister to the New Apostolic Reformation with its "prophets" and "apostles." The NAR and WOF false teachers not only preach another gospel, but they preach philosophies and practices derived from the occult. The Church must beware of the Christian and pro-family leaders who have given these groups credibility.

The "Christian" Version of the Law of Attraction

Although David Barton spoke for our Worldview Weekend conferences for many years, I stopped inviting him after he helped organize Glenn Beck's 8-28 rally in August 2010. Subsequently, I also discovered that David had participated in spiritual enterprises with members of the New Apostolic Reformation, or Word of Faith, and even appeared on a DVD that promotes the Law of Attraction. The same DVD praises the New Age book and DVD *The Secret*.

I bring this up as an example of how Christians should respond to aberrant teachers. Worldview Weekend discontinued carrying Barton's radio program on our website, offering his books and DVDs, and featuring him at our conferences. And it was a very hard thing to do. David Barton had been a close friend for many years, but my ultimate commitment must be to the Word of God. It is really difficult to see people you have admired taking part in activities that are clearly a violation of biblical theology and doctrine.

In March 2008, a Christian talk-show host called to tell me that David Barton was appearing on a DVD called *The Source of the Secret* that described how Christians could benefit from the Law of Attraction. That "Law" is one being widely promoted by New Agers on *The Oprah Winfrey Show*. I immediately called David and explained to him that Oprah was promoting the "Law of Attraction" and that perhaps he did not know this to be a blatantly New Age concept. David explained that he believes Oprah's teaching is unbiblical but that what he and the other presenters were talking about on the DVD is the biblical manner in which Christians could benefit from "the Law." I explained my biblically based objections and implored David to remove himself from this documentary before it was released. But three years later, I found out that, in May 2010, the documentary had aired on Trinity Broadcasting Network (TBN). It overtly promotes a so-called "Christian" version of the Law of Attraction.

David Barton's April 4, 2011 radio program description noted, "Culture can be divided into 7 pillars of influence, Family, Religion, Education, Media, Entertainment, Business and Government."[491] These are exactly the same pillars of C. Peter Wagner's New Apostolic Reformation "Seven Mountain Mandate." In a May 31, 2007 letter, C. Peter Wagner wrote:

> In my view it is not possible to get an operational handle on how to initiate corporate action toward social transformation without taking into account the seven mountains or what I like to call "molders of culture." The seven are religion, family, business, arts & entertainment, government, education, and media.[492]

Barton appears to have identified himself with the dominion theology crowd by promoting what he called the seven pillars on his radio program.

I am sad to see my friend of many years go in the theological direction he is now headed. Another syndicated Christian talk-show host also told me she had warned him in an email exchange at about the same time of my first warning to David. Our pleas were to no avail, and Barton appeared in the documentary that featured a lineup of Word of Faith, name-it-and-claim-it teachers including the now-deceased Oral Roberts and an orthodox Jew who talked about how the Law of Attraction works. Apparently, faith in the Lord Jesus Christ was not required to make "the Law" bring you what you desire.

The Source of the Secret DVD seems contradictory. It praises the Law of Attraction, praises *The Secret,* and then it warns about potential dangers before praising both *The Secret* and the Law of Attraction again.

Author and pastor Kerry Shook also appears on the DVD with David Barton and claims:

> I have talked to a lot of people who said *The Secret* has forever changed my life, and I agree that it has. Because they're putting biblical principles into their life whether they realize it or not, it is going to change their life. Now I want them to take a step further and give credit to the source, and the source is Jesus Christ.[493]

How can these people say *The Secret* is a good thing when it is clearly false teaching? How can people appearing in *The Source of the Secret* say you need to look behind the source of the false teaching to Jesus Christ or to God? What Jesus or God are they talking about? It is certainly not the Jesus or God of the Bible. Only a false teacher would say the source behind *The Secret* is the God of the Bible.

The DVD alleges that the concept of *The Secret* is positive but that people need to meet the "God" behind the Law of Attraction. Does this not reveal just how far the Church and its leaders in America have sunk?

In 1 Kings 18:20–21, Elijah declares to the Children of Israel, who mingled worship of God with pagan spirituality, that they must choose to whom they will pledge their allegiance. Elijah asked the Israelites, "How long will you falter between two opinions? If the Lord is God, follow Him; but if Baal, follow him."

In 1985, Dave Hunt warned that such New Age teachings as the Law of Attraction would soon become mainstream in evangelicalism:

> Today's church is being swept by a revival of New Thought, now called Positive Thinking, Possibility Thinking, Positive Confession, Positive Mental Attitude, and Inner Healing. We are very concerned that this time New Thought, which represents inside the church what New Age is in the secular world, will not be forced out, but will remain within the evangelical church to contribute to the growing confusion and seduction. One of the most basic New Thought techniques is visualization, which is now firmly entrenched within the church. Even after it was forced

out of mainstream Christianity early in this century, New Thought survived on the fringes of the church in extreme Pentecostalism.[494]

This "extreme Pentecostalism" is no longer considered extreme but is openly embraced by the New Religious Right and neo-evangelicals. Thus, the New Age philosophies and practices of the NAR and WOF are also embraced whether the New Religious Right and neo-evangelicals are willing to admit it or not.

Bob Harrison, "America's Increase Activist," appears on *The Source of the Secret* DVD and proclaims:

> Knowing that millions of copies of *The Secret* book and video have been sold, and people have listened to it and read, I feel it is a positive thing because it can introduce them to the Law of Attraction, one of the principles that cause them to have greater success. But the danger is it's not going to take them far enough unless they learn the Source.[495]

How can it be a positive thing that people are reading false teaching? The danger is that people who meet the source of *The Secret* will be meeting demons. First Timothy 4:1 warns: "Now the spirit expressly says that in latter times some will depart from the faith, giving heed to deceiving spirits and doctrines of demons."

The DVD never mentions the Gospel. No one in the DVD—not the producer or anyone he interviews—ever explains the way to meet this God they claim is the source behind the secret. The message is simply that the source of the secret is God and that the original book and DVD did not go far enough.

Shad Wehrli, life coach and co-creator of *The Source of The Secret,* says:

> The source to "The Secret" is God and a relationship with Him. He is the source for everything. And that's when I saw the initial "Secret." I saw that it was incomplete because it talked about the universe but not The One who created the universe, talked about creation, but not the Creator. And so, I saw that it was absolutely incomplete. The source is God. I mean, af-

ter all, the Law of Attraction sounds good, but how can you have a Law without a Lawgiver?[496]

The Source of the Secret features several Word of Faith false teachers, and there is very little difference between Oprah Winfrey's New Age Law of Attraction and the Word of Faith Law of Attraction.

To help you grasp the scope of this problem, here is a listing of some of the other individuals and their statements that appeared on *The Source of the Secret:*

> *Ron McIntosh, executive director Victory Bible Institute*—"What I love about *The Secret* is the Law of Attraction. It is an automatic law. It works whether you believe it or not. You are applying the Law of Attraction by manifesting your dominant thoughts, whether you realize it or not."

> *John Bevere, best-selling author and international speaker*—"The Law of Attraction and all the laws described in *The Secret* work, because they are laws that have already been established by God."

> *Ed Gungor, NY Times best-selling author and speaker*—"You can be an agnostic, you can be an atheist, you can be a whatever, a pagan, and you can learn the laws of sowing and reaping as well as the Law of Attraction. And you can bring good into the world. And God designed it that way."

> *Alex Loyd ND, PhD, founder of "The Healing Codes"*—Rhonda Byrne [author of *The Secret* book] filmed me to be part of *The Secret*, but I was left on the editing floor. And I believe it was because I talked in that interview so much about how the Law of Attraction, yes, is real. But the thing that determines whether the Law of Attraction is going to work in your life or not is the condition of your heart."

> *Kerry Shook, pastor and author of* One Month To Live—"At the end of the day after you close *The Secret*

book, are you going to follow just principles, the Law of Attraction and the Secret? Or, are you going to follow the Real Secret, Jesus Christ?"

The DVD narrator concludes by saying:

> The discovery of the Law of Attraction is just the beginning. The journey can and must go deeper. Be inspired to continue your own journey as you search for and discover the Source behind these laws. For when you seek, you will find. And, through this journey, come face-to-face with a loving God, the true Source of Life, Love, and all the good you have ever known.

Unfortunately, the Law of Attraction is extremely attractive to some dynamic leaders who do an all-too-good job attracting others to themselves.

Joel Osteen's New Age Life Now

The Source of the Secret offers the same message promoted by Joel Osteen. At the time of this writing, Osteen is pastor of the largest church in America, with a weekly attendance of 43,000 people. Osteen's books have sold millions of copies, and his church service is viewed by millions each week.

People have been serving up heretical ideas for centuries, of course, so in a way, Osteen's is nothing new. But there is something new we must say about his teachings—something New Age, that is.

On January 1, 2012, I was scanning television channels only to see the smiling heretic Joel Osteen. I stopped to watch, and my wife and I, along with my parents who were visiting in our home, discussed Osteen's totally New Age sermon, which included, as Osteen often does, his taking Scripture completely out of context. The sermon was titled "Speak Faith into Your Future." His website summarizes the sermon as follows:

> What are you saying about your life and your future? Words of faith and victory? Or words of lack and despair? In order to be all that God has created you to be, it is imperative to get into agreement with what his Word says with your words. With your words, you are either blessing or cursing your future. Proverbs

18:21 says, "Life and death are in the power of the tongue." To walk in victory, you can't talk defeat. To experience abundance, you can't talk lack. Even during tough times, instead of using your words to describe the situation, use your words to change the situation. Joel 3:10 says, "Let the weak say, 'I am strong!'" Not, let the weak talk about their weakness. If you will train yourself to only speak victory to bless your future, then God is able to release His goodness in greater ways in your life. Make sure the words you are sending out are in the direction you want your life to go![497]

It is standard Word of Faith heresy to declare that our words have the power to create. While words can harm people—the Bible does speak about the power of the tongue in James 3:2–8—the Bible does not teach that our words have creative power. Only God has the power to create. Our words cannot create our futures for good or ill.

In November 2011, New Age life coach Osteen delivered a pep talk (I cannot bring myself to call it a sermon) called "The Power of I Am." Osteen continued to spew the heresy that our words have creative power. Osteen's website describes the talk this way:

God created our words to have creative power. What follows the two simple words, "I Am," will determine what type of life you have and will either bring success or failure in your life. Instead of saying negative "I Ams"—"I am unfocused. I am never going to succeed"—say what God says you are. Declare "I am blessed, confident, loved, accepted." When you change your "I Ams," your life will change for the better. The seeds of greatness God's placed on the inside will spring forth.[498]

"Whatever you conceive you can achieve." With this favorite "karma-changing" promise, New Agers believe you need only use the "unlimited" power and consciousness of your mind to bring about all your dreams, desires, and wishes. Cloaked in a "Christian" designer suit and tie, Joel Osteen's *Your Best Life Now* bears an uncomfortable and dangerous similarity to this most popular of New Age claims. Here are a few examples of the Osteen version:

- "You will produce what you're continually see-ing in your mind. If you foster an image of defeat and failure, then you're going to live that kind of life. But if you develop an image of victory, success, health, abun-dance, joy, peace, and happiness, nothing on earth will be able to hold those things from you."[499]

- "You must conceive it in your heart and mind before you can receive it."[500]

- "You must look through your 'eyes of faith' and start seeing yourself as happy, healthy and whole."[501]

- "What you will receive is directly connected to how you believe."[502]

- "We receive what we believe."[503]

- "Learn how to conceive. Keep the image of what you want to become in front of you. You're going to become what you believe."[504]

Osteen now travels the country, packing out stadiums with his happy talk. But I'd like to see Osteen pay a visit to China, preach his "your best life now" drivel, and see how Christians there respond. Let Osteen look into the eyes of Pastor Lei, who has been repeatedly arrested and beaten for preaching the Word of God in his church—a church not licensed by the Chinese government. How would Ameri-cans' best life work out for Pastor Lei and his congregation? Perhaps their jail time for the Gospel would give them time to assess Reverend Osteen's claims.

Have these and countless other persecuted Christians been beat-en, jailed, and murdered because they "received what they believed," or did these terrible things happen to them because they did not "de-velop an image of victory, success, health, abundance, joy, peace, and happiness"? Were eleven of Jesus' disciples martyred because "they received what they believed"? Were the disciples living under a "curse of poverty and defeat," as Osteen says of so many? Here's a roll call of questions I'd like to ask Mr. Osteen. Why is it, Joel, that:

- Paul and Matthew were beheaded?
- Barnabas was burned to death?
- Mark was dragged to death?
- James, the less, was clubbed to death?
- Peter, Philip, and Andrew were crucified?
- Thomas was speared to death?
- Luke was hung by the neck until dead?
- Stephen was stoned?

How would these disciples take to the Best Life message?

Yes, I know: Joel's promises sound so much better to American ears than all those warnings from Jesus about being hated by most people for Jesus' sake. But it remains that, in large measure, Joel's offering can be described as blasphemy. On page 36, he claims, "God has a big dream for your life." On page 56: "God sees you as a champion. He believes in you even more than you believe in yourself!" And on page 110: "God has confidence in you."

Osteen does not provide a single Bible verse to back up these statements—because there are none. Nowhere in the Bible do we read that God believes or has confidence in us. He loves us but does not believe in us. On the contrary, He knows all too well how unbelievably fickle and untrustworthy we humans actually are. The truth is not like Joel describes on page 57: "Believe it or not, that is how God sees you, too. He regards you as a strong, courageous, successful, overcoming person."

Furthermore, God does not define our success in materialistic terms as Joel does. God is interested in our obedience above all. On page 63, Joel writes: "As long as you are pressing forward, you can hold your head up high, knowing that you are a 'work in progress,' and God is in the process of changing you. He's looking at your last two good moves."[505]

Where in the Bible do we read that God is not looking at our last two bad moves but our last two good moves? Isaiah 64:6 says that even our righteous deeds are like filthy rags or wickedness to God because He is so holy. Even if God did look at our last two good moves, He would still see filthy rags.

Or how about this Osteen gospel gem from page 95: "Be the best you can be, then you can feel good about yourself."

Where in the Bible do we find this teaching? What if your best is getting drunk just once a week instead of twice a week? Should you still feel good about yourself?

But wait. I've saved Osteen's most outrageous statement for last (drumroll, please). On page 144, Joel elevates us to the heavenlies by pointing out that "you may even need to forgive God."

Whoa! And exactly what would we be forgiving God for? As I recall, forgiveness is for sins—or at least mistakes. But which of those has God made? Not a one according to any Bible I've ever read.

Oswald Chambers offers a perspective on the kind of thing the Osteens of the world do to Christians: "Satan's great aim is to deflect us from the center. He will allow us to be devoted to the death to any cause, any enterprise, to anything but the Lord Jesus." Hebrews 13:9 instructs us not to be carried away by all sorts of strange teachings (deflected from the center), but, sadly, that is exactly what is happening for many at the hands of Joel Osteen.

Instead of pursuing our best life now, we should pursue the things of the Lord so we can have our best life *later*. I fear that for many who follow Joel's false teaching, this life is the best they will get. The false gospel proclaimed by Joel Osteen and others and accepted as truth by millions may allow many to achieve what they can conceive of the things in this world, but true to Jesus' promise, they may lose their souls in the pursuit.

Many people over the years have told me that while they do not believe in extrabiblical revelation, they do believe God has spoken to them. I try to clarify the claim by asking if they really mean God spoke to them through the study of the Bible or that the Holy Spirit convicted them of sin or brought Scripture they had studied to their remembrance or the Holy Spirit helped them understand what they were reading as they studied God's Word. The answer I typically receive is that they actually heard the voice of God. If they are hearing an audible voice, whether in or outside of their minds, then we have a problem, biblically speaking, as they are now entering the realm of mysticism. Pastor Jack Hughes explains:

> So when someone says "God spoke to me," the question to ask is, "How did God speak to you?" Are you using "to speak" metaphorically? Do you mean you had an experience and you think it was from God? Do you mean that you received revelation about God, by observing creation and what has been made, or through

His law written in your heart, or through your conscience, i.e., by general revelation? Was it information about God? If not, it wasn't general revelation. If you believe you have received information about God, through general revelation, you should not live by that revelation, or act on it, since it is subjective, distorted by your sin nature, and the source of what you have experienced is unverifiable. The book *Experiencing God* teaches God speaks to us, but it does not qualify or meet the criteria for general revelation. Therefore, if it is not general revelation, it must qualify as special revelation.

Maybe you believe God gave you special revelation. When you say, "God spoke to me," do you mean He literally spoke? Was it an act of "inspiration"? Did the Holy Spirit move you to receive the perfect inerrant Word of God? The problem with claiming to receive special revelation is that the Bible canon is closed and we cannot add to it (Deut. 4:2; 12:32; Prov. 30:5–6; Rev. 22:18–19; Jude 3). We must not follow the cults who claim to have revelation apart from the completed biblical canon. The cults typically place their experiences above or on an equal plane with Scripture.

If God did not speak to you through inspiration, then the only other kind of special revelation left to consider is a direct encounter with God, i.e., a theophany or christophany. Are you saying that God appeared to you? Did you see the Shekinah glory, a burning bush, or a post-resurrection appearance of Christ and have God verbally speak to you? These questions must be answered.

Most people who claim to have had a "word from God" are not brazen enough to claim they have received special revelation in any of the ways described above. They want to claim that God "spoke to them," but they must invent a new type of revelation that is not general, special, or orthodox. Yet, it is revelation from God that is able to guide them, give them direction and able to lead them through life. There is a term for this; it is called "mysticism." Mysticism is the belief that direct knowledge of God and His will are received by our spirit, through experience, apart from the Word of God.[506] When a Christian begins to live and make decisions by intuition, hunches, feelings, perceptions, or things they "sense," then they have become "mystics." Mysticism is pagan. To depart from living by the objective revelation of God's Word is to depart from God's will (Deut. 8:3; Matt. 4:4; II Pet. 1:2–4).[507]

Southern Baptists Now Embrace Word of Faith Teachings?

Lest you think Word of Faith teaching is limited to Word of Faith teachers, think again. For about five years, I monitored the teachings of well-known Southern Baptist ladies Bible study teacher Beth Moore. For the most part, I refrained from speaking publicly about Moore in hopes she would make a course correction. However, I have not seen a change for the better and have seen what appears to be further veering into the Word of Faith camp through her teaching and weekly television appearances with Word of Faith sympathizer James Robison.

I recognize that Moore has Bible studies that have been very popular. However, something seems to have changed in her theology. In an online video clip, Beth Moore declares that God is speaking to her: "[God] began to say to me, 'I'm gonna tell you something right now, Beth, and boy you write this one down, and you say it as often as I give you utterance to say it...'"[508]

Let me be very clear: God is not verbally speaking to people today, and if He is, then the canon is open, but that cannot be because Jude 3 tells us the Word of God was once for all delivered to the Saints:

> Beloved, when I gave all diligence to write unto you of the common salvation, it was needful for me to write unto you, and exhort you that ye should earnestly contend for the faith which was once delivered unto the saints (KJV).

Proverbs 30:5–6 also makes it clear we are not to be adding to the Word of God: "Every word of God is pure: he is a shield unto them that put their trust in him. Add thou not unto his words, lest he reprove thee, and thou be found a liar" (KJV).

Deuteronomy echoes this truth in 12:32: "Whatever I command you, be careful to observe it; you shall not add to it nor take away from it."

Similarly, Deuteronomy 4:2 says: "You shall not add to the word, which I command you, nor take from it, that you may keep the commandments of the Lord your God which I command you."

Beth Moore even seems to embrace the idea of positive confession, also known as "Name It and Claim It." In describing Matthew 17:20–21, she says:

> Look carefully at what that verse is saying. He said, "and you can say to the mountain." For some reason ordained by God alone, He tells us that when we want something to move, we are to tell it to. That we are to open our mouths and say to the mountain, "Move it! You're in my way!"
>
> Now I can tell you what's going on right now. Some people are thinking, they're already shutting off right here. Because they're thinking, "Well, that is not for today." Then why in the world did He leave us this word? Why in the world did He leave us this word? We are to confess with our mouths. He said, "Open your mouth and say." When He spoke the worlds into existence, He didn't just think them. He spoke them! And He set a precedent, and He's saying to us, "My words are omnipotent, but your words are potent!" You stir up the faith within you, you look at that mountain, and you say, "Move it!"
>
> I've got to tell you something. God has been teaching me how to move some mountains with my voice.[509]

Pay close attention to what Moore says here: "When He spoke the worlds into existence....He set a precedent." God speaking the world into existence is not a precedent for *us*. God can create with His words, but we cannot. Standard Word of Faith heresy teaches that man's words can create. That is not only heresy, it is shamanism; it is pagan; it is taught within the occult.

Matthew 17:20–21 and a corresponding passage of Mark 11:23–24 are not talking about our moving mountains with our words but about Christians praying and having faith that God can do things that we see as impossible. It is not you or I that move the mountain with our words, but it is God Who does what we think is impossible. Context is vital. Look at Matthew 17:20–21 in context:

> So Jesus said to them, "Because of your unbelief; for assuredly, I say to you, if you have faith as a mustard seed, you will say to this mountain, 'Move from here to there,' and it will move; and nothing will be impossible for you. However, this kind does not go out except by prayer and fasting."

Notice, the important word is "however," and then comes the full context: this is done through prayer and fasting. Look at Mark 11:23–24:

> For assuredly, I say to you, whoever says to this mountain, "Be removed and be cast into the sea," and does not doubt in his heart, but believes that those things he says will be done, he will have whatever he says. Therefore I say to you, whatever things you ask when you pray, believe that you receive them, and you will have them.

Again, the mountains or obstacles in our life may or may not be moved by God as we pray and God's will is done. We have to have faith that God will do what He knows is best for us, and if it is God's will, then He will do what we think is impossible, such as moving a mountain. God is the object and source of our faith. It is not having faith in the power of our words.

We must use Scripture to interpret Scripture. First John 5:14–15 tells us that whatever we ask has to be in accordance with God's will:

> Now this is the confidence that we have in Him, that if we ask anything according to His will, He hears us. And if we know that He hears us, whatever we ask, we know that we have the petitions that we have asked of Him.

Luke 1:37 tells us, "For with God nothing will be impossible." Nothing is impossible for God, but that does not mean God will always do what we ask. That is where true faith is revealed. True faith does not just believe God can do something, but true faith is content and trusts Him even when He does not do what we want or ask. We know His ultimate will is what is best for us.

There is serious danger with what Moore is teaching, and sadly, too many pastors are more interested in appeasing the sheep than in protecting them. Instead of warning the women in their churches about Moore's unbiblical proclamations, most will keep silent. After all, Moore is very popular, and to present the documented facts of what she has taught in light of what the Bible teaches would be too controversial. It might even start a stampede of the sheep to another shepherd's field, and no hireling wants to take that risk. But this is a perfect opportunity to separate the shepherds from the hirelings. True shepherds put the well-being of the sheep before anything else, and sometimes it's surprising which "true" shepherds end up being not-so-true.

Credibility for Crouch

California pastor and author David Jeremiah has spoken for several Worldview Weekend events, and one of the last times he spoke, I talked with him privately about what is happening in evangelicalism with regard to the Emergent Church and the New Spirituality. I challenged him to be careful about those with whom he associates so as to preserve the integrity of his teaching.

Sadly, like so many I have pleaded with, the warning seems to have fallen on deaf ears.

Dr. Jeremiah has offered credibility to Trinity Broadcasting Network (TBN), one of the world's largest Word of Faith television networks. On March 5, 2012, he participated in TBN's *Praise-a-Thon* fundraising broadcast where he praised not only God but TBN and delivered a troubling message on sowing and reaping. His comments included this plea for financial contributions to TBN:

> Well, you probably have a big harvest coming because God's saving the best... You only reap what you sow. Let me ask you this: Do you get blessed by this network [TBN]; by watching the teaching programs and the music and the things that come to your life?...

Do you get blessed by this ministry?... If you wanna get blessed by TBN, then the problem you have to solve is, "How am I investing in TBN?" Let me tell you something, we have this incredible network today because people before us—for many, many years before us—have invested their dollars, their time, their effort, in this network so that it could be what it is today. So, I wanna stop right now and ask you to do this; if you've been blessed by TBN this year—and you haven't called to say, "I wanna be a part of TBN going forward"—I want you to go to your phone and find out how you can help make this network even more successful than ever before.[510]

Why would David Jeremiah associate himself with TBN? Why would he want to support a network that promotes some of the worst false teachers in the history of the world, such as Benny Hinn, Paula White, Creflo Dollar, Kenneth Copeland, and Jesse Duplantis? His *Praise-a-Thon* participation demonstrates that some of evangelicalism's most well-known and trusted teachers are giving credibility to the religious Trojan horse. It's time they remind themselves of 2 Corinthians 11:3–4:

> But I am afraid that just as Eve was deceived by the serpent's cunning, your minds may somehow be led astray from your sincere and pure devotion to Christ. For if someone comes to you and preaches a Jesus other than the Jesus we preached, or if you receive a different spirit from the Spirit you received, or a different gospel from the one you accepted, you put up with it easily enough. (NIV)

On the program, Dr. Jeremiah declared that *God* had given Paul Crouch the vision for TBN:

> I'm so amazed at the vision God has given to this man... I want to be a part of helping him continue... I hope you will do that, too. Be a part of what's happening at TBN. And let's pray together that God will enable you to do more than you even thought...

[A]fter you support the [local] church, you need to support the ministries that feed your soul.[511]

Jeremiah persists in giving God the credit for TBN's growth and success:

> So tonight, I wanna encourage you, with all of my heart, to understand your part in the ministry of TBN... Everybody needs to do it [send money], and especially now... It's really encouraging to hear Paul talk about how God has sustained [TBN], and it hasn't gone backwards. But unless everybody who's involved in this ministry gets underneath it and says, "This is part of my life"—I mean, if you sit and watch this program [Praise The Lord] at home—if you use this to grow spiritually, then the Bible says you should be involved with it. You should invest in it. You should make it part of what you do for almighty God.[512]

Really? God gave Crouch the vision to build a network on which to promote false teachers? Only if you think God is helping build a religious Trojan horse.

CHAPTER 11

Christian Mysticism Goes Mainstream

Many pro-family and Christian leaders of today are waging war on the secular world for its values and lifestyles, much of which stem from paganism. Ironically, many of these same leaders are either embracing pagan spirituality or embracing those who promote it.

As we discussed earlier, an abundance of today's Christian and pro-family leaders have openly embraced the New Apostolic Reformation or Word of Faith movement, which openly promote pagan spirituality, Gnosticism, or mysticism. My friend T. A. McMahon of the *Berean Call* asks and answers a very important question:

> What can be done to stem the tide? Nothing that the Bible seems to indicate. On the other hand, God has given believers orders that appear to be designed more for a rescue operation than for a reversal of widespread apostasy.[513]

The falling away from biblically held truths is the apostasy of today predicted in the Word of God thousands of years ago. Our responsibility is to preach the Gospel to the lost, warn the Church of wolves inside the flock, and to rebuke ignorant sheep who feed on the spiritual poison served up by hirelings masquerading as shepherds.

Some of these evangelical and pro-family leaders about whom we must give warning are false converts. Others are simpletons that blindly go along with their unsaved colleagues. Together, these people are enemies of the cross. They make way for ecumenicalism, mysticism, moralizing, and, perhaps worst of all, the mainstreaming of these beliefs among otherwise well-meaning believers.

Taste and See What's Wrong

Mystical practices that have gone mainstream in evangelical circles include:

- "Christian" yoga,
- Contemplative prayer, and
- Soaking prayers or breath prayers (which are nothing less than transcendental meditation).

Many within "evangelical" churches embrace the idea of being a mystic Christian, which fosters the merger with pagan spirituality. Yoga, transcendental meditation, and walking an occultic labyrinth are becoming increasingly popular practices in both emergent and mainline churches. So much so that even secular media are taking notice. The September 14, 2008, issue of Nashville's *Tennessean* newspaper featured an article entitled "Meditation Goes Mainstream," which reported:

> Joe Scott, 61, got hooked on meditation in yoga classes about 16 years ago. At the time, he was an opinionated workaholic who had a need to always be right. "I used to be a very angry, intense person," says Scott, who works in the quality assurance department at HCA. Thirty minutes of meditation first thing in the morning completely changed his life, says Scott, who also meditates with members of Self Realization Fellowship in Berry Hill, which incorporates readings from the Bible and the Hindu holy book in their Sunday services. For Carolyn Goddard of Nashville, she was drawn to centering prayer, a form of contemplative prayer, to deepen her connection with God. A Colorado monk revived this ancient ritual of "resting in God" in the 1970s as an alternative for Christians lured to transcendental meditation.[514]

Notice that this writer observes, as I have said, that transcendental meditation has simply been renamed.

A Deeper Response

I've already touched on the problem of Christian leaders participating in gatherings of a generally spiritual nature, but let's take a further look at the August 6, 2011, prayer rally hosted by Texas governor Rick Perry. The Response website lists the leadership team for the event, and it includes several people associated with the International House of Prayer in Kansas City. As I've already pointed out, IHOP-KC has been described by numerous researchers and theologians as "cult-like." One IHOP leader who appeared on the platform at The Response was the group's founder, Mike Bickle. A quick review of the IHOP website bookstore reveals the unbiblical philosophies embraced by Pastor Bickle and his organization. Yet, the president of the American Family Association wrote me a four-page letter in the month of the event, ridiculing me for warning Christians of the unbiblical nature of The Response. Not surprisingly, his organization had assisted in organizing and promoting the event.

This pro-family leader sent his letter not only to me but to my pastor, several of my friends, and a few of my Worldview Weekend speakers. Since he chose to make the letter public, I have no hesitation in sharing parts of it with you.

The letter argued that "the International House of Prayer and Cindy Jacobs ministries have statements of faith that are solid." I will tell you, though, that it is not uncommon for false teachers to have statements of faith on their websites that pass muster with the undiscerning who look no further. But from further research, I can say that even a cursory review of the writings and teaching of Cindy Jacobs and Mike Bickle reveal that neither Jacobs nor Bickle teach a biblically solid faith.

My personal warnings to this and other pro-family leaders concerning the false theologies of Jacobs and IHOP-KC were ignored. Let me share with you, though, some of the information the folks I cautioned have ignored in order to justify uniting and partnering with participants of the New Apostolic Reformation and Word of Faith movements.

A Manual for Mysticism

The book *Fire Within: St. Theresa of Avila, St. John of the Cross, and the Gospel on Prayer*, written by Catholic priest Thomas Dubay, promotes spiritual mysticism and contemplative prayer. Yet, Mike Bickle is quoted on the IHOP website as stating, "I want this book to be the manual for IHOP-KC."[515]

Amazon.com describes *Fire Within* this way:

> This book is the fruit of Fr. Dubay's many years of study and experience in spiritual direction and in it he synthesizes the teachings on prayer of the two great doctors of the Church on prayer—St. John of the Cross and St. Teresa of Avila—and the teaching of Sacred Scripture.

Why would Bickle want a book that promotes the mysticism of St. Theresa of Avila "to be the manual for IHOP-KC" unless he is committed to mysticism. An online encyclopedia explains that "Saint Teresa of Avila....was a prominent Spanish mystic, Roman Catholic saint....and theologian of contemplative life through mental prayer."[516]

Under a section entitled "mysticism," an online encyclopedia reports: "The kernel of Teresa's mystical thought throughout all her writings is the ascent of the soul in four stages."[517] The four stages include "mental prayer," "prayer of quiet," "devotion of union," and "devotion of ecstasy or rapture."

The fourth stage, "devotion of ecstasy or rapture," is described by St. Teresa in her book *Interior Castle*:

> The fourth is the "devotion of ecstasy or rapture," a passive state, in which the consciousness of being in the body disappears (2 Corinthians 12:2–3). Sense activity ceases; memory and imagination are also absorbed in God or intoxicated. Body and spirit are in the throes of a sweet, happy pain, alternating between a fearful fiery glow, a complete impotence and unconsciousness, and a spell of strangulation, intermitted sometimes by such an ecstatic flight that the body is literally lifted into space. This after half an hour is followed by a reactionary relaxation of a few hours in a swoon-like weakness, attended by a negation of all the faculties in the union with God. From this the subject awakens in tears; it is the climax of mystical experience, productive of the trance.[518] Cathleen Medwick's *Teresa of Avila: The Progress of a Soul* recounts that Teresa at times levitated during this process:

Teresa's rapture became so frequent as to be almost commonplace... The occasional visitor, like Bishop Alvaro de Mendoza, might be astonished to see the prioress, her hands pressed forward in prayer and her eyes rolled up to heaven, rise a foot or more off the ground. Teresa ordered that any sister who happened to be present during one of these levitations was to grab hold of her habit and try to hold her down. This, of course, was impossible, obedience being no match for celestial magnetism.[519]

Interior Castle is described on Amazon.com as follows:

Celebrated for almost five centuries as a master of spiritual literature, St. Teresa of Avila is one of the most beloved religious figures in history. Overcome one day by a mystical vision of a crystal castle with seven chambers, each representing a different stage in the soul's spiritual quest for union with God, Teresa recorded her vision in this now classic text. Probably her most important and widely studied work, *The Interior Castle* guides the spiritual seeker through each chamber of the castle to the center and the soul's final union with the divine.

Free of religious dogma, this contemporary rendering is a beautiful and practical set of teachings for seekers of all faiths in need of guidance. Mirabai Starr's introduction places this classic in a contemporary context, reasserting its spiritual and literary importance close to five hundred years after it was first published.[520]

When I typed "contemplative prayer" into an the search engine of an online encyclopedia, St. Teresa of Avila and St. John of the Cross were key figures in the site's three-page report. The word "mysticism" was used numerous times in their description of contemplative prayer. This online encyclopedia offers an eye-opening description of Teresa's four stages of prayer:

Saint Teresa of Avila described four degrees or stages of mystical union:

1. incomplete mystical union, or the prayer of quiet or supernatural recollection, when the action of God is not strong enough to prevent distractions, and the imagination still retains a certain liberty;

2. full or semi-ecstatic union, when the strength of the divine action keeps the person fully occupied but the senses continue to act, so that by making an effort, the person can cease from prayer;

3. ecstatic union, or ecstasy, when communications with the external world are severed or nearly so, and one can no longer at will move from that state; and

4. transforming or deifying union, or spiritual marriage (properly) of the soul with God.[521]

Notice again the fourth stage includes becoming one with God and becoming divine. This is not so surprising if you are aware that the Church of Rome has for years promoted the idea that man can become as God.

The Catholic Catechism, item #460, declares:

> The Word became flesh to make us "partakers of the divine nature." "For this is why the Word became man, and the Son of God became the Son of man: so that man, by entering into communion with the Word and thus receiving divine sonship, might become a son of God." "For the Son of God became man so that we might become God." "The only-begotten Son of God, wanting to make us sharers in his divinity, assumed our nature, so that he, made man, might make men gods."[522]

The IHOP's website also promotes a CD set by Mike Bickle entitled "Contemplative Prayer: The Journey into Fullness." In it, Bickle declares:

> ...mystics is a legitimate term... I don't want to fight the war....so I'm just *saying* contemplative prayer, but I *mean* the mystics—even here at IHOP I say, let's just stay with contemplatives ...I don't have time to argue... so I call them the contemplatives... I don't want to go into the semantics, the debates....so, I'm

calling it the contemplatives... I don't have time to argue... but I mean the *mystics*.

...a study of the lives of the mystics, the contemplatives, through history, and clearly the most inspiring, compelling examples of history, in my world, have come out of the Catholic dark ages. I can't find anything like it in modern times, in America, in the Protestant world.[523]

And the bookstore also offers Henri Nouwen's *Clowning in Rome* for which the product description describes Nouwen as "renowned contemplative author." Despite what members of today's New Religious Right declare, IHOP-KC and Bickle are not promoting a biblical faith.

Mystic Is as Mystic Does

In May 2012, *Christianity Today* featured a cover story about Heidi Baker, who, with her husband Rolland, operates a "ministry" in Mozambique. The subtitle of the article announced, "There are credible reports that Heidi Baker heals the deaf and raises the dead,"[524] and the text goes on to explain:

We are in the dusty village of Chiure, Mozambique... Heidi Baker, known worldwide for her healing miracles, spends a third of every year on the charismatic speaking circuit, where people routinely fall to the floor in unconscious bliss or shake and laugh uncontrollably. They come, enthralled, to hear of Baker's miracles in places like Chiure.[525]

The article reports that Baker "...claims, scores have risen from the dead, food has been multiplied, the crippled and blind have been restored..."[526]

Reading the *CT* story immediately brings to mind the question: Why don't we have video documentation of the "scores" who have been raised from the dead? Certainly such scenes would be worthy of a few YouTube views. But perhaps it's easier to perpetrate a falsehood in writing than it is on video. And why are these reports always overseas in some third world country—away from scrutiny?

Christianity Today describes a time when Baker was sick and her husband, Rolland, visited

> ...the Toronto Airport Vineyard Christian Fellowship (now known as Catch the Fire), where the controversial Toronto Blessing revival of the mid-1990s had broken out. It was marked by ecstatic manifestations of the Holy Spirit, most notably "holy laughter." Hearing his report, Heidi became convinced that she desperately needed to visit Toronto.[527]

CT explains that "One night, she had a vision of Jesus in which she literally ate his flesh and drank his blood."[528] And "Heidi speaks of ministry flowing from 'your secret place' in a love experience with Jesus so potent it verges on the erotic."[529]

The article also reports that, back in Mozambique: "Heidi prophesied to two of the pastors that they would raise people from the dead. Soon there were reports of a district official rising from her deathbed after two hours of prayer."[530] The article further reports "Scholar McClymond describes Heidi as a 'practical mystic, like Teresa of Avila.'"[531]

"Mystic" is a good description of Heidi Baker, given that she does things like this:

> On Tuesday and Thursday mornings, Heidi teaches local student pastors and visiting Westerners at the Harvest School in Pemba. They gather in a large, hillside shed, a concrete slab with a roof for shade. To face the heat, students wear shorts or loose-fitting skirts, T-shirts, and flip-flops. They sit on the floor or stretch out as a guitarist leads in the ultimate worship song of three chords, four words, repeated 50 times. "Welcome in this place," words addressed to Jesus, are repeated without variation at least 200 times, lasting for 30 minutes. Some students kneel with eyes closed and hands lifted high, swaying themselves into a trance.[532]

Can you say, "Mantra"? If you study transcendental meditation, or contemplative prayer, this is the technique used to enter into a "trance" or altered state of consciousness. Sometimes mystics simply go into the silence. The Bible in Matthew 6:7, however, specifically commands against repetitive babbling: "And when you pray, do not use vain repetitions as the heathen do. For they think that they will be heard for their many words."

Baker also:

> slips in behind the guitarist, placing herself prone on the floor, her arms outstretched. Several women gather to lie beside her, massaging her and praying. She does not move as the song endlessly repeats. Then, slowly, she raises herself to her knees and leads a continuation of the music, improvising words in a strong, deep voice.[533]

Christianity Today mentions the New Apostolic Reformation but tries not to connect Baker to the NAR. Baker, though, works with many prominent NAR personalities, and she is a co-author of *The Reformer's Pledge* with Cindy Jacobs, C. Peter Wagner, Bill Johnson, James Goll, Lance Wallnau, John Arnott, Chuck Pierce, Lou Engle, and Jim Garlow.[534] Baker and her husband Rolland are also listed as part of Revival Alliance, which is made up of NAR proponents such as Bill and Beni Johnson, Che and Sue Ahn, Randy and DeAnne Clark, Georgian and Winnie Banov, and John and Carol Arnott.[535]

Sadly, in May 2012 it was not just *Christianity Today* bringing Heidi Baker to the attention of Christians but also groups like the American Family Association and American Family Radio Network. AFR's website posted a May 22, 2012, interview between Tim Wildmon, president of the American Family Association and AFR, and Heidi Baker.[536] True Christians should grieve at how self-professing groups and individuals are helping to bring false teaching into the mainstream—whether they know it or not.

I have stated many times that New Agers, the New Apostolic Reformation, neo-evangelicals, the New Religious Right, and the Emergent Church are merging. For example, the "Flame of Love Project" is described on the University of Akron website as

> ....a four-year collaborative effort by researchers at the University of Akron and The Institute for Research on Unlimited Love, funded by the John Templeton

Foundation, that will provide the scientific and theological foundation for a new interdisciplinary field of study; the science of Godly love.[537]

John Templeton, as you'll recall, wanted to establish a world religion "about God that doesn't rely on ancient revelations or scripture."[538] Under the heading "Exemplar Biosketches," the Flame of Love website lists those involved in the project, including such New Apostolic Reformation personalities as:

- Che Ahn
- Sue Ahn
- John Arnott
- Carol Arnott
- Heidi Baker
- Jay Bakker (son of Jim and Tammy Faye Bakker)
- Bill Johnson
- Peter Wagner[539]

Under "Social Justice Ministries," you'll find Emergent Church folks like Jim Wallis, Shane Claiborne (who did a year's internship with Bill Hybels at Willow Creek), and Tony, Peggy, and Bart Campolo.[540] Ironically, with respect to the Flame of Love, the most loving thing we can do is point out those who are promoting false teaching and false teachers so we can defend the Gospel and see people spared from the flames of an eternal hell.

Reformed Preachers Promoting a New Counter-Reformation?

While many discerning Christians are not surprised that heretics who make up the Word of Faith movement and the New Apostolic Reformation have embraced occultism and mysticism, it may come as a surprise that this same occultism and mysticism is becoming popular even within the Reformed theology camp. These are the folks I believe who pride themselves on being smarter, more discerning, and more biblically pure than non-Calvinists.

Please understand that some of the men warning of false teaching and heresy in the Reformed community are genuine adherents to Reformed theology. One such "watchman on the wall" is John MacArthur, who explains:

> There is this growing sort of acquisition of Reformed soteriology among these young guys. And it seems to me the mood is, that if you have a Reformed soteriology, you get a pass on everything else... In other words, how in the world can you have a true, Reformed view of the doctrines of grace that relate to salvation, and then think that having holes in your jeans and an Abercrombie & Fitch t-shirt and a can of beer in your hand somehow gave you access to the lost? And what the fear is, is that the power of the world's attraction is gonna suck these guys—and every generation after them—more and more into the culture and we're gonna see a reversal of the Reformed revival.[541]

(Soteriology is the study of "theology dealing with salvation especially as effected by Jesus Christ."[542])

In other words, many of the Reformed guys profess salvation through Jesus Christ alone but embrace additional philosophies not according to Christ but according to human thinking. So MacArthur is correct when he says we are going to see a reversal of the Reformed revival. I believe many well-known and lesser-known Reformed pastors who embrace mysticism—whether knowingly or unknowingly—actually assist in bringing about a new Counter-Reformation.

This Counter-Reformation will lead an apostate church right back into the arms of Rome, which I believe has been quietly infiltrating both Reformed churches and seminaries and non-Reformed churches and seminaries for hundreds of years in an attempt to re-introduce mysticism, pragmatism, social justice, communitarianism, dominion theology, and ecumenicalism.

John MacArthur details how many in Reformed circles compromise biblical truth and embrace the world and culture in order to attract a larger crowd:

> So what's gonna happen is, the world has already pulled them that far. It's pulled them into worldly music, R movies, all that stuff, and eventually I think it will pull them right away from their theology. I think for the time, it's even macho. I think there's a sense in which Reformed theology is kind of strong and manly, you know it's kind of airtight, and they like that. My fear is that the further this thing goes in trying to accommodate the culture, the less it's going to be able to hang on to that core doctrine. That's what I fear. And even when you have some of the people who are the most well-known for Reformed theology partner up in conferences with the people who are the most extreme pragmatists. I mean, this is happening. Who would have thought that, say, John Piper would have Rick Warren at a Desiring God conference? Those [teachers] seem like two completely polar opposites. So I don't know that the heart of this Reformed theology, kind of existing freestanding like an island, can really survive the pull of the culture which is attracting these young guys, and which these young guys are using to attract people.[543]

I believe we have now reached the point where some of the most popular Reformed preachers are a theological and doctrinal threat to the body of Christ. Many are knowingly or unknowingly part of the religious Trojan horse that is redefining and transforming Christianity away from a biblical ethos.

In an attempt to appeal to the culture's desire for a "spiritual" experience, many Reformed preachers openly promote pagan spirituality and mysticism in their churches. One such Reformed "superstar" is Timothy Keller, the founding pastor of Redeemer Presbyterian Church in New York City. In June 2012, Appraising Ministries posted an audio of Pastor Tim Keller praising Catholic mystics as follows:

> The best things that have been written, almost, are by Catholics during the Counter Reformation: Ignatius

of Loyola, St. Frances Sales, John of the Cross, St. Theresa of Avila....great stuff." [544]

For a time, Keller's church website featured a class entitled "The Way of the Monk." However, several discernment ministry websites reported on it, and it was removed. What was the problem with this course? The class description offers insight:

> Do you long for the great theology in your head to be more real to your heart? Come **discover age-old methods of contemplative prayer** and worship that can help you **encounter Christ in a more intimate, experiential way**. In this hands-on workshop, you will experience the ancient art of chanting the Psalms (they were meant to be sung!), embark on a **practice of** authentic Christian **meditation**, discover how a simple, time-honored tool can help unleash the prayer warrior in you, learn what **a typical monastic day** is like and how you can make your own private retreat at a monastery, and much more! [545]

Indeed, contemplative prayer was and is a practice of Catholic monks and mystics, but why would a Reformed pastor lead his church members back to the Church of Rome? Thousands of Christians died for the Gospel during the Catholic inquisitions that sought to stop the Reformation, and now Reformed and non-Reformed pastors alike are leading right back to the Roman Catholic Church. I believe, as do many researchers and theologians, that one of the institutions that make up the Great Harlot who rides the beast as described by John in the book of Revelation will be the Church of Rome. [546]

Numerous websites have archived the screen shots of "The Way of the Monk" class schedule. The website listed Susan Catillo as the instructor and stated:

> She wholly espouses Reformed Presbyterian theology while continuing to embrace her "inner monk." Sometimes referred to as "The Retreat Lady," she has been fleeing to monasteries to "honeymoon with Jesus" for over ten years. [547] "The Way of the Monk" class

included such topics as "Contemplative Practice" and "Centering Prayer" (another name for contemplative prayer).

Even though the class is gone, Keller's church website still offers questionable articles. One by Jan Johnson promotes *Lectio Divina*, which is another word for contemplative prayer. Johnson writes:

> As I tried to meditate on the discourse and poetic texts, such as the New Testament letters and Old Testament poets and prophets, I found that another classical method helped me: lectio divina. This kind of meditation has been used widely among believers since the sixth century.[548] An online encyclopedia defines Lectio Divina as representing, "a traditional Catholic practice of prayer and scriptural reading intended to promote communion with God."[549]

Pope Benedict XVI affirmed the validity of this approach in September 2005:

> I would like in particular to recall and recommend the ancient tradition of *Lectio divina*: the diligent reading of Sacred Scripture accompanied by prayer brings about that intimate dialogue in which the person reading hears God who is speaking, and in praying, responds to him with trusting openness of heart (cf. Dei Verbum, n. 25). If it is effectively promoted, this practice will bring to the Church—I am convinced of it—a new spiritual springtime.[550]

Given the Catholic teaching that Jesus wants to make gods out of us, would you be shocked that the Church of Rome for hundreds of years has promoted a practice such as contemplative prayer that is found in the occult of Eastern mysticism—a practice designed to facilitate a person's becoming divine? In the book *Open Mind, Open Heart: The Contemplative Dimension of the Gospel*, Catholic priest Thomas Keating wrote:

> The following principles represent a tentative effort to restate the Christian spiritual journey in contemporary terms. They are designed to provide a conceptual background for the practice of centering prayer. They should be read according to the method of lectio divina. The fundamental goodness of human nature, like the mystery of the Trinity, Grace, and the Incarnation, is an essential element of Christian faith. This basic core of goodness is capable of unlimited development; indeed, of becoming transformed into Christ and deified.[551]

In January 1979, at the "World Congress on Hinduism" in Allahabad, India, a speaker declared: "Our mission in the West has been crowned with fantastic success. Hinduism is becoming the dominant world religion and the end of Christianity has come near."[552]

While God's Church will not be defeated, the reality is that Christianity has been replaced in many churches by the practices of Hinduism. Many once-biblical churches have embraced the mysticism of contemplative prayer, "Christian" yoga, and walking a labyrinth. They are no longer biblical churches and are no longer preaching and teaching biblical Christianity but the Eastern mysticism of Hinduism.

Jan Johnson's article "Meditation: Not So Mysterious," posted on Keller's church website, shows how this occurs:

> One of the best-known ways to ponder God's character, works, and ways is a format originated by Ignatius Loyola, founder of the Jesuits. Loyola's methods, recorded in his book *Spiritual Exercises*, have been used for hundreds of years. He urged people to enter into Scripture with all five senses: sight, hearing, taste, touch, and smell.[553]

There's an interesting connection between Ignatius Loyola and the Counter-Reformation idea I mentioned earlier: Loyola's Jesuit Order was founded specifically to oversee the (original) Counter-Reformation.

Jan Johnson explains that mystic Richard Foster, who also writes positively of Ignatius of Loyola, assisted her in using her imagination in meditation: "But since I read Richard Foster's words about 'sanctifying the imagination' many years ago, I've asked God to purify my imagination along with my heart, mind, and will."[554] In his book *Celebration of Discipline,* Foster writes about the importance of the imagination. However, as researcher Bob DeWaay points out, "A search of the KJV [King James Bible] for 'imagination' yields 14 verses, and in each case it is a bad thing."[555]

Yet Richard Foster recommends:

> The inner world of meditation is most easily entered through the door of the imagination. We fail today to appreciate its tremendous power. The imagination is stronger than conceptual thought and stronger than the will.[556]

Foster proclaims that through the use of one's imagination, one can actually see and talk to Jesus Christ:

> As you enter the story, not as a passive observer but as an active participant, remember that since Jesus lives in the Eternal Now and is not bound by time, this event in the past is a living present-tense experience for Him. Hence, you can actually encounter the living Christ in the event, be addressed by His voice and be touched by His healing power. It can be more than an exercise of the imagination; it can be a genuine confrontation. Jesus Christ will actually come to you.[557]

Nowhere in the Bible are Christians instructed to use their imaginations to physically see and hear from the Lord. Yet Foster believes "as with meditation, the imagination is a powerful tool in the work of prayer."[558]

Foster embraces the "if you can conceive it, you can achieve it" philosophy of shamanism when he writes, "Imagination opens the door to faith. If we can 'see' in our mind's eye a shattered marriage whole or a sick person well, it is only a short step to believing it will be so."[559] Foster even believes you can use your imagination to be involved in what sounds like astral projection or astral travel:

> In your imagination allow your spiritual body, shining with light, to rise out of your physical body. Look back so that you can see yourself lying in the grass and reassure your body that you will return momentarily.

> Imagine your spiritual self, alive and vibrant, rising up through the clouds and into the stratosphere… Go deeper and deeper into outer space until there is nothing except the warm presence of the eternal Creator. Rest in His presence. Listen quietly, anticipating the unanticipated.

Note carefully any instruction given.[560] Note carefully any instruction given? So people are to listen for an audible voice? And just who or what would be talking to them? Could it be demons?

Foster actually warns of the possibility that those who practice contemplative prayer could encounter demons. In *Prayer: Finding the Heart's True Home,* he cautions:

> I also want to give a word of precaution. In the silent contemplation of God, we are entering deeply into the spiritual realm, and there is such a thing as supernatural guidance that is not divine guidance. While the Bible does not give us a lot of information on the nature of the spiritual world, we do know… there are various orders of spiritual beings, and some of them are definitely not in cooperation with God and his way! …But for now I want to encourage you to learn and practice prayers of protection…"All dark and evil spirits must now leave."[561]

Foster admits he was influenced by Agnes Sanford:

> The advice….[of] prayer through the imagination….picture the healing….and much more, was given to me by Agnes Sanford. I have discovered her to be an extremely wise and skillful counselor….Her book *The Healing Gifts of the Spirit* is an excellent resource.[562]

Sanford taught many pastors and self-professing Christians her philosophy of prayer, but it is clearly steeped in paganism. For example, Sanford recounts:

> Wise men of India for many centuries have trod the lofty peaks of meditation, developing their psychospiritual powers and giving birth to their oversouls. Spirits

of those [dead] for whom we have prayed on earth are working through us… One conveys that healing force to the inner being [of the sick] through the law of suggestion… He [the person doing the healing] has made a thought-track between his spirit, subconscious mind and body; and the body, the subconscious mind and the spirit of the patient…[563]

Shamanism and Eastern mysticism are twin sisters, and Foster seems to have no problem with the latter when he writes:

No doubt part of the surge of interest in Eastern meditation is because the churches have abrogated the field. How depressing for a university student, seeking to know the Christian teaching on meditation, to discover that there are so few living masters of contemplative prayer and that nearly all of the serious writings on the subject are seven or more centuries old. No wonder he or she turns to Zen, Yoga, or TM.[564]

Foster thinks we need spiritual "masters" in our churches? Would Jan Johnson from Keller's church teaching "The Way of the Monk" class be an example of what we need in our churches? This creates a downward spiral of sorts. As Bob DeWaay points out:

Once mysticism and the supposed need to gain personal revelations from God are embraced, there arises a need for new "masters" who are better at navigating the spirit world. Pagan societies have always had such persons. They are called "shamans." Eastern religion calls them "gurus." Deceived Christians call them "spiritual directors."[565]

One reason so many churches now have "spiritual directors" that teach "spiritual formation" or "soul care" is that too many church leaders have read Richard Foster's book. They buy his contention that "in the Middle Ages not even the greatest saints attempted the depths of the inward journey without the help of a spiritual director."[566]

Tim Keller is not the only Reformed theology leader to embrace Richard Foster. Donald Whitney, a Reformed theologian who has taught in a Reformed seminary, also appreciates Foster:

> Richard Foster's *Celebration of Discipline* has been the most popular book on the subject of the Spiritual Disciplines in the last half of the twentieth century. The great contribution of this work is the reminder that the Spiritual Disciplines, which many see as restrictive and binding, are actually means to spiritual freedom.[567]

John Piper is another popular Reformed pastor who promotes Richard Foster. In his sermons "Prayer, Meditation, and Fasting, Part 1" and "Man Shall Not Live on Bread Alone," Piper quotes Foster in a positive light.[568] In another sermon, "When the Bridegroom Is Taken Away, They Will Fast—With New Wineskins," Piper also affirms Foster and references *Celebration of Discipline*:

> Richard Foster, who wrote the book *Celebration of Discipline*, said in his chapter on fasting of Matthew 9:15, "That is perhaps the most important statement in the New Testament on whether Christians should fast today." That's probably true. So let's give close attention to this text and ask the Lord to teach us from it what we should know and what we should do in regard to fasting.[569]

And Foster is not the only off-base teacher cited by John Piper. In his sermon "Tell How Much the Lord Has Done for You!," Piper recommends C. Peter Wagner's book *The Crest of the Wave*: "It may mean getting up in the middle of the night and listening to a John Michael Talbot album like Tom did, or reading *The Crest of the Wave* (Peter Wagner)."[570]

As I have already explained, Wagner is founder of the New Apostolic Reformation network. The NAR promotes mysticism, Gnosticism, and extrabiblical revelations that are declared equal to the Word of God. So why would Piper give credibility to Wagner? Does he agree with Wagner's theology? Does Piper not realize his recommendation of Wagner's book could cause readers serious spiritual consequences?

On this point, I was able to "get a little help from my friends." Phil Johnson, on his website, PyroManiacs, explained where Piper is coming from: "John Piper was openly intrigued with the Toronto Blessing when it was at its peak. (If he ever denounced it as a fraud, I never heard or read where he stated that fact publicly.)"[571]

In his book *When I Don't Desire God*, Piper also quotes Richard Foster concerning "new prophets to arise in our day," and Piper responds by writing, "And when they arise, one way that we fight for joy in God is to read what they write."[572]

Why would John Piper encourage anyone to read self-proclaimed, modern-day prophets who believe in extrabiblical revelations? He offers credibility to the religious Trojan horse of mystic Richard Foster as well as C. Peter Wagner and his "prophets" who make up the New Apostolic Reformation.

Piper does not seem to be finishing his race very well. Besides encouraging Foster and the like, he invited Rick Warren to speak for his Fall 2010 Desiring God conference, and in April 2011, Piper invited Warren to speak for a Desiring God conference reportedly cosponsored by Warren's church. At the conclusion of the conference, Piper videotaped an interview with Rick Warren about *The Purpose Driven Life* in which he said, "I read *The Purpose Driven Life* very carefully...And one of my agendas is to do an appreciative critique." I think Piper's other agenda was to try and prove that his critics were wrong to argue against his uniting with Rick Warren in spiritual enterprises.

Piper did not ask Warren why he positively cited nine different mystics in his book. He did not ask why Warren invited Drs. Oz, Amen, and Hymen to his church when all are promoters of the occult and Eastern mysticism. Piper did not ask why Warren would speak at a conference sponsored by the radical Center for American Islamic Relations (CAIR), a front group for the Muslim Brotherhood. Piper did not ask Warren why his Daniel Plan includes promoting hypnosis and meditation. He did not ask Warren why he has had Richard Foster speak at his church. He did not ask Warren why he sits on the advisory board of Tony Blair's Faith Foundation.

Piper has given aid and comfort to someone I believe is one of the most dangerous false teachers ever to arise within evangelicalism. I don't believe we can accept the excuse that Piper just does not understand Warren's worldview. C. Peter Wagner, Richard Foster, and Rick Warren have all been involved in the promotion of mysticism, and now Piper has promoted them. As I said, mysticism is going mainstream.

Another significant "mainstreamer" in recent years is Robert Schuller of the famed Crystal Cathedral. He advocates a mystic mush derived from an assortment of questionable sources:

> A variety of approaches to meditation....is employed by many different religions as well as by various non-religious mind-control systems. In all forms... TM, Zen Buddhism, or Yoga or...meditation....of Judeo-Christian tradition...the meditator endeavors to overcome the distractions of the conscious mind... It is important to remember that meditation in any form is the harnessing, by human means, of God's divine laws....We are endowed with a great many powers and forces that we do not yet fully understand. The most effective mantras employ the "M" sound. You can get the feel of it by repeating the words, "I am, I am," many times over... Transcendental Meditation or TM....is not a religion nor is it necessarily anti-Christian.[573]

I believe there may even be a connection between Schuller's and Rick Warren's embracing of mysticism. In the November 2002 issue of *Christianity Today*, Rick Warren's wife, Kay, spoke of the "profound" influence Schuller had on her husband:

> During his last year in seminary, he and Kay drove west to visit Robert Schuller's Institute for Church Growth. "We had a very stony ride out to the conference," she says, because such nontraditional ministry scared her to death. Schuller, though, won them over. "He had a profound influence on Rick," Kay says. "We were captivated by his positive appeal to nonbelievers. I never looked back."[574]

The article continues: "Imitating Schuller, Warren walked the (then unincorporated but fast-growing) town of Lake Forest, asking what kept people from going to church."[575] Schuller himself states that Warren's success was due to this imitation of Schuller's methods:

This spirit is the underlining principle that we have taught to over 50,000 pastors who over the years attended the Institute for Successful Church Leadership. These pastors returned home and built upon it and even surpassed what they learned from me. Bill Hybels, Rick Warren, and many other pastors of most of the biggest churches today are a result of applying that principle.[576]

The Crystal Cathedral website also confirms the influence of Schuller on Rick Warren:

Since 1970, Dr. Schuller has taught more than 20,000 church leaders this approach to church growth at the Robert Schuller Institute for Successful Church Leadership. Institute alumni include pastors Bill Hybels and Rick Warren.[577]

These are the nine mystics Rick Warren quotes affirmatively in *The Purpose Driven Life*:

Thomas Carlyle (page 27);
Bernie Siegel (page 31);
Henry David Thoreau (page 32);
Brother Lawrence and Benedictine monks (pages 88–89);
Gary Thomas (pages 102–103);
St. John of the Cross (page 108);
Henry Nouwen (pages 108, 269);
Madame Guyon (page 193); and
William James (page 285).

Of Catholic monk Brother Lawrence, Warren writes: "The classic book on learning how to develop a constant conversation with God is *Practicing the Presence of God*. It was written in the seventeenth century by Brother Lawrence, a humble cook in a French monastery."[578] Another proponent of Brother Lawrence was C.S. Lovett, who wrote:

Around 300 years ago there was a French monk by the name of Brother Lawrence, who...developed the art of visualizing the Lord Jesus, and it revolutionized his life....

THE MOST NOBLE AND GLORIOUS PURPOSE OF THE IMAGINATION IS GVING REALITY TO THE UNSEEN LORD!...

As you know, many tend to be superstitious about picturing the Lord.... But you see, the Lord doesn't care ONE BIT how we visualize Him.... Picture Him any way you wish, but love Him.... I know from experience your enjoyment of Him is going to be greatly enhanced by giving Him arms with which to hold you. [emphasis in original][579]

The Wrong Channel

If you have read *Grave Influence*, you will remember my pointing out that Helen Schucman wrote *A Course in Miracles* starting in 1965 while associate professor of medical psychology at Columbia University in New York. Her book was based in large measure on her experiences channeling "a New Age Jesus" whom she believed would teach mankind how to live in these difficult times. Her Jesus taught a "new gospel," and he dictated the contents of the course over a seven-year period.

Schucman took shorthand as "the voice" spoke. Then she read the messages to William Thetford, a colleague at Columbia University, who typed the daily notes from Schucman. As in the case of Alice Bailey, I contend Schucman was hearing from a demon (or demons). The book was released in 1976, and this 600-plus page transcription of these teachings is described by some as the "Bible" of the New Age movement.

At the risk of shocking some folks: I believe many who think they are encountering God are, like Schucman, actually hearing from a demon. Remember that even Richard Foster warned of this possibility and cautioned his readers to be careful as they entered the spiritual world.

Occult expert Dave Hunt warns that this attempt to visualize Jesus is clearly occultism:

In visualizing "God" or "Jesus" or the thing being prayed for, the average Christian is not aware that he is following the same procedure that shamans insist opens a "magic doorway" in the mind that leads to the sorcerer's world. This simple but powerful technique (long used by shamans for entering the spirit realm in order to contact and bargain with spirit entities) has gained acceptance in today's medicine, psychology, success/motivation, and education. It is also being promoted and taught by an alarming and increasing number of Christian leaders, who urge us to visualize our concept of "Jesus" and promise that the image we create in our minds will become the real Jesus, who will then make genuine contact with us.[580]

Nowhere in the Word of God are we called to visualize Jesus Christ. After His resurrection, when Jesus appeared to people, it was not because they were involved in visualization. Saul, who became Paul, encountered the risen Lord while walking on the road to Damascus.

Mary Magdalene encountered the risen Lord at the empty tomb and did not even know Who it was until He told her. Martha certainly was not in a peaceful state and seeking to enter into the silence when she encountered the resurrected Christ. In fact, Martha was walking around in a state of panic at the thought that the body of Jesus was missing. The real story is recorded in John 20:11–16:

> But Mary stood outside by the tomb weeping, and as she wept she stooped down *and looked* into the tomb. And she saw two angels in white sitting, one at the head and the other at the feet, where the body of Jesus had lain. Then they said to her, "Woman, why are you weeping?" She said to them, "Because they have taken away my Lord, and I do not know where they have laid Him." Now when she had said this, she turned around and saw Jesus standing *there,* and did not know that it was Jesus. Jesus said to her, "Woman, why are you weeping? Whom are you seeking?" She, supposing Him to be the gardener, said to Him, "Sir, if You have carried Him away, tell me where You have laid Him, and I

will take Him away." Jesus said to her, "Mary!" She turned and said to Him, "Rabboni!" (which is to say, Teacher).

When Jesus appeared to the disciples—minus Thomas—in the evening of the day of His resurrection, they were not in a calm state of meditation. Scripture makes it clear they were worried about being attacked or arrested by the Jewish leaders who had crucified Jesus. John 20:19–20 recounts:

> Then, the same day at evening, being the first *day* of the week, when the doors were shut where the disciples were assembled, for fear of the Jews, Jesus came and stood in the midst, and said to them, "Peace *be* with you." When He had said this, He showed them *His* hands and His side. Then the disciples were glad when they saw the Lord.

Each time we see the risen Lord appearing to individuals or groups, they are not meditating or seeking to visualize Jesus. Jesus appears on His own without their help.

It was after the ascension of Jesus Christ, on the day of Pentecost, that the Holy Spirit came to dwell in those who become His children through faith and repentance. After His ascension, there is never again a mention of Jesus Christ appearing to anyone, except to Paul on the Damascus road. In Acts 1:9–11, the disciples were told by two angels that Jesus would come again the same way they saw Him leave:

> Now when He had spoken these things, while they watched, He was taken up, and a cloud received Him out of their sight. And while they looked steadfastly toward heaven as He went up, behold, two men stood by them in white apparel, who also said, "Men of Galilee, why do you stand gazing up into heaven? This *same* Jesus, who was taken up from you into heaven, will so come in like manner as you saw Him go into heaven."

The two angels did not tell the disciples, "Hey, guys, if you want to see Jesus again, just find a quiet place, close your eyes, quote a mantra over and over, enter into the silence, and Jesus will appear to you." No! The disciples were told to stop gazing up into heaven. He is gone, but He will return someday in the same manner as described in Daniel 7:13, Matthew 24:30, Matthew 26:64, and Revelation 1:7; 14:14. The return is the Second Coming when Jesus Christ sets up His Kingdom on earth. And, by the way, do not confuse the rapture of the Church with the second coming of Jesus Christ. The Second Coming is described in these verses and is when Jesus Christ will literally put His foot on the earth again.

First Peter 1:8 does not say, "whom we see whenever we want through visualization" but rather: "whom having not seen you love. Though now you do not see *Him,* yet believing, you rejoice with joy inexpressible and full of glory, receiving the end of your faith—the salvation of *your* souls."

In 2 Corinthians 5:6–8, Paul also gives us more biblical proof that while on this earth in our temporal bodies, we do not see the Lord but walk by faith:

> So *we are* always confident, knowing that while we are at home in the body we are absent from the Lord. For we walk by faith, not by sight. We are confident, yes, well pleased rather to be absent from the body and to be present with the Lord.

In Philippians 1:22–24, Paul again talks about not seeing the Lord in his fleshly body while here on earth:

> But if *I* live on in the flesh, this *will mean* fruit from *my* labor; yet what I shall choose I cannot tell. For I am hard-pressed between the two, having a desire to depart and be with Christ, *which is* far better. Nevertheless to remain in the flesh is more needful for you.

After His ascension into heaven, Scripture tells us over and over that the only way a Christian will see the Lord is either upon his death or if he is alive at the time of the rapture or Second Coming.

Pornographic Divination

In September 2011, Phil Johnson posted an article called "Pornographic Divination." In it, he exposed Mark Driscoll's preaching about spiritual warfare. Unless Phil had provided the actual video of Driscoll's sermon, I am not sure I would have believed what I was reading. Driscoll told those in the audience that some of them had such a gift of discernment it would include having visions of things that had happened in people's pasts.

I played the audio of Driscoll's shocking comments on my radio program, and the phone lines lit up. Here is a partial transcript of what Driscoll said:

> Some people actually see things. This may be a gift of discernment. On occasion, I see things. I see things. Uh, like I was meeting with one person and they—they didn't know this, but they were abused when they were a child. And I said, "When you were a child you were abused. This person did this to you, physically touched you this way."
>
> He said, "How do you know?"
>
> I said, "I don't know. It's like I got a TV right here. I'm seeing it."
>
> He said, "No, that never happened."
>
> I said, "Go ask him. Go ask him if they actually did what I think they did and I see that they did."
>
> They went and asked this person, "When I was a little kid did you do this?"
>
> And the person said, "Yyyyeah, but you were only like a year or two old. How do you remember that?"
>
> He said, "Well, Pastor Mark told me."
>
> I'm not a guru. I'm not a freak. I don't talk about

this. If I did talk about it everybody'd want to meet with me and I'd end up like one of those guys on TV. But some of you have this visual ability to see things.

Um, uh, there was one woman I dealt with. She never told her husband that she had committed adultery on him early in the relationship. I said, "You know—" (she's sitting there with her husband). I said, "You know I think the root of all this—I think Satan has a foothold in your life because you've never told your husband about that really tall blonde guy that you met at the bar. And then you went back to the hotel. And you laid on your back. And you undressed yourself. And he climbed on top of you. And you had sex with him. And snuggled up with him for a while. And deep down in your heart, even though you had just met him, you desired him because secretly he is the fantasy body type." I said, "You remember that place; it was that cheap hotel with that certain-colored bedspread. You did it—you had sex with the light on because you weren't ashamed and you wanted him to see you. And you wanted to see him."

She was just looking at me like—

I said, "You know, it was about ten years ago."

"I see everything."

She says—she looks at her husband. He says, "Is that true?"

She says, "Yeah."

"He was 6'2", blonde hair, blue eyes?"

"Yeah."

Some of you when you're counseling you will see

things. I mean you will, you will literally have the gift of discernment to see things. I can't explain it. It doesn't happen all the time.

Sometimes your counselee, they will see things. Ye—eh—there's pa— I found this with people—ok, now let me—I'm gonna ask the demon questions. You tell me what they say."

"They don't say anything."

I say, "What do you hear?"

And they say, "Nothing." They say, "But I'm seeing stuff."

"Oh, oh, well, tell me. What's that?"

"I'm seeing—you know when I was little my grandpa molested me. I didn't know that."

I said, "Well, let's not assume it's true. Go ask your grandfather."

Grandpa says, "Yyyeah, when you were little I molested you." Grandpa was assuming they'd be too young to remember. So he'd only molest grandkids up to a certain age. But they saw it.

It's the supernatural. It's, it's, it's the whole other realm. It's like the Matrix. You can take the blue pill, you take the red pill. You go into this whole other world. And, and, and that's the way it works.

So I say—tell me everything you hear, tell me everything you see. And sometimes I see things, too. I see things, too. I've seen women raped. I've seen children molested. I've seen people abused. I've seen people beaten. I've seen horrible things done. Horrible things done. I've seen children dedicated in occultic groups and demons come upon them as an infant by invitation. And I wasn't present for any of it, but I've seen it visibly.

Upon occasion when I get up to preach I'll see— just like a screen in front of me—I'll see somebody get raped or abused and then I'll track 'em down and say, "Look, I had this vision. Let me tell you about it." All true. One I had—I was sitting in my office at the old, uh, Earl Building. This gal walks by. Nice gal, member of the church. This is when the church was small. And it's just like a TV was there and I saw the night before her husband threw her up against the wall, had her by the throat, was physically violent with her.

And she said, "That's it, I'm telling the pastors."

And he said, "If you do I'll kill you." He was a very physically abusive man.

She was walking by, and I just saw it. It was like a TV. And I said, "Hey, come here for a second." I said, "Last night did your husband throw you up against the wall and have you by the throat, physically assault you and tell you if you told anyone he would kill you?"

And she just starts bawling. She says, "How did you know?"

I said, "Jesus told me."

I call the guy on the phone: "Hey, I need you to come to the office." Didn't give him any clue.

He comes in and I said, "Dude, what'd you do to your wife last night? Why'd you do this? Why'd you throw her up against the wall?"

And he gets very angry. They're sitting on the couch and he says, "Why did you tell him?"

I said, "She didn't. Jesus did. Jesus did."

...And there are some people that have real gift of discernment, and I'm not saying I'm a hundred percent always right with it, but some of you are going to have the gift of discernment, and you need to—you need to learn to grow in the use of that gift. And sometimes people will hear things. Sometimes people will see things.[581]

Part of the problem here is that I believe Driscoll dwells on the demonic while we are called to focus on what is godly:

Finally, brethren, whatever things are true, whatever things are noble, whatever things are just, whatever things are pure, whatever things are lovely, whatever things are of good report, if there is any virtue and if there is anything praiseworthy—meditate on these things. (Philippians 4:8)

Who, then, is imparting these images to Mark Driscoll? What Driscoll is saying sounds similar to the kind of images Word of Faith heretic Kenneth Hagin claimed to have experienced. Driscoll alleges that he sometimes has these visions while preaching in his church.

John MacArthur addressed this issue in *Charismatic Chaos*: "Hagin claims God miraculously transported him out of church on Sunday, right in the middle of the sermon. Worst of all, Hagin was the preacher delivering the sermon."[582]

Hagin had described his "revelation" this way:

Suddenly I was gone! Right in the middle of my sermon, I found myself standing along a street in a little town fifteen miles away—and I knew it was Saturday night. I was leaning against a building, and I saw this young lady come walking down the street. About the time she got to where I was standing, a car came down the street. The driver pulled up to the curb, sounded the horn, she got into the car. He backed out, turned the other direction, and started out of town—and suddenly I was sitting in the back seat!

They went out in the country and committed adultery. And I watched them. I was still in the cloud. Suddenly I heard the sound of my voice, and the cloud lifted. I was standing behind my pulpit. I didn't know what to say, because I didn't know what I had been saying, so I just said "Everyone bow your head," and we prayed. I looked at my watch, and...I'd been gone about fifteen minutes in the cloud.

While I was shaking hands with people as they went out the door, this young lady came by. I said, "We missed you last night." She said, "I was over in _____" (and she named the little town). I said, "Yes, I know."[583]

Whether it is the revelations reported by Driscoll or Hagin, I find nowhere in the Scriptures that, after the apostolic age, anyone receives visions and extra-biblical revelation from God. There would be no reason for it because the Word of God is complete according to Jude 3, Revelation 22:18–19, and 2 Timothy 3:16. Scripture is all we need in order to be *thoroughly equipped* for every good work.

Many self-professing Christians have become rip-*out* artists. They are great at ripping Scripture out of context in order to justify unbiblical theology and often an unbiblical lifestyle. Numerous people have emailed Joel 2:28 to me to tell me their dreams and visions that include extrabiblical revelations are viable today. There is, however, a serious problem with their interpretation. Joel 2:28 describes something that happens during the tribulation to the house of Israel alone, as it refers to "your sons and your daughters":

And it shall come to pass afterwards that I will pour out my Spirit on all flesh; Your sons and your daughters shall prophesy, Your old men shall dream dreams, Your younger men shall see visions.

The word "prophesy" in this verse means to speak forth truth contained in God's Word. It is not referring to an ability to predict the future.

Many people who take Scripture out of context have bought into what is called "replacement theology." This is the belief that when the Word of God speaks of Israel in the New Testament it really means the Church. However, this false idea has caused many to believe they will also receive dreams and visions.

Whether they know it or not or intend to or not, I believe Piper, Keller, Warren, Schuller, Bickle, and Driscoll give credibility to incredibly destructive and unbiblical teachings. These are teachings that in many ways are rooted in the goals and objectives of those who desire a Counter-Reformation leading back to the extrabiblical revelations, new experiences, mysticism, ecumenicalism, and social justice of the Church of Rome and her Maryknoll Jesuit Order.

CHAPTER 12

Man-Centered from Both Sides:
The Social Gospel, Right and Left

Should Christians promote righteousness within our nation and be concerned about the worldview our various levels of government and education promote?

Of course.

After all, it is God Himself Who drew the borders of nations and chose the very nation in which each man and woman would be born. God created government.

Because we are Christians, we must judge everything against the Word of God, which is a reflection of God's character and nature. Therefore, Christians should support legislation and initiatives that reward the righteous and punish the wicked, purposes for which God created government (Romans 13).

God designated civil, family, and Church governments with different spheres of influence. His assigned role for civil government is to restrain evil and to make a stable, just society so the family and the Church can fulfill their God-given mandates. The government is called to be the government, and the Church is called to be the Church. The two institutions are to complement one another, according to God's plan, but the Church is not to become the government, and the government is not to become the Church. In light of this division of responsibility, Christians must remember that their first priority and ultimate calling is to preach the Gospel as well as the whole counsel of God (Acts 20:27). We must not replace the biblical Gospel with any sort of "social gospel."

The Social Gospel of Moralizing

The religious right of the 1970s and 1980s has drastically changed and is now a New Religious Right, embracing and participating in many unbiblical activities and projects as I noted in chapter 7. Consistent with this misdirection, many within the NRR seem more interested in being the civil government than in being the Church. I contend the primary reason for this is that many within the New Religious Right are not committed to the Gospel. Some NRR adherents are seemingly so shallow in biblical knowledge and discernment that they fail to recognize the error of their commitment to a social gospel. Among other problems, the New Religious Right embraces ecumenicalism in order to build political coalitions, to increase revenues to their organizations, and because they simply are not committed to biblical theology and doctrine.

I believe most pro-family organizations claim to be Christian and boast that they embrace "Christian values" because the majority of their donors call themselves "Christian." When it comes to defining what it means to be a Christian, however, most of the New Religious Right will not reflect biblical Christianity because they don't want to offend their Catholic, Mormon, Word of Faith, or New Apostolic Reformation donors. So, in the end, the New Religious Right betrays the Gospel in deference to "another" gospel embraced by these disparate groups.

But is "another" gospel of the New Religious Right any different from "another" gospel of the religious left?

From whichever side a social gospel originates, it is always man-centered. Its basic claim says man needs to fix or improve his condition through social activism, Christian activism, philanthropy, and good works. A social gospel leaves out the preaching and teaching that sin is the primary reason for the problems of our world. Rick Warren's social gospel, for instance, involves leaving out the biblical Gospel so he can work with Muslims and other world religions to improve education, address poverty, combat disease, and promote globalism.

The social gospel from the New Religious Right is primarily about lowering taxes, decreasing the size of government, and giving people more political and economic liberty. But accomplishing these goals—as laudable as they may be—will not solve man's root problem of sin and rebellion against God. Our problems will not be addressed by more liberalism or more conservatism but only through the proclaiming of the biblical Gospel. If 80 percent of a society's problems and heartaches are directly related to the demise of the family unit, one merely has to ask why the family is in decline. The answer will quickly ring up "sin."

Unfortunately, for many within the New Religious Right, it is too late. They have already compromised the Gospel by their willingness to unite with false teachers such as the New Apostolic Reformation and the Word of Faith movements. Certain members of the New Religious Right have admonished me and some of my friends not to expose the unbiblical theology of Mormonism or Catholicism or liberation theology on the NRR airwaves. Such biblical truth offends the unbeliever and causes these ministries to lose donors.

What the NRR does not seem to understand is that the culture war is really only a symptom of the serious spiritual problem from which man suffers, and only the preaching of the Gospel will cure this disease. Even if the New Religious Right could implement every law it wants and turn America into one great big town of Mayberry, the result would simply be a more comfortable and moral America from which millions of people could enter hell.

While many Christian news and public policy organizations are clueless about the overall failure of modern-day evangelicalism and pro-family groups due to their moralizing, the secular website of *National Review* published an insightful article about this very issue. David French's article "Evangelicals' Collapsing Cultural Infleunce" notes:

> We are more focused on meeting the material needs of the poor than their spiritual needs. Spend much time in the evangelical community, and you'll soon learn that the old-fashioned Gospel-focused mission trip is largely a thing of the past. Now, you go build schools. Now, you go dig water wells. Now, you repair houses. These are worthy goals, all, but service projects by themselves don't change hearts and minds; they often make (frequently) self-inflicted misery more bearable. Service must be accompanied by intentional, vocal evangelism and discipling.[584]

French comes to the same conclusion I announced in the first five words of *Grave Influence*: "We've lost the culture war." Mr. French explains why:

> I once heard it said that following the social and political disruptions of the 1960s and early 1970s,

religious conservatives decided that they had to win elections, while secular leftists decided to win the culture—and both groups succeeded. So now here we are, enjoying unprecedented influence on presidential outcomes even as our cultural foundation rots away beneath our feet. Not even the best presidential candidate will fix the family, nor will our most generous service project save a soul.[585]

Good on the Surface

In Matthew 23, Jesus calls the religious leaders of His day "whitewashed tombs." They looked good on the outside. They thought they were promoting morality, but they were dead spiritually. Jesus warned that they would strain out a gnat but swallow a whole camel. And, indeed, the New Religious Right is notorious for such activity. The Southern Baptist Convention called for a boycott of the Disney Company, for instance, but in 1993 refused to pass a resolution at their national convention condemning the occultism of Freemasonry. Instead, the denomination passed a resolution stating that there are aspects of Freemasonry consistent with Christianity. (Compare this stance with Ezekiel 5:11–16; 8:5–18 to see the Old Testament attitude toward aberrant systems such as Freemasonry.)

The New Religious Right will boycott a company whose unsaved executives promote the homosexual agenda but will themselves promote and give credibility to false teachers who preach another Jesus and another gospel. Both the executives and false teachers are wrong, but purchasing a hammer from a hardware chain that supports immorality is not going to result in someone going to hell. Promoting and giving credibility to false teachers and their false gospel can certainly result in people spending eternity in hell.

In Matthew 23:13–29, Jesus uses the word "woe" eight times when speaking to the scribes, Sadducees, and Pharisees. "Woe" means "judgment upon you," and Jesus pronounced judgment on them because they were more interested in moralizing and legislating morality than in understanding, accepting, and preaching the life-changing Gospel of Jesus Christ.

In similar whitewashed-looking causes, the New Religious Right has chosen:

1. Family values over biblical doctrine.

The NRR united in spiritual enterprises with false teachers, despite their attacks on the Word of God, simply because members of the New Apostolic Reformation and Word of Faith claim to be pro-life and opposed to same-sex marriage.

2. Moralizing over evangelizing.

Instead of making their primary focus the proclamation of the Gospel to the unsaved world by which to change hearts and minds, the New Religious Right focuses on moralizing, which has proven to be a failure since the 1980s.

3. Prosperity over sacrifice.

The New Religious Right has united with the New Apostolic Reformation and Word of Faith movements, giving credibility to the prosperity gospel where the Gospel of Jesus Christ calls for sacrifice. The NRR is obsessed with the need for America to maintain economic prosperity by electing the right people to political office. While I am all for liberty and economic freedom, financial prosperity is not going to solve America's spiritual problem of rebellion against God. Many pro-family groups raise millions of dollars each year, and yet with that prosperity, few in the NRR have proclaimed a biblical Gospel but rather have compromised the Gospel. The NRR deliberately avoids proclaiming biblical truth so as not to offend Mormon and Roman Catholic donors. This is how many within the NRR have chosen prosperity over the sacrifice that Christians must make when they lovingly speak truth.

4. Christian activism over biblical discipleship.

Most of the New Religious Right has focused on creating Christian activists rather than biblical disciples according to the mandate of the Great Commission in Matthew 28.

5. Compromise over commitment.

The New Religious Right is identified by its willingness to compromise biblical truth for political and financial pragmatism.

6. The flag over the cross.

Patriotism (the love of country) is one thing, but nationalism (the love of government) is a sin. The New Religious Right has moved from patriotism to nationalism and has raised the flag over the cross. The NRR focuses on cultural activism, returning to the Founding Fathers' "original intent," and "reclaiming America" instead of preaching the cross. Nationalism is defined in part by a belief that the state is of primary importance.[586] In brief, nationalism is a theory of political legitimacy, which requires that ethnic boundaries should not cut across political ones. To many NRR members, the state is of primary importance because they believe they must implement the Kingdom of God on earth before Jesus Christ comes to rule His Kingdom. Nationalism emphasizes collective identity—a "people" must be autonomous, united, and express a single national culture.[587] This definition certainly applies to NRR members committed to implementing "kingdom values" so they can transform the culture and establish dominion through a theocratic or "Christian" government.

7. The White House over the Church house.

The New Religious Right is more committed to reclaiming or maintaining the office of U.S. president than in reclaiming Church offices from false teaching. Instead of defending the Church from false teachers, the NRR unites with them. The result is that many of NRR members become false teachers themselves.

8. The wolves over the sheep.

I have personally witnessed members of the New Religious Right criticize and shun Christians who

warn of false teachers. I've experienced the "soft persecution" of criticism from members of the NRR that
choose to unite with the very wolves about which I
warned. Members of the NRR often partner with the
wolves at the expense of the sheep.

9. An earthly kingdom over the Kingdom of God (1 Corinthians 9:16).

Many members of the New Religious Right are
hostile to the biblical Gospel of the Kingdom of God
and instead are committed to building an earthly kingdom. Some are not openly hostile to the message of
Christ, but they have no commitment to defending or
proclaiming the Gospel because their primary goals re-
volve around the culture war and dominion theology.

The Dangers of Moralizing

On my June 20, 2012, radio program, John MacArthur made an
extremely important biblical and historical point about the perils of
moralizing:

The Pharisees and the Sadducees had created in the
land of Israel a moral culture—the Pharisees in particular.
The Bible describes the Pharisees as the rabbis. They had
created a moral culture. In other words, they had created
a fastidious culture in which all of the normal categori-
cal sins were excluded from society. They had a kind of
"form of godliness" the Apostle Paul called it. I would say
that based upon, sort of Old Testament moral standards,
that the culture of Israel when our Lord came was the
most moral culture in the history of Israel and therefore,
more moral than any other culture, because they at least
had the Bible to base it on, the Old Testament to base
it on. They'd gotten rid of idolatry after the Babylonian
captivity. There were no idols in the land. They were living fastidiously by the law. The Pharisees were in control,
and they were the rigid legalists. They had disseminated
this religion throughout the land of Israel.

And Jesus came into that situation and basically condemned the entire thing, and said this is what is going to send you to hell. And Paul picks up on that and says that they're going about establishing their own righteousness. They don't know how holy God is. They don't know how unholy they are (Romans 10). The only way to be saved is to call on the name of the Lord.

So what do you get when you're done reclaiming the culture? What have you got? You've got first century Judaism, and Jesus came and said your house has left you desolate. You're going to be destroyed.

And in 70 AD the Romans were God's divine weapon that came in and massacred and Josephus says that, we don't know if the number's exactly accurate, a million Jews were killed, 985 towns in Israel were sacked and people were slaughtered. The divine judgment fell on the most moral society maybe that the world has ever known based on the Old Testament morality and superficiality. So what do you get when you get a moral society? You get a society of people insulated against the true understanding of their own wretched hearts.[588]

The Real Meaning of Salt and Light

The New Religious Right uses the biblical theme of salt and light to argue that we are called to focus time, energy, and money on Christian activism. Yet the overarching message of Matthew 5:13–16 is not about Christian activism but about proclaiming the Gospel. In Matthew 5 Jesus says: "You are the light of the world... Let your light shine before men, that they may see your good works and glorify your Father in heaven."

Christians should be involved in good works such as defending the lives of the unborn, caring for widows and orphans, and running crisis pregnancy centers. The reason, though, is that people will see the transforming power of the Gospel in our lives. Good works when used as a platform for the Gospel offers unbelievers the chance to see the light of Christ within our lives and to give glory to our heavenly Father.

Christian activism apart from the Gospel has no eternal value and is, in fact, a sin because we are not obeying God and fulfilling the Great Commission. When Christians call on unbelievers to conform to a certain "religious standard" without faith and repentance in Jesus Christ, we run the risk of leading them to believe that becoming a Christian means simply living a good life. This ignores the central fact that "there is none that are good, no, not one" (Romans 3:10).

Christians and the Church, not the civil government, are called to be salt and light. Romans 13 declares that government and laws exist to deter evil. The government causes lawbreakers to fear the consequences of their actions, but just because a man is afraid of the law and so decides not to steal, rape, or murder, that does not save him from the eternal wrath of God. No matter how many pieces of legislation become law and no matter the number of laws to which the unsaved conform, they are still lost in sin and need to hear the Good News of salvation through Jesus Christ.

When the Church takes on the role of morality police to penalize with a loss of sales, for example, the immoral actions of a company run by unbelievers, we are only addressing the symptoms of their unsaved condition. On the other hand, when Christians are spiritual lifeguards who preach the Gospel instead of moralism, we address the root cause of man's immoral actions.

Getting to this root of the problem is the world's only hope. How can people change their values and conduct unless they change their worldviews? Jeremiah 13:23 echoes this impossibility: "Can the Ethiopian change his skin or the leopard its spots? Then may you also do good who are accustomed to do evil?"

How can the unregenerate be anything less than they are? Their worldviews are the foundation of their values, and their values are the foundation of their conduct. Until their unbiblical worldviews are transformed into a biblical view through faith and repentance in Jesus Christ, they are slaves to sin.

Moralism is just as dangerous and deadly as outright liberalism. As John MacArthur has said:

> It makes no difference if an unsaved person is for
> or against abortion, a political liberal or a conservative,

a prostitute or a police officer, he will spend eternity apart from God unless he repents and believes the gospel.[589]

The hardest people to reach with the Gospel are not prostitutes, drug addicts, or reprobates who know they deserve to go to hell, but the morally upright who think they are good people that *deserve* heaven.

The Biblical Gospel

The late Dr. Francis Schaeffer was one of the greatest defenders of the Christian faith in the 20th century. He predicted the American church would become inconsequential because of a false concept of spirituality. Self-professing Christians would talk about and proclaim a belief in God while rejecting the God of the Bible. They would, instead, follow a man-made, New Age god.

I believe one of the main reasons we have a crisis in the American church, that Christians poll no differently from the world, and that students are leaving the church in large numbers is that we have an epidemic of false converts in American congregations. People call themselves Christians but do not believe in many, if any, of the essential Christian doctrines.

To bring clarity to this issue, let me outline the biblical Gospel and explain the problem of false converts who fill many churches. It is precisely because so many self-professing Christians are false converts that they have been captured by the lies of the religious Trojan horse.

In several books, from the Worldview Weekend platform, and in various articles, I've sounded an alarm about the sorry state of the worldviews held by many evangelical Christians. Numerous studies—perhaps the most stunning of which was done by the Southern Baptist Church of its own youth—reveal that the lifestyles, values, and resulting worldview of most of those who attend "evangelical churches" are no different from the world and that a large majority of students leave the church after graduating from high school, never to return.

While these studies may reveal the problem, they don't explain what has caused it, but I believe I know. Our churches are filled with false coverts. And it's a problem I identify with all too readily because, despite being raised in a Christian home, taught in a Christian school, and belonging to a Bible-believing church, I was a false convert myself until adulthood. And the especially scary part is that it's not all that hard to do!

I played the "game" (even though I didn't know I was playing a game). I thought I was saved because I believed in Jesus Christ, had prayed the "sinner's prayer," walked the aisle, and had been baptized. I was "sorry" for my sins, but it was not the kind of sorrow that produced repentance unto salvation.

My wake-up call came when I read the book of 1 John and recognized ten clear signs of a true convert but saw very few of those signs manifested in my life. After searching the Scriptures further, I discovered in 2 Corinthians 7:9–10 the source of my dysfunctional attempt at Christianity:

> Now I rejoice, not that you were made sorry, but that your sorrow led to repentance. For you were made sorry in a godly manner, that you might suffer loss from us in nothing. For godly sorrow produces repentance leading to salvation, not to be regretted; but the sorrow of the world produces death.

True repentance was missing from my heart and, hence, my life! "Godly sorrow" causes a person to turn and go in the opposite direction of a willfully sinful life. True repentance leads to a change in someone's priorities and desires, and it produces God-honoring fruit.

Many people say they believe in Jesus, but this does not make them saved. The Bible says demons believe in Jesus (James 2:19), but theirs is not a saving belief.

Too often people think they are saved because they are sorry for the bad things they do, but they continue to willfully practice sin. (Can you say, "Sunday Christian"?) The 2 Corinthians passage makes clear there is a worldly sorrow that leads to death and another, godly, sorrow that produces repentance leading to salvation.

What caused me to realize I was not a good person, that I was totally depraved and deserved hell, was when I encountered the biblical teaching and doctrine of the moral law. Considering the Ten Commandments made me realize that only a godly sorrow leads to repentance and true salvation. The moral law revealed my true condition: extreme sinfulness and depravity.

While my study of the moral law revealed I was not a good person, it was when I opened the book of 1 John and underlined every sign of a true convert that I realized I did not measure up to even half of the signs. To my dismay, I recognized myself as a false convert.

First John 5:13 tells why the book of 1 John was written: "These things I have written to you who believe in the name of the Son of God, that you may know that you have eternal life." So here are 1 John's ten signs of a true convert, so you can, indeed, know that you have eternal life (you might want to compare yourself to make sure you're where you think you are):

1. A true convert admits he or she is a sinner. He does not believe he can go to heaven by being a "good" person. She understands her totally depravity (1 John 1:8).

2. A true convert lives a life of obedience by *keeping* God's commandments more often than *breaking* them. A true convert is not a habitual sinner. There's a difference between stumbling into sin and jumping in with both feet. While true converts may sin as part of the struggle with our sin nature, the life of a true convert is marked by a desire to pursue holiness and walk in obedience to God's Word (1 John 2:3–6, 3:6, 5:2).

3. A true convert does not harbor hate for his brother but offers forgiveness, love, and compassion (1 John 2:9, 2:11, 3:15, 4:16, 4:20).

4. A true convert does not love the world or the things of the world, nor the world's system of evil, ruled by Satan (1 John 2:15).

5. A true convert proclaims Jesus Christ as the Son of God and defends the exclusivity of Christ in a world of multiple religious systems (1 John 4:15).

6. A true convert hopes and longs for the return of the Lord (1 John 3:2–3).

7. A true convert desires to serve and help other Christians 1 John 3: 14,17).

8. A true convert loves being with other believers and hearing the Word taught (1 John 5:1).

9. A true convert rejects false teaching (1 John 2:22–23).

10. A true convert remains in the truth and perseveres in the faith (1 John 2:24).

Sadly, repentance is *not* a Christian doctrine taught often enough (many churches *never* teach it), and as a result, the church is filled with false converts. This dire reality should concern all of us. Scripture is forthright about how important this is:

- The word "repent" and its various forms are used more than 100 times in the Bible.

- John the Baptist preached in the wilderness, "Repent, for the kingdom of heaven is at hand!" (Matthew 3:2).

- Jesus preached this same message of repentance. Mark 1:14, 15 says, "Now after John was put in prison, Jesus came to Galilee, preaching the gospel of the kingdom of God, and saying, 'The time is fulfilled, and the kingdom of God is at hand. Repent, and believe the gospel.'"

- In Mark 6, Jesus sends out the 12 disciples, two by two. Verse 12 recounts, "So they went out and preached that people should *repent*" (italics mine).

Every day 150,000 people step into eternity, and a frightening percentage of them fall into eternal judgment. Many who wind up under judgment are likely shocked when they realize their situation. They will have thought they lived a good life as defined by today's standards. They went to church, perhaps even walked the aisle and were baptized. Some even taught Sunday school. But Jesus warned this would happen:

> Not everyone who says to me, "Lord, Lord," will enter the kingdom of heaven, but the one who does the will of my Father who is in heaven. On that day

many will say to me, "Lord, Lord, did we not prophesy in your name, and cast out demons in your name, and do many mighty works in your name?" And then will I declare to them, "I never knew you; depart from me, you workers of lawlessness." (Matthew 7:21–23)

The e-mail below reveals that when we are faithful to proclaim truth and what it really means to be a Christian, people like Nick (and me!) will listen, open God's Word, be convicted, and come to a place of godly sorrow that produces repentance unto salvation.

Dear Mr. Howse,

I took your worldview test a few years ago and ranked as a secular humanist worldview thinker. At the time, I got mad at it and mad at your organization. I took the test again just a few weeks ago and ranked as a strong biblical worldview thinker. I knew I'd changed vastly in recent times, but never how much. I've become a new man since those few years back, and I'm happy for it.

I was raised by a Lutheran father and non-denominational Christian mother. I'd always been a strong believer in God's existence and the salvation found in Christ. However, I realize now that I never really understood it during all of those years. Even though I accepted the Bible as truth, looking back I realize how much I twisted meaning to find what I wanted to see instead of what was there. This "liberal theology" is due a lot, I believe, to the media and societal structure in which we live. I have seen many, many others fall victim to it, as well as false doctrines such as theistic evolutionism. Thankfully, those misinterpretations are in my past, and I now stand with the real truth in hand.

I attend one of the largest evangelical churches in the Las Vegas area. As I silently observe my college contemporaries, I see that they are like I once was— having a terribly skewed interpretation of God's Word or in many cases, even worse, they deny the Lord outright. Watching this, along with an even greater passion for the lost, inspired me to begin studying for the ministry. I'd spent about 12 years of my life preparing for and gearing towards becoming an attorney. Now, all I want to do is spread the message of our Lord.

In any case, I just wanted to let you know how much I've changed and how much more biblical I've become. Praise the Lord for that.

Sincerely, Nick

Remember, your faithfulness to proclaim truth may very well help someone pass the true/false converts test once and for all. I thank God someone once spoke doctrine into my life and revealed the true condition of my heart and mind so as to allow me to understand I was a false convert. I pray that this explanation of the biblical Gospel will either confirm your salvation or reveal to you your great need to repent and place your faith and trust in Jesus Christ as Lord and Savior.

Active for the Gospel

Supporting legislation and initiatives to fulfill the God-given purpose of government or opposing legislation that perverts God's intent is fine when in balance. But we must never lose sight of the reality that legislation and morality do not save people. The power of the Gospel transforms lives, families, churches, communities, states, and nations. As 2 Corinthians 5:17 declares: "Therefore, if anyone is in Christ, he is a new creation; old things have passed away; behold, all things have become new."

The Great Commission is our ultimate mission, not political activism and moralizing. In Matthew 28:19–20 Jesus commands, "Go therefore and make disciples of all nations, baptizing them in the name of the Father and of the Son and of the Holy Spirit, teaching them to observe all things that I have commanded you."

If Christians would spend 10 percent of their time on biblically based Christian activism, and 90 percent of their time on preaching a biblical Gospel to make disciples, the eternal impact would be immeasurable. What is happening within American churches and denominations is not new. Dietrich Bonhoeffer noticed that those committed to a social gospel were co-opting the liberal American churches in 1930 when he observed:

> In New York they preach about virtually every-
> thing, only one thing is not addressed, or is addressed
> so rarely that I have yet been unable to hear it, namely,
> the gospel of Jesus Christ, the cross, sin, and forgive-
> ness, death and life.[590]

Today it is both the liberal and "conservative" denominations and Christian leaders that are co-opted by a social gospel. Eric Metaxas, in his book *Bonhoeffer*, also recognized the problem in Bonhoeffer's time:

> Seeing an opportunity to knock out fundamental-
> ism in New York, the Rockefeller Foundation promptly
> funded the construction of a church for Fosdick [a lib-
> eral pastor], one that would serve as a proper platform
> for his "progressive" modernist views.[591]

Progressives for years have sought to co-opt Christianity for their own political, progressive agenda. The Rockefellers helped establish the United Nations, and I have discussed how, more recently, the Southern Baptists' Ethics and Religious Liberty Commission is a Unit-ed Nations NGO (non-governmental organization). America's largest Protestant denomination is aligned with the godless United Nations!

According to the United Nations website, an NGO must "sup-port and respect the principles of the Charter of the United Nations." Richard Land, head of the ERLC, is also a member of the globalist organization, the Council on Foreign Relations. Are we to accept that SBC leaders "support and respect the principles of the Charter of the United Nations," which includes the quest for world government? If so, I, and many others, may need to resign our memberships in SBC churches. If SBC leaders do endorse the UN charter, then something must change. Meanwhile, I would make sure 100 percent of the con-tributions to your local SBC church remain local and do not go back to the SBC cooperative program, which contributes to the work of the Ethics and Religious Liberty Commission.

The story is really the same as what Bonhoeffer saw in 1930: glo-balists and progressives are using the Church to give themselves cred-ibility while they push their anti-biblical worldview. But where are the American Bonhoeffers? Why do Christians attack people like you and me when we simply point out the facts about what the Bible instructs?

A few Christians may be disappointed that I quote Bonhoeffer because they have read he was not a conservative. But having researched this issue, I believe that many years ago liberals set out to hijack Bonhoeffer's legacy and make him their poster child for social justice. If you read Bonhoeffer's own words, you will see that he was offended by those who preached social justice. What's more, Bonhoeffer remains a rare example of a pastor who refused to go along with Hitler's nationalism, racism, socialism, and the use of the Church for Hitler's political and social gain.

Perhaps what is happening in the American Church is the same thing Bonhoeffer noticed among ministers and seminary students in New York in 1930. He saw that "without doubt the most vigorous... have turned their backs on all genuine theology and study many economic and political problems. Here, they feel, is the renewal of the Gospel for our time."[592] He also noted their "self-assurance which lightly makes mock of any specifically theological question [as] unwarranted and naïve."[593]

Today if you question—even with Scripture as your basis—one of the "celebrities" of evangelicalism, do not be shocked if you're called a "pinhead." Many who heard Land's national radio program of October 9, 2010, believe I was the pinhead to whom Land referred, since it was one of my articles he was responding to when he used the term. I had dared to raise theological issues regarding the economy, politics, and pragmatism.

Bonhoeffer observed the same flippant, condescending response by those in Church leadership, ministry, and seminary when he wrote: "They become intoxicated with liberal humanistic phrases [and] laugh at the fundamentalists..."[594] Bonhoeffer also warned of "the secularization of Christianity in America." He believed most American Christians and churches had forgotten the real calling of Christians:

> So what stands in place of the Christian message? An ethical and social idealism born by a faith in progress that—who knows how—claims the right to call itself "Christian." And in the place of the church as the congregation of believers in Christ there stands the church as a social corporation. Anyone who has seen the weekly program of one of the large New York churches, with their daily, indeed almost hourly

events, teas, lectures, concerts, charity events, opportunities for sports, games, bowling, dancing for
every age group, anyone who has heard how they try
to persuade a new resident to join the church, in-
sisting that you'll get into society quite differently by
doing so, anyone who has become acquainted with
the embarrassing nervousness with which the pastor
lobbies for membership—that person can well assess
the character of such a church. All these things, of
course, take place with varying degrees of tactfulness,
taste, and seriousness; some churches are basically
"charitable" churches; others have primarily a social
identity. One cannot avoid the impression, however,
that in both cases they have forgotten what the real
point is.[595]

With each passing day, I am more and more thankful for the example of Pastor Bonhoeffer, a man I am sure would be marginalized
and criticized by America's Christian celebrities if he were living in
America today. Bonhoeffer was a man of deep conviction, willing to
leave America and return to Germany in order to call the Church to
be the Church. Bonhoeffer knew if he returned to Germany he risked
arrest, and indeed, he eventually was arrested.

Bonhoeffer wanted to fight the Christianity in Germany that had
been replaced by Germanism, and pastors and religious leaders by the
thousands turned their backs on him. In the end, most of his friends
abandoned him, and Bonhoeffer was hung to death by a piano wire at
the hands of a government that had co-opted the Church.

Evangelical Christianity in America certainly seems to be proclaiming strange assortments of "another gospel." The left pushes
a bigger government and progressive agenda while the right pushes
smaller government, man-centered moralizing, and a false nationalism that has already said "no" to God in a thousand ways. Both sides
are increasingly hostile to Christians who hold to biblical theology
and make proclaiming the Gospel and the Great Commission their
first priority.

The stage is set for the coming persecution of the West as true
believers in Jesus Christ are targeted by both the left and the right. Do
not be shocked when Christian leaders position themselves so they

can be thought well of by the powers that be. Neither be surprised when members of the remnant are criticized and mocked by these same leaders.

Bonhoeffer was not certain he could remain faithful in the face of persecution, but because of God's grace and strength, he persevered till the end. Perhaps you, like Bonhoeffer, wonder if you can remain faithful when you lose relationships with longtime friends or even family because you stand for biblical truth. I pray that 2 Corinthians 4:7–9 will encourage you for the spiritual battle that is heating up even within our own churches and denominations:

> But we have this treasure in earthen vessels, that the excellence of the power may be of God and not of us. We are hard-pressed on every side, yet not crushed; we are perplexed, but not in despair; persecuted, but not forsaken; stuck down, but not destroyed.

ENDNOTES

[1] Pastor Jim Bublitz from his website: www.oldtruth.com.

[2] Alice Bailey, *The Rays and the Initiations* (1934–1947), 109.

[3] Alice Bailey, *The Reappearance of the Christ*, 1st ed. (1948), 164–65.

[4] Jerry Falwell, Jr., posted at: http://www.glennbeck.com/content/articles/article/198/42325/

[5] Alice Bailey, *The Externalisation of the Hierarchy*, 1st ed. (1957), 589–590.

[6] David Breese, *Seven Men Who Rule the World from the Grave* (Chicago: Moody Publishers, 1992), 221.

[7] science.jrank.org/pages/7686/Existentialism.html.

[8] Ibid.

[9] Walter Kaufmann, *Existentialism: From Dostoevsky to Sartre* (Cleveland: The World Publishing Company, 1956), 11.

[10] John MacArthur sermon, "God's Plan for Younger Women, Part 1," March 7, 1993, posted at: http://www.gty.org/resources/sermons/56–14/Gods-Plan-for-Younger-Women-Part-1-1-of-2.

[11] Andy Crouch, "The Emergent Mystique," *Christianity Today*, November 1, 2004.

[12] Friedrich Nietzsche, *The Twilight of the Idols,* written in 1888 and published in 1889.

[13] Friedrich Nietzsche, *Beyond Good and Evil*, Walter Kaufman, trans. (New York: Vintage, 1966).

[14] Ibid., section 228.

[15] William S. Lind, *Further Readings on the Frankfurt School,* chap. VI (Free Congress Foundation), http://www.freecongress.org/centers/cc/pcessay6.aspx.

[16] Ibid.

[17] Chuck Morse, *"Enthralled by Cultural Marxism,"* posted at: http://www.tysknews.com/Depts/society/cultural_marxism.htm.

[18] George J. Marlin, "The Anti-Church of Antonio Gramsci," August 24, 2011, posted at: http://www.thecatholicthing.org/columns/2011/the-anti-church-of-antonio-gramsci.html.

[19] Herbert Marcuse in William Lind, ed., "'Political Correctness': A Short History of an Ideology," November 2004, posted at: http://www.discoverthenetworks.org/viewSubCategory.asp?id=552.

[20] Gerald L. Atkinson, "What Is the Frankfurt School?," August 1, 1999, posted at: http://www.newtotalitarians.com/index_files/FrankfurtSchool.htm.

[21] Benjamin Wicker, *10 Books That Screwed Up the World: And 5 Others That Didn't Help* (Washington DC: Regnery Publishing, Inc., 2008), 219.

[22] Daniel Horowitz, *Betty Friedan and the Making of "The Feminine Mystique": The American Left, the Cold War, and Modern Feminism* (Amherst, MA: University of Massachusetts Press, 1998) for a study of Friedan's leftism and pro-Communist views.

[23] MacArthur, "God's Plan for Younger Women."

[24] John MacArthur, "What Is Pragmatism & Why Is It Bad?," January 20, 2010, posted at: http://www.gty.org/resources/Questions/QA209/What-Is-Pragmatism--Why-Is-It-Bad.

[25] Deace Show podcast, 01-02-12, posted at: http://stevedeace.com/news/national-politics/deace-show-podcast-01-02-12/.

[26] Adrienne S. Gaines, "Christian Leaders Call for 40-Day Fast in Run Up to Election,"*Charisma Magazine*, September 16, 2010, posted at: http://www.charismamag.com/index.php/news-old/29264-christian-leaders-call-for-40-day-fast-in-run-up-to-election.

[27] Jim Garlow, "Evangelicals and Glenn Beck," posted at: http://www.onenewsnow.com/Perspectives/Default.aspx?id=1144072.

[28] "Glenn Beck: A Vatican-approved, 'Wildly Important' Warrior Against Forces of 'Great Darkness'?" audio clip, posted at: http://mediamatters.org/blog/201004220063.

[29] "Beck's Europe Trip Sets the Stage for Religious Freedom Coalition and International Tea Party Movement," *The Blaze.com*, February 20, 2012, posted at: http://www.theblaze.com/stories/becks-europe-trip-sets-the-stage-for-religious-freedom-coalition-intl-tea-party-movement/.

[30] Ibid.

[31] Malachi Martin, *The Jesuits* (New York: Simon & Schuster, 1987), 20.

[32] Daniel Libit, "The End of Community Organizing in Chicago?" posted at: http://www.chicagomag.com/Chicago-Magazine/April–2011/The-End-of-Community-Organizing-in-Chicago/.

[33] Brian Tashman, "Garlow Warns Religious Right Voters That Only Gingrich Can Defeat Romney," January 3, 2012, posted at: http://www.rightwingwatch.org/content/garlow-warns-religious-right-voters-only-gingrich-can-defeat-romney.

[34] John MacArthur, "What's Inside the Trojan Horse?," posted at: http://www.gty.org/resources/Articles/A333/Whats-Inside-the-Trojan-Horse.

[35] Saul Alinsky, *Rules for Radicals* (New York: Vintage Books, 1972), dedication page.

[36] Peter Gay, *Freud: A Life for Our Times* (New York: W.W. Norton, 1998), 526.

[37] Ibid., 527.

[38] Benjamin Wiker, *10 Books That Screwed Up theWorld: And 5 Others That Didn't Help* (Washington, DC: Regnery Publishing, Inc, 2008), 168.

[39] Ibid., 167.

[40] Sigmund Freud, *The Future of an Illusion*, James Strachey, trans. (New York: W.W. Norton, 1961), 13.

[41] Wiker, *10 Books*, 169–70.

[42] John MacArthur sermon, "Fundamental Christian Attitudes: Self-Discipline, Part 2," posted at: http://www.gty.org/resources/sermons/90-131/Fundamental-Christian-Attitudes-SelfDiscipline-Part-2.

[43] Erich Fromm, *You Shall Be as Gods* (New York: Holt, Rinehart and Winston, 1966), 7.

[44] Noebel, *Understanding the Times*, 228.

[45] John MacArthur sermon, "Fleeing from Enemies," posted at: http://www.gty.org/resources/sermons/50–35/Fleeing-from-Enemies.

[46] Marx and Engels, *Collected Works*, vol. 3 (New York: International, 1976), cited in Noebel, *Understanding the Times* (2006), 67.

[47] Congressional testimony of Richard Wurmbrand, May 6, 1966, posted at: http://richardwurmbrandbio.info/communist.html.

[48] Ibid.

[49] Daniel M. Bell, *Liberation Theology after the End of History* (London: Routledge, 2001), 104.

[50] J. Zajda, S. Majhanovich, V. Rust, *Education and Social Justice* (2006). ISBN 1-4020-4721-5.

[51] Carl Teichrib, *The Fallacy of Social Justice: All for One and Theft to All*, posted at: http://www.worldviewweekend.com/worldview-times/article.php?articleid=6585.

[52] J. Edgar Hoover, *Masters of Deceit* (New York: Pocket Books, 1958), 90.

[53] "Karl Marx," *World Eras*, vol. 9: *Industrial Revolution in Europe, 1750–1914* (Gale Group, 2002).

[54] Ibid.

[55] Townhall.com, March 31, 2012.

[56] Yahoo!Canada Co., April 4, 2012.

[57] Richard Owen, "Vatican thumbs up for Karl Marx after Galileo, Darwin and Oscar," *The Times Online*, October 22, 2009.

[58] Teichrib, *The Fallacy of Social Justice*, posted at: http://www.worldviewweekend.com/worldview-times/article.php?articleid=6585.

[59] Mark W. Hendrickson, "The 'Social Justice' Fallacy? Wolves in Sheep's Clothing," posted at: http://www.worldviewweekend.com/mobile/view-article.php?articleid=7849.

[60] Henry Lamb, "An Unseen Enemy of Freedom," WorldNetDaily.com, September 13, 2008, http://www.wnd.com/index.php?pageId=75118.

[61] Wurmbrand, *Marx and Satan*.

[62] Fred C. Schwarz and David Noebel, *You Can Still Trust the Communists (to be Communists)*.

[63] Charles Darwin, *Origin of Species* (New York: Mentor, 1958), 29.

[64] Ibid., 177.

[65] Tim Stafford, "Evangelical Evolutionists Meet in New York," *Christianity Today*, March 30, 2012, posted at: http://www.christianitytoday.com/ct/2012/marchwebonly/biologos-new-york.html.

[66] Ibid.

[67] Albert Mohler, "No Pass from Theological Responsibility—The BioLogos Conun-

drum," November 9, 2010, posted at: http://www.albertmohler.com/2010/11/09/no-pass-from-theological-responsibility-the-biologos-conundrum/.

[68] Ibid.

[69] John UpChurch, "The Danger of BioLogos," September 23, 2011, posted at: http://www.answersingenesis.org/articles/am/v6/n4/blurring-the-line.

[70] John Templeton Foundation page, posted at: http://www.templeton.org/what-we-fund/grants/the-language-of-god-biologos-website-and-workshop.

[71] Dave Hunt, Occult Invasion (Eugene, OR: Harvest House Publishers, December 1997), 531–35.

[72] Alicia Doyle, "Bestselling Author to Give Free Lecture at CLU," The Ventura County Star, September 24, 2011.

[73] Ibid.

[74] Ibid.

[75] Marilyn Ferguson, The Aquarian Conspiracy (Los Angeles: J.P. Tarcher, 1980), 418-20.

[76] Teilhard de Chardin, The Future of Man (San Francisco: Harper & Row, 1959), 23, 34–35.

[77] Al Gore, Earth in the Balance: Ecology and the Human Spirit (New York: Penguin Books, First Plum Printing, 1993), 263.

[78] Video posted at: http://www.youtube.com/watch?v=I2sWPkioVoU.

[79] Ibid.

[80] Ibid.

[81] Ibid.

[82] Ibid.

[83] Ibid.

[84] Alice Bailey, Education in the New Age, 1st ed. (1954), 88.

[85] Alice Bailey, Esoteric Healing, 1st ed. (1953), 393.

[86] Bob DeWaay, The Emergent Church: Undefining Christianity (St. Louis Park, MN: Bob DeWaay, 2009), 68–69.

[87] Bob DeWaay, Fighting Spiritual Evolution in the Emergent Church, posted at: http://apprising.org/2010/10/18/fighting-spiritual-evolution-in-the-emerging-church/.

[88] Ibid., 23.

[89] Jurgen Moltmann, The Crucified God: The Cross of Christ as the Foundation and Criticism of Christian Theology (Fortress Press, 1993), 5.

[90] John Strachey, Contemporary Capitalism, (New York: Random House, 1956), 310.

[91] John Maynard Keynes, Economic Consequences of the Peace (New York: Harcourt Brace, 1920).

[92] Walter Williams, "Counterfeiting Versus Monetary Policy," December 17, 2008, posted at: http://townhall.com/columnists/walterewilliams/2008/12/17/counter-feiting_versus_monetary_policy.

[93] Zygmund Dobbs, "Sugar Keynes," The Review of the News, June 23, 1971.

94 "About LSE- Students and staff," posted at: Jobs.ac.uk. http://www.jobs.ac.uk/enhanced/employer/london-school-of-economics-and-political-science/.

95 "2008 Sunday Times University Guide – LSE Profile," *The Times (London)*, 2007-09-23, posted at: http://www.timesonline.co.uk/tol/life_and_style/education/sunday_times_university_guide/article2496158.ece.

96 James McGregor Burns, *The Power to Lead* (New York: Touchstone Publishing, 1984), 189.

97 CNBC interview on floor of New York Stock Exchange, January 2009, posted at: http://www.youtube.com/watch?feature=player_embedded&v=GThfWVCfjVo.

98 Jonathan Weisman, "Wider U.S. Interventions Would Yield Winners, Losers as Industries Realign," November 20, 2008, posted at: http://online.wsj.com/article/SB122714374260443023.html

99 Mikhail Gorbachev, "A New International Agenda," *International Herald Tribune*, January 1, 2009.

100 Ibid.

101 Henry Kissinger, "The Chance for A New World Order," *International Herald Tribune*, January 12, 2009.

102 Dick Morris, "European Socialism to Run Our Financial System," www.newsmax.com, April 7, 2009.

103 Gideon Rachman, "And Now for World Government," *Financial Times*, December 9, 2008.

104 Lyubov Pronina, "Medvedev Shows Off Sample Coin of New 'World Currency' at G-8," Bloomberg.com, July 10, 2009.

105 James Simpson, "Barack Obama and the Strategy of Manufactured Crisis," worldviewtimes.com, March 9, 2009.

106 Heather Heidelbaugh "Obama Is Governing as a Community Organizer," Washington Examiner.com, August 21, 2009.

107 Saul Alinsky, *Rules for Radicals* (New York: Vintage Books, 1972), 3.

108 Ibid., 25.

109 Ibid., 7.

110 Ibid., 3.

111 Ibid., 61.

112 "I am a Communist but not a member of the Communist Party. Stalin is a first-rate Fabian. I am one of the founders of Fabianism and, as such, very friendly to Russia." Source: Reported in the Evening Herald (Dublin), Feb. 3, 1948, quoted by Butler, p. 11.

113 "Wheaton College to Become the First American Associate University of the Tony Blair Faith Foundation," posted at: http://www.tonyblairfaithfoundation.org/news/2010/12/03.

114 **Roger Oakland, "Globalization: A Special Report," posted at:** http://www.understandthetimes.org/commentary/c86.shtm.l.

[115]Joseph Farah, "Rick Warren: Is He or Isn't He?" posted at: http://www.wnd.com/2007/01/39612/.

[116] Carroll Quigley, *The Anglo-American Establishment* (G S G & Associates Pub, 1981), 168.

[117] Dennis Cuddy, "The Power Elite Exposed," posted at: worldviewweekend.com, March 25, 2010.

[118] Council on Foreign Relations Address by Secretary of State Hillary Clinton, July 15, 2009, posted at: http://www.cfr.org/diplomacy/council-foreign-relations-address-secretary-state-hillary-clinton/p19840.

[119] Richard N. Haas, "Sovereignty and Globalization," February 17, 2006, posted at: http://www.cfr.org/sovereignty/sovereignty-globalisation/p9903.

[120] John Ensor Harr and Peter J. Johnson, *The Rockefeller Century: Three Generations of America's Greatest Family* (New York: Charles Scribner's Sons, 1988), 156.

[121] John D. Rockefeller, quoted in James W. Wardner, *Unholy Alliances: The Secret Plan and the Secret People Who Are Working to Destroy America*, 1996 (privately published).

[122] David Rockefeller, *Memoirs* (New York: Random House, 2002), 404–05.

[123] Dennis Cuddy, "The Rockefeller Plan," January 12, 2009, posted at: http://www.worldviewweekend.com/worldview-times/article.php?articleid=8316.

[124] Ibid.

[125] John Stormer, *None Dare Call It Treason* (Florissant, MO: Liberty Bell Press, 1964), 125.

[126] Edgar C. Bundy, *Collectivism in the Churches: A Documented Account of the Political Activities of the Federal, National, and World Councils of Churches* (Wheaton, Illinois: Church League of America, 1957), 97.

[127] *A Yearbook of the Church and Social Service in the U.S.*, Federal Council of Churches, 1916, 23.

[128] Bundy, *Collectivism*, 101.

[129] Committee on Un-American Activities of the U.S. House of Representatives, 83rd Congress, in July, 1953, page 2229, cited in Bundy, 127–28.

[130] July 7, 1953 testimony before House Committee on Un-American Activities

[131] Barry Goldwater, *With No Apologies: The Personal and Political Memoirs of United States Senator Barry M. Goldwater* (William Morrow and Company, 1979).

[132] Don Koenig, "The Woman on the Beast in End Time Prophecy Has Dominion Theology," posted at: http://www.thepropheticyears.com/comments/The%20woman%20on%20the%20beast%20in%20end%20time%20prophecy%20has%20dominion%20theology.htm.

[133] Al Dager, *Vengeance Is Ours: The Church in Dominion* (Sword Pub., 1990), 87. This book is a historical "encyclopedia" of the history of modern dominionism, clearly demarking the various sects. Dager approaches the subject from a Christian perspective. His book is available through http://www.discernment-ministries.org.

[134] Robert Crabtree, "New Wave Theology" (privately printed paper, 1987), 19–20.

[135] John D. Rockefeller, quoted in James W. Wardner, *Unholy Alliances: The Secret Plan and the Secret People Who Are Working to Destroy America,* (privately published 1996).

[136] "The Evangelicals Engaged In Spiritual Warfare," NPR, August 24, 2011, posted at: http://www.npr.org/2011/08/24/139781021/the-evangelicals-engaged-in-spiritual-warfare.

[137] C. Peter Wagner, May 2007 letter, posted at: http://www.erwm.com/ApostolicLetter.htm.

[138] C. Peter Wagner at Arise Prophetic Conference, October 19, 2004, Gateway Church, San Jose, CA.

[139] C. Peter Wagner interview, "A Leading Figure in the New Apostolic Reformation," NPR, October 3, 2011, posted at: http://www.npr.org/2011/10/03/140946482/apostolic-leader-weighs-religions-role-in-politics.

[140] National Day of Prayer website statement under the headline "Why Pray?" posted at: http://nationaldayofprayer.org/about/what-is-prayer/.

[141] David Barton on the television program of Kenneth Copeland, posted at: http://www.worldviewweekend.com/worldview-times/article.php?articleid=7555.

[142] Thomas Kidd, "The David Barton Controversy," World, August 7, 2012, posted at: http://www.worldmag.com/webextra/19820

[143] Ibid.

[144] 'Lost confidence' by Thomas Kidd, Worldmag.com, August 9, 2012 posted here: http://www.worldmag.com/webextra/19840

[145] Stephanie Samuel, "Are Evangelicals Seeking 'Dominion' Over Politics, Government?" *Christian Post*, posted at: http://www.christianpost.com/news/are-evangelicals-seeking-dominion-over-politics-government-54726/.

[146] Jeffrey Kofman, "Thousands Flock to Revival in Search of Miracles," July 9, 2008, posted at: http://abcnews.go.com/Nightline/FaithMatters/story?id=5338963&page=1.

[147] Video of C. Peter Wagner installing Todd Bentley as a "prophet," posted at: http://worldviewweekend.com/worldview-times/article.php?articleid=8263.

[148] Transcript of program posted at: http://crystalcathedral.org/print/index.php?contentid=2838.

[149] Rabbi Bruce Lustig, opening remarks at the National Day of Prayer, May 1, 2008.

[150] The Dobsons can be seen at Lou Engle's "The Call" in San Diego in 2008, video posted at: http://www.youtube.com/watch?v=DQp-K6stkss&feature=results_main&playnext=1&list=PLADFD6935C9EA006F.

[151] C. Peter Wagner, "Warfare Prayer" excerpt, posted at: http://www.christian-faith.com/articles/citytaking-peterwagner.html.

[152] Dale Neill, speech given at International Coalition of Workplace Ministries banquet, October 2004.

[153] Robert Crabtree, posted at: http://herescope.blogspot.com/2006/02/dominion-ism-and-kingdom-now-teachings.html.

[154] George Wood, "Kingdom Now and Missions," *Mountain Movers*, 1989.

[155] C. Peter Wagner, May 31, 2007, letter as chancellor, Wagner Leadership Institute.

[156] John MacArthur, "Christians and Politics, Part 4," posted at: http://www.gty.org/Resources/Articles/A127.

[157] Alice Bailey, "The Spiritual Hierarchy," posted at: http://www.lucistrust.org/en/service_activities/world_goodwill/world_goodwill_literature_on_line/the_spiritual_hierarchy.

[158] W. Howard, *Despatch Magazine* 12:1, March 2000.

[159] Alice A. Bailey, *The Externalisation of the Hierarchy* (New York: Lucis Trust, 1982), 513.

[160] *Engaging the Enemy*, (Ventura, CA: Regal Books, 1991), 15–16, posted at: http://www.wrs.edu/journals/jour298/engaging.html.

[161] George Wood, "Kingdom Now and Missions."

[162] Brochure for Brisbane 2000, as cited in Hughie Seaborn, "Jumping on the Bandwagon—Australian Christian Churches Seduced by the Beat of a Different Drummer?," 1999, posted at: http://members.ozemail.com.au/~rseaborn/bandwagon.html.

[163] John MacArthur, "The Gifted Man, Part 1: Apostles and Prophets," posted at: http://www.gty.org/Resources/Sermons/1851.

[164] Ibid.

[165] Transcribed from a YouTube video posted at: http://www.youtube.com/watch?v=YEwsG4lsXq4.

[166] C. Peter Wagner, *On the Crest of the Wave*. (Ventura, CA: Regal Books, 1983), 131–32.

[167] Tribute: "A Collection of Thoughts and Memories of the Late John Wimber," posted at: http://vineyardcommunitychurch.org/about/tribute.htm.

[168] C. Peter Wagner, as cited in John F. MacArthur Jr., *Does God Do Miracles Today?*, 1991, posted at: http://www.gty.org/resources/sermons/90-56/does-god-do-miracles-today.

[169] C. Peter Wagner, CBN interview, January 3, 2000.

[170] George Wood, "Kingdom Now and Missions," *Mountain Movers* (1989), posted at: http://georgeowood.com/?TargetPage=97BDC859-8385-49F2-AFE3-8A25587CED0C.

[171] Jewel Grewe, "Joel's Army," Discernment Ministries, 1991, posted at: http://www.worldviewweekend.com/worldview-times/article.php?articleid=7345.

[172] Rick Joyner, "Paul Cain, Part 1, 2004 Special Bulletin #6," posted at: http://www.morningstarministries.org/resources/special-bulletins/2004/paul-cain-part-1.

[173] Paul Cain, "My Father's House," November 1988 recording. Quoted in Mainstream, Spring 1995, posted at: http://letusreason.org/Latrain5.htm.

174 Bob Jones, cited in Al Dager, *Vengeance Is Ours* (Sword Pub., 1990), 146.

175 Bill Hamon, *Prophets and the Prophetic Movement* (Destiny Image Publishers, Inc., 1990).

176 Bill Hamon, *The Eternal Church* (Christian International Publishers, 1981), 385.

177 "Dr. Bill Hamon Answers Your Questions about the Eternal Church," posted at: http://www.thevoicemagazine.com/ApoMoments_BillHamon.htm.

178 Jewel Grewe, "Joel's Army," Discernment Ministries, 1991, white paper posted at: http://www.worldviewweekend.com/worldview-times/article.php?articleid=7345

179 Ibid.

180 School for Prophecy, Session 7, Vineyard Ministries, 1989, cited by Jewel Grewe in "Joel's Army," posted at: http://herescope.blogspot.com/2005/12/why-prayer-warfare-is-heresy.html.

181 "Earl Paulk dies at 81; progressive evangelical's legacy fell to sex scandals," *Los Angels Times*, April 2, 2009, posted at: http://articles.latimes.com/2009/apr/02/local/me-earl-paulk2.

182 October 3, 2011, NPR interview with C. Peter Wagner.

183 Earl Paulk, "The Handwriting on the Wall," tract published by Chapel Hill Harvester Church, 20.

184 Bill Hamon, "God's Wave of Restoration for the 1980s," *Thy Kingdom Come* 9, (August 1987): 11.

185 Earl Paulk, *Unity of Faith*, n.d., tract published by Chapel Hill Harvester Church, 4.

186 Ibid.

187 Tommy Ice and H. Wayne House, *Dominion Theology: Blessing or Curse?* (Portland, OR: Multnomah, 1988), appendix A that was not included in the book but was given to me by Dr. Ice.

188 Benny Hinn, *Our Position in Christ*, Orlando Christian Center, Tape #A031190-1.

189 "Praise-a-Thon," TBN, recorded November 12, 1990.

190 Kenneth Copeland, *Believer's Voice of Victory Magazine* (August 8, 1988): 8.

191 Ibid.

192 John MacArthur, *The MacArthur New Testament Commentary for Philippians* (Chicago: Moody Publishers, 2001), 126.

193 Copeland, *Believer's Voice of Victory Magazine*.

194 Barbara Marx Hubbard, *The Book of Co-Creation: The Revelation—Our Crisis Is a Birth, "The Christ" Comments on Rev. 10:8–11* (Novato, CA: Nataraj Publishing, 1993), 158.

195 "Barbara Marx Hubbard the Armageddon Alternative," p.49 quoted by Brooks Alexander, Vol. 19:2/3, 1995).

196 Brian McLaren, comment posted at: http://www.brianmclaren.net/archives/000226.html.

[197] C. Peter Wagner, "Another New Wineskin…The New Apostolic Reformation," *Next*, January–March 1999.

[198] Ibid.

[199] Brian McLaren, interviewed on *Bleeding Purpose Podcast,* posted at: http://www.enteuxis.org/leifh/bleedingpurple21b.mp3.

[200] George Wood, "Kingdom Now and Missions."

[201] Orell Steinkamp, "The Apostles Are Coming to Your City, Ready or Not," *The Plumbline* 6, no. 2, (March/April 2001): .

[202] Rick Joyner, *The Harvest* (New Kensington, PA: Whitaker House, 1997), 36–38.

[203] Ibid.

[204] Bill Randles, *Beware the New Prophets: A Caution Concerning the Modern Prophetic Movement*, July 1999, 39.

[205] Rick Joyner, *The Final Quest*, 37.

[206] Robert Crabtree, report of January 13, 1987.

[207] Wagner, cited in MacArthur, "The Third Wave," sermon, August 15, 1991, posted at: http://www.gty.org/Resources/Sermons/90-57.

[208] Ibid., 290.

[209] C. Peter Wagner, *Your Church Can Grow* (Ventura, CA: Regal, 1976), 161.

[210] C. Peter Wagner, "Another New Wineskin…The New Apostolic Reformation."

[211] Charles Spurgeon, "Christ's Universal Kingdom and How it Comes," sermon no. 1535, delivered on Lord's Day morning, April 25, 1880.

[212] General Presbytery of the Assemblies of God, "Report on Apostles and Prophets," August 6, 2011.

[213] John MacArthur, "The Gifted Men, Part 1: Apostles and Prophets," posted at: http://www.gty.org/Resources/Print/Sermons/1851.

[214] John MacArthur, "The Gifted Men." The Gifted Men, Part 1: Apostles and Prophets, posted at: http://www.gty.org/resources/sermons/1851/the-gifted-men-part-1-apostles-and-prophets.

[215] Rick Joyner, "The Prophetic Ministry," *Morningstar Prophetic Newsletter* 3, no. 2, (): 2.

[216] Ibid.

[217] Ibid.

[218] Iain Murray, *Evangelicalism Divided: A Record of Crucial Change in the Years 1950 to 2000* (Nashville: Thomas Nelson, 2000), 20.

[219] Union University Press Release, March 3, 2011, posted at: http://www.worldviewweekend.com/worldview-times/article.php?articleid=7025/day/2011/04/6.

[220] Mikhail Gorbachev, *The Search for a New Beginning: Developing a New Civilization* (San Francisco: Harper San Francisco and the Gorbachev Foundation/USA, 1995), 60–62.

[221] William F. Jasper, "Gorbachev: Pushing New World Order," *World Government*, November 3, 2011 posted at: http://thenewamerican.com/usnews/politics/9626-

gorbachev-pushing-new-world-order-world-government.

222 Slogan posted on conference website at: http://www.globalfaithforum.org/.

223 Global Faith Forum website, sponsors posted at: http://www.globalfaithforum.org/sponsors.

224 Speaker biographies listed on Global Faith Forum website and posted at: http://www.globalfaithforum.org/speakers.

225 Slogan printed on Global Faith Forum under "About," posted at: http://www.globalfaithforum.org/about.

226 David A. Noebel, "Barack Obama's 'Red' Spiritual Advisor," posted at: http://www.worldviewweekend.com/worldview-times/article.php?articleid=4767.

227 Stephanie Samuel, "Evangelicals Join 'Religious Left' to Defend Poor Against Budget Cuts," *Christian Post*, April 28, 2011.

228 Ibid.

229 Ibid.

230 Robert Rector, "How 'Poor' Are the Poor?" August 28, 2007, posted at: http://archive.frontpagemag.com/readArticle.aspx?ARTID=27923.

231 Aaron Klein, "Is Obama's GOP Prayer Partner a Dem Wolf in Sheep's Clothing?" June 1, 2011, posted at: http://www.wnd.com/index.php?fa=PAGE.view&pageId=305845.

232 Ibid.

233 Ibid.

234 Brannon Howse, *Grave Influence* (Collierville, TN: Worldview Weekend Publishing, 2009), 26.

235 Kate Galbraith, "The Three Horsemen of the Third Way," *Slate*, September 29, 1998, posted at: http://www.slate.com/id/1001976.

236 Dana Milbank, "Needed: Catchword for Bush Ideology; 'Communitarianism' Finds Favor," *The Washington Post*, February 1, 2001.

237 Neela Banerjee, "Pastor Chosen to Lead Christian Coalition Steps Down in Dispute Over Agenda," *New York Times*, November 28, 2008.

238 Alex Spillius, "US Religious Right Concedes Defeat," April 10, 2009. *The Telegraph*, posted at: http://www.telegraph.co.uk/news/worldnews/barackobama/5136050/US-religious-Right-concedes-defeat.html.

239 *World Magazine*, June 4, 2011.

240 David Wright and David Patten, "Robertson's Regret: Less Politics, More Ministry," April 23, 2011, posted at: http://www.newsmax.com/Headline/Easter-PatRobertson-BillyGraham/2011/04/23/id/393870.

241 David Noebel, "Barack Obama's 'Red' Spiritual Advisor," May 5, 2010, posted at: http://www.worldviewweekend.com/worldview-times/article.php?articleid=4767.

242 David Noebel, "Tony Campolo, Jim Wallis: The Marxist Delusion and a Christian Evangelist," February 19, 2008, posted at: http://www.worldviewweekend.com/worldview-times/article.php?articleid=1597.

[243] Tony Campolo, "What's a 'Red-Letter Christian'?", February 27, 2006, posted at: http://www.sojo.net/index.cfm?action=news.display_article&mode=s&NewsID=5270.

[244] *MacArthur Study Bible* (Nashville: Thomas Nelson, 1997), 125.

[245] David Noebel, "Tony Campolo, Jim Wallis: The Marxist Delusion and a Christian Evangelist," February 19, 2008, posted at: http://www.worldviewweekend.com/worldview-times/article.php?articleid=1597.

[246] "The Mavens' Word of the Day," posted at: http://www.randomhouse.com/wotd/index.pperl?date=20001214.

[247] In the CBI Bulletin of Dave Hunt's, 12/89.

[248] Tony Campolo, in *A Reasonable Faith* responding to secularism, p.59 also documented at: http://letusreason.org/Popteac27.htm.

[249] Brian McLaren, *The Secret Message of Jesus*, (Nashville: Thomas Nelson, 2006), 7.

[250] Ibid., 169–170.

[251] Brian McLaren, interviewed on Bleeding Purpose Podcast, posted at: http://www.enteuxis.org/leifh/bleedingpurple21b.mp3.

[252] Statement found on the Interfaith Youth Core in 2010 and documented on this website: http://www.odysseynetworks.org/channel/interfaith-youth-core.

[253] Bob Smietana, *USA Today*, "Muslims in USA face fears, bias to build, expand mosques," posted at: http://www.usatoday.com/news/religion/2010-07-05-new-mosques04_ST_N.htm.

[254] Diane Macedo, "Plans to Build Massive Islamic Centers Raise Concerns in Tennessee," FoxNews.com, August 09, 2010, posted at: http://www.foxnews.com/us/2010/08/09/plans-build-tennessee-islamic-centers/.

[255] Adelle M. Banks, "Southern Baptist Leader Resigns Interfaith Coalition Supporting Mosques," Religion News Service, posted at: http://www.christiancentury.org/article/2011-01/southern-baptist-leader-resigns-coalition-supporting-mosques.

[256] Robert Spencer, "Obama Adviser Loves Sharia," *Human Events*, October 13, 2009.

[257] Ibid.

[258] Ibid.

[259] Art Moore, "Interfaith Meeting Rocked by Terror Accusations: Muslim Leader Unexpectedly Confronted with Group's Ties to Parent of al-Qaida," WorldNetDaily.com, May 14, 2010.

[260] U.S. Muslim Engagement Initiative Report Endorsements, posted at: http://www.usmuslimengagement.org/index.php?option=com_content&task=view&id=22&Itemid=51.

[261] Laurie Goodstein, "Obama Wins Unlikely Allies in Immigration," *New York Times*, July 18, 2010, posted at: http://www.nytimes.com/2010/07/19/us/politics/19evangelicals.html.

[262] *Matthew Henry Commentary* posted at: http://www.biblestudytools.com/commentaries/matthew-henry-complete/leviticus/19.html?p=5

[263] http://evangelicalimmigrationtable.com/

[264] Trevor Loudon, "Communist Rosalio Munoz on Exploiting Mexican Americans to Further Revolution," July 6, 2010, posted at: http://www.worldviewweekend.com/worldview-times/article.php?articleid=6257.

[265] "Glenn Beck and Obama's Christianity: NPR's Robert Siegel Talks to Richard Land," August 30, 2010 posted at: http://www.npr.org/templates/story/story.php?storyId=129535008.

[266] Bob Allen, "Richard Land Announces Retirement," The Associated Baptist Press, August 1, 2012, posted at: http://www.abpnews.com/ministry/organizations/item/7668-richard-land-announces-retirement.

[267] Julian Huxley, *UNESCO: Its Purpose and Its Philosophy* (Washington, DC: Public Affairs Press, 1947), 61.

[268] Schwarz and Noebel, *Trust the Communists*, 179f.

[269] Richard Rorty in Mark Edmundson, ed., "Trotsky and Wild Orchids," *Wild Orchids and Trotsky: Messages from American Universities*, (New York: Penguin Books, 1993), cited in Noebel, *Understanding the Times*, 388.

[270] Robert E. Klenck, "How Diaprax Manifests Itself in the Church," posted at: http://www.crossroad.to/News/Church/Klenck3.html.

[271] A Christian Response to "A Common Word Between Us and You," posted at: http://www.yale.edu/faith/acw/acw.htm.

[272] Jeffery Sheler, "Preacher with a Purpose," *U.S. News and World Report*, October 31, 2005.

[273] Ibid.

[274] Rick Warren, "Myth of the Modern Megachurch," Biannual Faith Angle Conference on Religion and Politics and Public Life, Key West, Florida, May 2005. www.pewforum.org/Christian/Evangelical-Protestant-Churches/Myths-of-the-Modern-Megachurch.aspx.

[275] Jake Tapper, "Rick Warren Takes On His Critics: 'I'm a Big Target'," ABC News, August 15, 2008, posted at: http://blogs.abcnews.com/politicalpunch/2008/08/rick-warren-tak.html.

[276] Ken Witty, "Peter Drucker's Search for Community," *Businessweek*, December 24, 2002.

[277] Peter Drucker, "Modern Prophets: Schumpeter and Keynes?," 1983, posted at: http://www.peterdrucker.at/en/texts/proph_01.html.

[278] Emerging Partnerships: New Ways in a New World: A Symposium organized by the Peter F. Drucker Foundation for Nonprofit Management, sponsored by the Rockefeller Brothers Fund, December 1996, posted at: http://leadertoleader.org/forms/partners.pdf.

[279] *Forbes* magazine, October 5, 1998.

[280] Peter Steinfels, "A Man's Spiritual Journey from Kierkegaard to General Mo-

tors," *New York Times*, November 19, 2005, posted at: http://www.nytimes.com/2005/11/19/national/19beliefs.html?pagewanted=all.

[281] Peter Drucker, *Landmarks of Tomorrow* (Transaction Publishers, 1996), 264–65.

[282] James S. Bowman and Dennis L. Wittmer, "The Unfashionable Drucker: Ethical and Quality Chic," *Journal of Management History* 6, no. 1, 2000): 35–36.

[283] http://en.wikipedia.org/wiki/Confucious.

[284] Interview with Peter Drucker, December 5, 2001, posted at: http://ccdl.libraries.claremont.edu/cdm/singleitem/collection/dac/id/2176/rec/1.

[285] "Management's New Paradigms," *Forbes*, October 5, 1998.

[286] Peter Drucker quote posted at: http://quotationsbook.com/quote/7293/.

[287] Bob Buford, *Halftime*, dedication, Zondervan; also reported in this article (May 4, 1997) at: http://www.crossroad.to/News/Church/Klenck2.html.

[288] *Leadership Network-Advance*, November 14, 2005, posted at: http://www.pursuantgroup.com/leadnet/advance/nov05o.htm.

[289] Originally posted on Leadership Network website, this quote has been removed but is referenced in numerous other articles such as the one posted at: http://www.crossroad.to/News/Church/Klenck2.html.

[290] Chris Rosebrough, "The Druckerites Must Issue a Safety Recall for Their 'Emerging Church' Product Line," posted at: http://www.extremetheology.com/2010/02/the-druckerites-must-issue-a-safety-recall-of-their-emerging-church-product-line.html.

[291] Originally posted in "The Leader to Leader Institute Vision 2010" at: http://drucker.org/about/vision.html.

[292] Brian McLaren, comment posted at: http://www.brianmclaren.net/archives/000226.html.

[293] Jason Carlson, "My Journey Into and Out of the Emergent Church," February 26, 2006, posted at: http://www.worldviewweekend.com/worldview-times/article.php?articleid=514.

[294] Cameron Crabtree, "Church Growth Scholar Advocates Radical Change in New Millennium," *Baptist Press,* Nov 23, 1998.

[295] Jim Belcher, *Deep Church: A Third Way Beyond Emerging and Traditional* (Downers Grove, Illinois: Intervarsity Press, 2009), 13, 15.

[296] "Evangelicals and Catholics Together," document posted at: http://www.leaderu.com/ftissues/ft9405/articles/mission.html.

[297] Belcher, *Deep Church,* 28.

[298] Richard Mouw, "The Orthodoxy of Rob Bell," March 15, 2011, blog posted at: http://www.netbloghost.com/mouw/?p=188.

[299] Ibid.

[300] Desmond Doig, *Mother Teresa: Her People and Her Work* (Harper & Row, 1976), 156.

[301] Ibid., endorsement page.

[302] Cameron Crabtree, "Church Growth Scholar Advocates Radical Change in New

Millennium," November 23, 1998, posted at: http://www.baptistpress.org/bpnews. asp?ID=4888.

303 Ibid.

304 Harlan Cleveland, *The Third Try at World Order* (Aspen Institute for Humanistic Studies, 1977).

305 Peter Drucker, "Management's New Paradigms," *Forbes*, October 5, 1998. Article posted at: http://www.forbes.com/forbes/1998/1005/6207152a.html.

306 Bill Hybels, *Mastering Contemporary Preaching*, (Multnomah / Christianity Today, 1995), 27; also quoted in Bill Hybels, "Speaking to the Secular Mind," *Christianity Today*, March 7, 2007, posted at: http://www.christianitytoday.com/biblestudies/ articles/evangelism/070307.html?start=2.

307 Maria Kefala, "Pastor Argues Faith Is Missing Link," February 5, 2008.

308 Ibid.

309 Jeffery L. Sheler, "Preacher with a Purpose," *U.S. News & World Report*, October 31, 2005, posted at: http://www.usnews.com/usnews/news/ articles/051031/31warren.htm.

310 William Still, "The Work of the Pastor," *Exhortations for Pastoral Preaching in Reformation and Revival* 1:4 (Fall 1992): 68.

311 Rick Warren and Pastors.com, "Becoming a Purpose Driven Church, Part Two," posted at: http://www.cbn.com/spirituallife/ChurchAndMinistry/warren_purpose_ driven_churchb.aspx.

312 Tim Stafford, "Business of the Kingdom," *Christianity Today*, November 15, 1999, posted at: http://www.christianitytoday.com/ct/1999/november15/9td042. html?start=8.

313 Rick Warren, *The Purpose Driven Church* (Zondervan Publishing, 2007), 327.

314 Erika Ritchie, "Rick Warren, Dr. Oz to Partner on Health Plan," *The Orange County Register,* January 11, 2011.

315 Mehmet Oz, MD, with Jonathan S. Rose, PhD, and Lisa Oz, "Mehmet Oz Finds His Teacher," *Spirituality and Health,* November/December 2007.

316 Daniel Amen, *Change Your Brain, Change Your Body* (Crown Archetype, 2010), 283.

317 Ray Yungen, *For Many Shall Come in My Name* (Lighthouse Trails Publishing), 115.

318 Daniel Amen, *Change Your Brain, Change Your Body* (Crown Archetype, 2010).

319 Eckhart Tolle, *The Power of Now: A Guide to Spiritual Enlightenment* (Novato, CA: Namaste, 1999), 104.

320 Phylameana lila Desy, *The Everything Reiki Book* (Avon, MA: Adams Media, 2004), 144.

321 Endorsement by Dr. Oz on front cover of *The Instruction* by Ainslie MacLeod. Sounds True, Incorporated, cover can be seen here: http://www.amazon.com/The-Instruction-Ainslie-MacLeod/dp/1591797209/ref=sr_1_1?s=books&ie=UTF8& qid=1338413078&sr=1-1.

[322] Amazon.com product description for Ainslie MacLeod, *The Instruction*, posted at: http://www.amazon.com/The-Instruction-Ainslie-MacLeod/dp/1591797209/ref=sr_1_1?ie=UTF8&qid=1337220831&sr=8-1.

[323] Robert E. Klenck, cited in "How Diaprax Manifests Itself in the Church," posted at: http://www.crossroad.to/News/Church/Klenck3.html.

[324] Merrill F. Unger, "The Need of Expository Preaching in the Twentieth Century," *Bibliotheca Sacra 111*, July–September 1954, 231.

[325] International Church of the Nazarene, "Creation Care" document.

[326] David Noebel, "Pastor Bill Hybel's Wife and Willow Creek Are Proud of the 'Social Justice' of Rev. Jim Wallis?," May 5, 2010, posted at: http://worldviewweekend.com/worldview-times/article.php?articleid=6064.

[327] Ibid.

[328] David Noebel, "A Communist Rally in Washington, D.C.," October 12, 2010, posted at: http://worldviewweekend.com/worldview-times/article.php?articleid=6570.

[329] David Noebel, "The President of the United States Is a Socialist and Some 'Evangelicals' Are Helping Him," January 1, 2011, posted at: http://worldviewweekend.com/worldview-times/article.php?articleid=6773.

[330] Ibid.

[331] Brannon Howse, "'Evangelical' Leaders Form Unholy Alliance with Pro-gay, Pro-abortion, Globalists to Fight Global Warming?," February 13, 2006, posted at: http://www.worldviewweekend.com/worldview-times/article.php?articleid=486.

[332] *Global Warming, a Scientific and Biblical Expose of Climate Change* (Hebron, KY: Answers in Genesis, 2008), 83. Can be purchased here: http://www.answersingenesis.org/PublicStore/product/Global-Warming-Pocket-Guide,5742,228.aspx.

[333] Tom DeWeese, "Teachers, Preachers and Greens: The Unholy Alliance to Transform America," February 19, 2008, posted at: http://www.worldviewweekend.com/worldview-times/print.php?&ArticleID=1597.

[334] Ibid.

[335] Declaration of the "Mission to Washington," posted at: http://nrpe.org/interaith/statements/mission-washington?layout=item.

[336] Rankings posted at: http://epi.yale.edu/Countries.

[337] Ibid.

[338] Ibid.

[339] Ibid.

[340] Facts about Tides Foundation at Discover the Networks, posted at: http://www.discoverthenetworks.org/funderprofile.asp?fndid=5184.

[341] Facts posted at: http://www.discoverthenetworks.org/individualProfile.asp?indid=1673.

[342] A Directory of Environmental Activities and Resources in the North American Religious Community, Summer 1992, p. 27.

[343] John Tierney, "Recycling Is Garbage," *New York Times,* June 30, 1996, posted at: http://www.nytimes.com/1996/06/30/magazine/recycling-is-garbage.html?src=pm.

[344] Ibid.

[345] "Recycling Can Be a Waste of Money," letter to the editor, *Bismarck Tribune*, December 13, 2007, posted at: http://www.bismarcktribune.com/news/opinion/mailbag/article_8d775476-0f8b-51f2-bf8d-a4d98a860a0f.html.

[346] Benny Avni, "Mayor Compares Threat of Global Warming to Terrorism," *New York Sun*, February 12, 2008, posted at: http://www.nysun.com/national/mayor-compares-threat-of-global-warming/71103/

[347] "NASA Chief Questions Whether Global Warming Is a Problem," Foxnews.com, June 1, 2007, posted at: http://www.foxnews.com/story/0,2933,276722,00.html. Read more: http://www.foxnews.com/story/0,2933,276722,00.html#ixzz1wOIepsMh.

[348] Tom DeWeese, "Fanatics, Heretics and the Truth about Global Warming," posted at: www.ammericanpolicy.org.

[349] Ibid.

[350] Interview with Dr. S. Fred Singer, *Nova* on PBS, March 12, 2000, posted at: http://www.independent.org/newsroom/article.asp?id=1938.

[351] Richard S. Lindzen, "Why So Gloomy," *Newsweek International,* April 16, 2007.

[352] DeWeese, "Fanatics, Heretics and the Truth about Global Warming."

[353] Ibid.

[354] Ibid.

[355] "Baliunas Says Global Warming Related to the Sun," posted at: http://www.tylerpaper.com/article/20080213/NEWS08/802130360.

[356] Statement posted on the website: www.frcaction.com/twoweeks

[357] John MacArthur on Worldview Weekend Radio with Brannon Howse, June 20, 2012.

[358] Helen Schucman, *A Course in Miracles,* (Foundation for Inner Peace).

[359] Glenn Beck's Divine Destiny: Frequently Asked Questions, posted at: http://www.glennbeck.com/content/articles/article/198/44012/.

[360] 8-28 Rally Update, posted at: http://www.glennbeck.com/content/articles/article/198/44048/.

[361] Website of former Mormon Ed Decker on Mormon theology: http://www.saintsalive.com/resourcelibrary/mormonism.

[362] Ibid.

[363] Ibid.

[364] Ibid.

[365] Ed Decker, "The Massive Mormon Scriptures Mess," posted at: http://worldviewweekend.com/worldview-times/article.php?articleid=8281.

[366] Dan Gilgoff, "Some Evangelicals on Defensive Over Partnering with Glenn Beck, a Mormon," August 27, 2010, posted at: http://religion.blogs.cnn.com/2010/08/27/some-evangelicals-on-defensive-over-partnering-with-glenn-beck-a-mormon/?hpt=C2.

[367] "Some Evangelicals on Defensive Over Partnering with Glenn Beck, a Mormon," August 27, 2010, posted at: http://religion.blogs.cnn.com/2010/08/27/some-evangelicals-on-defensive-over-partnering-with-glenn-beck-a-mormon/?hpt=C2.

[368] Jay Richards speaking at Skyline Wesleyan Church in San Diego on April 22, 2012, along with Jim Garlow, Glenn Beck, and James Robison, audio clip played on *Worldview Weekend Radio* with Brannon Howse on April 23, 2012.

[369] Glenn Beck speaking at Skyline Wesleyan Church in San Diego on April 22, 2012, audio clip played on *Worldview Weekend Radio* with Brannon Howse on April 23, 2012.

[370] Ibid.

[371] Ibid.

[372] Ibid.

[373] David Barton, *Life Today TV*, September 20, 2010, posted at: http://www.youtube.com/watch?v=LWf_jx49PzM.

[374] Ibid.

[375] Glenn Beck in TV interview "Mormon Glenn Beck on Successful Marriage," posted at: http://www.youtube.com/watch?v=2uKvve0ffss&feature=related.

[376] Schwarz and Noebel, chapter 14.

[377] *Journal of Discourses* 1: 230. Available online at: http://www.journalofdiscourses.org/volume-01/.

[378] Ed Decker, "The Mormon Plan for America and the Rise of Mitt Romney," February 2007. Available at: http://www.worldviewweekend.com/worldview-times/article.php?articleid=6317.

[379] Ezra Taft Benson Mormon, LDS President, in the speech, "Our Divine Constitution."

[380] Greg West, "Glenn Beck and the 'Restoring Honor' Rally," *LDS Church Examiner*, August 28, 2010, posted at: http://www.examiner.com/lds-church-in-national/glenn-beck-and-the-restoring-honor-rally.

[381] Glenn Beck on Fox News Sunday with Chris Wallace on August 29, 2020 posted here: http://www.foxnews.com/on-air/fox-news-sunday/transcript/glenn-beck-039restoring-honor039-rally-america039s-future-and-his-critics

[382] Understanding the connection between your Higher Self, Cosmic Consciousness, and Universal Mind posted here: http://thevoiceforlove.com/higher-self.html

[383] Glenn Beck declared this blasphemous, New Age teaching during his commencement address at Liberty University, which is supposed to be a Christian university. Glenn Beck: A big dose of Common Sense posted on Beck's Website here: Transcript posted here: http://www.glennbeck.com/content/articles/article/199/44635/ Video posted here: http://www.youtube.com/watch?feature=endscreen&v=z4rwEEGbGu4&NR=1

[384] Ibid., 17.

[385] Ed Decker, "Some Unanswered Questions of the Mormon Gospel," posted at: http://worldviewweekend.com/worldview-times/article.php?articleid=8282.

386 A megachurch pastor responding to concerns from one of his church members, personal email to me from the church member.

387 Glenn Beck and Keith Ablow, *The Seven Wonders that Will Change Your Life* (New York: Simon & Schuster Inc., 2012), 85.

388 Russell Goldman, "New Alabama Gov. Criticized for Christian-Only Message," *ABC News*, January 19, 2011, posted at: http://abcnews.go.com/US/alabama-gov-robert-bentley-criticized-christian-message/story?id=12648307.

389 "Glenn Beck Criticizes Alabama Governor Robert Bentley's Remarks on Non-Christians," Press Register, January 24, 2011, posted at: http://blog.al.com/live/2011/01/political_skinny_glenn_beck_cr.html.

390 Glenn Beck, "We Are All Brothers and Sisters," January 20, 2011, posted at: http://www.glennbeck.com/2011/01/20/glenn-to-gov-bentley-we-are-all-brothers-and-sisters/.

391 Grace Wyler, "Meet the Radical Evangelical Army Behind Rick Perry," *Business Insider*, July 21, 2011, posted at: http://www.businessinsider.com/rick-perry-the-evangelicals-behind-the-response-2011-7-21.

392John MacArthur, "The Nature and Sufficiency of Scripture," posted at: http://www.gty.org/Resources/Sermons/GTY111_The-Nature-and-Sufficiency-of-Scripture?q=simpleton.

393 Originally posted on Hagee's church website at: http://www.sacornerstone.org/difference/feast-of-tabernacles-midway-oct-28-2011.

394 Anugrah Kumar, "'Romney Not Cultist,' Fuller President Says Cautiously," October 10, 2011, posted at: http://www.christianpost.com/news/romney-not-cultist-fuller-president-says-cautiously-57688/.

395 Ibid.

396 Ibid.

397 Billy Graham, *Just As I Am* (London: Harper Collins, 1997), 450.

398 Henri Nouwen, *Sabbatical Journey* (New York: Crossroad, 1998), 51.

399 As posted on The Response website and printed out and saved in the Worldview Weekend files.

400 Joseph Farah, "Rick Perry Fooled Me," WorldNetDaily.com, July 27, 2011, posted at: http://www.wnd.com/index.php?fa=PAGE.view&pageId=%20326665.

401 Ice and House, *Dominion Theology: Blessing or Curse?*, 418.

402 Gary North, *Unholy Spirits: Occultism and New Age Humanism* (Forth Worth: Dominion Press, 1986), 388–89.

403 Ice and House, appendix A, not included in the book but given to Brannon Howse by Dr. Ice.

404 Gary North, "The Three Legs of Christian Reconstruction's Stool," in *Backward Christian Soldiers?* (Tyler, TX: Institute for Christian Economics, 1984), 146, 150.

405 Robby Dean, letter of warning posted at: http://www.worldviewweekend.com/worldview-times/article.php?articleid=7374.

406 James Robison, article posted at: http://jamesrobison.net/?q=node/88.

[407] Video clip of Creflo Dollar on *Life Today with James Robison*, posted at: http://www.youtube.com/watch?v=W0v-urU5Wtk.

[408] Video clip of Jonathan Morris on *Life Today with James Robison*, posted at: http://www.oneplace.com/ministries/life-today/listen/father-jonathan-morris-happiness-242065.html.

[409] *Life Today with James Robison* clips posted at: http://www.youtube.com/watch?v=8jYJyJ8wN6Q.

[410] Morris on *Life Today with James Robison*.

[411] Ibid.

[412] Signers were listed online at: http://www.torenewamerica.com/pray-and-act.

[413] Adrienne S. Gaines, "Christian Leaders Call for 40-Day Fast in Run Up to Election," September 16, 2010, posted at: http://www.charismamag.com/index.php/news-old/29264-christian-leaders-call-for-40-day-fast-in-run-up-to-election.

[414] Ibid.

[415] John MacArthur, "The Modern Blasphemy of the Holy Spirit," sermon from October 23, 2011, posted at: http://www.gty.org/resources/sermons/90-415/the-modern-blasphemy-of-the-holy-spirit.

[416] Ibid.

[417] *One News Now*, December 20, 2011, posted at: http://www.onenewsnow.com/Politics/Default.aspx?id=1500430.

[418] Steve Farrell, "Gingrich, Toffler, and Gore: A Peculiar Trio," posted at: http://www.themoralliberal.com/2010/01/30/gingrich-toffler-and-gore-a-peculiar-trio-steve-farrell/.

[419] Ibid., Farrell quoting Newt Gingrich and Dick Armey, *Contract with America* (New York: Times Books, 1994), 186.

[420] Ibid.

[421] Newt Gingrich in Alvin and Heidi Toffler, *Creating a New Civilization: The Politics of the Third Wave* (Turner Publishing, 1995), foreword.

[422] Steve Farrell, "Groveling in the Gutter of the Gulags," posted at: http://www.themoralliberal.com/2010/02/08/groveling-in-the-gutter-of-the-gulags-steve-farrell/.

[423] Ibid.

[424] Steve Farrell, "Eradicating the U.S. Constitution by Design," posted at: http://www.themoralliberal.com/2010/02/16/eradicating-the-u-s-constitution-by-design-steve-farrell/.

[425] Alvin Toffler, *The Third Wave* (New York: Bantam Books, 1984), 417.

[426] Farrell, "Groveling."

[427] Ibid.

[428] Rebecca Terrell, "Newt Gingrich: The Establishment's Conservative," November 27, 2009, posted at: http://www.thenewamerican.com/usnews/politics/2396-newt-gingrich-the-establishments-conservative?showall=1.

[429] Ibid.

430 Ibid.

431 AP source: "Another $5M donated to pro-Gingrich PAC," posted at: http://www.cbsnews.com/8301-505245_162-57364635/ap-source-another-$5m-donated-to-pro-gingrich-pac/.

432 Sam Blumenfeld, "Newt Gingrich and the Tofflers," *American Thinker*, January 11, 2012, posted at: http://www.thenewamerican.com/opinion/sam-blumenfeld/10488-newt-gingrich-and-the-tofflers.

433 Mark Leon Goldberg, UN Dispatch, "Newt Gingrich: United Nations Champion," November 21, 2011, posted at: http://www.undispatch.com/newt-gingrich-united-nations-champion.

434 Daniel Sayani, "Newt's Contract with the Earth: Pseudo-Science, Big Government," February 15, 2011, posted at: http://thenewamerican.com/reviews/books/6323-newts-contract-with-the-earth-offers-pseudo-science-big-government-and-earth-worship.

435 The Freedom Federation website, posted at: http://freedomfederation.org/content/members.

436 The Freedom Federation website, posted at: http://freedomfederation.org/content/awakening_2012_speakers.

437 Ibid.

438 Ibid.

439 Ibid.

440 Common Good website, posted at: http://www.commongoodonline.com/index.php.

441 J. Zajda, S. Majhanovich, and V. Rust, "Education and Social Justice," Wikipedia, 2006.

442 Generals International website notice posted at: http://us2.forward-to-friend.com/forward/show?u=2c8533b164a12dac690d3544f&id=bb611955c7.

443 Tony Perkins, "Perkins Perspective: The Call," August 22, 2008,

444 "A Covenant for Civility," posted at: http://www.sojo.net/index.cfm?action=action.display&item=100308-civility-covenant.

445 Tony Perkins on MorningStartv.com, video comment (approximately at 8:00 mark), posted at: http://www.morningstartv.com/oak-initiative/christians-effect-government.

446 Video of speech at Oak Initiative, posted at: http://www.youtube.com/watch?v=hfNVgJ4rwMo.

447 Vance Havner, *Playing Marbles with Diamonds* (Grand Rapids: Baker Books, 1985), 61.

448 Wikipedia, posted at: http://en.wikipedia.org/wiki/NARAL_Pro-Choice_America.

449 "Come Let Us Reason Together: A Governing Agenda to End the Culture Wars," posted at: http://comeletusreason.org/wp-content/uploads/2009/09/Come_Let_Us_Reason_Together_Governing_Agenda_Addl_Statements.pdf.

[450] Wikipedia, posted at: http://en.wikipedia.org/wiki/People_for_the_American_Way.

[451] "Come Let Us Reason Together."

[452] "Come Let Us Reason Together: A Fresh Look at Shared Cultural Values Between Evangelicals and Progressives," The Governing Agenda, posted at: http://comeletusreason.org/?page_id=73.

[453] Ibid.

[454] "What Is the Circle of Protection?," posted at: http://www.circleofprotection.us/.

[455] Focus on the Family press release, January 19, 2011, posted at: http://www.focusonthefamily.com/about_us/news_room/news-releases/20120119-focus-national-hispanic-leadership-conference-to-join-forces.aspx.

[456] Information posted at: http://www.focusonthefamily.com/about_us/events/date-night-challenge.aspx.

[457] Posted at: http://action.afa.net/Detail.aspx?id=2147516172.

[458] Sarah Posner and Anthea Butler, "Beyond Alarmism and Denial in the Dominionism Debate," August 29, 2011, posted at: http://www.religiondispatches.org/archive/atheologies/5026/beyond_alarmism_and_denial_in_the_dominionism_debate/.

[459] Warren Throckmorton, "American Family Association Targets Radio Hosts Over Association with Critic," September 30, 2011, posted at: http://www.religiondispatches.org/dispatches/guest_bloggers/5203/american_family_association_targets_radio_hosts_over_association_with_critic.

[460] James Robison website, posted at: http://jamesrobison.net/?q=node/88.

[461] Ibid.

[462] Ibid.

[463] As posted at: www.dfw.undergodindivisible.org

[464] Ibid.

[465] Ron Carlson and Ed Decker, Fast Facts on False Teachings, (Eugene, OR: Harvest House Publishers, 1994), 170-171.

[466] Posted at: http://www.ldschurchtemples.com/independence/.

[467] White Horse Prophecy explained by pro-LDS website, posted at: http://www.ldsresources.net/white-horse-prophecy/

[468] John MacArthur, MacArthur's New Testament Commentary: 1 Corinthians (Chicago: Moody Press, 1996), 305.

[469] Matthew Henry's Biblical Commentary on Acts, posted at: http://www.christnotes.org/commentary.php?b=44&c=16&com=mhc

[470] John MacArthur, MacArthur's New Testament Commentary: Acts (Chicago: Moody Press, 1996), 102.

[471] MacArthur, 1 Corinthians, 305.

[472] Video of speech, comment made between 7:25 and 7:51, posted at: http://www.glennbeck.com/2012/07/28/witness-the-third-great-awakening-glenn-beck-

brings-the-movement-of-peace-and-freedom-into-a-new-age/

473 "The Coolest Moment of My Life," posted at: http://www.glennbeck.com/2012/07/30/the-coolest-moment-of-my-life/

474 Cathy Lynn Grossman, "Survey: 72% of Millennials 'More Spiritual than Religious'," USA Today, posted at: http://www.usatoday.com/news/religion/2010-04-27-1Amillfaith27_ST_N.htm.

475 Carlson and Decker, Fast Facts on False Teachings, 179.

476 Havner, Playing Marbles with Diamonds, 61

477 Dave Hunt and T. A. McMahon, The Seduction of Christianity (Eugene, OR: Harvest House Publishers, 1985), 149.

478 Ibid., 157.

479 Ibid., 101.

480 Video posted at (go to the 4:55 mark): http://www.worldviewweekend.com/worldview-tube/play.php?id=cwnVideo-4460.

481 Justin Peters, interview on Worldview Weekend Radio.

482 Video posted at (go to the 9:47 mark): http://www.worldviewweekend.com/worldview-tube/play.php?id=cwnVideo-4460.

483 Ibid.

484 Peters, interview on Worldview Weekend Radio.

485 John Hagee, video posted at (go to the 42:12 mark): http://www.worldviewweekend.com/worldview-times/article.php?articleid=8283.

486 Kenneth Copeland, Southwest Believers Convention, Ft. Worth, TX, August 3, 2009, as documented by Justin Peters of www.justinpetersministries.org.

487 Peters, interview on Worldview Weekend Radio.

488 Ibid.

489 Ibid.

490 Video posted at (go to the 43:29 mark): http://www.worldviewweekend.com/worldview-times/article.php?articleid=8283.

491 Right Wing Watch, "David Barton Advocates Seven Mountains Dominionism" posted at: http://www.rightwingwatch.org/content/david-barton-advocates-seven-mountains-dominionism.

492 C. Peter Wagner, letter dated May 31, 2007, posted at: http://www.erwm.com/ApostolicLetter.htm.

493 The Source of the Secret DVD, Gaiam Studio.

494 Hunt and McMahon, 151.

495 The Source of the Secret DVD, Impact Productions, promo DVD clips posted at: http://www.worldviewweekend.com/worldview-times/article.php?articleid=8284.

496 The Source of the Secret DVD.

497 Joel Osteen website, posted at: http://www.joelosteen.com/pages/podcastitem.aspx?pid=26&video=true.

498 Ibid.

[499] Joel Osteen, *Your Best Life Now* (New York: FaithWords, 2007), 5.

[500] Ibid., 6.

[501] Ibid., 15.

[502] Ibid., 22.

[503] Ibid., 72.

[504] Ibid., 8.

[505] Ibid., 63.

[506] Ronald B. Mayers, cited in Jack Hughes, "*Experiencing God* by Blackaby and King: Is God Speaking to Us Today? A Critical Evaluation," posted at: http://www.jackandlisahughes.com/storage/Experiencing-God.pdf.

[507] Hughes, "*Experiencing God* by Blackaby and King."

[508] Video posted at: http://worldviewweekend.com/worldview-times/article.php?articleid=7882.

[509] Beth Moore video clip, posted at: http://www.worldviewweekend.com/world-view-times/article.php?articleid=7870.

[510] TBN *Praise-a-Thon*. March 2012, video posted at: http://apprising.org/2012/05/16/southern-baptist-david-jeremiah-praises-vision-god-gave-to-tbns-paul-crouch/.

[511] Ibid.

[512] Ibid.

[513] T. A. McMahon, "From Oprah to Oz and Beyond," *Berean Call Newsletter*, September 30, 2011.

[514] Bonna Johnson, "Meditation Goes Mainstream," *The Tennessean*, September 14, 2008, posted at: http://www.appliedmeditation.org/About_IAM/articles/Tennessean.html.

[515] IHOP website bookstore, posted at: *http://store.ihop.org/store/product/163/Fire-Within/*.

[516] Wikipedia, posted at: http://en.wikipedia.org/wiki/St._Teresa_of_Avila.

[517] Ibid.

[518] St. Teresa of Avila, *The Interior Castle*, (Trinity Press, 2011).

[519] Cathleen Medwick, *Teresa of Avila: The Progress of a Soul* (Knopf, 1999), 93.

[520] Product description, *Interior Castle*, St. Teresa of Avila, posted at: http://www.amazon.com/The-Interior-Castle-ebook/dp/B002IPZJ92/ref=sr_1_3?ie=UTF8&qid=1315165631&sr=8-3.

[521] "Contemplative Prayer," Wikipedia, posted at: http://en.wikipedia.org/wiki/Contemplative_prayer.

[522] *Catholic Catechism*, #460, posted at: http://www.catholicdoors.com/catechis/cat0422.htm#456.

[523] As sited by numerous writers, including Joel Landon Watts, posted at: http://unsettledchristianity.com/2010/01/mike-bickle-on-contemplative-prayer/.

[524] Tim Stafford, "Miracles in Mozambique: How Mama Heidi Reaches the Aban-

doned," *Christianity Today*, May 18, 2012, posted at: http://www.christianitytoday. com/ct/2012/may/miracles-in-mozambique.html?start=1.

[525] Ibid.

[526] Ibid.

[527] Ibid.

[528] Ibid.

[529] Ibid.

[530] Ibid.

[531] Ibid.

[532] Ibid.

[533] Ibid.

[534] Information about *The Reformer's Pledge* and its authors posted at: http://www. amazon.com/Reformers-Pledge-Bill-Johnson/dp/0768432693/ref=sr_1_1?ie=UTF 8&qid=1338429421&sr=8-1.

[535] See Revival Alliance website, posted at: http://revivalalliance.com/.

[536] A portion of this interview is posted on YouTube at: http://www.youtube.com/ watch?v=t6dont3GOY8.

[537] The Flame of Love Project website, posted at: http://www3.uakron.edu/sociol-ogy/flameweb/index.html.

[538] Dave Hunt, *Occult Invasion* (Eugene, OR: Harvest House Publishers, 1997), 531–535.

[539] The Flame of Love Project website.

[540] Ibid.

[541] From a discussion with Christianity.com editor Alex Crain and Grace to You's John MacArthur, discussing Dr. MacArthur's 2011 book *Slave: The Hidden Truth about Your Identity in Christ,* video clip posted at: http://www.worldviewweekend. com/worldview-times/article.php?articleid=7474.

[542] *Merriam-Webster Dictionary*, posted at: http://www.merriam-webster.com/dic-tionary/soteriology.

[543] John MacArthur, video clip, posted at: http://www.worldviewweekend.com/ worldview-times/article.php?articleid=7474.

[544] Ken Silva, "Tim Keller Teaching Roman Catholic and Quaker Mysticism to His RPC Leaders," Appraising Ministries, June 15, 2012, posted at: by http://apprising. org/2012/06/15/tim-keller-teaching-roman-catholic-and-quaker-mysticism-to-his-rpc-leaders/.

[545] Screen shots of "The Way of the Monk" course description from Redeemer Pres-byterian Church website, posted at: http://apprising.org/2011/01/27/tim-keller-recommending-roman-catholic-mysticism/.

[546] For more detail, see Dave Hunt's book, *A Woman Rides the Beast* (Eugene, OR: Harvest House Publishers, 1994), available at: http://www.thebereancall.org/con-tent/woman-rides-beast-1.

547 Screen shots of "The Way of the Monk."

548 Jan Johnson, "Meditation: Not So Mysterious," website of Redeemer Presbyterian Church in New York, NY, posted at: http://www.redeemer.com/connect/prayer/prayer_johnson_article.html.

549 Wikipedia, posted at: http://en.wikipedia.org/wiki/Lectio_Divina.

550 Ibid.

551 Thomas Keating, *Open Mind, Open Heart: The Contemplative Dimension of the Gospel*, (Continuum, 1994).

552 January 1979, VHP-sponsored second "World Congress on Hinduism" in Allahabad.

553 Johnson, "Meditation."

554 Ibid.

555 Bob DeWaay, "Richard Foster—Celebration of Deception, Evangelical Mysticism," *Critical Issues Commentary*, May/June 2009.

556 Richard Foster, *Celebration of Discipline: The Path to Spiritual Growth* (San Francisco: Harper, 1978), 22.

557 Ibid., 26.

558 Ibid., 36.

559 Ibid., 36.

560 Ibid., 27, 28.

561 Richard Foster, *Prayer: Finding the Heart's True Home* (San Francisco: Harper, 1992), 157.

562 Foster, *Celebration of Discipline*, 36.

563 Agnes Sanford, cited in Hunt and McMahon, *The Seduction of Christianity*, 127.

564 Ibid., 14.

565 DeWaay, "Richard Foster—Celebration of Deception, Evangelical Mysticism."

566 Foster, *Celebration of Discipline*, 159.

567 Donald Whitney, cited in DeWaay, "Richard Foster—Celebration of Deception, Evangelical Mysticism."

568 John Piper sermon "Man Shall Not Live on Bread Alone," posted at: http://www.desiringgod.org/resource-library/sermons/man-shall-not-live-on-bread-alone.

569 John Piper sermon "When the Bridegroom Is Taken Away," posted at: http://www.desiringgod.org/resource-library/sermons/when-the-bridegroom-is-taken-away-they-will-fast-with-new-wineskins.

570 John Piper sermon "Tell How Much the Lord Has Done for You!," transcript posted at: http://www.desiringgod.org/resource-library/sermons/tell-how-much-the-lord-has-done-for-you.

571 Phil Johnson, "Pornographic Divination," posted at: http://teampyro.blogspot.com/2011/08/pornographic-divination.html.

572 John Piper, *When I Don't Desire God*, 193; also documented in Gary Gilley, "*When I Don't Desire God* by John Piper," posted at: http://www.svchapel.org/re-

sources/book-reviews/4-christian-living/203-when-i-dont-desire-god-by-john-piper.

[573] Robert Schuller, *Peace of Mind Through Possibility Thinking* (Grand Rapids: Fleming H. Revell, 1977), 131–132.

[574] Tim Stafford, "A Regular Purpose-Driven Guy," *Christianity Today*, November 18, 2002.

[575] Ibid.

[576] Crystal Cathedral website, comment posted at: http://www.crystalcathedral.org/hour_of_power/pastors/index_lc.php?contentid=3391.

[577] Crystal Cathedral website, posted at: http://www.crystalcathedral.org/about/purpose.php.

[578] Warren, *The Purpose Driven Life,* 88.

[579] C. S. Lovett, *Longing to Be Loved* (Personal Christianity, 1982), 13–16, 87–90.

[580] Hunt and MacMahon, *The Seduction of Christianity*, 160.

[581] Phil Johnson, "Pornographic Divination," posted at: http://www.worldviewweekend.com/worldview-times/article.php?articleid=7427. A video of Driscoll saying these things posted at: http://worldviewweekend.com/worldview-times/article.php?articleid=8285.

[582] MacArthur, *Charismatic Chaos*, 56.

[583] Kenneth E. Hagin, *The Glory of God* (Tulsa: Faith Library, 1987), 14–15.

[584] David French, "Evangelicals' Collapsing Cultural Infleunce," *National Review*, March 14, 2012, posted at: http://www.nationalreview.com/corner/293457/evangelicals-collapsing-cultural-influence-david-french.

[585] Ibid.

[586] Ernest Gellner and John Breuilly, *Nations and Nationalism* (Ithaca, NY: Cornell University Press, 2009), 1.

[587] John Hutchinson and Anthony D. Smith, ed., *Nationalism,* Oxford Readers (Oxford: Oxford University Press, 1994), 4–5.

588 John MacArthur on Worldview Weekend Radio with Brannon Howse, June 20, 2012.

[589] John MacArthur, "Christians and Politics, Part 4," posted at: http://www.gty.org/Resources/Articles/A127.

[590] *Dietrich Bonhoeffer's Works*, vol. 10 (Barcelona, Berlin, New York: 1928–1931 and Fortress 2008), 313.

[591] Eric Metaxas, *Bonhoeffer* (Nashville: Thomas Nelson, 2010), 102.

[592] Ibid., 104–105.

[593] Ibid., 105.

[594] Ibid., 104.

[595] Ibid., 107.

Twenty Characteristics of False Teachers Embraced By the False Church

1. **False teachers are insincere and use God's Word for personal gain.**

   2 Corinthians 2:17: "For we are not as so many peddling the word of God; but as of sincerity, but as from God, we speak in the sight of God in Christ."

2. **False teachers appeal to the flesh and sin nature of people.**

   2 Peter 2:18: "For when they speak great swelling words of emptiness, they allure through the lusts of the flesh, through lewdness, the ones who have actually escaped from those who live in error."

   "Actually escaped" is better translated "trying to escape or barely escaping." These are often people who are not saved but are seeking through man-centered efforts to escape consequences of their sinful lives, only to be deceived by false teachers.

3. **False teachers deliberately take Scripture out of context to attract a following.**

   Acts: 20:30: "Also from among yourselves men will rise up, speaking perverse things, to draw away the disciples after themselves."

4. **False teachers have a form of godliness but deny God.**

2 Timothy 3:5: "[H]aving a form of godliness but denying its power. And from such people turn away!"

5. **False teachers openly reject truth.**

2 Timothy 4:4: "[A]nd they will turn their ears away from the truth, and be turned aside to fables."

6. **False teachers willingly embrace unbiblical philosophies.**

2 Timothy 4:4: "[A]nd they will turn their ears away from the truth, and be turned aside to fables."

The word *fables* refers to philosophies.

Colossians 2:8: "Beware lest anyone cheat you through philosophy and empty deceit, according to the tradition of men, according to the basic principles of the world, and not according to Christ."

7. **False teachers are arrogant and self-righteous.**

2 Timothy 3:2–5: "But know this, that in the last days perilous times will come: For men will be lovers of themselves, lovers of money, boasters, proud, blasphemers, disobedient to parents, unthankful, unholy, unloving, unforgiving, slanderers, without self-control, brutal, despisers of good, traitors, headstrong, haughty, lovers of pleasure rather than lovers of God, having a form of godliness but denying its power. And from such people turn away!"

8. **False teachers embrace mysticism.**

Colossians 2:18: "Let no one cheat you of your reward, taking delight in false humility and worship of angels, intruding into those things which he has not seen, vainly puffed up by his fleshly mind."

9. **False teachers sound educated and speak with persuasive words, but they speak error.**

Colossians 2:4: "Now this I say lest anyone should deceive you with persuasive words."

Colossians 2:8: "Beware lest anyone cheat you through philosophy and empty deceit, according to the tradition of men, according to the basic principles of the world, and not according to Christ."

10. **False teachers are flippant in their attitude and dealings with demons.**

2 Peter 2:9–12: "[T]hen the Lord knows how to deliver the godly out of temptations and to reserve the unjust under punishment for the day of judgment, and especially those who walk according to the flesh in the lust of uncleanness and despise authority. They are presumptuous, self-willed. They are not afraid to speak evil of dignitaries, whereas angels, who are greater in power and might, do not bring a reviling accusation against them before the Lord."

Jude 8: "Likewise also these dreamers defile the flesh, reject authority, and speak evil of dignitaries."

Many theologians believe these dignitaries are fallen angels or demons.

Notice that Jude 9 tells us that Michael the archangel did not get into an argument with Satan over the body of Moses. If Michael the archangel did not rail against Satan, should we? Our response is found in Zechariah 3:2, where we read that the Angel of Lord said to Satan, "The LORD rebuke you." Our response is also found in James 4:7: "Therefore submit to God."

To submit to God means to line up under His authority. A Christian who lines up under God's authority can then resist

470

or take his stand knowing that he is secure under God's authority and protection, which results in the devil fleeing.

We are not called to bind Satan. Word of Faith and New Apostolic Reformation members use Matthew 16:19 and Matthew 18:18 out of context. These verses have nothing to do with binding Satan or demons but speak to the issue of church discipline.

Luke 11:22 is also another verse often taken out of context. The strong man in this verse is Satan, but the stronger man is Jesus Christ (not man), who defeated Satan through His death, burial, and resurrection.

11. False teachers promise liberty or freedom from spiritual bondage, but they are themselves in bondage as children and servants of Satan.

2 Peter 2:19: While they promise them liberty, they themselves are slaves of corruption; for by whom a person is overcome, by him also he is brought into bondage.

12. False teachers have heard the Gospel but reject it.

2 Peter 2:20–21: "For if, after they have escaped the pollutions of the world through the knowledge of the Lord and Savior Jesus Christ, they are again entangled in them and overcome, the latter end is worse for them than the beginning."

13. False teachers embrace moralizing.

2 Peter 2:20–22: "For if, after they have escaped the pollutions of the world [through moralizing and man-centered efforts] through the knowledge of the Lord and Savior Jesus Christ, they are again entangled in them and overcome, the latter end is worse for them than the beginning. For it would have been better for them not to have known the way of righteousness, than having known it,

to turn from the holy commandment delivered to them. But it has happened to them according to the true proverb: 'A dog returns to his own vomit,' and, 'a sow, having washed, to her wallowing in the mire.'"

Jesus spoke a parable of the dangers of moralizing in Matthew 12:43–45. When an unbeliever seeks to clean up his life without the Gospel message of faith and repentance, he can end up in a worse condition than before he attempted self-improvement through man-centered methods.

14. **False teachers rise from within the Church, and others seek to infiltrate the true Church.**

2 Peter 2:1: "But there were also false prophets among the people, even as there will be false teachers among you, who will secretly bring in destructive heresies, even denying the Lord who bought them, and bring on themselves swift destruction."

Jude 4: "For certain men have crept in unnoticed, who long ago were marked out for this condemnation, ungodly men, who turn the grace of our God into lewdness and deny the only Lord God[a] and our Lord Jesus Christ."

Acts: 20:30: "Also from among yourselves men will rise up, speaking perverse things, to draw away the disciples after themselves."

15. **False teachers cause personal and doctrinal division within the Church.**

Romans 16:17: "Now I urge you, brethren, note those who cause divisions and offenses, contrary to the doctrine which you learned, and avoid them."

Jude 19: "These are sensual persons, who cause divisions, not having the Spirit."

1 Corinthians 11:18: "There must be division among you to know who is approved of God."

16. False teachers preach a different Jesus, and demons can take on the form of their false god.

2 Corinthians 11:3–4: "But I fear, lest somehow, as the serpent deceived Eve by his craftiness, so your minds may be corrupted from the simplicity that is in Christ. For if he who comes preaches another Jesus whom we have not preached, or if you receive a different spirit which you have not received, or a different gospel which you have not accepted—you may well put up with it!"

1 Corinthians 10:20: "Rather, that the things which the Gentiles sacrifice they sacrifice to demons and not to God, and I do not want you to have fellowship with demons."

17. Some false teachers perform signs and wonders through demonic power.

Matthew 24:24: "For false christs and false prophets will rise and show great signs and wonders to deceive, if possible, even the elect."

True believers will not follow a false shepherd or false teachers. (see John 10:4–5).

False teachers can be demonically controlled and used to perform signs and wonders. Exodus 7:10–11: "So Moses and Aaron went in to Pharaoh, and they did so, just as the LORD commanded. And Aaron cast down his rod before Pharaoh and before his servants, and it became a serpent. But Pharaoh also called the wise men and the sorcerers; so the magicians of Egypt, they also did in like manner with their enchantments."

18. False teachers are part of God's judgment on a people and nation.

1 Kings 22:21–23: "Then a spirit came forward and stood before the Lord, and said, 'I will persuade him.' The Lord said to him, 'In what way?' So he said, 'I will go out and be a lying spirit in the mouth of all his prophets.' And the Lord said, 'You shall persuade him, and also prevail. Go out and do so.' Therefore look! The Lord has put a lying spirit in the mouth of all these prophets of yours, and the Lord has declared disaster against you."

2 Thessalonians 2:11: "The coming of the lawless one is according to the working of Satan, with all power, signs, and lying wonders, and with all unrighteous deception among those who perish, because they did not receive the love of the truth, that they might be saved. And for this reason God will send them strong delusion, that they should believe the lie."

19. False teachers can be a test from God of our faithfulness and to reveal true and false converts.

Deuteronomy 13:3: "[Y]ou shall not listen to the words of that prophet or that dreamer of dreams, for the LORD your God is testing you to know whether you love the LORD your God with all your heart and with all your soul."

20. False teachers deny the deity of Jesus Christ.

1 John 4:2–4: "By this you know the Spirit of God: Every spirit that confesses that Jesus Christ has come in the flesh is of God, and every spirit that does not confess that Jesus Christ has come in the flesh is not of God. And this is the spirit of the Antichrist, which you have heard was coming, and is now already in the world. You are of God, little children, and have overcome them, because He who is in you is greater than he who is in the world."

When a false teacher redefines God as does the Word of Faith Movement (also known as prosperity preachers), New Apostolic Reformation, neo-evangelicals, Mormons,

New Agers, the Emergent Church, etc., they are no longer speaking of the God of the Bible, and thus they are denying the deity of Jesus Christ, because if you redefine God you redefine Jesus, Who is God incarnate.

Many within the Word of Faith movement and NAR teach that Jesus Christ has not always existed as part of the triune God but was created by God as a separate entity to come to earth. This teaching denies the deity of Jesus Christ. It is called Arianism and comes from Arius, who died in 336 A.D.

Appendix 2

Glossary of Terms

active euthanasia: *Voluntary, active euthanasia* occurs when a doctor uses medical means to take the life of a patient at the request of the patient. *Involuntary, active euthanasia* occurs when a doctor uses medical means to take the life of a patient without the patient's permission.

Agenda 21: A nearly 400-page document on how to use "sustainable development" as the framework for global governance. *Agenda 21* is the global plan to implement a one-world economy, a one-world government, a one-world religious system, and radical environmentalism (see below for definition of "sustainable development"). Mikhail Gorbachev and Maurice Strong were involved in the 1992 United Nations' Earth Summit in Rio de Janeiro, where *Agenda 21* was unveiled.

agnostic: A person who believes it is impossible to know whether or not there is a God.

apologetics: The discipline of defending, contending for, and explaining the truth and validity of biblical Christianity.

atheism: The denial of a supernatural being known as God.

atheist: A person who believes there is no God. A Secular Humanist is an atheist.

change agent: A person posing as a "Christian," evangelical, or neo-evangelical in order to infiltrate the Church from within. Change agents are rabid haters of Christians, the Gospel, and the Bible and know how to manipulate a church for their own ends. Many change agents co-opt religious organizations and institutions in order to turn them toward pagan spirituality, ecumenicalism, liberation theology, dominion theology, and the creation of a New World Order. A significant goal of change agents is to transform the Church so it is no longer an obstacle to the New World Order but an active participant and builder of it.

communitarianism: A blend of socialism and capitalism; also referred to as "Communism lite" (see also "Fabian socialism" below).

contextualizing the Gospel: The idea that the Church must dilute the Gospel to make it more appealing to contemporary culture. Contextualization, as practiced by the false church, does not involve preaching the biblical Gospel that transforms people who live within the culture but is the preaching of a social gospel by people who have instead been transformed by their culture.

Cosmic Humanism: The belief that only the spiritual world is real and that the natural world is an illusion; also called the New Age movement. Cosmic Humanists generally believe in reincarnation.

cultural Marxism: The state in which an all-powerful and intrusive government eliminates personal freedoms under the guise of political correctness. Cultural Marxism intends to destroy Christianity in all areas of life because elimination of the Christian worldview will create the chaos necessary for the implementation of socialism (redistribution of wealth). Cultural Marxism was introduced in America when the faculty of the Frankfurt School was welcomed to America by John Dewey in 1933. Dewey and his cohorts specifically targeted education and media as the means by which to inculcate their worldview into American culture. Cultural Marxism is taught through educational programs that emphasize feminism, diversity, multiculturalism, and tolerance.

deist: A person who believes that God created the world but does not intervene in the affairs of mankind.

diversity: A masking term for the promotion of homosexuality, bisexuality, transgender sexuality, and the transvestite lifestyle.

dominion theology: The belief that God gave Adam and Eve a type of legal authority over the earth. The dominion interpretation of mankind's mandate from God wrongly assumes a legal authority instead of the actual intent that we are to be stewards of the world. Adherents to dominion theology believe they must establish the Kingdom of God on earth before Christ can return. As a result, its proponents work to place Christians in control of every earthly institution and area of influence. This belief is reflected in the "Seven Mountain Mandate" (see definition below).

dualism: The belief that man has a mind/soul and a body, which are distinct from each other. Christians believe the mind/soul lives forever.

ecumenicalism, ecumenism: The merging in spiritual and theological issues with other religions for the accomplishment of certain spiritual objectives. Ecumenicalism often involves Protestants joining in spiritual enterprises with Catholics, Mormons, Muslims, and New Agers.

Ecumenicalism was greatly advanced through the 1994 document "Evangelicals and Catholics Together."

Emergent Church: Although difficult to define because proponents believe truth is subjective (which results in a fluid belief system), the Emergent Church is marked by a rejection of the authority of God's Word, of the exclusivity of salvation through grace and faith in Christ alone, and of traditional, orthodox Christianity. The Emergent Church embraces postmodernism, existentialism, Gnosticism, and mysticism. Like many liberal, mainstream churches, the Emergent Church rejects the idea of the return of Jesus Christ and His judgment of the world. Instead, they believe it is their responsibility to build God's Kingdom through utopian ideals of the redistribution of wealth, the social gospel, disarmament, and a world community committed to social justice and pluralism.

"Evangelicals and Catholics Together": A 1994 document declaring that Catholics and Protestants are both Christian groups, and thus evangelicals should stop trying to convert Catholics. Chuck Colson and two Jesuit priests were the main influencers in drafting this heretical document.

existentialism: The central tenet of existentialism is that there is no absolute truth. "Christians" practicing existentialism introduced what is called neo-orthodoxy. The American version of this movement grew popular in the 1960s and virtually took over in the '70s and '80s. Søren Kierkegaard and Friedrich Nietzsche are considered by many to be the most influential promoters of existentialism. Nietzsche applied the idea of subjective truth to the natural world as an atheist, while Kierkegaard applied subjective truth to his brand of spirituality and called himself a Christian.

Fabian socialism, Fabianism: The system by which socialism is implemented through evolution, not revolution (as distinct from communism, which advocates revolution). Fabian socialism started in London in 1883. It is not merely national socialism but globalism. Fabianism dovetails with corporate fascism, the merging of big government and big business. Keynesian economics (see definition below) is tied directly to Fabian socialism and communitarianism. The ultimate goal is global governance, a one-world economic system, and a one-world government. Communitarianism and Fabian socialism are twins, but communitarians are generally not referred to as Fabian socialists because most have never belonged to the Fabian Socialist Society.

feminism: The belief that women are equal in all ways to men. The primary thrust of feminism, though, is not about gaining equal rights for women but about the feminization of the American male. Feminism is an anti-family and anti-father movement—and virtually guarantees the wholesale destruction of the traditional family. The champions of feminism have included Gloria Steinem, Elizabeth Cady Stanton, and, most prominently, Betty Friedan. Friedan was the co-founder of the National Organization of Women (NOW), one of America's most radical feminist organizations. Gnosticism (see definition below) and pagan spirituality are inextricably linked to feminism through the promotion of worshipping the female goddess Gaia or Mother Earth. Gnosticism elevates women to the role of savior of mankind. As a result, the worship of Mary is prevalent in the Gnosticism of the Catholic Church.

Gnosticism: The belief in discovering hidden spiritual knowledge through mystical practices often associated with Eastern religions. Gnosticism holds that salvation is not gained exclusively through the death, burial, and resurrection of Jesus Christ and that truth can be obtained through mystical experience and practices. Gnosticism includes the worship of angels,

hedonism: The belief that the pursuit of pleasure is the goal or purpose of life.

Hegelian Dialectic Process: Bringing about social and cultural change through creating conflict between opposites. The thesis, an idea, and the antithesis, an opposite idea, fight, conflict, synthesize, and merge together to produce a third option or Third Way, or a mixture of both. This process is used in many areas—including economics, law, government, and religion—to manipulate the populace. It is not only a favorite tool of communitarians, Fabian socialists, neo-evangelicals, and Marxists but also of the Church of Rome and its Jesuit Order.

Humanist Manifestos: Documents that detail the worldview of Secular Humanism and its application in many disciplines of life such as law, science, economics, history, religion, family, and education. *Humanist Manifesto I* was written in 1933, *Humanist Manifesto II* in 1973, and *Humanist Manifesto 2000* was written in 2000.

intolerance: Any belief that stems from a morally absolute foundation or worldview. Christianity is considered intolerant because it claims Jesus is the only way to God and that truth consists only in that which is consistent with the character and nature of God as revealed in the Christian Scriptures.

karma: That which determines how a person evolves through the process of reincarnation. Good karma allows a person to ascend to a higher order in the reincarnation process, and bad karma causes one to descend to a lower level.

Keynesian economics, Keynesianism: A philosophy of economics that calls for the continuous inflation or creation of money. It is named for John Maynard Keynes, who first articulated the system. Keynes was a Fabian socialist, and as a result, Keynesianism is tied directly to Fabian socialism and communitarianism. The creation of fiat money, a cornerstone of Keynesianism, generates inflation which steals people's wealth or the purchasing power of their money by devaluing currency. Keynesian economics also holds that debt is beneficial and that the dollar (or any other currency) should not be backed by gold or silver, thus allowing the government to print as much money as desired. The alternative economic philosophy is referred to as Austrian or classic economics. A classic economist, among other things, disapproves of debt, believes money should be backed by a hard asset such as gold or silver, and that the market should not be manipulated by a central government.

knowledge: An acquired body of truth.

legal positivism: The application of moral relativism to the law. Secular Humanism and its core beliefs of moral relativism and Darwinian evolution are the new, postmodern foundation on which America's courts and law schools are built. Legal positivism says that as society and morals evolve, so should the law.

Michael Foucault: French philosopher considered to be a key founder of postmodern thinking. Among his ideas, Foucault believed that homosexuality is a species, not an action.

monism: The belief that all is one. In regards to humanity, it is the belief that the body and the mind are not separate and both stem from a naturalistic process. There is no spiritual aspect to man, and he does not have a soul. The mind, thoughts, and ideas have no ultimate meaning or purpose. The mind as well as the body evolved through a random process known as Darwinian evolution.

moral absolutes: Beliefs that are considered true for all time, people, and places.

moral relativism: The belief that everything is relative and there are no absolute truths for all time, people, and places.

multiculturalism: Revisionist history that is anti-American and which promotes the liberal, leftist view of tolerance, pluralism, moral relativism, and socialism. Multiculturalism pits one cultural or ethnic group against another and has no desire to make America one nation out of many—contrary to the American motto *e pluribus unum*.

neo-evangelicals: Self-professed Christians who accept postmodernism and deny the inerrancy and authority of the Word of God in favor of man-centered reasoning or moral relativism. Many neo-evangelicals embrace the economic philosophies of Karl Marx in the form of "social justice" (see definition below) as well as many of the heresies handed down by their forerunners who embraced "neo-orthodoxy."

New Apostolic Reformation (NAR): A movement that believes in extrabiblical revelation, prophets, apostles, and other similar heresies. NAR proponents include Bill Johnson, Lance Wallnau, Chuck Pierce, C. Peter Wagner, John Arnott, Cindy Jacobs, James W. Goll, and Lou Engle. The New Apostolic Reformation is an outgrowth of the Latter Rain Movement of the 1940s, the Kansas City Prophet movement of the 1980s, and the Word of Faith movement that includes the prosperity gospel ("Name It and Claim It"). The New Apostolic Reformation is helping build the "new order" or "new world order" of the antichrist.

New Religious Right (NRR): Contemporary proponents of what was previously known as the Religious Right. The Religious Right developed in the mid-1970s. Its founders include the late Pastor Adrian Rogers of Bellevue Baptist Church in Memphis, Tennessee, and former president of the Southern Baptist Convention; the late Dr. D. James Kennedy of Coral Ridge Presbyterian Church in Ft. Lauderdale, Florida; and the late Dr. Jerry Falwell of Thomas Road Baptist Church and Liberty University in Lynchburg, Virginia. New Religious Right leaders, unlike the previous generation, have largely abandoned the original leaders' commitment to biblical theology and doctrine, and as a result they unite openly with false teachers when it furthers NRR political and cultural goals.

nihilism: The belief that life has no meaning and that nothing can be known for sure.

open theism: The belief that God is not sovereign and does not know the future.

panentheism: The belief that God is in everything, including all of nature and every individual human being.

pantheism: The belief that God is all and all is God.

passive euthanasia: *Voluntary, passive euthanasia* occurs when a patient has left a specific request for doctors not to take extraordinary measures to keep the patient alive—such as a feeding tube or artificial respiration—but instead allows nature to take its course. *Involuntary, passive euthanasia* occurs when a patient has not left any specific requests and cannot communicate with the doctors, but doctors allow nature to take its course based on their own evaluation or at the request of a family member.

pluralism: The belief that all religions and beliefs are equal.

political correctness: Speech required by the cultural elite that denies the character and nature of God. Related to compromise, collectivism, socialism, tolerance, and moral relativism, political correctness is a masking term for the beliefs and ideas that stem from humanism and socialism; also known as cultural Marxism.

postmodernism: The belief that truth (and the consequent reality) is not discovered but is created by mankind. A postmodern worldview allows that two opposing truth claims can be equal—unless one of the views is based on a fixed moral standard. An "absolute" view is not seen by the postmodernist as being equal but as being unacceptable because it is "intolerant."

pragmatism: The belief that a given end result justifies any necessary action or activity. Moral relativism and situational ethics are tied to pragmatism.

presuppositional worldview: The foundational idea upon which a person's understanding of the world is based. Every person must begin with one of three possible presuppositions: that God is, God is not, or that His existence cannot be known. From that presupposition, a person builds his or her worldview as the basis of his or her values and actions.

Reconstructionism: Dr. Tommy Ice defines reconstructionism as the belief that "…God will bless the church's effort to Christianize the earth. Since God's kingdom was established at Christ's first coming, godly dominion will be mediated through the church before the return of Christ. The victory of God's kingdom on earth will be during and continuous with this present era."*

reincarnation: The belief that a person's soul passes repeatedly from one body to another at death. The process continues until the soul reaches a state of perfection when its good karma (good deeds) outweigh its bad karma (bad deeds). Accumulating good karma results in a soul being reincarnated into a more desirable state. If someone accumulates bad karma, he or she will be reincarnated into a less desirable state.

religion: "A set of beliefs" (*Random House Unabridged Dictionary of the English Language*); "a system of belief" (*Webster's New World Dictionary*).

Secular Humanism: The belief that there is no God. People are the highest order of creature, and there is no such thing as the spiritual world. Only the natural world exists. A Secular Humanist believes people die, and that is it—there is nothing beyond the grave.

Seven Mountain Mandate: The goal of those who believe in dominion theology. They hope to win the culture war by taking control of the power centers of the culture. The seven mountains of influence to be taken by Christians are religion, family, business, arts & entertainment, government, education, and media. They believe through these seven power centers they can legislate "kingdom values." Many proponents of the Seven Mountain Mandate want to rule the world under Old Testament Law. Detractors have referred to those who hold to the Seven Mountain Mandate as a "Christian Taliban."

social gospel: Social justice (see definition below) advocated and implemented by the Church. While its proponents call it a "gospel," the social gospel is simply socialism wrapped in religious terminology and unbiblical theology.

social justice: A masking term for the economic philosophies of

---

* H. Wayne House and Thomas Ice, Dominion *Theology: Blessing or Curse?* (Portland, OR: Multnomah, 1988), 418.

communism and socialism. Social justice promotes the redistribution of income in the name of "the common good." Among world influencers, "common good" is used regularly by the Vatican and the pope.

socialism: The belief that the outcome of everyone's work can and should be equal. Socialism advocates the elimination of private property and seeks to redistribute wealth. It is consistent with the humanist worldview because humanists deny the sin nature of mankind and as a result believe socialism will work if people simply try hard enough to implement its principles. In reality, people are sinful from birth, battling greed, selfishness, pride, anger, bitterness, envy, laziness, and dishonesty. All of these sinful human qualities prevent a system of economics based on equal work, equal income, and shared benefits from working.

sovereignty: An attribute of God that relates to His ultimate authority, control, and supremacy in all areas. God is not surprised or shocked; nothing happens that God could not have prevented.

spiritual evolution: A common belief within Fabian socialism, the Emergent Church, the communitarian church-growth movement, and the New Age movement that everything is biologically and spiritually spiraling up to a condition of perfection that will allow mankind to usher in a New Age—a New World Order or God's Kingdom on earth. Spiritual evolution teaches that mankind can save himself as he discovers and embraces his own divine nature and the common ground in all religions. "The Father of the New Age Movement" was Jesuit priest Teilhard de Chardin, a major promoter of spiritual evolution.

sustainable development: The framework for global governance. Sustainable development is a code term for restraining developed countries through multinational power. The system promotes abortion on demand, population control, socialized medicine, social justice, welfare programs, public housing, and elimination of national sovereignty, parental authority, and religious liberty. One of its tenets is the criminalization of Christianity. A variety of UN-aligned organizations uses sustainable development as the framework for bringing about global governance.

syncretism: The belief that religious worldviews once thought incompatible can actually merge. The end result of syncretism will be the creation of a one-world religion. Syncretism is possible because modern-day evangelicalism has embraced mysticism and pagan spirituality while rejecting the authority of God's Word.

theistic evolution: The belief that God used Darwinian evolution to produce the world we know today.

theistic worldview: The understanding of the world that holds there is only one God and that there are both a spiritual world and a natural world.

theology: The person's view of God.

Third Way: See "Hegelian Dialectic Process" above.

truth: Fidelity to the original; that which is consistent with the character and nature of God.

useful idiot: A person manipulated into introducing socialism or communism into an arena where it would otherwise be rejected; a historic term created by Josef Stalin to describe those who gave him credibility.

wisdom: The application of truth.

worldview: The "lens" through which a person views the world. It is the foundation of values that determines how a person acts and lives his or her life. Whether conscious of it or not, every person has a worldview. A worldview answers such questions as where did we come from, why are we here, and what happens after we die? A worldview can be applied to life disciplines such as law, science, economics, history, religion, family, and education.